0

.5.

,72

,5

2000.

The Black Image in the White Mind

Studies in

Communication,

Media, and

Public Opinion

+

A series edited by

Susan Herbst

and

Benjamin I. Page

The Black Image
in the
White Mind

Media and Race in America

Robert M. Entman
and
Andrew Rojecki

THE UNIVERSITY OF CHICAGO PRESS

Chicago and London

ROBERT M. ENTMAN is professor and head of the Department of Communication at North Carolina State University. He is author of *Democracy without Citizens* (1989), coauthor of *Media Power Politics* (1981), and coeditor of the forthcoming *Mediated Politics*. ANDREW ROJECKI is assistant professor of communications at the University of Illinois, Chicago, and author of *Silencing the Opposition* (1999).

The University of Chicago Press, Chicago 60637
The University of Chicago Press, Ltd., London
© 2000 by The University of Chicago
All rights reserved. Published 2000
Printed in the United States of America

09 08 07 06 05 04 03 02 01 00   1 2 3 4 5
ISBN: 0-226-21075-8 (cloth)

Library of Congress Cataloging-in-Publication Data

Entman, Robert M.
    The black image in the white mind : media and race in America / Robert M. Entman, Andrew Rojecki.
        p.   cm.—(Studies in communication, media, and public opinion)
    Includes bibliographical references and index.
    ISBN 0-226-21075-8 (cloth : alk. paper)
    1. Afro-Americans in mass media.   2. Mass media and race relations—United States.   3. United States—Race relations.   I. Rojecki, Andrew, 1946–   II. Title.
III. Series.

P94.5.A372U55   2000
302.23´089´00973—dc21   99-086742

⊗ The paper used in this publication meets the minimum requirements of the American National Standard for Information Sciences—Permanence of Paper for Printed Library Materials, ANSI Z39.48-1992.

For Emily

—RME

For Susan

—AR

Contents

vii

Tables and Figures

Tables

Figures

Preface

This study attempts to say something new about race and about the media, two subjects that have generated more scholarly and journalistic writing, and more public concern and even outrage, than most. Why another book? Although we build upon the wisdom and insight of many who have gone before us, we believe there is still too little understanding about race or media and, especially, about the relationship of the two. We try to analyze dispassionately Whites' complicated sentiments toward African Americans, to describe not only the well-known negatives but the poorly recognized positive yearnings and tentative hopes. We explore the many ways that television news, entertainment, and advertising, as well as Hollywood film, register and help both to alter and to perpetuate White America's racial disquiet. We write in hopes of influencing scholars' understanding of the vital intersection between culture and race relations. But we also take our responsibilities as public intellectuals seriously, and present our findings and analysis in a form we intend to influence the wider public discussion.

We should explain the almost exclusive focus on African Americans. We do not have much to say about minority groups subject to many of the same cultural and political forces as Blacks, such as Latinos, Asian immigrants, and Native Americans. Certainly the media influence the dominant group's ideas about the other groups too. And we fully recognize that members of these other groups can suffer gravely from Whites' stereotyping and negative emotions.

We focus on Blacks for four basic reasons. The first is national political significance: Blacks are the most consistently visible subjects of political discourse about non-Whites in the United States. Other groups are more geographically concentrated and that makes them less universally potent as political symbols. The importance of anti-*Black* sentiments to American politics throughout the country, even in places where few live, has been documented repeatedly.[1] Second, no other group except Native Americans possesses the long history of discrimination that includes slavery and genocidal oppression, a history that helps explain the first point. Third, available methodologies allow for more reliable study of African Americans. Quite simply, in analyzing media content, we can usually identify Black persons, and thus draw comparisons to depictions of Whites. Classifying Latinos, Asians, and Native Americans cannot be done with nearly the same reliability. The final reason is parsimony: the subject of African Americans is complicated and multifaceted enough. Trying to explore mediated communication on all ethnic minorities is beyond the scope of any one study of this type.[2]

The Other Side of the Equation

Assuming the legitimacy of focusing on Blacks and Whites, what about the other side of the chasm—"Black racism" or animosity? Blacks can be racist in ideology but rarely have individual or collective power to translate the ideology into racist outcomes; few African Americans occupy positions that allow them systematically to enforce discriminatory resource allocations. To cite a few examples of the power differential, when this book was completed in 2000 there were no black U.S. senators or governors, and the first black editor-in-chief of a major national news outlet had just been appointed (Mark Whitaker of *Newsweek*). No African American had ever served as chief executive officer of a major mainstream media corporation. Just one African American headed a Fortune 500 corporation, and he took the helm only on 1 January 1999 of the anomalous, government-chartered Federal National Mortgage Assurance Corporation (Fannie Mae). No Black has been a chief justice of the U.S. Supreme Court, a speaker of the U.S. House, or a majority leader of the Senate. (For that matter, no Jewish and hardly any Catholic Whites had reached these pinnacles.) Nor had an African American ever held the presidency of an elite private university—or, of course, of the United States. All this 137 years after the Emancipation Proclamation.

There remains a large difference in social status, economic resources, cultural influence, and political power between White Americans as a whole and Black Americans as a whole, which makes the political import of Whites' racial sentiments fundamentally different. The far more urgent questions revolve around Whites' sentiments toward Blacks, and, for us in particular, the ways that mass communication reflects and affects them. For all intents and purposes, when we are speaking about the United States as a whole, it seems to us misleading to equate White and Black racism, even if in scattered cities or organizations Blacks might have the power to carry out a racist agenda. In reaching this conclusion we do not mean to minimize the deleterious impacts of perceived and actual hostility, resentment, stereotyping, and other negative sentiments among African Americans toward Whites.

An example clarifies the priority of studying White racial animosity: there is essentially no way to insult former president George H. W. Bush, his son, Texas governor George W. Bush, Bill Clinton, or Al Gore, to take a few Whites every reader knows about, based on their ethnicity or race. No ethnic insult exists, no term equivalent to "nigger," in the English language can be hurled at members of the culturally dominant Anglo-Saxon ethnic group. Nor does the culture supply any anti-Anglo-Saxon stereotype on any seriously valued attribute; about the strongest epithet one might find is "repressed." Perhaps Clinton could be called a "redneck," but that is a regional or class insult, not an ethnic one. Calling him "White trash" marks the idea that the targeted person is exceptional as "trash," and indeed the term "Black trash" does not exist. We have more to say on the associations of African Americans and dirt in chapter 10, on advertising.

As we move downward from the core cultural group to less assimilated White groups, we find words and stereotypes that can injure by contributing to others' prejudices, and might ultimately be translated into adverse resource allocations for group members. Anti-Jewish or Polish stereotypes still have some sting, can harm members' self-concepts and deepen others' prejudices, thereby increasing the possibility that power will be used against them. But in most cases the effects will be marginal. As demonstrated by studies that ask for rankings of ethnic groups, Blacks are generally the most vulnerable, though this varies somewhat by locale and circumstance. Moreover, as Winant[3] points out, unlike Whites, African Americans have little control over society's group identification of them; most are visibly marked as African Americans, and most Whites are hyperconscious of each individual's racial membership. This renders Blacks uniquely vulnerable to any discriminatory actions that dominant group members may carry out.

Caveats

Encouraged by those who read this book in manuscript form, we have attempted simultaneously to satisfy the exacting standards for support and verification that characterize scholarly research, and the rather opposed if equally demanding standards of public intellectual discussion. Normally, to transcend the halls of academe and enter this wider public sphere, a book must offer jargon-free, declarative prose; it should eschew the detachment and cautious qualification of claims typical of academic studies; and it must base its arguments far more on logic and reason than on statistics and tables. We believe our subject is important enough to make its study worthy of attention by those who do not normally look at academic books—though we also believe our book merits the interest of those whose job is to expand knowledge and build theory.

We earnestly hope the approach we settled upon will help the book reach audiences inside and out of academia, and we ask for patience from those used to reading only one type of book or the other. This approach places numbers in the background; most tables and methodological discussions appear in endnotes or in the appendix, although data essential to the main points of the argument appear in the body of the book. Some of the finer methodological details are not enumerated in the book at all but are found on the authors' web pages on the Internet, <http://www.raceandmedia.com>. Here readers will also find links to related sites on the Internet, updated comments from the authors, and other material designed to engage readers in a continuing dialogue, which we pledge to keep readily available in whatever future form the technology of networked information storage and retrieval may offer.

We have tried to avoid jargon, no doubt with only partial success. We attempt to write clearly, though we simply cannot avoid a degree of qualification and caution, because this is not an area that readily yields up definitive findings and indisputable answers and because the truth as we see it is too complicated to permit unqualified declarations.

Speaking of readability, a word about the book's title: It comes from a sentence in Donald Kinder and Lynn Sanders's fine book, *Divided by Color.* We thank them for the inspiration. The subtitle requires a bit more explanation. The original subtitle was "Television and Race in America." Some might argue we should not have changed "television" to "media." We did so not only because the book includes a chapter on Hollywood film and touches upon print media at various points throughout, but also because the revised subtitle is clearer and more forceful. We acknowledge that some readers will think that a book about "media" should include more analysis of newspapers and magazines, and perhaps of radio. But we feel the book already covers sufficient ground for one volume. Moreover, the subject of race is peculiarly visual, so it makes sense to focus a study of media and race on the most visually oriented outlets. We admit to a degree of internal debate about using the term *media*, not only in the title but also throughout the book. Yet writing something more precise like "broadcast network television, some cable networks, Hollywood film, and some print media" on the book's cover or throughout the text violated our hope to offer readers as clear a trip through this complicated field as possible.

Acknowledgments

One of the most difficult challenges facing authors is avoiding cliché in the acknowledgments section. But we think it more important to thank the many people and institutions who helped us than to avoid overly familiar phrases.

Robert Entman would like to thank first of all those providing support for the research. They include the Markle Foundation, whose grants have sustained two book projects, and whose former president, Lloyd Morrisett, board chairman, Joel Fleishman, and program officer, Cathy Clark, have all been indispensable supporters. The Chicago Community Trust's Human Relations Foundation provided several grants; special thanks to Clarence Wood, head of the foundation, and chairman of the Chicago Human Relations Commission, and Terri Johnson. They have worked tirelessly and effectively to build racial comity, and have supported Entman's work for almost as long as the Markle Foundation. They have been invaluable friends, informants, and backers of this project. The Aspen Institute's Communications and Society Program and its head, the inestimable Charlie Firestone, have also long supported Entman's work in the field. In addition, the Woodrow Wilson International Center for Scholars provided Entman a Guest Scholar slot in 1989, and it was in the comfortable halls of the Smithsonian that this project was hatched. The Gannett Urban Journalism Fund and the Center for Urban Affairs and Policy Research at Northwestern University also provided critical early funding. Thanks especially to former Journalism Dean Michael Janeway and former Speech Dean David Zarefsky, and to Professors Susan Herbst and Ben Page.

Entman's current institution, North Carolina State University, provided a sabbatical in 1997–98; thanks to Dean Margaret Zahn for responding affirmatively, and to colleagues in the Department of Communication for their congeniality and critique. The Kennedy School of Government at Harvard University appointed Entman to the Laurence Lombard Visiting Chair during the fall semester, 1997, an experience that offered many stimulating opportunities and provided some outstanding research assistance for the book. Harvard graduate students Debbie Burns Melican, Irma Munoz, Charles Merritt, Brian Kenner, and Judith Gaddie, and law students Simone Boayue, Caryn Kennedy Groce, and Anita Raman contributed significantly to several of the data analysis projects reported here, in the course of compiling a joint report to President Clinton's Initiative on Race. Professor Christopher Edley at Harvard Law School drew Entman and the Harvard students into the work of the president's Initiative. Marvin Kalb, Pippa Norris, and Tom Patterson at the Shorenstein Center for the Press, Politics and Public Policy all offered insight and friendship. Professor Constance Book of Elon College has been a good colleague and deserves credit for stimulating Entman's interest in pursuing the issue of skin color in advertising. Many other research assistants and students at Northwestern and N.C. State, too numerous to mention, have helped over the years. Thanks to one and all. Entman's old friend, Professor Clay Steinman, read and commented upon the entire manuscript with great care and perspicacity. John Tryneski, our editor at the University of Chicago Press, offered insight, patience, and good humor.

Shifting to the first person for a moment, first Entman, then Rojecki: The research on race and media began just weeks after Emily Hope Seymour Entman was born, on September 11, 1989. Although I am proud of this book's development over the past decade, that feeling is as nothing compared to the pride and inexpressible pleasure I have taken in Emily's unique presence on this earth. Three others, older but every bit as dear to me, deserve my unending gratitude too: my son Max, my wife Francie Seymour, and my father Bernie Entman. They are, respectively and quite simply, the best son, spouse, and father a guy could have. All four have put up, usually in good cheer, with the standard litany of tortures imposed by writers upon their families. Sadly, my mother, Rose, died just before the book's completion. Along with my father, she always encouraged my interest in social justice and thus bears some responsibility for what appears here.

Andrew Rojecki warmly thanks Clarence Wood of the Chicago Community Trust's Human Relations Foundation for two grants and Terri Johnson for arranging several stimulating forums. I would also like to thank the Bureau of Media Research at Indiana University for two summer grants and the school of journalism for a reduced course load that permitted me to come up to speed at the outset of this project. My gratitude to colleagues Jane Rhodes and David Weaver for their comments on early versions of chapters in the manuscript.

Acknowledgments

Students figured prominently in this project as well. My appreciation to graduate students Susan Zuckerman and George Sullivan for their patient and solicitous interviewing of our Indianapolis respondents and also to the undergraduates of the spring 1997 public opinion class for their diligent phone work. My thanks also to graduate students John Hostler and Nabil Echchaibi for their rapid turnaround of untimely and unreasonable research requests in the last hectic stages of the project.

I dedicate this book to my wife, Susan Estes, who offered insights and helpful criticism and had a knack for asking the right question when some knotty problem stopped the flow of writing.

1 The Racial Chameleon

SSESSING THE STATE OF RACE RELATIONS in the United States at the beginning of the twenty-first century, scholars, intellectuals, and ordinary citizens disagree on the extent of the breach between Blacks and Whites. While some argue it has narrowed substantially, others claim it is as wide as ever. There is evidence to support both positions. Material conditions for African Americans have undoubtedly improved since the major legal and political reforms in the 1960s. Yet racial identity remains an important component of social appraisal, and this continues to disadvantage Blacks while benefiting Whites.[1] Though at century's end a few African Americans had crossed over to highly visible acceptance, even veneration, among Whites, most Blacks still lived apart from Whites and lagged seriously behind in income, housing, health, and education.[2]

Beyond the conflicting evidence, we believe that some of the disagreement over the state of racial matters results from new, less apparent forms of differentiation that sustain race as a social marker. These are more difficult to detect in part because they are no longer based on biological understandings of race and the overt stereotypes and caricatures that grew out of them. Since the end of World War II, these have gradually disappeared from public view. Although race clearly remains a strong predictor of life chances, the public face of race is now cloaked in a chameleon-like form, an ever-changing camouflage that obscures its force. The unresolved conflicts over facts and their interpretation, disseminated by the media, result in the kind of ambivalence evident in this exchange between a citizen and President Bill Clinton:

MR. MORGAN: Yes, I do honestly think that there is still discrimination in this country to a point. There are a lot of prejudiced people out there that still remain. . . . And I think it has been ironed out in our generation.

THE PRESIDENT: Do you think it's because of personal experiences, do you think it's because you've had more direct personal experience with people from

1

different age groups? Or do you think it's because you grew up in a different time where the climate, the legal and the political and the social climate, was different?

MR. MORGAN: I think it was because I grew up in a different time. We grew up watching television. The *Cosby* show was my favorite show. (Laughter.)

THE PRESIDENT: So, therefore, if you worked at a bank and a Black person came in with a check you wouldn't necessarily think it ought to be held because you saw Bill Cosby and he was a good role model? (Laughter.) No, this is important. No, no, this is important.

MR. MORGAN: Yes, I don't think I would give him a hard time. But at the same time, I have my own prejudices, whereas if I'm walking downtown on a street and I see a Black man walking towards me that's not dressed as well, I may be a little bit scared. So, I mean, at the same time I have those prejudices.

THE PRESIDENT: Do you think that's because of television crime shows, or because of your personal experience?

MR. MORGAN: It would have nothing to do with my personal experience. Just from the media, television shows and things that I have heard.

Appropriately enough, this discussion occurred on 3 December 1997 in Akron, Ohio, during the first town meeting of the President's Initiative on Race. Our findings suggest this young man's experience is typical. Like many Whites, he is ambivalent, "a little bit scared" of some Blacks and admiring of others—more on the basis of what he learns from the media than personal experience, understandably so since most Blacks and Whites in the United States continue to live their private lives apart from one another.[3] And even if they increasingly work together, formal, role-structured job contact with isolated individuals does little to modify preexisting feelings among Whites. Racial isolation heightens the importance of the messages Whites receive about Blacks from the mass media, and especially from the most widely consumed source—television. Its constant stream of messages designed to inform, pleasurably distract, and, above all, put targeted audiences in the mood to buy creates two influential roles for television. Along with other media, it is both a barometer of race relations and a potential accelerator either to racial cohesion or to cultural separation and political conflict. Because Whites control mass media organizations, and because Whites' majority status makes their tastes the most influential in audience-maximizing calculations, media productions offer a revealing indicator of the new forms of racial differentiation. Beyond providing a diagnostic tool, a measuring device for the state of race relations, the media also act as a causal agent: they help to shape and reshape the culture.

In the following chapters, building upon a large body of research, we employ close analyses of media content along with interview data to show the subtle way that racial images on television (and to a lesser extent other mass media) reflect and possibly influence Whites' ways of thinking on racial matters. What is most fascinating about the present situation is that media producers have, like the great majority of Americans, rejected the most blatant forms of racial differentiation to a point some critics have derisively described as "political correctness." Yet racial differentiation lives on nonetheless. Its new forms and the methods by which the media sustain them—in large part inadvertently—are the principal subjects of this book.

White Attitudes and the Paradox of Racial Progress

We believe the majority of White Americans experience ambivalent thoughts and feelings about African Americans, a complex mixture of animosity and yearning for racial harmony. The ambivalence emerges, in part, from a paradox of racial progress. Lacking political or economic clout, Blacks long functioned in the mainstream national culture (outside the White-dominated South) largely as quaint symbols of nostalgia and innocence. Blacks' new political assertiveness and power after World War II, and their large-scale emigration from the South, spread White anxiety and resentment throughout the nation, even as it rendered open proclamations of racial inferiority passé. Thus it is possible that old-fashioned racism, wrong as it was on every level, coexisted with rather positive emotions among many Whites. If Blacks couldn't be expected to achieve, if they were naturally inclined to slow-wittedness and laziness, then they could be regarded with paternal fondness, so long as they showed proper deference. Growing beyond the myths of genetic racial hierarchy, the current culture rejects the most overt claims of Black inferiority—and this ironically cultivates White impatience and hostility.

The contrast becomes clear when we compare Hollywood's submissive, jolly Black mammies and uncles of the 1930s or 1940s[4] with the aggressive Black characters in such hit films of the 1990s as *Independence Day* or *Jerry Maguire*, or compare beloved jazz maestro Louis Armstrong with rappers like Tupac Shakur or Snoop Doggy Dog. Deferential behavior on the part of members of the out-group stimulates affectionate condescension among the in-group; assertiveness does not.

At the outset we need to register an important qualification. This book explores the implicit and explicit meanings and images transmitted by the media that reflect and reinforce the attitudes, assumptions, anxieties, and hopes Whites have about themselves and African Americans.[5] We emphasize White perceptions and sentiments not out of White chauvinism, but because that group holds by far the dominant share of cultural, social, economic, and political power in the United States. When Whites exhibit racism, hostility, or misunderstanding toward other groups, they are uniquely able to act on their negative views in ways that harm those groups and their own interests in a just, efficient, and effective national community.

Questions and Evidence for Answers

The specific questions that guide our study include the following: Assuming that much positive change occurred over the second half of the twentieth century, what is the current state of White beliefs, attitudes, and emotions toward Blacks? How do the media influence the culture in which these have emerged? What are the new hidden codes of racial difference and hierarchy? Why, after decades of heightened awareness and vigilance that have expunged the most overt and offensive stereotypes, do media often convey problematic images of African Americans? How can we "read" these new codes—discern the chameleon—and can anything realistically be done to hasten improvements?

In hunting for answers we naturally begin with overt images and plainly spoken statements, but we also look for comparisons, exclusions, classifications, relationships, and boundaries. Others have written insightfully on media, culture, and race.[6] We hope to advance understanding by studying the way images and words supply information and stimuli to audiences, how they set up implied contrasts and critical omissions, and how they selectively frame the world. Mediated information includes not just what media explicitly tell us but how a given message compares with previous ones and with potential material on the same subject. Mediated information is inherently comparative: audiences interpret a narrative or image through filters shaped by other media content and, of course, by direct experience. Measuring only what appears on the screen or page does not offer a comprehensive picture of its nature and potential impacts. It is the totality of presences and absences that constitutes the mediated communication.

For this reason, we look beyond single genres of media content and, unlike most previous studies of mediated racial politics, beyond news. Not only do most people see far more than news (if they see any at all), but television viewers rarely confine themselves to one kind of show, sitcoms for example. They are as likely to watch dramatic programs and one or two news or "infotainment" programs and, despite the handy remote control, certainly cannot avoid the numerous ads—now crafted precisely to keep their clickers at bay. Many also go to movies, especially the big hits that cross-owned television and print outlets do so much to promote.

For these reasons we study a broad range of media to illuminate the current culture of race; to reveal important influences that media may have on this culture; to suggest how much subtle material pertinent to Black–White relations structures all media productions; and therefore to support the need for a new understanding of the political nature and effects of news, entertainment, and advertising, all the more so as accelerating economic competition blurs the lines between these genres.[7] We hope this understanding might help to inform public debate and perhaps promote changes in the practices of those who shape media products—and of those who consume them.

Unlike most research, our study spans a range of fields from critical and cultural studies to political and other social sciences. It attempts to cross lines that normally separate disciplinary orientations and opposed scholarly discourses. We do this because no single method seems satisfactory by itself to do justice to this complex and emotionally freighted topic. Take, for example, the controversy in political science regarding the adequacy of using standardized attitude statements for detecting and measuring racial prejudice. Researchers have over the years developed inventive techniques for getting respondents to say what they really think about racial matters in a time when such candor is socially discouraged. These measures have revealed continuing negative racial attitudes grouped under such rubrics as "racial resentment," "symbolic racism," "modern racism," and "aversive racism." We believe that a broad grasp and analysis of media content, informed by the insights of such scholarship, promises further advances in understanding this unwieldy and troubling problem.

In the end, our goal is the same as those who use survey research exclusively: to outline the elusive shape of what has largely become a private discourse on a sensitive topic. By *discourse* we simply mean how people understand, think, and talk about something, be it an issue or a category of people. It is of course possible to grasp these ways of thinking by asking people to state their level of agreement or disagreement with a survey item, but the item itself is an economical statement of some common understanding. Despite the prodigious and productive effort to make these summary items accurate and reliable reflections of everyday thinking, they remain volatile. As Schuman et al. show in their comprehensive historical review of racial attitudes[8] (discussed further in chapter 2), survey questions change their meaning over time as common-sense understanding changes. Media content, even of the most fanciful variety, partakes of the same common-sense thinking and thus offers a rich store of the patterns that underlie ways of understanding that often remain undetected until they change and suddenly appear visibly offensive or merely quaint.[9] In this study we propose to raise the grain of these patterns, to enrich our understanding of White racial attitudes, and thereby also to pose new questions.

By revealing the open and covert racial themes in media content—the assumptions or suspicions that permeate American life and shape Whites' hearts and minds—we hope to advance knowledge of mediated communication in ways useful to all concerned. At the same time, we hope this book will add something new to the understanding of race relations more generally.

Discerning the Chameleon

Our findings show that in a variety of ways across the diversity of genres and outlets, the mass media convey impressions that Blacks and Whites occupy different moral universes, that Blacks are somehow fundamentally different from Whites.[10] This is not the only lesson, for the media also convey images of harmony and similarity, and we shall document the complexities and contradictions. But, having only limited personal experience with Blacks, and raised in a culture where race is highly salient and Black persons rest at the bottom of the social hierarchy, Whites may be more likely to remember the negative than the positive in all the unplanned, media-generated impressions. Psychologists have found more generally that people remember negative information most readily.[11] By what they both do and do not convey, the media can stimulate Whites' tendencies to imagine, exaggerate, and misunderstand group differences.

We also find a major difference between the surface and the deeper levels of media content. At the surface, any examination of the media reveals evidence of enormous progress since the days of the widely cited 1968 Kerner Report[12]: greater media visibility for Blacks than ever, even overrepresentation by some measures. Yet at deeper levels, negative images abound. One point of this book is to show how discussions of social and political effects of media, and any resulting policy issues, must be informed by more thorough understanding of media content. We seek to move beyond current, limited understandings of exactly what constitutes the politically influential material in media texts, understandings that distort critical discussions about what makes for "accurate" or "objective" news.

The heart of this book outlines the shape and describes the patterns of the new forms of racial differentiation present in the minds of White Americans and throughout the media. In chapter 2 we first review the recent scholarship on racial attitudes and suggest a model that we believe clarifies Whites' often complicated and conflicted racial sentiments. We emphasize the need to get beyond any simple scheme that categorizes Whites as either racist or not. We then describe a survey and in-depth interviews of Indianapolis residents that illustrate the contradictory nature of White Americans' thinking about Blacks and the part the mass media play in that thinking. The products of the mass media do not fall on the receptive minds of a wholly accepting, ingenuous audience; they interact with personal experience, mainly impersonal, distant contact. As we will show, Whites' attitudes on race and perceptions of Black behavior reveal a necessarily simplified but understandable mode of thinking that arises from the absence of regular, close interaction and from largely hidden but lingering cultural influences. As one would expect, their perceptions and sentiments are particularly responsive to media imagery that reinforces their outlooks.

Chapter 3 explores the national survey data and the scholarship on White racial opinion. It explains the social psychological consequences of limited interpersonal contact with Blacks on White Americans and sets out a cultural framework for interpreting the habits of thought that result. The main argument is that Blacks now occupy a kind of limbo status in White America's thinking, neither fully accepted nor wholly rejected by the dominant culture. The ambiguity of Blacks' situation gives particular relevance and perhaps potency to the images of African Americans in the media.

Our analysis of media content is reported in chapters 4 through 11. We begin in chapter 4 with the network news, where we find that the broad patterns of roles assigned to Blacks fall into a limited range, mainly crime and sports. Politically Blacks are depicted as sources of disruption, as victims, or as complaining supplicants. One gets the impression from the overall pattern in these reports, in other words, that—although they do entertain us in songs and games—in what really counts, Blacks are takers and burdens on society. Turning to the positive side of the societal supply and demand ledger, we also study the racial patterns in the range of experts that appear on newscasts to offer their authoritative and persuasive views.[13] Here we find that Blacks are rarely consulted for their considered opinions. On these dimensions the news rarely publicize Blacks' contributions to America's serious business, making the images that do appear all the more suggestive of a generally irresponsible clan seizing more than their share of generosity's bounty. We set out for the first time in this chapter as well our model to account for the multiple causes of media content. The model points to five forces that interact to produce race-based differentiation: the mainstream culture; the creative needs, limitations, and professional norms of individual media personnel and their organizations; the evolving economics of media industries; the agendas of political elites; and the changing national and international economic structure and the requirements of its healthy growth.

Chapter 5 shows how local television news portrays Blacks in urban communities with a limited palate that paints a world apparently out of control and replete with danger. Here victimizers are more often Black and victims more often White. Racial coding also applies to alleged lawbreakers: White victimizers appear as personalized, named individuals while Black victimizers are more often depersonalized, nameless threats depicted in mug shots cut from a generic stripe of common criminal. Accused Blacks are also far more often shown restrained and in police custody. The accumulated impression from these images is that race alone suffices for comprehensive identification of criminals—that being African American is almost tantamount to guilt.

The average White mistakenly believes that Blacks constitute one-third of the American population, a majority of the poor, and the bulk of welfare rolls. No wonder, perhaps, so many Whites resentfully overestimate government attention and spending on poverty. Their misimpressions may be reinforced by images—and voids—in the media. Television news tends to illustrate welfare and poverty by portraying urban Blacks rather than the (actually more numerous) rural Whites, furnishing symbolic resources many Whites use to justify resentments. In chapter 6 we show that television news often equates Blacks with poverty, turning the mere appearance of African Americans into a coded signal of poverty. We also show how news content leads to public ignorance of poverty's origins through repeated use of dramatic visual symptoms rather than explanations of their underlying causes. In its reporting on poverty, television paints a Bosch-like landscape of social disruption and danger in which the principal actors, mainly Black, are visually associated with poverty as threat. Lacking a consistent thread explaining how poverty symptoms like unemployment, dilapidated housing, and crime connect to each other and to a set of causes and potential solutions, the media provide White audiences little way of resolving any contradictory tugs between fear and sympathy.

Although the reporting on poverty may function largely to keep it off the political agenda, other reports affect perceptions of policy issues that do garner explicit official attention. Chapter 7, on affirmative action, shows how news production processes and political ambitions can combine to stimulate racial misunderstanding on public policy. News organizations, ostensibly disinterested bystanders, do have an agenda: most prefer dramatic conflict that can be packaged in visually interesting, emotionally engaging ways. Add to this the limited ability of most news reports to convey intricacy and nuance, and the incentives of politicians either to board any apparent bandwagon or get out of its way. The result has been a thoroughly misleading depiction of public opinion and the group interests at stake in affirmative action policy. Despite many media depictions of a zero-sum Black–White contest, the chapter argues that affirmative action distributes costs and benefits in complicated ways that cross racial (and gender) lines. And, fed by the incendiary comments of some politicians and the silence of others, we find many news reports that constructed a Black–White brawl on the issue that is repudiated by survey research. The overlap between Black and White opinion is substantial. With exceptions, news reports and editorials obscured the common ground and accentuated the discord.

Black political power in the news is the subject of chapter 8. We begin with an extended case study that illustrates how television's interest in conflict and drama exaggerated the political significance of Louis Farrakhan, leader of the Nation of Islam, by repeated attention to his association with the Reverend Jesse Jackson. This coverage elevated the importance of the racially symbolic aspects of Jackson's presidential candidacy over the issues and interracial coalition he promoted. It repeatedly tied Jackson to an icon of racial menace as it unwittingly provided Farrakhan with a national forum, enhancing his political credibility and potential power. We then turn to a local setting where we see how these news conventions work to produce an impression of Blacks as significantly more self-seeking and vocally demanding than Whites. The implicit comparison portrays White politicians as more public spirited and politically altruistic in their balance of concerns than Blacks.

In chapter 9 we turn from information and politics to the pleasing but revealing distractions of television entertainment. Producers of shows most popular with White audiences cast the few Black actors who appear in superior organizational positions to their White counterparts. Thus we see Blacks as chief residents, police captains, and corporate managers. This well-intentioned utopian reversal imposes a formal distance between Black and White actors that hobbles the development of interracial intimacy and the enlargement of the audience's sympathetic imagination. Meanwhile, shows with mostly Black casts appear on niche broadcast or cable networks. Ironically, entertainment television mirrors a racially segregated real world.

In chapter 10 we probe advertising, the fuel that drives "free" television. The creative talent in advertising is exquisitely sensitive to popular culture and its connection with social trends, to the mainstream as well as its titillating borders. Analyzing the broad patterns of ad content reveals that, contrary to the time of the Kerner Report, Blacks commonly populate the attractive world of the television commercial. A Black person appears somewhere in over a third of primetime ads. Although ads eschew most stereotypes, on less overt dimensions a more subtle pattern emerges: Blacks attain less visibility than Whites in ads for luxury products such as perfume and jewelry and fantasy-related products like vacations; in other words, those where advertisers are selling myths and promising fulfillment of especially vague needs. For such products, advertisers cannot hope to boost sales simply by giving information about how well it satisfies a commonplace need. The distance and subtle differentiation evident here is echoed in the absence of interracial contact in ads. Several measures testify to advertisers' belief, no doubt backed by some combination of intuition and audience research, that, racial progress notwithstanding, many Whites remain troubled by contact with Blacks.

Our final analysis of media content in chapter 11 covers Hollywood movie hits. Here the story is mixed: heartening progress combined with continued subtle stereotyping and distancing or exclusion of African Americans. The token integration and emotional distance between White and Black characters prevalent on primetime television tends to prevail on the big screen as well. Although a handful of African American stars have demonstrated bankable crossover appeal, this is mainly in broadly comic or super-masculine action hero formats that recollect traditional stereotypes of clowning minstrels or menacing brutes. Interracial love is virtually absent, though friendship is more common than on television, and longer running time and more complex story lines do allow some movies to provide perhaps the most socially beneficial, even "accurate," impressions of African Americans of any media form.

After documenting and developing an understanding of the media's subtle reflections and influences upon racial harmony, illustrated by these and other examples, the book suggests a reorientation in the professional thinking and practices of media personnel. Chapter 12 urges a reexamination of such goals as truth and accuracy, and even profit. In conjunction with this effort we propose systematic monitoring and vigorous public discussion of the media's impacts on Black–White relations. The vision here is of an undertaking as well-funded and as visible to government and industry leaders as the nation's long-standing dialogue about media and violence. We are under no illusions about the ease of reforming the media's activities in the area of race. Images of violence are certainly still with us, as is superficial, distracting campaign news, to take two primary deficiencies for which media have long been criticized. On the other hand, when it comes to matters of race, market incentives and other influences may point media more decisively toward reform.

The Normative Ideal

What goal, then, would we want the media to pursue if they were to contribute more positively to race relations? Always implicit and sometimes explicit in this kind of research is a baseline standard by which the conditions described and explained can be judged. Our normative ideal is what used to be called "brotherhood." That word, a casualty of the shift toward gender-neutral language, captures the sentiments needed to overcome America's legacy of racism. We propose to use the more modern term *racial comity*. The *Oxford English Dictionary* defines comity as "courtesy, civility; kindly and considerate behavior towards others." Comity would allow Whites and

Blacks to see common interests and values more readily and thus to cooperate in good faith to achieve mutually beneficial objectives. Research on "social capital" and trust strongly suggests that trustful and cooperative interaction among group members enhances a society's material and physical (not to mention spiritual) well being.[14] Furthermore, comity is self-reinforcing: the more trustful the interaction, the more good results and the higher the incentives for even more cooperation and trust. A context of comity can nurture a virtuous circle of respect, empathy, and generosity to replace the vicious circle of suspicion, separation, and stinginess.

Framing the concern with race relations in terms of racial comity highlights the shared self-interest of all Americans in understanding and healing the continuing breach. It avoids moral exhortation or implicit calls for Whites to feel collective guilt, which generally produce resentment, not repentance. Although racial comity means something more than mere tolerance, it does not require that members of the two groups no longer identify as such, only that they act kindly and empathetically enough to see beyond skin color to their own shared interests in a more effective and harmonious society.

Conditions of empathy and trust illustrate more concretely what might be meant by racial and ethnic "reconciliation," promoted by President Clinton's Initiative on Race during 1997–98. For Whites consistently to support genuine reconciliation, they need to possess a nuanced, contextualized understanding that Blacks are fundamentally "just like" Whites, and yet, because of racism's legacy and persistence, profoundly different. The absence of such an empathetic understanding, the frequent White ignorance and obliviousness to a larger vision of racial justice, variously disappoints or enrages many Blacks, further compounding mutual alienation, the opposite of racial comity.

Still, the puzzles here are deep and complicated. Even if we somehow had the power to transform the communication industry, the grip of racialized thinking upon White (and Black) Americans, uncertainties about how mediated communications influence this thinking, and the difficulty of devising palliative messages, let alone ensuring their consistent provision, would remain. Our purpose is to illuminate these relationships and dilemmas, not to pretend that they can be easily or conclusively understood and set right.

The Racial Chameleon

A Caveat for Scholars

When we began this study of media and race, we soon realized it would require a substantial degree of interpretation and choice—for example, what counts as an important media "text," and what aspects of it do we analyze? Inescapably, when selecting what to analyze, we made assumptions about potential meanings for audiences, their possible impacts on thoughts and emotions. Indeed, we often made those inferences on a preliminary basis—that is, hypothesized them—before undertaking the analysis.

Consider, for example, portrayals of Blacks and Whites on network news. If we assume it is worthwhile to study these in detail, we need to decide exactly what aspects to explore. One element we believed important as an indicator of Blacks' cultural status, and thus a potential shaper of some Whites' sentiments, was representation of Blacks as experts. We began with an assumption that seeing mostly White persons and few Blacks acting as experts in network news might have a common meaning for many audience members who share similar sentiments—say, those who have ambivalent or hostile feelings about African Americans. That is why we recorded the race of every expert who appeared in a large sample of news programs. We thought a dominance of Whites and scarcity of Blacks could confirm many Whites' sense that the natural order of expertise is White-dominated, that Black expertise is exceptional. For some of them, we thought, that sense might bolster a belief or suspicion of Whites' racial superiority.

Others might find other potential meanings in the networks' representations of Blacks for White audiences, or might prefer to analyze aspects we omitted. And of course actual audience members can and do read texts in a multitude of ways. Those individuals might fail entirely to register, consciously or unconsciously, elements of the texts that our analysis highlights. But we know of no way to undertake a systematic study of media and political communication in the area of race without making some assumptions about which aspects of the texts have potential political significance for large segments of the audience. We ground those assumptions in our conceptualization of White racial thinking, laid out in chapter 2. We use that understanding, based on decades of research into race relations, to guide us to those aspects of media texts that might resonate with and affect in some way the belief systems of significant segments of the audience.

Many scholars prefer to see experiments, surveys, or other methods that yield quantitative data on audience responses to media before drawing any inferences as to their meaning for audiences. But in practice, the media texts that researchers use as stimuli, and the data on responses, remain selective and susceptible to different interpretations. Definitive proof that particular media messages have caused specific behaviors or thoughts among audiences has long eluded social scientists. Thus a general theory that predicts precisely what dimensions of mediated texts create, reinforce, or change specific sentiments among particular audience groups remains unavailable to guide the present study. However, researchers *have* provided strong evidence for media influence at a more general level of analysis of media content and audience thinking.[15] This body of work guides our assumption that the patterns we find do at least have the potential to affect audiences' sentiments.

In most of our analyses of media content, then, we rely upon the following argument to guide our focus on specific elements of the text and our discussions of their *potential* political significance. Its logic goes like this:

1. From the vast empirical literature on information processing, we know that people use mental shortcuts (such as stereotypes) to interpret communications, even as mediated communication influences development and use of the shortcuts.

2. And we know from the large body of research on Whites' racial attitudes that significant portions of White Americans, probably a majority, hold negative sentiments toward Blacks often summarized and encoded in shorthand appraisals and stereotypes.

3. Our understanding of information processing, public opinion, and media influence can guide our analysis of media content to reveal patterns likely to resonate, either consciously or unconsciously, and thus to affect White thinking about race.

4. Granting the important cautions previous scholarship raises about inferring media effects, we avoid any strong claims about them. But a combination of empirical data and logic strongly suggests that mediated communications may indeed stimulate similar (*not* identical) responses among large blocks of audience members, and that the content patterns we find are therefore at least potentially significant for race relations.

The preceding section was intended for many of our fellow researchers in the social sciences. But others who study mass communication, those with orientations generally identified with cultural studies, might argue that this whole paradigm of emphasizing media effects unduly limits our understanding. They might deny that only empirical demonstrations of statistically significant "media effects" on the mass public's opinions can justify the study of mass media. For one thing, the flow of influence between media content and audience sentiments is reciprocal. Media producers constantly probe and respond to their targets' thinking, even as media products help shape that thinking. Moreover, although each individual is socially conditioned and socially positioned to some degree, each nonetheless helps to construct his or her own meanings from the media. The "effects" of media reside in the ongoing relationship between individuals' consciousness and what they notice, process, interpret, remember, and discard in the media. All this mutual influence blurs the lines sufficiently to make statistical demonstrations difficult and their results suspect.

We hope in this book to reach those committed to both the social scientific and the cultural or critical study of the media and race. We do not think it necessary to take sides, and so we employ methodologies and insights drawn from both groups and, we hope, build fruitfully upon both.

2 White Racial Attitudes in the Heartland

N THIS CHAPTER we try to account for the surprising amount of ambiguity in the massive body of writings on the attitudes of Whites toward African Americans and offer a clarifying model of racial thinking. The model focuses on the broad array of racial sentiments among Whites and emphasizes not the minority of outright racists but the perplexed majority. The more subtle forms of racial thinking that have evolved over the past thirty years, illustrated here by probing a sample of Whites from Indianapolis, have left most Whites with a complex amalgam of ideas and feelings better labeled as ambivalence or animosity than racism.

Scholarly Disagreement on White Racial Attitudes

Recent scholarship on U.S. race relations offers convincing evidence for both pessimism and optimism. Some observers believe White racism continues to suffuse politics and social relations.[1] Others insist that a remarkable decline of stereotyping and a reduction in desired social distance is the real story.[2] Still others fall between these poles.[3]

Aside from the differences in conceptualization that may be responsible for the disparate conclusions by scholars, it is apparent that White racial attitudes have undergone a change that is neither insignificant nor yet fully consummated. We argue that White racial thinking now spans a spectrum that runs from *racial comity* and understanding to *ambivalence*, then to *animosity*, and finally to outright *racism*. The bulk of Whites exhibit ambivalence that may be tipped toward comity or hostility depending on the interaction of political climate, personal experience, and mediated communications. Although boundaries between the orientations are blurry, we distinguish three dimensions of belief and one of emotional response that array Whites along a continuum of racial sentiments. One taps the degree to which Whites attribute *homogeneity in negative traits to African Americans*. The second belief component measures the degree to which Whites deny the *existence of discrimination*. Denial of discrimination is perhaps the most politically significant because it is often sufficient for White opposition to progressive racial policy. The third is *the degree to which Whites see themselves as having group interests that conflict with those of Blacks.* The fourth dimension measures the *degree and direction of emotional responses to Blacks as a group.* The four dimensions are correlated but independent.

Politically significant racial sentiments frequently combine both negative ideas and negative emotions about Blacks. Thus we deal in analytically separable but parallel tracks of cognitions and emotions, while recognizing that the two intermingle in human consciousness. How people interpret their emotions, what kinds of thoughts the emotional state produces, critically shapes behavior in social and political life. We illustrate the continuum of attitudes in table 2.1, which readers should study carefully.

The graphical presentation of these ideas does not imply the existence of sharply demarcated categories of thoughts and feelings. At the *comity* end of the spectrum would be a White person who believes it is not possible to generalize about African American individuals any more than about Whites. Such Whites acknowledge the continued, varied forms and legacies of discrimination that impede Black progress; fail to see politics as an arena where Black and White group interests must clash; and have either neutral or positive feelings toward Blacks as individuals or as categories in their political thinking.

We think this multidimensional concept a more useful way to understand Whites' racial thinking than alternatives that tend to draw more rigid lines, often suggesting Whites are either racist or not. A White might view Blacks as possessing generally negative traits yet still acknowledge widespread discrimination, for example, or may see great variety among Blacks yet consider African American political activity a threat to the interests of Whites and acknowledge little present-day discrimination. In fact, by arguing that Whites are often ambivalent though readily pushed by environmental stimuli toward animosity, we are saying precisely that such complicated, dimension-scrambling mixtures are common. For instance, one influential theory called "aversive racism"[4] proposes that many Whites consciously adhere to egalitarian ideals and regard themselves as nonracists, yet have unrecognized negative feelings about Blacks that can lead to prejudiced behavior. This would place them at some point between the extremes on the scale from racism to comity.

At the other end of the spectrum, full-blown *racists* believe Blacks and Whites are fundamentally different. In their view, Blacks (rare exceptions

Table 2.1 Spectrum of White Racial Sentiment

	← **Comity**	**Ambivalence**	**Animosity**	**Racism** →
	Individual Diversity	*Negative Tendencies*	*Stereotyping*	*Hierarchy*
Negative Homogeneity	Individual Blacks, like Whites, vary widely in traits	Black individuals tend more than Whites to exhibit negative traits	Most Blacks share a syndrome of negative traits	Blacks are a lower order of humanity than Whites, with consistently negative traits
	Empathy	*Underestimation*	*Denial*	*Separation & Discrimination*
Structural Impediments	Discrimination remains prevalent, causing great harm to equal opportunity	Discrimination may occur in isolated individual instances	Anti-Black discrimination is a thing of the past; Whites now experience more racial discrimination	Blacks cannot attain equality no matter what society does; discrimination is therefore necessary
	Political Acceptance	*Political Concern*	*Political Rejection*	*Political Aggression*
Conflicting Group Interests	Fundamental interests of Blacks and Whites do not differ; cooperation possible and desirable	Black political power sometimes creates trouble for Whites as a group; cooperation suspect	Black political power extracts advantages at White expense; cooperation rarely to mutual advantage	Black political power poses grave dangers to Whites as a group; cooperation dangerous
	Comfort	*Disquiet*	*Fear & Anger*	*Hatred*
Emotional Responses	Low intensity, positive or neutral feelings	Low intensity oscillation from neutral to positive to negative	Largely negative, moderately intense emotions	Intensely and globally negative emotions toward Blacks

aside) share such homogeneously negative characteristics that they must be an inferior rank of human against whom discrimination is inevitable and justifiable. Embedded in racist ideas are the assumptions that human beings fall into natural and distinct racial categories akin to species, with identifying biological and behavioral traits that reliably distinguish members of one race from members of the other; that the races can be ranked in order of inherent ability and social desirability; and that race is therefore a legitimate basis for discriminatory distribution of valued resources. We adapt this standard definition of racism,[5] add the dimension of negative emotions, and situate racism at one pole of the broader continuum outlined in table 2.1, with special emphasis on its political implications.

Racial *animosity* occupies an important step short of racism. Although those exhibiting animosity often get labeled as racists, they do not see their stereotyped anti-Black generalizations as adding up to a natural racial order that places Whites on top and legitimizes discrimination. Rather, animosity consists of less intense and all-encompassing stands on the four dimensions. As indicated in table 2.1, animosity boils down to stereotyping, denial, political rejection and demonization, and fearful, angry emotions. Those characterized by animosity tend to overestimate group-linked differences between Whites and Blacks. They underestimate shared values while perceiving outgroup members as largely if not homogeneously possessing negative traits.

Whites who exhibit animosity deny discrimination and other structural impediments to Blacks' social mobility. Denial is rooted partially in sheer ignorance: many Whites simply do not realize that despite civil rights laws and highly visible progress in such areas as higher education and the entertainment industry, Blacks still face massive discrimination in employment, housing, and medical care, among other fields.[6] Many are also unaware of how structural changes in the economy, such as the loss of entry-level manufacturing jobs in the core cities of most metropolitan areas, disproportionately affect Blacks.[7] Nor do the subtle but systematic advantages conferred by the legacy of White privilege register with most Whites.

The gap in Whites' understanding of past and present life for African Americans tends to support their beliefs that laziness and weak will are now the chief impediments to Blacks' social mobility.[8] Such moral judgments from those Whites who are simply misinformed as to the true state of discrimination against Blacks are thus analytically distinct from those of Whites who are simply rationalizing their hostility.

The third dimension taps the political salience to the White person of racial group membership. Whites characterized by animosity feel that belonging to the White "race" establishes group interests that must be defended in politics against those exerting political power who are Black. Politics to them is generally a zero-sum game pitting Black interests against White.

The fourth dimension involves negative emotional responses to Blacks. High sensitivity to racial classifications often yields negative emotions, especially anger or resentment toward Blacks as a group, and fear or anxiety about being close to Black individuals. Whites exhibiting animosity feel threatened by Blacks as a group and as individuals.[9] Notice that for those with animosity, such negative emotions do not necessarily involve a conviction that Blacks are inferior as a group, nor are the feelings typically as intense and central to the political and social worldview of their holders as for racists.

A White can feel more or less animosity depending on the particular information circulating in his or her environment and on current conditions. For example, a White person alone in a city at night might feel more fearful of a Black stranger than a White, or believe most Blacks are on welfare or face no racial discrimination, thus exhibiting *a degree* of animosity according to our definition. And many Whites who do not necessarily believe in Black inferiority, who may even live near or socialize with African Americans, nonetheless reject the legitimacy and moral status of Blacks' political claims and demands. If we were arraying people on the continuum from mild to strong animosity, we would probably want to add such different components of animosity and rank people according to how many they exhibit. Whites whose animosity is inflamed—including ambivalent Whites responding to specific situations and stimuli—become receptive to coded campaign appeals designed to mobilize them into coalitions with traditional racists.[10] In this sense, the fact that the majority of Whites are not racist can become less relevant to political outcomes than the fact that so many can be induced to vote alongside racists.

Racial animosity hinders coalition building between working- and middle-class Blacks and Whites who might otherwise support policies that produce more equality in allocation of valued resources. A vicious cycle ensues, with heightened inequality and unresponsiveness to Blacks' need for new government policies inducing hopelessness, alienation, and damaging behavior especially among the Black persons most salient to Whites possessing animus, the so-called underclass. Actions by members of this group, both perceived and real, further confirms in those Whites the tendency to overestimate Black pathology and burden on White-dominated society,[11] aggravating their tendency toward political demonization and rejection.

While those with racial animosity often experience some of these negative feelings, they do not always hold consistently to all their antagonistic sentiments. That is to say, *they are susceptible to change.* Much animosity is rooted not in the seemingly intense personality needs and motivations that explain racism, but in ignorance, confusion, and anxiety. These conditions can be ameliorated, and they can be understood by Blacks as creating animosity, something promisingly different from (even if nearly as damaging as) racism. Once African Americans (and Whites of good will) recognize that some Whites who sound and act a lot like racists have the potential to move toward ambivalence and even comity, that understanding can itself contribute to positive evolution.[12]

And what of *ambivalence*, the point on our spectrum between comity and animosity? As the interviews will show, the specific content and shape of ambivalence varies considerably from individual to individual. Whites bring complicated combinations of assumptions, misinformation, emotional needs, experiences, and personality traits to their thinking about race. For instance, a White may oppose increased welfare spending, but on grounds that emphasize a consistent philosophy of individual self-reliance. She may be convinced, based on some amalgam of ignorance, exposure to media stereotypes, and salient examples in her own personal experience that most Blacks do not work hard and so are not deserving. If she further believes that most welfare spending goes to Blacks, this naturally heightens her opposition to welfare expenditures. Yet that same White woman may feel that in the exceptional case when a Black individual *is* deserving, he would merit aid. Moreover, as our interviews suggest, this White person may well acknowledge after some careful questioning that a lot of Blacks do face discrimination, which may explain why some stop trying to get ahead, so that judging whether people *deserve* assistance becomes more difficult than it seems at first.

This book considers such reasoning to be an example of the complex ambivalence, shading often into animosity, that most frequently characterizes the majority group. Again, this portrayal implies that correcting Whites' ignorance holds considerable promise for enhancing racial comity. On the other hand, the ignorant assumptions may themselves constitute a manifestation of underlying racism or animosity. The ease with which so many Whites seem to believe Blacks to be undeserving suggests as much. Still, we want to argue that most Whites are not incurably racist. Instead, a complicated ambivalence characterizes the bulk of the White citizenry as it does the bulk of our interviews, with individual variation that places some closer to racial comity and others to animosity.

The reason for all this conceptualization of racial thinking is that animosity and racism are reflected in political decisionmaking. The higher a White person scores on a hypothetical animosity / racism scale, the more they tend to oppose remedial policy attention from government.[13] We do not suggest that opposition, say, to busing for school integration or to affirmative action in itself indicates racial animosity. People might and do oppose such policies for other reasons. But animosity tends to be associated with Whites' rejection of *open-minded deliberation on racial inequality as a high priority public policy problem.*

An end to denial and a growth toward empathetic understanding might not yield a happy consensus among Whites and Blacks on policy remedies. Yet it would by definition encourage the public and government to place a higher priority on discourse aimed not at expressing resentments, finding scapegoats, or repeating comfortable shibboleths, but at discovering ways to ameliorate the obstacles African Americans still face, encumbrances that ultimately diminish the entire society.

The Indianapolis Study

We now turn to examine at close hand racial attitudes and images among a group of White Indianapolis residents. We first analyze the results of a standardized telephone survey of this group and then follow up with an analysis of face-to-face, in-depth interviews to see what underlies their racial thinking. Our goal was to trace the origins and consequences of the most recent wave of White attitudes toward Blacks, with special attention to the role of the media in tipping conflicted and ambivalent sentiments toward animosity.

In exploring decades of poll data on White racial attitudes, Schuman et al.[14] empirically reveal Whites' ambivalence. They find that cause for optimism or pessimism depends on the specific questions selected for analysis. White attitudes on inherent racial differences and the desirability of the principle of integration have clearly changed in a positive direction. But if one looks specifically at White attitudes toward implementation of these high-minded principles, a less hopeful picture emerges. Thus even interpretation of some poll results comes into doubt as survey questions, though precisely reproduced in studies over time, change meaning in the minds of respondents. For example, the term *equality* has a very different meaning today—freighted as it is by negative associations with affirmative action—

than it did in the civil rights era when northern Whites reacted to the oppressive treatment of Blacks by southern racists.[15] Schuman et al. call for greater effort at asking respondents for their interpretations of the questions and their answers as one way of advancing knowledge in this area. One goal of our study was to contribute to this effort by asking respondents specifically about the foundations of their beliefs, the sources of information for their attitudes, and their understanding of these questions. If, as Kinder and Sanders say, Whites' attitudes are powerfully influenced by their mental images of Blacks, then we need to address their sources.[16]

To assess some of the reasons for White attitudes—what influences them and, especially, how people arrive at them—we undertook a telephone survey of a random sample of Indianapolis residents during spring 1997 (N = 251). The survey included a question about willingness to participate in a longer face-to-face interview. Ultimately we conducted twenty-five such interviews, with a subsample of the volunteers in respondents' homes, in bookstores, and in coffee shops.

The Survey

Because denial of continuing discrimination has such potent political implications, we selected it as the centerpiece of the survey and as an entry point into a discussion with our respondents on their broader racial attitudes. We selected five items to measure the belief that because no significant impediments to Black progress remain, Blacks' success or failure can be traced to individual character flaws or lack of effort. The items comprise a set of conventional measures used in the National Election Studies (NES) and other national surveys. Following are the item-by-item responses from the Indianapolis study, stated as the percentage that responded "strongly agree" or "agree." Full data and comparative results from prior national surveys can be found in the appendix, table A.1.

1. Irish, Italians, Jewish, and many other minorities overcame prejudice and worked their way up. Blacks should do the same without any special favors: 76.8 percent strongly agree or agree.

2. Most Blacks who are on welfare programs could get a job if they really tried: 77.8 percent.

3. If Blacks would only try harder they could be just as well off as Whites: 58.2 percent.

4. Black neighborhoods tend to be run down because Blacks simply do not take care of their property: 50.2 percent.

5. A history of slavery and being discriminated against has created conditions that make it difficult for Black people to work their way up: 50.9 percent.

An analysis of these five statements indicated they all tapped a common underlying sentiment, or attitudinal dimension.[17] (The full survey and interview protocols are displayed on the book's website.) Accordingly, we combined the items into a sixteen-point index of racial denial and divided the respondents into three groups based on their scores: those scoring highest (11–15), those in the middle (6–10), and those with the lowest scores (0–5). Figure 2.1 shows the distribution of scores. Note here the predominance of those who fall into the middle, or what we call the "conflicted" or "ambivalent" group. It is this group that is politically most significant and thus the focus of the follow-up interview analysis.

When we analyze the data to find the factors that predict denial, a mixed but potentially hopeful picture emerges.[18] The four major predictors of denial are ideology (measured by self-designation as liberal, moderate, and conservative), age, education, and knowledge. These are illustrated in the left-hand side of appendix figure A.1. Ideology's impact is expected, as conservatives are philosophically more prone to individual-level explanations

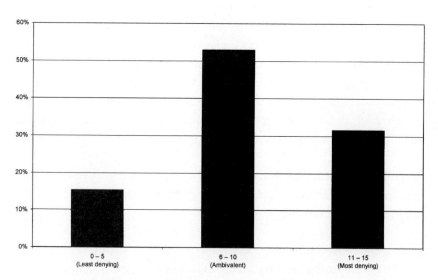

Figure 2.1 Racial Denial Groups (average score = 8.8)

for success and failure.[19] Age is also an expected predictor as older people were socialized when traditional, biological notions of racism were commonplace. Because ideology and age are slightly correlated—some people become conservative as they grow older[20]—there is a bit of good news here: to the extent that these are indeed generational effects, the passage of time and maturation of new generations could reduce denial.

The best news comes in the influences of education and knowledge, the two most powerful predictors of denial. In the survey we asked people to estimate the percentage of Blacks in the U.S. population and the percentage of the U.S. budget going to welfare. We combined these into a three-point index of racial knowledge such that the higher one's score the more accurate one's estimates. In general, the levels of knowledge in these areas are not impressive. For example, the respondents' average estimate of the percentage of Blacks in the population was 30 percent, two and one-half times the actual number, and a fifth of the sample estimated it at 40 percent or higher. These findings resemble those in national surveys.[21] Respondents' estimates of the welfare budget were somewhat better. Here, in contrast to the two-thirds that had overestimated the percentage of Blacks in the population, "only" about half overestimated the size of the welfare budget, but this was going by the most generous definition, which includes Aid to Families with Dependent Children (AFDC), Medicaid, food stamps, and disability (12 percent of the federal budget). Only one in ten of the sample got the right answer to both questions. By contrast, 40 percent grossly exaggerated both the size of the Black population and the size of the welfare budget, which many associate with Black poverty that seems both incurable and—by common argument—traceable to moral and individual causes.[22]

As education goes up, the tendency to deny continuing racial discrimination diminishes. More interesting, knowledge also exerts an influence independent of education. In other words, once the influence of education has been factored out, knowing more about Blacks still leads Whites to engage in less denial. The sunny interpretation of this is that even well-educated respondents have potential reservoirs of sympathy that may be tapped simply by correcting their misimpression of a massive Black population feasting on a swollen welfare budget. The alternative, less optimistic explanation is that denial is the cause of these exaggerated estimates, that the inflated perceptions suggest a siege mentality on the part of those Whites who see Black threat and dependency everywhere, especially in the media.

The Effects of Denial

To illustrate the political implications of denial, we undertook the analysis of Indianapolis respondents illustrated in the right side of the diagram in appendix figure A.1. Those implications are decisive and strong. In the survey we asked respondents about their support for increased federal spending on programs targeted to help Blacks. Two variables influence this attitude: ideology and denial. We expected the influence of ideology, but an even stronger association arose with denial (with the effects of ideology factored out). We also asked respondents whether they would favor a hypothetical, temporary (five-year) tax increase that would "guarantee a 50 percent reduction" in Black welfare and unemployment. Denial has an influence here as well, but it is weaker. This may be because respondents were less willing to see themselves as mean-spirited. Or it may show that, given the premises of the question—a "guarantee" of success—even denial-prone Whites are willing to open their wallets for racial progress. Also, since the effects of ideology on support for this policy are statistically insignificant once the effects of denial are held constant, at least in theory, even conservatives might be willing to contribute to a program that deals effectively with the problem. The looming obstacle here, however, is that interviewees—even the most liberal—were in fact skeptical about the effectiveness of government programs, possibly because of their underpublicized success at reducing welfare and poverty.[23]

The Interviews

Though standardized surveys are valuable for tracing connections between attitudes and such structural variables as ideology, age, and gender, the deeper sources of racial attitudes and their character often lay hidden from public view and emerge only in private moments. As Fowler puts it: "Most overt racist discourse is likely to take place behind closed doors or in the company of sympathetic listeners. . . . [T]he discreet face of racism is not responsive to established research methodologies. . . ."[24] It is for this reason that we asked respondents whether they would be willing to follow up with face-to-face interviews where we hoped such private moments would encourage candid discussion. For these interviews, we revisited key parts of the survey and asked our respondents to explain their answers. In particular we looked for the reasoning that led to their answers, and especially for the sources of the beliefs and feelings supporting their denial. We cannot claim equivalency between the face-to-face interviewees and the larger sample of which they are a self-selected part. The face-to-face sample is somewhat older and, thus, wealthier and more conservative than the larger Indianapolis group. There is, nevertheless, close similarity on education and on denial, the centerpiece of our analysis. A comparison of the larger with the smaller sample can be found in appendix table A.2.

To begin our discussion, we asked respondents to account for their agreement or disagreement with two attitude items: "If Blacks would only try harder, they would be just as well off as Whites," and "Irish, Italian, Jewish, and many other minorities overcame prejudice. Blacks should do the same without any special favors."

After the conversation flagged, we next asked about two of the knowledge items that predict racial denial—the percentage of Blacks in the population and the percentage of the federal budget going to welfare. We also asked respondents for the reasoning behind their support for or opposition to affirmative action and finally media-related questions about sources of information and general impressions of Blacks they got from television. The idea throughout was to encourage people to say whatever was on their minds, hoping that one or more of the questions would stimulate an open, candid discussion. This strategy worked well in nearly every interview. Guarded responses gave way to easy discussion, sometimes emotional, and in several cases the interviewees revealed that they rarely talked about these issues despite their interest in them.

For the most part the denial scale did a good job of discriminating significant differences among respondents' feelings and racial beliefs: those low on the denial scale were genuinely sympathetic toward Blacks and spoke with conviction about their observations of continuing racial discrimination. Those in the conflicted group—by far the largest in our sample—had predictably mixed feelings. They generally recognized the discrimination and continuing disadvantage suffered by Blacks and offered more or less sympathetic reactions; but there were limits to their sympathy and understanding. These limits offer tantalizing clues to the sources of beliefs and feelings that shift the tenuous balance from consideration to indifference and even animosity. Finally, those who scored highest on the scale proved to be quite confident in their vision of a White world endangered by the encroachment of Blacks on White privilege. Only one of the twenty-five respondents escaped proper categorization by the scale. The scale identified him as ambivalent (he scored 8 on the denial scale), but the respondent, a fifty-four-year-old painter, regarded race mixing as a plot to increase racial strife and thus government power: "Multiculturalism is against reason, against God, against humanity."

We also detected a potentially serious problem with one of the scale items, the often-used racial denial statement, "If Blacks would only try harder, they would be just as well off as Whites." The statement is intended to measure the belief that Blacks exhibit less than a normal amount of motivation, perhaps a euphemism for the stereotype of Black laziness. This was indeed the case for most respondents. But six of the twenty-five interviewees had another interpretation of the statement: they recognized that since discrimination is a realistic fact of life for Blacks, greater effort is needed to overcome it. Far from measuring belief in the stereotype, the item for the six respondents tapped an assessment of continuing White opposition to avenues for Black achievement, though not all were sympathetic to Black complaints about this, arguing that more effort would be more productive than complaining. And another respondent disagreed with the statement because he felt some Blacks were less inherently capable and thus additional effort would be wasted. We do not know the extent of this ambiguity among the other respondents in the larger sample nor, obviously, in the larger University of Michigan studies that have used this item on a regular basis; it suggests, however, the great care that is necessary when interpreting survey responses, especially on matters of race, and the need for alternative measurement strategies.[25]

To summarize our general findings, the interviewees tended to rely on personal experience to explain their denial, often from a few vivid examples, but they also relied on the mediated reality of local news and entertainment television. In effect, the mediated images supplied authoritative bolstering evidence for their attitudes. In some cases the process worked in reverse, however. Here people discounted personal experience that offered demonstrable proof of Black effort and hard work—no different from White—in favor of television images, often vague, of welfare cheats and Black violence. In either case, media serve as resources for perpetuating racial animosity. What did not arise much, unsurprisingly in view of the media images we document later, was interviewees drawing on television or other media for evidence that pulled them *toward* comity. None cited evidence from media that Blacks are essentially the same in character, morals, and capabilities as Whites, and that the main racial distinction is the heritage and present reality of discrimination faced by African Americans. When present, this absolutely essential information came overwhelmingly from personal experience.

Those Whites who harbored negative feelings selected Blacks they knew, often at work, to illustrate their claims that Blacks in general do not deserve any special consideration. This was typically a two-part argument that also relied on mediated information. The first part is that a Black co-worker, or perhaps several, use race as a way of extracting concessions or as a smoke screen for covering personal failure. This is not true for all Blacks they know, just the few salient examples that sanction their opposition to group remedies. The second part of their argument relies on examples of successful Blacks—Oprah Winfrey, Tiger Woods, and Michael Jordan were often named—to prove that Blacks can make it if they only try harder. By inference if other Blacks don't make it, that means they must not care to work hard and thus don't deserve to make it. Nor do they merit sympathy or government assistance.

When we probed for respondents' source of evidence for their typically inflated estimates of Blacks in the population, we found that many simply generalized from their own experience as they walked and drove through Indianapolis. Others remarked on the number of Blacks they had seen on local news, the familiar crime stories that portrayed Blacks as victims or perpetrators. These vivid and memorable examples ran together into a quasi-statistical critical mass, one that elicited both fear and denial, albeit couched in restrained terms. In the absence of more definitive information, respondents simply relied on what was readily available from their experience.[26]

And now to the more detailed analysis. To simplify our task we divide our respondents into three groups identified in figure 2.1 based on their racial denial scores: those scoring highest (11–15), those in the middle (6–10), and those with the lowest scores (0–5). Those in the middle comprised the largest group, fifteen people, or 60 percent. Those with the highest scores comprised the next highest number, seven people, or 28 percent. Only three (12 percent) fell into the lowest scoring category of those Whites who generally acknowledged the barriers that still confront African Americans.

The High Denial Group

In a way, those in the high denial group are somewhat easier to describe because they either subscribe to old-fashioned biological racism rooted in the dominant culture of their youth or because they hold extreme political or religious beliefs (e.g., prohibitions against race mixing). In short, they are bound to a worldview that denies racial equality. Of the seven in this group, five were female and two male.

Only one person in the group openly professed beliefs in inherent racial biological differences, an eighty-two-year-old woman who offered a theory of racial superiority based on European facial features and skull shape. She like many others in this group confidently denied the continuing existence of discrimination, while two conceded that though it may continue to exist, it is more than balanced by Black discrimination against Whites. These claims were based on first-hand experience readily generalized to group identity rather than to individual behavior, an ironic position in light of the common argument among this group that Blacks needed to be treated as individuals when it came to matters of affirmative action. For those in high denial, negative experiences with individual Blacks redound to the discredit of the entire group, but public policy must treat everyone in that group as unconnected individuals. This pattern is also observed by social psychologists who find that the "best" members of an out-group (e.g., Oprah Winfrey, Bill Cosby, Colin Powell) are praised lavishly while the worst are caricatured as villainous.[27]

Others among these respondents were not even this generous. They avoided biological explanations for what they found offensive or irritating in Black behavior, attributing it instead to individual cases of perceived abuse of privilege or of the use of race as a ruse for gaining undeserved advantage. (A forty-two-year-old postal worker referred to this as the "two-hundred-year-old excuse.") Each person in this group recalled individual instances of Blacks who had either offended or insulted or taken unfair advantage. In one case, Amy, a twenty-nine-year-old woman who worked at an automobile auction, referred to a Black co-worker who claimed racial discrimination when he was left behind when others had gone to appraise some cars: "No one likes him, no one gets along with him. He's just rude and obnoxious and acts like he thinks people owe him things because he's Black and been discriminated against." Paradoxically, this same woman, a single mother, also praised a Black child who had befriended her son. Amy also applauded two Black families who lived down the street for keeping tidy houses and yards, even though she strongly agreed with a survey statement that Black neighborhoods are rundown because Blacks do not take care of their property. After some discussion she conceded that Blacks were as varied as Whites in their abilities and motivations. She nevertheless rejected affirmative action on the basis of group advantage but readily accepted it when applied to the poor, Black and White alike. The malleability and openness to some reasonable concession to reality of even someone who scored high on denial—15, the highest possible—suggests the importance of probing beneath survey questions.

The aforementioned postal worker justified his attitudes by reference to personal experience as well: "In the post office, you can't fire them. They can have ten times the violent incidences. They can be late, sick and still keep their job. I've seen Blacks fired and rehired three or four times; Whites were just booted. Nobody wants to rock the boat, plus you got Blacks on the EEO committee. The ones that do that, make racism a big problem; that's what causes greater problems at work."

The striking (and sobering) common element among people in this group is the absolute confidence with which they approach a world in which there are so many with conflicted or opposite beliefs regarding issues of racial equality. One suspects, along with Kinder and Sanders[28] and others, that the racial animosity or outright racism that such persons exhibit—the combined denial, stereotyping, and negative emotion—play a role in their psychic economies that does not hold for the other respondents.

The Low Denial Group

Those with the lowest denial scores make up the smallest group both in our face-to-face interviews (three people, or 12 percent) and in the larger survey sample (15 percent). These people agreed on several crucial points: continuing discrimination against Blacks, categorical rejection of Black stereotypes, accurate knowledge of Black population and welfare statistics, and a common, sophisticated reading of media images. This group is also the best educated and the least conservative politically.

Beverly, a forty-year-old college-educated hospital employee, remarked that although she had not witnessed any racial discrimination, she assumed it was as common as her experience of being discriminated against as a woman. As evidence she mentioned that she had heard racially disparaging remarks and jokes from fellow employees, and denial when the company she worked for brought in Black managers who then promoted Blacks: "Well the only reason he got that job is because he's Black." Yet even this generous, sympathetic woman favored affirmative action for the poor in general rather than being racially targeted. As she put it, "I've been there." Beverly opposed affirmative action because she regarded as unfair the idea that Blacks gain at White expense. Her mild racial animus was thus confined to only a single dimension and unaccompanied by strong negative feeling. It nevertheless demonstrates the divisive potential of racial issues framed in a way that inflames even the most racially sympathetic Whites.

An older widow noted the difficulties some Blacks have qualifying for mortgages: "They're strait-jacketed in some situations—color is something they can't hide." She also rejected comments by friends and others who repeated Black stereotypes, for example the idea that Black welfare mothers have large families to get bigger welfare checks. As unprejudiced as this woman was, she did not hide behind conventional sentiment and safe points of view. She was dismayed, for example, at Black professional couples whom she had known in Cleveland who had been rejected by their Black friends for acting "White." "They weren't Black any more; they had gone over to the White side."

Finally, Stuart, a fifty-two-year-old Libertarian, noted that no one could understand Black frustration and anger unless he or she stood in line in bureaucracies and saw how people are treated. "If you don't have a mechanism for dealing with it, you get angry." Moreover, such anger was necessary, he felt, to correct the source of continuing Black disadvantage: "Irish-Catholics were aggressive at the turn of century. Progress is not possible without it. Lots of liberal people have more money than they need, but they will get upset if it's taken away."

The critical perspective of these three people on matters of race also translated into relatively sophisticated critiques of television conventions in both news and entertainment. Beverly, the hospital worker, commented on the unrealistic quality of the news focused on criminal behavior and drug problems rather than the "nitty-gritty of home life" that is at the source of these pathologies. On entertainment she noted that television shows like *Cosby* make it seem "so easy" for Blacks and that the media portray the Black man as "very loose and rather immoral. . . . They make it seem like everybody's doing it."

Stuart noted how television uses what he called "political correctness" to create a semblance of concern that concealed its genuine interest in "competing on sensationalism," exploitative images of violence and death. As for entertainment, he perceived a "hip-jive culture that only exists on television." This respondent argued that television's power (as of other media) arises from reflecting culture back to people, which has a small but persistent influence in the long run. When asked to give an example of the "hip-jive" culture, he mentioned the "Murdoch network [Fox]and to a lesser extent the WB [Warner Brothers]."

To be sure, those with the lowest scores constituted a very small group in our interview sample from which it would be foolhardy to generalize uncritically. Nevertheless their overall sympathy to race-based politics and sensitivity and resistance to media conventions distinguish them from the larger sample in unique and revealing ways.

The Ambivalent Majority

By far the largest and the most politically important group in our interview sample gave such conflicted responses that the group can most accurately be characterized as ambivalent: Whites who do not generally harbor deep-seated fears or resentment, who sometimes recognize that discrimination continues to be a fact of life for many Blacks, but who also sometimes lose their patience over racial issues. They constitute the most important group because they are the "swing" group in the population of constituents for race policy. It is their opinion that is crucial to building support for ameliorative policy or in the alternative for what Daniel Moynihan, then working for the Nixon administration, called the policies of "benign neglect." That said, there are also wide variations in this group that tap the multiple origins of racial attitudes.

In the analysis of this pivotal group, we search for themes, ideas, images, and symbols that tend to reinforce one or more of the four dimensions of racial thought described in our model: (1) stereotyping, the belief that Blacks share some negative group attribute; (2) the belief that racial politics is a zero-sum game; (3) a visceral negative reaction to Blacks that overcomes reasoned beliefs that might otherwise create sympathy and goodwill; and of course (4) denial, the belief that discrimination no longer poses a significant problem to Blacks. We are, in other words, in search here of one or more precipitating factors that comprise a "tipping point" for their frustration, for shifting racial ambivalence to animosity along any of these four dimensions, and of the role of mediated information and images (or their absence) in this process.

To generalize, the ambivalent majority are people with good intentions who are somehow stymied from achieving them. One example illustrating these conflicted feelings: "I think generally Blacks have maybe one or one and a half strikes against them to begin with just based on the attitudes of the population. I think also, however, that sometimes they use that as a crutch." And the following:

> If you had the opportunity to go to school and you don't take advantage of it, whose fault is that? . . . Of course I don't know, if you didn't get a good night's sleep and had to worry about somebody shooting your windows out and you weren't being well nourished and you had a lot of contributing factors. . . . But I don't know, they've got free lunch and they're trying to compensate for that at least, you know, to a certain extent. You know Head Start and stuff like that. But on the other hand it's like . . . they've still got to go home and live in that. So that's got to have an effect on the way you're going to function the next day in school. You know, my son, he doesn't have to worry about anything. He comes home . . . at night and plays Nintendo and horses around and you know, he doesn't have a care in the world as far as I know.

The ambivalence in these comments, repeated in one guise or another among many in this group, rests on the belief that Blacks sometimes use race to gain undeserved advantage by exaggerating the significance of slights or discriminatory practices. And yet there is also a sympathetic understanding that is overwhelmed occasionally by unique, vivid personal experience and by impressions taken from local and national news of complaining Black ministers. Another overwhelming factor is media images of Blacks on welfare, of Black violence on local news, and of crude behavior—open sexuality and insolence—in entertainment television. The mediated experience rises just above a critical threshold where these ambivalent respondents say they do know better intellectually, from coming into contact with a variety of Black people who offer compelling evidence to the contrary, but nevertheless feel themselves being taken in by the flood of images.

One example is Larry, a forty-six-year-old janitor, who followed international news from a cable feed of ITN world news and his local news from what he called the local "fish wrapper" and the local evening news:

> Q: When you think of welfare, do you think of it being primarily a problem of Blacks?
>
> A: No. Cause the majority of the people are White on welfare. So I think . . . I guess in my mind I probably think of Black people though when I think of

welfare. Possibly, although I know intellectually in my mind that there's more White people. . . .

Q: Why do you think that is?

A: Well, I think, I don't know, maybe some of it's media. You know, I mean I don't want to blame them, and if this is something that I'm generating I guess I'm guilty too, but it seems like we do see it—if it's something about poor people, you know they're in Chicago—you know, no offense, but if they're in Cabrini Green [a Chicago housing project] or some place, you don't . . . they're in some project or something, or in D.C. or something. . . . there was a lot of stuff about people being murdered up there.

Another respondent, a forty-five-year-old woman:

Q: What kind of picture do you think TV news gives of Black people? What do we learn about Blacks from TV news?

A: I think most of it's a lot of negatives.

Q: In what way?

A: Just the violence and the welfare stories are always negative about Blacks. And I think they get a lot of bad press. Because I don't see that in the people that I deal with. And I think that's unfair that they do get a lot of negative press. But then a lot of the violence and stuff they do to themselves!

Q: So you think those stories are accurate?

A: I think for the most part they're accurate, but I think they bring it on themselves.

The respondent, a teacher's aide, had known many Blacks and realized they were not all the same, but her experience was at war with her mediated view of reality, which seemed compelling, especially when reinforced with a frightening drive-by shooting she had witnessed in Indianapolis. The responses of these people cohere with the findings of Gilens that news coverage of poverty features images of Blacks at twice the rate predicted by their representation among welfare recipients and depicts Blacks in more negative contexts than Whites.[29] An accretion of consistent, race-dominated imagery from newscasts has created in these respondents' minds an enduring stereotype that defeats their otherwise sympathetic impulses.

The most reasoned, least emotional respondents in the ambivalent group are, in general, the best educated. At the heart of their ambivalence is doubt about what constitutes effective help. As one respondent, a retired marine officer put it, "I think there has to be some middle ground that can help 'em without handing it to 'em on a platter. . . . That's the nut of the thing, how do you help them without hurting them by helping too much?" Another respondent, an old-line Democratic liberal, said that she did not disagree with the concept of affirmative action but that "sometime you've got to stop this because the people who DO make it on their own are always, then, regarded as somehow inferior. So it perpetuates this concept that some people have, that Blacks can't make it, or that they don't have the ability to do this." She, like two others in the ambivalent group, took the statement "If Blacks would only try harder, they would be just as well off as Whites" in two ways: disagreeing with the statement's presumed assumption that Blacks were unmotivated but then agreeing that realistically Blacks would have to try harder to overcome continuing patterns of discrimination.

The conflicted attitudes of this group appear most dramatically on the issue of affirmative action. Here people recognize continuing discrimination against Blacks but find themselves opposed on a gut level to affirmative action policy. The attempts to square this circle reveal the contradictions and the paradox at the core of White ambivalence. The most articulate statement of this view came from a former supervisor at Pillsbury who took some role in hiring. He recognized the continued existence of discrimination:

> I kept myself as color blind as I could. But it seemed to me, at least in one organization, if I recommended a colored person, a Black person, it would be somewhere up line—one of the big psychologists or somebody would say, "Well, he doesn't fit our profile." And I knew—pretty certain—that color was in the thing somewhere, and somebody was exercising prejudice. And I felt I missed a lot of very good potential employees, colleagues.

He nevertheless rejected affirmative action on the job as a solution because he saw that under-qualified employees performed at a subpar level, making it easier for those "up the line" to reject further Black hiring. He, like others in this group, recommended that Blacks ought to be better prepared before taking a job, but rejected affirmative action in education, thus begging the question as to where such preparation was to take place. When pressed on this point, he said that government-mandated programs are doomed to fail (several others pointed to the failures of the Great Society) and that Blacks ought to take a greater role in managing them at a local level. Aside from the failures of past federal programs, he said the programs attracted self-interested figures whose power functionally rested on Black dependency.

Here was the first and decisive element in the shift from ambivalence to animosity—the mention of Black leaders, and especially Jesse Jackson who embodied the idea of opportunism and selfishness. His name came up spontaneously in a third of the interviews as the respondents became increasingly impatient with and emotional about Black problems. Larry (the janitor) expressed typical frustration: "I mean when comes the point where it's like 'Okay . . . is the playing field ever going to be balanced and fair?' I don't know, but I can't see sitting around whining and moaning about it." Jackson was regarded by one respondent as a "2-percenter" who won't be satisfied with anything less than 100 percent equality. Jackson is thus associated with the White attitude that Blacks complain more than other groups. Another noted that "[h]e's not doing it for mankind. He's not doing it for anyone but himself." Another put it simply, "It stirs me up." Here was a key indirect indication of a media-related factor, the negative image of Black leadership and its association with a zero-sum view of Black–White politics.

Respondents also referred to the more subtle effects of what they regarded as media reluctance to make common-sense judgments on matters of fact. As an example, one respondent faulted the media for their deferential reference to Louis Farrakhan as an "alleged anti-Semite" and thus offering him and others such as Al Sharpton undeserved access to public forums for "hate peddling." As argued by Stuart (from the low denial group), the media use such nonjudgments to hide their true motives of trading on sensationalism and conflict to draw curious audiences. Lily, a thirty-four-year-old mother with a Black brother-in-law, noted that the less sophisticated afternoon talk shows offered forums for Blacks who willingly demeaned themselves in front of the camera: "They really make Black people look bad, and I know they are not representative of every Black person. I mean you get these Black guys that get on stage and brag about cheating on their spouse several times and it's like yes, I know that happens in the White community also and you have people that are too dumb to know they look dumb. But they seem to have an overabundance of them on talk shows and you just can't help but get that opinion of them, but I know you see the absolute worst selection there."

For some respondents, the perception of restraints on public discourse makes them angrier and more resentful, a feeling that they cannot express their frustration publicly. In part, they seem fearful of angering those few Blacks they know personally, whom they believe use race as a stratagem for avoiding responsibility or advancing a false claim of racial discrimination to gain some undeserved advantage. It is in large part these experiences (which may well be accurate reports or may be distorted perceptions arising from prejudice) coupled to examples of Black success in the media—as well as their deep suspicion of government—that work against these respondents' acceptance of public policy remedies. Nor, of course, do these people make analogies between Blacks milking dubious charges of discrimination and White workers taking advantage of whatever levers they might have to get ahead in the organization (personal connections, flattery, expensive gifts, credit-hogging). And of course none of these respondents saw the Federal Housing Administration (FHA), mortgage tax deduction, or other government programs as affirmative action for Whites.

The sensational media images are rejected as too simplistic by the more sophisticated ambivalents. These people, though well read, nevertheless remain unaware of the daily abuses Blacks continue to endure in a White-dominated society, conditions that could help explain both the Black reaction to the O.J. Simpson verdict and the White puzzlement to it. Two respondents, well-educated, upper-middle-class women, both with a history of social activism, were confounded by Black reactions to the O.J. Simpson verdict. Dianne, a junior college English teacher, simply did not know what to make of it: "I think the one thing it pointed out to me that the whole Civil Rights movement achieved was that we no longer feel free and comfortable to be racially vocal—vocal about racism. But that it didn't really change maybe the lives of as many people as we thought—or their hearts and minds." The other illuminated the problem this way: "How do you have an intelligent discussion with people who are really angry and upset and maybe don't even have an accurate picture of the way things really are?" Here the influence of mediated reality is apparent only indirectly.

Other effects are more overt and can be established more confidently. The long-term unintended effects of the media's hunt for sensationalism and conflict provide fodder for the less educated (and perhaps less sympathetic) who use the images to support their worst suspicions. The instinctive reaction, the one that bypasses thoughtful analysis and even first-hand experience, is based on a more compelling, sensational mediated reality, as in the case of Larry, who knew better than to think of welfare as a Black problem.

In case after case, it was the respondents who did not have a history of close relationships with Blacks who were most susceptible to mediated information. By contrast, take the case of Marianne, a twenty-six-year-old mother who had gone to an integrated Florida high school and who grew up with several close Black friends. She explained her deeper, more textured understanding this way: "I think there's probably more White people on welfare than there are Black people. I do believe that. And I know that a lot of people find that very hard to believe, but I mean there's so many White people that are poor, that are out in America and we don't see. Black people that are poor live in the city and you see 'em every time you go to the city. So it's a different thing." Thus a forty-five-year-old mother with several children in the Indianapolis school system was very sympathetic to the plight of welfare mothers who needed money for childcare so that they could work, but her sympathies ebbed when she thought of those who did not want to work but were content to stay on welfare. She had no firsthand evidence of such cases, just a vague awareness that they were rampant. Her experience with Blacks, parents of her children's schoolmates, told her that Blacks do not feel discriminated against. Therefore, those others who are on welfare simply wanted a handout, leading her to conclude that it was a choice: "It's just what you want to do." The available firsthand evidence offered proof of the merits of hard work and thus tacit evidence of the laziness and preference for criminality among others who had failed.

Few in this group took much notice of Black images in entertainment television, though those who remembered watching shows with Black casts preferred *Cosby*. Three in the ambivalent group noted in passing the images in all-Black sitcoms (six others in the face-to-face group also referred to these shows). There were two general reactions to these programs: those with high denial scores cited them in circumspect ways as evidence for their worst beliefs about Blacks; those in the ambivalent group were irritated by what they regarded as behavior that perpetuated such stereotypes. One woman said the shows perpetuated language differences that put Blacks at a disadvantage. Another woman, one who fell into the ambivalent group, agreed: "Well as you flip the channels you see some of these stupid situation comedies which are sort of stereotypical Black people, but I flip right past all of those. . . . I think they're being exploited and reinforcing people's notions of group memberships." Those most sympathetic are offended by the stereotypes. Regardless of sympathy, however, both groups are put off by what they regard as open sexuality and insolent behavior, particularly on the part of young actors, and the language they use. Beverly, the hospital worker who scored low on denial remarked that television "portrays Black men very loose and rather immoral and I don't see that as the case. In the Fox shows they are so sexual toward each other. I don't see that in my personal experience. . . ." Marianne, the Floridian who had grown up with close Black friends, noted the distance maintained between Black and White characters that she conceded reflected real life: "In some situations they're definitely in competition with each other. In other situations they are . . . I can't say that they are friends. They don't hang out. They don't go to places together. They don't have anything to do with each other in life. They work together and that's about it." Thus the distance between the White and Black worlds implied by the entertainment media's distinctions in language and sexual behavior is heightened by the paucity of Black–White socializing.

Those who have interacted with Blacks on an intimate basis beyond the workplace are most resistant to media conventions, a finding that comports with studies of the "group contact hypothesis." Researchers find that casual interracial contact in mainly impersonal settings does not necessarily increase intimacy because it lacks one or more necessary components—equal status; common goals; intergroup cooperation; and support by authorities, law, or custom.[30] Few of these traits are likely to characterize work settings.[31] Outside of work, two respondents in this ambivalent group had Black brothers-in-law and another had grown up in a racially integrated environment.

The most animated in this group was Marianne. Here was a case of someone whose political conservatism and strict application of a fairness norm for rejecting affirmative action was genuine and not merely a screen for racial animosity. She cited examples of Blacks she had known who had become moderately successful and others who despite their middle-class backgrounds had gone on welfare. In short, while Marianne made no categorical racial distinctions, ideologically she had little sympathy with programs targeted specifically for Blacks ("If you're going to thrive, you're going to thrive in whatever situation you're in"). Thus her observations on the media were especially noteworthy. She regarded the news as interested in only the last stage of a complex developmental process, the one most easily sensationalized: "What you see on TV, when the person is being carted off to jail, or a five-year-old girl is killed in a drive-by shooting. Nobody thinks about what drew that person to do that thing." When we asked her if she discussed racial issues with her neighbors (she lived in an all-White Indianapolis suburb), she responded that she did not, that these discussions only came up in response to crime reports on the evening news:

> If news has top 5 stories that are of crimes that happened downtown, what is the perception of a person who has lived away? People aren't willing to look at the big picture. The end result is what you see. It's ugly. Nobody thinks about what brought this up. The news presents a horrible picture of Blacks. I know that crime is a huge problem in Black communities but there has to be good people in Black communities or they would have died off a long time ago. I think that they think it's easier to be involved in a gang or whatever the criminal activity is that goes on, than to go out and work and build something for yourself. And it may be easier to do those things. Growing up in that environment, it may be easier to do those very things. But you don't wake up one morning normal and say, "I think I'll go join a gang." You don't wake up one morning on the farm (laughs) basically, and say "I think I'll go try selling drugs on the corner—where will I get some?" I mean you wake up and decide that you're going to sell drugs because your mom has 'em in the other room. Or your next door neighbor has 'em and asked you yesterday, and the day before, and the day before, and the day before, and the day before if you wanted it. So I think that they're [news media] not very concerned about what those reasons are.

In general, those Whites in our sample who shared some intimacy with Blacks saw local news stories as the end point of a long process that remained largely invisible to those Whites whose experience was more restricted. For these latter, media reports of Black crime helped rationalize fear, anger, and denial.

Conclusion: Media Resources for Highlighting Group Differences

As we review the interview transcripts, particularly of the conflicted group, we note the following common examples of White racial thinking and feeling. The most common negative Black stereotypes derive from mediated impressions of laziness, murderous violence, and sexual intemperance. Judgments of laziness derive mainly from global judgments of welfare cheats. These are clearly media-fed impressions, since only one of our interviewees was personally acquainted with this population, the twenty-six-year-old Floridian. Indeed, those in our interview sample who had had regular face-to-face contact with Blacks contrasted their exemplary behavior—tending their children, keeping tidy yards—with the generic, irresponsible Blacks they heard about from television news reports. Firsthand experience in the workplace registered impressions of Black slackness from examples of individuals who had used their race as a stratagem to shirk responsibility. However authentic, these reports were readily generalized to category membership rather than to garden-variety human failing. This easy lapse into old stereotypes of conniving laziness suggests the power of culture; the newest permutations of stereotypes seem to draw from the same traditional sources, a topic we take up in chapter 4.

Affirmative action stimulated the most visceral responses on racial politics as a zero-sum game. Virtually everyone in our sample, including the most sympathetic, opposed it with some heat. To be fair, some were antagonistic because they had lost faith in the federal government to do any good whatsoever, but the frequent ardent reactions suggested that the affirmative action debate had reconfigured the coordinates of their political worlds; here undeserving Blacks gained at White expense. In no case were these losses felt personally, however, strongly suggesting that media reports played an important role in their thinking.

As we have suggested, the media's influence encompasses relevant information they fail to convey as well as material they pass on. Most important of the voids, in our view, is the almost total absence, in media and in our respondents' thinking, of the recognition that Whites continue to gain from pervasive racial privilege. Among these benefits are neutral or positive expectations among those occupying most social roles, from school teachers to sales clerks to police; availability of pride-generating, detailed information on ancestors' roots and achievements; and the self-esteem and confidence borne of membership in a majority group that provides almost all of society's top leaders.

These advantages in turn rest upon a foundation of public policy decisions. White people have long enjoyed rewarding forms of affirmative preference across the range of social and economic life. These have included government-subsidized mortgages and highways for all-White suburbs, subsidies that cost vastly more than housing and transit programs serving poor minorities; government-sanctioning of all-White unions that blocked occupational mobility for African Americans and of all-White neighborhoods that blocked geographical mobility;[32] and tax exempt and subsidized private and public universities throughout the region of highest Black population (the South) that enforced 100 percent White quotas for a century or more.[33] Such facts rarely appear in public discourse, yet discussing race without them is like discussing a book after reading only every sixth page.

Not surprisingly, then, few respondents could support with statistics or some other authoritative source of information their belief that discrimination no longer posed a significant problem to Blacks. Most referred to cases of individual Blacks whom they had known to take advantage of gullible Whites or use Equal Employment Opportunity Commission (EEOC) regulations to lodge nuisance charges of racial discrimination. For these Whites, such vivid personal examples and the general flow of the affirmative action debate suggested a topsy-turvy world, a kind of racial dystopia where Blacks had somehow gotten the upper hand on Whites. The contrary evidence of higher Black unemployment, lower income, poorer education and health, and higher mortality compared to Whites was not a part of their everyday understanding of the world—except perhaps as tacit evidence for Blacks' inferiority.

Denial of anti-Black discrimination (and of White privilege) seems to us the most critical component of animosity. It is by rejecting the ideas that structural impediments persist—and that Whites' own status and achievements rest in some measure upon a legacy of racial preference—that Whites most strikingly diminish the potential for racial harmony. Whites' denial feeds negative emotions and the tendency to become impatient and angry at Blacks' behavior and to reject political demands perceived as benefiting African Americans. Equally important, the denial of discrimination in turn undermines trust of Whites among Blacks. It implicitly indicts African Americans; it obdurately ignores and refutes the plain facts that most Blacks understand and live.

To be sure, persons of good will may reasonably argue that discrimination, though heinous, does not relieve individual Blacks of obligations to society and its values. Hardly anyone would deny that individual African Americans have a range of choices and hold a share of responsibility for whatever befalls them. True enough; but impediments rooted in White-dominated culture and society do limit the life chances and impinge upon the daily lives of most African Americans. Denials of these structural barriers tend to exonerate the system, assume the openness and efficiency of the economic market, and locate problems and solutions almost exclusively within the ambit of individual activity. Not particularly amenable to change through empirical data,[34] this constellation of ideas therefore falls short of the empathetic attempt to understand the lives of African Americans from those persons' own perspectives.

Analysis of these interviews leads us to conclude that the media play an ancillary but nonetheless important role in depleting racial understanding, tipping the balance toward suspicion and even animosity among the ambivalent majority of White Americans. The habits of local news—for example, the rituals in covering urban crime—facilitate construction of menacing imagery. The interviews suggest the role played by such coverage in creating in some respondents' minds a quasi-statistical "irresponsible Black world hypothesis."[35] We note also, however, that the mental ground from which these ideas emerge is far from being uncorrupted. It has within it seeds sown by culture, which require minimal nourishment to produce new but not entirely unfamiliar forms of racial thinking. The power of such forms is evident in the fact that the reality created by news coverage is compelling enough to override lived experience, especially of those in our study who cannot critically deconstruct the images nor appreciate the cost-effective economics of such coverage for local television stations.[36]

This finding is perhaps not unexpected, but what is noticed and discounted by the more sophisticated Whites in this study fails to plumb what is more significant. These televised images shared influence with firsthand experience even among sophisticated ambivalents. A prime example of the media influence, here as often residing in voids rather than presences, comes from Whites who were surprised and shocked by Blacks' reactions to the outcome of the O.J. Simpson trial. Taken aback by the deep frustration and anger at the root of these reactions, such Whites had been inadequately informed by a medium whose interest in Black problems began and ended at the agitated surface.

Of course television producers do not consciously create such imagery to draw down White sympathy; they are responding in an economically rational way to increased competition for audiences, arising from channel proliferation. Media operators have growing incentives to rely upon sensational news of violence and crime—and sensational entertainment employing exaggerated or stereotyped role play. Those incentives are fed by norms of objectively detached profit seeking that legitimize providing public forums to the marginal, the extreme, and the conflict-ridden while denying much exposure—whether in news or entertainment—to the serious, quiet lives of the majority.

In some ways the state of television today is more symptomatic than constitutive of interracial enmity. This is most evident in the operation of the marketplace where cable has lowered the break-even points for audiences and led to development of smaller networks—Fox, UPN, WB—that target minority audiences as attractive markets in their own right rather than as marginal additions to a majority White audience. The result has been a sort of mediated segregation that often leads to an exaggeration of cultural differences and supplies evidence to some Whites of their worst suspicions concerning Black behavior. Once again, those in our sample who have had intimate contact with Blacks see these shows as trading on exaggerated images; others who have little or no contact come away with silent confirmation of buried stereotypes.

The stereotypes may be missing from public discourse but they exert their power nonetheless in a political culture of distrust and wavering hostility that lies beneath surface politeness. This is, however, more accurately described as a disengagement, a truce of sorts that puts off work at solutions to what appear to be intractable problems. The evidence from the interviews is that the majority of Americans of all ideological hues yearn for some solution to a problem that has, for many, exhausted their patience.

3 Culture, Media, and the White Mind: The Character of Their Content

N THE EVIDENCE culled from our Indianapolis interviews, we conclude that the average White American is ambivalent toward African Americans, sometimes feeling animosity or racism, other times feeling quite friendly, and sometimes holding contradictory sentiments all at once. In this chapter we connect the findings from Indianapolis to the national surveys that have shaped scholarly understanding of Whites' racial opinions. Based on this understanding, we begin an explanation of Whites' thinking with particular reference to the wider American culture of race and, more generally, to the ways humans tend to separate the world into "us" versus "them." The hold of racial thinking is tenacious, the roots of racist conviction or suspicion deeply embedded. This means we must probe well beneath the manifest content to understand the media's embodiment of the culture and its potential influence on Whites. We find that Blacks occupy a *liminal* place in White-dominated media and society, neither fully accepted nor completely rejected.

White Public Opinion

Although surveys provide only imperfect indicators of Whites' racial thinking, a definitive review of just about all the national data convinced Howard Schuman, Charlotte Steeh, Lawrence Bobo, and Maria Krysan that ambivalence is the best way to describe the typical White person's attitudes. They write that this state is "probably closer to the truth than arguments over degrees of overt and covert prejudice."[1] A major indicator of ambivalence, Schuman et al. find, is that in matters of *principle* Whites show a clear positive movement since the 1950s toward greater tolerance, whether on intermarriage, residential integration, or voting for Black presidential candidates. But on matters of implementing *practice,* Whites evince less support. Thus we see less backing for government spending or affirmative intervention policies than for abstractions about equality.[2] According to Schuman et al., "There is no real sign that the larger White public is prepared to see norms of equal treatment reconceptualized to support substantial steps toward drastically reducing economic and social inequality in this country."[3]

Traditional racists who believe in Black inferiority and favor discrimination probably comprise about 20 percent of the White public. Though this represents a significant decrease since the middle of the twentieth century, there remain about three White racists for every two African Americans. Moreover, survey evidence involving race is notoriously unreliable: many Whites tend to disguise their true feelings, knowing the social undesirability of appearing to be racist. Whites' sentiments toward Blacks may therefore tilt more readily in the negative direction than surveys indicate[4]—racism and animosity are probably more widespread than immediately apparent.

As we found in Indianapolis, the most widely held explanations among Whites for Black disadvantage partake of the discourse of denial. Asked to explain Blacks' status and achievements, Whites most often cite low motivation. Schuman et al. found that 52 percent of respondents named this factor, compared with 45 percent citing no chance for education, 10 percent low ability, and 34 percent discrimination.[5] The authors go on to document that the large majority of Whites deny that racial discrimination persists as a major impediment to African Americans: "Thus an emphasis on past oppression of Blacks as a basic source of racial inequality has *lost* support over the past two decades. . . . [This] *probably reflects the fading of reports of obvious racial oppression from the media and their replacement by stories about forms of affirmative action intended to benefit Blacks*" (emphasis added).[6] After the late 1970s, about 75 percent of Whites rejected the idea that Blacks as a group face important barriers in jobs or housing.[7] The authors note that Blacks emphasize present discrimination more than past while Whites do the reverse: 81 percent of Blacks but 36 percent of Whites agree with the idea that Blacks have worse jobs, income, and housing "mainly due to discrimination."[8]

A large majority of Whites seem to tilt toward *denial*, the animosity end of the spectrum on the dimension that taps recognition of discrimination. This cannot be traced to *Rashomon*-like differences of interpretation. By any measure, discrimination does persist as a daily reality in Blacks' lives when dealing with White realtors, bank lenders, employers, physicians, teachers, and sales clerks, among others.[9]

To reiterate our multidimensional conception of racial thinking, White ignorance and denial of discrimination do not by themselves constitute racism. Nor do the desires of Whites to be in the majority in schools and neighborhoods—and legislatures.[10] As Schuman et al. note, the latter sentiments "are at least as much a matter of power and control and of fear of being *controlled by others* as they are of 'prejudice' as a separate and self-contained psychological state" (emphasis added).[11] Note, however, that this very sense that Blacks are "others," of distinguishing an "us" whose interests clash with "them," is a prerequisite for racial animosity. If one consistently groups individuals by racial membership, one is more likely to engage in stereotypical generalizations, experience negative feelings, and reject the political activities of that group's members.

The Origins of Ambivalence and Animosity

How do Whites' misapprehensions arise? Just about everyone has two paths of social information: personal experience (including formal education, socialization, and conversation) and mediated communication. For most Whites these exist in confusing combination: Most lack a theory or integrating perspective to harmonize the two streams. Combine this with what appear to be inherent tendencies in human mental processes to notice and respond negatively to group differences.[12] Add a culture, a stock of widely held and frequently reinforced ideas that emphasize racial difference, and imply a racial hierarchy with Whites on top. Stir in the psychic and other motivations Whites might have to maintain a sense of difference and superiority, such as a desire for group dominance.[13] The result is a recipe for continued interracial alienation.

Our discussion begins with mental process, specifically the truism that we do not create the world afresh each waking day. In the parlance of social cognition research, people are more "theory-driven" than "data-driven." That is, we more often approach life with assumptions that lead us to confirm expectations rather than to inscribe fresh interpretations of daily experience upon a blank mental slate. This tendency toward mental inertia is the joint product of cognitive economy and of cultural influence.

Cognitive economy is supplied by habits of thinking formed through the use of mental shortcuts like *schemas* and *frames*. A schema is a set of related concepts that allow people to make inferences about new information based on already organized prior knowledge. Schemas "abstract generic knowledge that holds across many particular instances."[14] For instance, mainstream U.S. culture includes a schema stored in many Americans' minds that associates the concept of success with other ideas such as wealth, hard work, educational attainment, intelligence, status, snobbery, fancy cars, and good looks. Images representing those related concepts readily come to mind when people hear the word or see a symbol that evokes the concept of success—a picture of a BMW, a mansion, a big executive office suite. A schema about "welfare" brought to mind by a television news story on welfare reform might trigger linked thoughts about the ideas "lazy," "Black person,"[15] "waste," "liberals," and "high taxes."

Frames are very much like schemas, except they reside within media texts and public discourse. Frames highlight and link data selectively to tell more or less coherent stories that define problems, diagnose causes, make moral judgments, and suggest remedies.[16] When we say a news report "framed" a drive-by shooting as a gang war story, we mean it selected certain aspects of the event that summoned an audience's stored schematic understandings about gang members. The story may have included visuals illustrating turf consciousness, exaggerated attachment to symbolic clothing, hand signaling, weapons, and aimless loitering. By highlighting this gang frame, the report obscures other possible mental associations such as, perhaps, the shooter's absent father, unemployment or low wages, and clinical depression. The gang frame makes these more sympathetic connections less available to the audience. The political significance of the frames derives from the underlying implicit moral judgment, in one case condemnation of threatening criminal behavior, in the other perhaps greater understanding of its deeper causes. Once again, the typical audience member's reaction when confronted with the gangbanger frame is to confirm long-standing expectations rather than to critically analyze the text for fresh insight.

This is where culture comes in. We define the mainstream culture as *the set of schemas most widely stored in the public's minds and the core thematic frames that pervade media messages.* Lacking much opportunity for repeated close contact with a wide variety of Blacks, Whites depend heavily on cultural material, especially media images, for cataloging Blacks. The mediated communications help explain the tenacious survival of racial stereotypes despite a social norm that dampens public admission of prejudice.[17] And they help explain pervasive White ambivalence that shrinks from open prejudice but harbors reactive fear, resentment, and denial that the prejudice itself widely exists.

Media frames evoke thoughts that have the potential for eroding or building racial comity. Racial comity betokens wide recognition that each person's way of behaving, viewing, and valuing the world overlaps and intermingles with that of others, that people in all groups can share similar schemas, understanding their society in common ways. Comity thus requires individuals to believe that group membership has limited rather than comprehensive significance, that boundaries between groups and individuals are blurry and permeable. Such a fluid perception of the social structure allows for subjective sharing, for empathy and trust. Racial animosity, on the other hand, arises from a sense that the out-group's members fundamentally differ from the in-group in their thinking and values, and that these differences impose unfair or even dangerous burdens on the dominant group.

The Cultural Sources of Habit

Individuals' schematic thinking, rooted in culture, reflects judgments of value while helping to impose a kind of mental order on an unstable world. To describe these influences and their cultural origins more precisely we draw upon Mary Douglas's anthropological studies of purity and danger. Douglas shows how cultural distinctions between the safe and the dangerous parallel distinctions between one's own group and the out-group. These symbolic differences, she argues, permeate virtually all cultures; all societies tend to erect cultural boundaries that link objects and ideas representing the realm of the pure and desired, and separate them from notions and things associated with the polluted and dangerous.[18] In our view, these separate realms of the pure and virtuous as contrasted with the impure and hazardous should be considered "meta-schemas," overarching associations between sets of schemas that link concepts of the good and the valued and distinguish them from the bad and feared. Thus in many Whites' minds, a meta-schema that registers the concept of "other" or "them" loosely links ideas like "Black," "poverty," "crime" and so forth, and clearly distinguishes from the more valued traits connected with "us." Pollution fears, and rules applied to keep pollution at bay, shape the way dominant groups deal with subordinate groups: "People really do think of their own social environment as consisting of other people joined or separated by lines which must be respected. Some of the lines are protected by firm physical sanctions. . . . But wherever the lines are precarious we find pollution ideas come to their support. Physical crossing of the social barrier is treated as a dangerous pollution. . . . The polluter becomes a doubly wicked object of reprobation, first because he crossed the line and second because he endangered others."[19]

Now this distinction between groups is not entirely, as it were, black and white. Rather, as cultural signifiers, Blacks now traverse an ill-defined border state, symbolically comprising an uneasy, contradictory mixture of danger/pollution and acceptability. As communicating cultural symbols, Blacks are in transition from being (consciously or unconsciously) perceived by most Whites as representing the realm of disorder and perhaps danger. Except for the confirmed racists, most Whites' belief systems contain examples of Blacks exhibiting valued traits, and include hesitations and uncertainties, suspicions rather than convictions of negative traits linked to Black persons. In other words, Blacks in American culture are now *liminal* beings.[20] Liminal people are by their nature *potentially* polluting, disruptive but not necessarily destructive of the natural order since they are "no longer classified and not yet classified," as Malkki describes the Hutu refugees in Rwanda.[21] Media culture reflects this in its melange of images, as does the largest segment of the White audience in its mixture of emotions, beliefs, hopes, and fears about Blacks.

A multidimensional hierarchy related to the purity/danger meta-schema establishes ideal human types in American culture. Black individuals may rank highly on some dimensions and approach the ideal, but rarely if ever achieve it. Nor can isolated individual examples generalize to undermine dominant understandings of Blacks or to modify the culture's ideal type. The hierarchy of ideal type attainment constrains all of us—not just Blacks. All individuals must try to adjust, but some of us can do so more easily, and have less to overcome in order to progress higher up the hierarchy. We might suggest a formula for social judgments of persons unknown or slightly known to us:

Ideal Type Attainment =
(Body traits + Communication behavior + Achievement-related status)

The continuum from body traits through communication to achievement runs from

- traits over which one has little or no control, signals one gives off because of cultural ascriptions to physical characteristics (such as skin color and hair texture); to
- traits that are communication signals that one can control if one is knowledgeable about their meaning and motivated to fit in (such as speech style, accent and grammar);[22] to
- traits that are substantive achievements especially valued by the culture, which are not in themselves communication behaviors (such as holding a high status job).

We know that people judge others using speech, nonverbal communication style, and the visual cues supplied by physical characteristics and dress. For example, physical beauty that proximates ideal body traits has been shown repeatedly to predict financial success, moral approval, and other positive outcomes.[23] Obviously, individuals attach different weights to different traits according to their own judgments; the mainstream is an average of thinking among individuals who comprise a culture. These average weights establish where an individual falls on a social hierarchy of judgment that runs something like this:

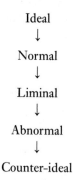

Ideal
↓
Normal
↓
Liminal
↓
Abnormal
↓
Counter-ideal

At the extremes of the hierarchy from the ideal to its opposite, this spectrum may be anchored by the general cultural tendencies Mary Douglas identifies in *Purity and Danger*. Still, the border between the two realms is not impermeable, but shades gradually through a series of other statuses. Those falling into the "normal" category—most Whites, actually—exhibit some though not all of the idealized traits. The liminal person has hints of these traits—some overlap with the positive end of the spectrum but some with the negative part as well. The signal of dark skin color is enough to trigger associations among many Whites with pollution and danger; even if African Americans dress and speak in a conventionally acceptable manner, employ a restrained verbal style, obtain degrees from Harvard and Yale, and run major corporations, they cannot totally surmount the barrier posed by Whites' automatic generalizations from physical traits to moral, behavioral, and intellectual qualities and achievements.[24]

The "abnormal" exists in opposition to the ideal traits: dark complexion, unconventional speech patterns and dress. The counter-ideal looks and acts in ways that overtly, and sometimes (through language and dress) deliberately, threaten dominant group members. Far from the ideal or normal, such types are regarded as posing a danger or burden to the dominant group (and perhaps other groups as well). William "Willie" Horton, a Black man convicted of murder who starred in George Bush's 1988 presidential advertising campaign,[25] offers a prime illustration of the counter-ideal in U.S. culture, and he would partake of the scariness of the defiled, polluted realm.

It is possible for a White to fall into liminality or beyond by unconventional communication behavior, weird dress, pronounced accent, and other cultural differences—for example, becoming a "street person." But the White majority will always see such individuals as exceptional, and no amount of media imagery of White street people can change this. It is quite the reverse for African Americans. Blacks are prisoners of the widespread acceptance by Whites of what is understood to be the prototypical—the most representative—Black person. For Whites, the prototype of the Black person is a lower class or "under" class individual of little economic attainment or status. That means Blacks of outstanding attainment in several of the dimensions will be seen as atypical, as the exception. However, the very fact that most Whites now recognize frequent exceptions evidences cultural progress—the movement of Blacks into liminality from the less desirable region of the hierarchy. Liminality describes the unsettled status of Blacks in the eyes of those who produce dominant culture and of those who consume it. The cultural liminality of Black persons leads us to expect contradictions and tensions in the media's texts, and in the White audience's reactions.

Still, the mainstream culture registers the continued power of unconscious prototypical thinking that considers Whites the normal, and prototypical, human. Newsmagazine covers offer a good illustration of the sway of the White image. Several times a year, *Time* and *Newsweek* select cover topics that call for a visual representation of a person symbolizing the prototypical American. For instance, on 10 May 1999, *Time* ran a story "Growing Up Online," which depicted a White boy of about 12 years old. On 19 October 1998, *Time* ran a story "How to Make Your Kid a Better Student." The cover showed a White boy who appeared to be about 10. In fact, between 8 January 1996 and 6 September 1999, *Time* ran 30 covers illustrated by one or two anonymous persons symbolizing the prototypical American child or adult. The topics ran from "Too Much Homework" and "Why We Take Risks" to "Taking Care of Our Parents" and "Forever Young." Every single image was of a White person. *Time* did feature individual Blacks on its cover during this period, of course—

Michael Jordan, Oprah Winfrey—but never to stand in for the prototypical American. *Newsweek,* checked for the period between 21 September 1998 and 6 September 1999, ran ten covers requiring this kind of anonymous representation. All, such as one on "Migraines," showed just one person, all White. A near-exception was one cover, on "Your Next Job," that showed more than two persons representing prototypical Americans. It depicted ethnic diversity: a Black woman, and two White men, one of whom may have been Latino.

What does all this tell us? When editors think "an American person," they automatically think "White." When they are trying to show a group of "American persons," they consciously recognize the need to show diversity and throw it in. In a sense this summarizes the duality of thinking among media workers, registering nicely the limits of cultural integration. Automatically, media personnel (most presumably White) think of the normal American as a White person. But when cued by the need to represent a *group* of Americans they realize they should add in some non-prototypical types, they recognize their responsibility to reflect America's ethnic diversity.[26] Seeing images like this tell White audiences (some of whom get annoyed at "political correctness") that America is indeed multi-hued: deal with it, these illustrations say. Yet, if genuine race-blindness ruled the day, if the covers represented a random sample of Americans, four or five of the forty covers would have shown a Black model.

However, such a pattern of choice would violate the very nature of prototypical thinking. For racial representation to rotate randomly, it would be as if one could think of the concept *bird* and sometimes the idea *robin* would pop up and other times, less often but occasionally, *penguin* or *ostrich* would come to mind. In fact, most people asked to name a typical bird consistently say *robin* or *sparrow.*[27] Prototypical thinking means a thinker will visualize a single fixed type every time a concept like *person* or *bird* comes up. So (mostly White) media workers and media content reflect the nature and limits of human thinking—no surprise there. What we need to do, however, is grasp the implications of these unavoidable characteristics for the way American society deals with race.

The Persistence of Memory

Our focus on the media notwithstanding, we fully recognize that memories and impressions of racial distinctions and racial hierarchy reside deep within the White American psyche as a persistent threat to the hope for racial comity. The psychology of this conundrum is summarized by Rothbart and John.[28] They describe how "minimal groups" form in lab experiments, where psychologists discovered it is easy to foment in-group/out-group prejudice. For example, subjects in a classic series of experiments[29] were told they either belonged to the group of persons who overestimate the number of dots in a pattern projected on a screen or to the group that underestimates dots. Subjects then developed an affinity for and identification with their presumed group: "In short, merely categorizing the subjects implicitly raised the expectation that 'we' are better than 'they' which resulted in subjects disproportionately remembering unfavorable behaviors associated with the outgroup."[30] People have a tendency to "maximize the difference between the boundaries of groups and often treat overlapping distributions of characteristics as if they were non-overlapping." In consequence, people tend to see members of other groups as pretty much all the same.[31] This means that favorable impressions of an out-group individual may cause more positive attitudes toward that individual, but will not generalize to challenge the negative group stereotype: *"[I]n effect, atypical category members are not category members at all. . . .* [W]e give too much weight to those individuals who confirm the stereotype and not enough weight to those who disconfirm the stereotype. This in turn implies that only a few stereotype-confirming individuals, against the background of many stereotype disconfirming individuals, would nonetheless serve to maintain the stereotype."[32]

The resistance to information that refutes stereotypes exemplifies and helps explain the invisible pull of deep-seated cultural judgments theorized by Mary Douglas.

Yet Whites have important motivations that may work in the opposite direction: maintaining a positive image of themselves as moral, and, relatedly, gaining the rewards that come from acting generously and making human connections to others. Support comes from a 1997 Gallup poll in which 75 percent of African Americans claimed they had a close friend who was White, and 59 percent of Whites claimed similar close friendships with African Americans.[33] Given population proportions, this claim, if true, would mean the average Black must have three or four close White friends. Although this seems highly unlikely (by our lights, few people have more than three or four close friends in total), the overestimation seems to reflect a *yearning for racial reconciliation.* And there are some harder data indexing progress: 12 percent of all new marriages by Blacks in 1993 were with Whites, which is four and one-half times the rate in 1970, and these unions are producing children at equal rates to unmixed marriages, unlike in the past.[34] Rates of interracial dating have also risen dramatically. In 1997, *USA Today* (3 November, p. 10A) reported that 57 percent of young people claimed to have dated persons of another race, a marked increase from 17 percent in 1980 (though other data suggest that younger Whites are less progressive racially compared to older generations).[35] Some real advances have occurred.

But even if more Whites than ever fantasize about having close Black friends or actually date or marry African Americans, political understanding remains underdeveloped. Steeped in individualist American culture, Whites are not predisposed to develop sophisticated structural explanations and solutions for conditions among Blacks.[36] That orientation renders them less ready to notice discrimination or accept political activity by Blacks as a group. When confronted either with factual data about group disparities, such as crime or poverty rates among Blacks, or with specific incidents conforming to stereotyped expectations, Whites, lacking an alternative way to make sense of the information, may readily develop animosity.

Thus Patterson notes that Black families are over three times more likely to be poor than White; that in 1995 single women accounted for 70 percent of African American births;[37] and that "on any given day almost one in three (32.2 percent) of Afro American men between the ages of 20 to 29 is under some form of criminal justice supervision, in either prison or jail, or on probation or parole. . . ."[38] As discussed further in chapter 6, media—reflecting the emphases and vacuums of elite discourse[39]—do not often provide White audiences a way of explaining such data without resorting to pejorative inferences. Animosity—fear, perhaps, or political rejection—in this light becomes an understandable, even rational, response to limited, conflicting, and often negative information and varied motivations. By subscribing to one or more of the sentiments that comprise the animosity syndrome, Whites, consciously at least, can avoid succumbing to a full-blown racist ideology they know is morally wrong.

What the Media Do

The years since the mid-1960s have seen enormous increases in the media presence of Blacks, visibility that inherently denies the precepts of traditional racism by showing capable, successful Blacks in a variety of roles from news anchors to fictional doctors, judges, and detectives. Across the genres, from big-screen productions like *Amistad, Beloved,* and *A Time to Kill* to the reverential paeans broadcast on Martin Luther King Day, media also take overt positions denouncing traditional racism and endorsing civil rights. Explicitly, media images deny White superiority and the legitimacy of White privilege. In their most obvious dimensions, they promote tolerance, inclusiveness, and (limited) acceptance by Whites of Blacks. At the same time, less overt media signals—and equally important, systematic absences from media content—may work against the development of greater interracial empathy and trust.

Beyond this, media images still contain traces of long-standing cultural presumptions not only of essential racial difference but of the hierarchy that idealizes "Whiteness." Many Whites lack a convincing schematic explanation for their negative social observations about Blacks, both factual— higher Black crime, lower occupational attainment—and fanciful. Suspicions that there may be something to the notions of essential racial difference and White superiority can easily fill the void. So, even though most media personnel oppose outright racism and may even consciously preach against it, media could nonetheless sustain the foundations of animosity. When they endorse racial difference and hierarchy, however subtly and unconsciously, the media may reinforce tendencies toward prejudiced thinking apparently built into human cognition.

In this chapter and throughout the book, we are concerned with the *dominant* tendencies in media, their causes, and their likely implications for society as a whole. Of course there is variation around the central tendencies. At times the media promote, or at least open a door to, increased empathy on the part of Whites. At other times, they can stimulate old habits of racist or ethnocentric thought. Quite often both these seemingly contradictory tendencies and others coexist in a single television show, news report, or film— and in the results of public opinion interviews. Media texts can do double and triple duty, and individual audience members can react in surprising or conflicted ways to them. That said, however, despite the potential for varied, idiosyncratic readings by disparate, unconnected, and unorganized individuals, most audience members, alone or in their like-minded families and peer groups, take the path of least cognitive resistance. Consequently, they do not actively resolve contradictions in media texts by developing their own new theories or modifying existing schematic understandings. Most often, they either miss the contradictions, noting just the material that confirms their existing thoughts and ignoring the rest, or they recognize the contradictions without changing their basic orientations.[40] If there is one overarching lesson of cognitive psychology, it is that most persons are "cognitive misers"[41] who do not exert much energy to resolve complexities and contradictions in the information that comes their way. Thus it seems to us legitimate to focus most intensively upon the frames, images, and themes that dominate the media by sheer quantitative count and by their powerful congruence with those racial schemas that research reveals to pervade the thinking of most White Americans.

We do not mean to suggest the media consistently promote a particular racial mindset. Still less do we want to imply that media workers are fully aware of their contributions to public thinking. Media images can promote Whites' acceptance of presumptions about Blacks without either their producers[42] or their audiences realizing it—without overt assertions, without obvious stereotyping.[43] Or media content can reinforce an audience member's guilty conjecture, rooted in centuries-old elements of Euro-American culture,[44] that certain unfavorable traits widely ascribed to Blacks *might* be true. Simply by failing to explain a pattern of such images as unkempt Black criminals or welfare mothers, media may bolster baleful thoughts. Yet given their conventional assumptions and practices, it is probably impossible for media to offer explanations, at least not with enough clarity, frequency, and vividness to challenge the sway of the deep-seated culture. And this is the dilemma: blame is not easy to assign, nor solutions easy to discern.

We shall write from here on of media material that, both by what it contains and what it omits, tends to encourage or discourage stereotyping, denial, political rejection, or negative emotional responses to Blacks. These are the major components of racial animosity, and their opposites the major components of comity.

The remainder of the book shines a broad light across the range of media outlets, genres, and images. Here are the issues and the chapters that focus most heavily on them:

- How might media contribute to Whites' *stereotyping* of Blacks? We explore media depictions of the social meanings and predictive value of race in chapter 4, comparing Black and White images in network news.

- Exactly how might news stimulate Whites' *negative emotional responses* to Blacks? This is our focus in chapter 5, a close look at images of violence and crime in local television news.
- Does the news tend to illustrate or to omit the African American experience of discrimination, thereby undermining or contributing to Whites' tendency to engage in *denial?* This question receives particular attention in chapter 6, an examination of poverty in the news.
- Relatedly, how might reporting practices heighten the salience of racial identity and boundaries between groups? Does coverage of problems experienced disproportionately by African Americans foster the *rejection* component of animosity by encouraging Whites to see themselves as sharing group interests in opposition to Blacks? We give particular attention to these questions in chapter 7, on affirmative action.
- With the exploration of images that may reflect and promote stereotyping, negative emotions, denial, and conflicting racial group identifications as a backdrop, chapter 8 offers a summary probe of the way news treats black political leadership and activity. Is Black power considered more threatening than White? Case studies of reporting on Jesse Jackson and Louis Farrakhan provide the focal point of the chapter.
- What about the majority of the content that Whites consume, entertainment and advertising? In exploring this material we are particularly concerned with the ways Blacks and Whites are shown interacting with each other and among their racial peers. In what manner might depictions of interpersonal contact reinforce or undermine the salience of racial classifications, prevalence of negative stereotyping, denial of structural impediments, and experience of negative emotions—and the suspicion of White superiority? How do these portrayals of interpersonal behavior mark the liminal status of Blacks, and do they indeed link Blacks symbolically to the dangers of pollution? These questions occupy center stage in chapter 9 on Black and White images and relationships in prime-time television entertainment, chapter 10 on television advertising, and chapter 11 on Hollywood film.

As the rest of the book will show, dominant patterns in the most widely distributed media provide less sustenance for racial comity than fodder for maintaining Blacks' liminality in the culture—for the ambivalence and animosity exhibited by Whites in Indianapolis and around the United States.

4 The Meaning of Blackness in Network News

MERICANS MAY WATCH local television news three times a week, and network news twice this week, six times next week, and just once the following week; they may read a newspaper on most days, or on few. They go to a movie occasionally, they watch television entertainment and advertising in prime time and on weekends. Their friends and co-workers do the same. Some individuals talk about what they see in the media all the time, others rarely. As we have seen, it is from this shifting and varied melange of images and ideas, combined with interpretations of direct observation and experience, that each individual builds his or her own impression of the world and, in significant measure, of race.[1] Given such a media environment, it would be a mistake to look at any one genre in isolation. But we must begin somewhere, so we launch the detailed exploration of the media's racial texts from the traditional platform in the field: network television news. We look particularly at the ways network news helps to construct Whites' sense of what blackness means, what traits a representative African American possesses. The news is not terribly good. But before we consider directly those troubling results, we need to make sense of how Whites develop schematic thinking along lines that create animosity or, in more extreme cases, racism.

Cognitive Inertia and the Rise of Prototypes

Prototypes encode habitual ways of thinking that help people make sense of a complicated and uncertain world. These are, however, often formed swiftly and inaccurately, which is understandable given the limited time people have to work through all the tacit assumptions prototypes embody: "[W]ere we to approach every induction task without preconceptions, the manifold hypotheses that we could come up with to be tested in any given set of data would make the inference process unmanageable."[2] Consequently, the judgments that result conceal complexity and make it less likely that people will notice exceptions to culturally driven, stereotyped expectation and understanding.

It is theoretically possible that people could overcome this downside of schematic thinking, with their thoughts driven largely by data, not by prototypes. If they operated this way, the world would imprint upon their minds unique memories of clarity and detail from which they would inductively build categorical understanding. As the details from continuing experience were added, people would readily and dispassionately reclassify the objects of their experiential world or mint fresh categories. In the real world, people *are* data-driven to a degree—they do change their assessments of reality based on their experience with an obdurate world. There is compelling evidence, however, that people more often make on-the-fly judgments using theories that satisfy pragmatic and emotional necessity rather then engage in exhaustive and dispassionate case-by-case analysis. Indeed, evidence from studies of social cognition paints a picture of flawed and fuzzy human judgment driven by convenience and emotion, and informed by deeper influences of culture and individual psychology.[3]

The work of psychologist Eleanor Rosch is suggestive of these twin influences. She has used individual perceptions and classifications of ordinary objects to determine how people think in categories. Contrary to what the data-driven model would predict, she found that some members of a category enjoy a privileged status. For example, people judge robins more representative of the category "birds" than chickens, penguins, or ostriches, and desk chairs more representative of the category "chair" than rocking chairs, beanbag chairs, or barber chairs. These most representative members are called *prototypical*. Prototype theory posits that people abstract out a central tendency—a summary mental representation of a concept—sometimes based on experience but often on ideal characteristics derived from cultural lessons.[4] Prototypes serve as ideal examples of categories and as such induce what are called "prototype effects." To use the bird example, prototypical thinking leads people to rate robins and cardinals as better examples of the category "bird," to reduce the time in assigning them to that category, and to ease their recall as examples.[5]

Prototypes are important in social cognition because they aid people in their appraisal of others. These appraisals are stimulated by characteristics perceived as marking category membership, as in the case, for example, of skin color.[6] Skin color is often sufficient to stimulate expectations of stereotypic behavior. Once activated, these expectations drive social perceptions and act as inertial restraints on peoples' ability to interpret behavior that is incompatible with their stereotypes. The ideal examples that structure the categories and expectations come from the culture, which as Douglas observes, establishes boundaries between things or persons valued and things or persons condemned or feared. These assessments are subconscious and manifest themselves in everyday mental shortcuts that lead us to make snap judgments that appear to be reasonable and natural—although they are in fact deeply problematic.

Prototype theory explains why Whites may assume that a Black person in a White-dominated, high-status setting—an exclusive restaurant, for example—is a waiter. Whites expect the typical Black, if not a criminal, to be a member of the serving class. Such humiliating cases of mistaken identity are frequently reported by Blacks with high achieved status, even when they attempt by dress, grooming, and other communication behavior to signal their acceptance of mainstream norms and strive toward similar cultural ideals as Whites. Cose describes the rage of a Black senior partner in a law firm accosted by a suspicious White junior associate when he came in to work early one day.[7] Notice that this does not mean the White attorney was a racist, although for the Black senior partner on the receiving end of the prototypical expectation and social judgment, he might as well have been. And such experiences, even if exceptional, don't have to happen very often to a Black before he or she is induced to see overt racism as more pervasive than it actually is—to see the prototypical White as racist.[8] In this way, prototypical thinking operates to diminish racial comity, feeding a vicious circle.

Black Representations in Network News

To probe the racial prototypes of network news, we rely upon two kinds of data sets: analyses of videotapes of the evening news shows on the three major networks and analyses of verbatim transcripts for ABC's *World News*. The main videotape sample encompasses four randomly chosen weeks of evening news from the ABC, CBS, and NBC networks in 1997.[9] Another videotape sample covers three ten-day periods of these nightly news programs taped during 1990. The full transcripts of the nightly ABC *World News* program cover two one-year periods, 1990–91 and 1997.[10] The three-network tapes provide a sense of the overall *visual* and *aural* (soundbite) representation of Blacks. The ABC transcripts allow us to determine which Black leaders are mentioned and the contexts in which they made the news. They also permit an in-depth examination of precisely how Black persons are portrayed when the words *Black* or *African American* are mentioned explicitly on *World News.*[11]

Videotape analysis included all stories in which Blacks caused or clearly helped cause the newsworthy event, or where Blacks were *centrally involved* in the story.[12] An overview of ethnic representation in the 1997 three-network sample is revealing. Approximately 75.5 percent of the stories focused exclusively on Whites. That is, three-fourths of the stories did not contain any clearly identifiable members of non-White groups in anything but peripheral roles (such as people in a crowd scene). Just 6.3 percent of the stories (Blacks 2.9 percent, Latinos 1.3 percent, and Asians 2.1 percent) focused on activities of non-White ethnics. The remaining 18.2 percent of stories were ethnically mixed, meaning they depicted central involvement of at least one identifiable member of an ethnic minority, but what is striking is how much the doings of Whites alone pervade the news. Whites were twelve times more likely to have a network news story to themselves than were all the other ethnic groups combined (75.5 percent versus 6.3 percent). The figures would be even more skewed if we excluded foreign news—most reports emphasizing Asians or Latinos concerned the members of these groups who are citizens of *other countries.* Incidentally, census figures break down the U.S. population as 72.1 percent non-Hispanic White; 12.1 percent non-Hispanic Black; 11.4 percent Hispanic; 3.7 percent non-Hispanic Asian and Pacific Islander; and 0.7 percent non-Hispanic American Indian, Eskimo, or Aleut (U.S. Department of Commerce 1997).

In one sense this pattern seems empirically and even symbolically "accurate": Whites do dominate nearly every arena of American society. On the other hand, as these images display America's status and power hierarchy, they also may serve to reinforce it. At the most general level the color pattern of the news conveys a sense that America is essentially a society of White people with minorities—the very word rings pejoratively—as adjunct members who mainly cause trouble or need help.[13]

What were the chief topics of stories that included Black or White voices? Consider table 4.1, which lists the soundbites attributed to Black and White persons in the 1997 three-network sample and the topic of the stories in which they appeared. A pattern can be distinguished among stories where Blacks receive voice and those where they do not. In our sample, only one Black person said anything in an economics story, compared with eighty-six soundbites uttered by Whites, and just one Black said something in foreign

Table 4.1 Topics of Soundbites for Whites and Blacks, 1997 Network Sample

Topic	White Soundbites	Black Soundbites	W:B Ratio
Sports/Entertainment	35	11	3.2
Discrimination	35	10	3.5
Human interest	106	23	4.6
Crime	149	24	6.2
Deaths/Rituals/Anniversaries	39	3	13.0
Court proceedings/Government hearings	254	12	21.2
Science/Technology	84	3	28.0
Disasters/Rescues and weather events	145	5	29.0
Economics	86	1	86.0
Health/Smoking	178	2	89.0
Foreign Affairs	99	1	99.0
Electoral politics	79	0	—
Total	1289	95	13.6

Source: Analysis of sources of all soundbites in three-network sample, 1997.

affairs coverage that featured ninety-nine White quotations. Not one Black person said anything, at least in this sample, in stories on electoral politics, while White voices were heard seventy-nine times. The lopsided disparities were nearly as great in coverage of science/technology; health/smoking; disasters/rescues and weather events; and deaths/rituals/anniversaries. Only in human-interest features, sports/entertainment stories, and discrimination reports did Black voices achieve more prominent access. Stories that either invoked the common experiences or interests of Americans as a whole (disasters, foreign affairs, politics, and deaths/rituals) or that involved technical expertise (science, economics) offered hardly any Black voices. Such patterns of racial inclusion and exclusion, if typical, would reinforce an image of Blacks as a distinct group whose identity, knowledge, and interests are both narrower and systematically different from Whites.

We see here the outlines of the way media help construct the prototypical Black person, that is, the traits characterizing the most representative members of the category.[14] He or she is an entertainer, sports figure, or object of discrimination. Unlike Whites in the news, the prototypical Black can be pigeonholed into a narrow array of roles and traits. We can suggest even more subtle ways that network news may provide a map of the cultural alienation of Blacks and Whites, framing Blacks as separate from the core (White) community, by looking at the distribution of the soundbites (figure 4.1).

Sixty-three stories featured at least one soundbite by a Black person; of these, more than half, thirty-five stories, contained just one quote by a Black.

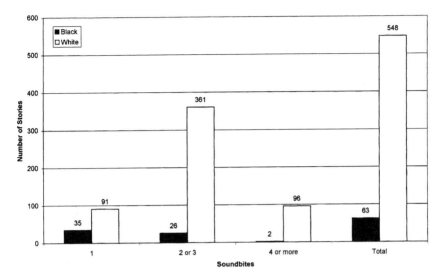

Figure 4.1 Numbers of Stories with One, Two or Three, and Four or More Soundbites, for Black and Whites

Only two stories had four or more Black soundbites, and twenty-six had two or three bites. In comparison, 548 stories transmitted a White person's words, and ninety-six offered four or more. In this sample, at least, viewers were forty-eight times more likely to hear four or more soundbites from White than Black persons in a news story. Hardly any stories were saturated with Black voices, if we define "saturation" as four or more soundbites (not counting reporters), whereas nearly a fifth (18.9 percent) of the stories include four or more instances of White voices. And the two stories with the heaviest presence of Black voices were features rather than hard news.

The Word Black

Beyond the constricted speaking roles for Blacks in network news, another dimension of representation comes in the uses of the word *black*. We recorded the subject of every story in which that word appeared on *World News* during the two transcript periods (1990–91 and 1997). ABC ran 214 stories explicitly mentioning Black *people* in the earlier year-long period, ninety-four in the more recent one. The decline is misleading. Much of the difference appears due to the virtual disappearance of South Africa as a subject by 1997. Representation of African *Americans* was about the same during the two periods (112 versus 94 stories), and it was considerable.

On the other hand, there was a noteworthy rise in the *nonracial* use of "black." In 1990–91, just 20 of the 234 uses of the word were nonracial. In 1997, "black" appeared in 167 stories, fully 73 of them with nonracial meaning. Repeated use of terms such as *blackmail, black hole,* or *black market* reflects the negative symbolic associations of darkness written deep in Western culture.[15] Whether the negative metaphoric connotations of the word *black* unconsciously spill over to Whites' thinking about Black persons is unclear, but the link cannot be very helpful. Strictly as a communication strategy, it might be worth considering replacement of "Black" with "Afro-American" as the preferred term for this ethnic group.[16]

We also looked more specifically at the topics of stories in which the word *black* or equivalents appeared. For this analysis, displayed in appendix table A.3, we also searched for the term *African American* and counted as equivalent the terms *inner city, ghetto, race, racial, racist, racism, underclass,* and *minority,* where the uses clearly (though not necessarily explicitly) referred to Black people. It is difficult to know if contrasts in story topics between the two samples represent random fluctuations or real trends.[17] However, network news throughout the 1990s generally moved toward lighter, more sensational fare and away from political, or policy-oriented stories. That movement seems compatible with our findings.

Proportionally, Blacks appeared three or four times more often than Whites in crime or sports stories in the later sample, and about one-third as much in political stories.[18] In a sense, then, the image of Blacks deteriorated: the network's coverage more heavily featured African Americans in stereotyped roles associated with crime and sports, as it less frequently depicted Blacks in political or governmental roles. On the other hand, ABC ran more stories on discrimination-related policy in 1997, reflecting in part the controversy over affirmative action.

We can more clearly see the Black image on ABC by considering the specific story topics in those reports that mentioned Blacks (or words connoting the group) explicitly. To conserve space, and readers' patience, we list in appendix table A.4 only the reports for the period from July to December of 1997. The list is rather depressing—as we suppose would be most enumerations of specific story subjects. No matter the ethnic group, quite generally, good news is not news. Nonetheless, we are struck by the paucity of neutral, let alone positive, contexts in which words referring to Black persons come up. For instance, not one political report and only two human interest stories appear in this list.

Can we generalize from the ABC data to the other two major networks? Researchers have found few if any systematic differences among the Big Three.[19] In our own three-network samples we found nothing to change this impression. For example, in the 1997 tape sample, African Americans were represented in 10 percent of the stories on ABC, 11 percent on CBS, and 14 percent on NBC. The same data set, on all three networks, also revealed a dearth of Blacks in stories that have as their central theme either Blacks as positive contributors to American society or as human beings whose racial identity is incidental. It therefore seems likely that, were transcripts of CBS and NBC news subjected to close analysis, they would reveal similar representations of Blacks.

Judging from the transcribed years of ABC, the network mainly discusses Blacks as such when they suffer or commit crime, or otherwise fall victim and require attention from government (and, perhaps, taxpayers). By tying appearances of Blacks so frequently to narratives of crime and victimization, the news constructs African Americans as a distinct source of disruption. Because stories featuring Whites in these circumstances are so much fewer as a proportion of all stories with Whites, the news can easily imply a baseline or ideal social condition in which far fewer serious problems would plague the society if only everyone in the United States were native-born Whites.

Incidentally, the portrayals of at least one other minority, Latinos, may be drawn similarly to that of Blacks, at least in some respects. Analyzing full-text verbal transcripts of every broadcast in a three-month subsample, we found that the word *Latino* appeared in just two stories and the word *Hispanic* in seven, all in relation to U.S. events. One of the two mentions of "Latino" came in a story on school segregation, the other in a report on diplomatic training where a man described as "Latino" played a terrorist in a simulation. "Hispanic" was mentioned in stories with the following topics: alleged vote fraud by Hispanics; segregation; the growth of Hispanic stars in baseball; police brutality against Haitian immigrant Abner Louima; the never-found third suspect in the terrorist bombing of the Oklahoma City federal building; school dropouts; and illegal immigration. The range of topics here too is narrow and arguably stereotypical.[20]

In such ways, the news may construct images that partake of the first component of racial animosity, the exaggerated sense of group differences recorded in negative stereotypes. Network news suggests that the distribution of traits characterizing representative Black persons coincides very little with the distribution of traits among Whites. And this fits right into the tendency noted by Rothbart and John: to "maximize the difference between the boundaries of groups and often treat overlapping distributions of characteristics as if they were non-overlapping."[21]

Blacks as Experts

Blacks do sometimes appear as knowledgeable persons with newsworthy, insightful things to say. Such people, by the very act of being consulted, show themselves to have positive social utility, to be valued parts of the community. This is particularly true when Blacks are not ghettoized as experts only on "Black" issues; therefore, we analyzed issues on which Black experts spoke as "Black-related" or not. The former covered racial discrimination, unemployment, homelessness, inadequate health care, welfare, crime and drugs, housing, gangs, and Martin Luther King (considered "Black" issues because television news discourse, visual and verbal, makes them so, as further documented in chapter 6).

Looking at the 1990–91 sample, the stories concerning "Black" issues featured thirty-three Black experts and twenty-seven Whites. In those stories about non-Black issues in which Blacks appeared, White experts markedly outnumbered Blacks—ninety-four to fifteen. Recall that this subsample consists exclusively of those stories that met our criteria for prominently featuring Blacks. In other words, that as many as fifteen Black experts appeared in this subsample is due largely to the fact that we looked only at stories in which Blacks played a prominent role.[22] So, within the total sample of 1,980 minutes of network news, Blacks spoke as experts outside the realm of Black-related issues little more than fifteen times, whereas Whites were likely quoted more than seven hundred times.[23]

These findings can be tested further using the 1997 network data, which Burns and Munoz coded for the ethnicity of the persons uttering every soundbite.[24] Appendix table A.5 lists the topics on which all Black persons commented, along with their apparent occupational status. The largest share of the 111 utterances by Blacks came from persons on the street, followed by government officials. Black experts (defined as scientists, professors, think tank personnel and the like, professional persons unaffiliated with government) spoke fourteen times. In comparison, White nongovernmental professionals made 496 assertions. The ratio of White to Black non-government experts is thus about 36:1 (496 to 14). In this sample the Black experts were not confined to "Black" issues, and of course the audience might have attributed expertise to some of the twenty-two quotes from Black government officials or to those in other roles. So images of knowledgeable Blacks are appearing on the networks. But there remains a relative dearth of high status, credentialed Black persons providing insight on the network news across a wide range of issues.

Although African American expert sources on television are few, the networks do feature Blacks as correspondents—experts in journalism itself. This turns out to be a slight exception to the general paucity of authoritative Blacks. For the 1997 network sample, the race or ethnicity of the correspondents for all nine hundred stories was coded. Non-White reporters covered about 8 percent of stories on ABC and 6 percent on CBS and NBC. As for reporting specifically by Blacks, ABC registered 6 percent; CBS, 4 percent; and NBC, just 2 percent. Blacks appeared underrepresented as reporters on all three networks, relative to their population percentage.[25] But for ABC and CBS, at least, the disparity with Whites was less when it came to interviewers (correspondents) than it was when it came to interviewees (expert news sources).

"Reality"

Some might explain disparities in the news as conveying "reality." If we divide news topics broadly into those involving persons suffering or perpetrating social problems and those involving all other newsworthy activities, we might expect such a racial disjunction. African Americans do experience many social ills at a higher rate than Whites, and their appearances in the news tend to involve those ills because they make minority individuals newsworthy in the first place. Members of the current majority group, on the other hand, control almost all newsworthy institutions—government agencies, legislatures, corporations, interest groups. As the dominant power holders, Whites naturally predominate in news reports not involving social problems because journalists focus most heavily—justifiably so—upon the most powerful individuals and institutions in the society. In those communities where African Americans (or Latinos or other non-White ethnic groups) control government or other important institutions—say, cities with Black mayors—we would expect exceptions to the pattern in the national news analyzed here.

These patterns can be traced in part to important elements of the structure of power in the United States, and they highlight the difficulty of changing the media's racial imagery as long as conventional journalistic forms and incentives remain in place. We reiterate that there are no villains in this piece. But even if the racial patterns are explicable and even defensible on these grounds, the story cannot end there.

The networks' choices are highly selective and incomplete. Consider the example of crime. We know many Whites tend to equate African Americans and crime, and feel intensely negative emotions—anger, fear, a desire for vengeance—more in the face of Black crime than of White crime. As a result, Black crime has long carried a potent political charge.[26] Although Blacks are indeed more likely to commit violent crimes than Whites, the difference declined after 1970 and the general trend in Black-committed violence has been downward since the early 1970s; further, some evidence suggests that Blacks are more likely to be arrested than Whites committing similar crimes, in which case the media might be accurately representing Blacks' higher *arrest* rate but exaggerating the comparative rate of *committing* violent or drug crimes.[27] Also, controlling for employment, there is no difference in crime rates: employed Blacks over the age of twenty-one are as law abiding as employed Whites, a message obscured by the typical representations in television news,[28] and one that establishes quite clearly the importance of unemployment to crime rates.

None of this is to deny that poor Blacks, especially males, engage in certain unlawful activities at a tragically and indeed frighteningly high rate, much higher than Whites on average.[29] But these same lawbreakers are subject to very much higher rates of discrimination, unemployment, ineffective schooling, single-parent upbringing, and other experiences that account for the difference in criminality. It is these experiences that tend not to be reported within the narrative of each specific crime. Stories that depict just the crimes themselves therefore provide a context-free version of Black crime, both in the aggregate and in the cases of individual defendants (and victims).

A Model of Racial Communication

How might we explain the Black presences and absences in the media documented in this and the following chapters? Why does network news select the elements it reports, such as Black crime, and leave others, such as the employment status or discrimination experience of Black defendants, out of the picture? The sources of the media's racial images are complicated and systemic. If anything, the average White media worker probably feels less racial animus than the average White American. But even if most media personnel actively sought to advance a progressive racial project through the media, perhaps even to promote awareness of the structural hindrances African Americans face, they would be impeded by the operation of the strong forces we identify in this section. (The concept of a "racial project," a strategically mounted effort to frame racial issues and relations in particular ways, comes from Omi and Winant.)[30] The *Cosby* show of the 1980s offers a prototypical case study of the way contradictory forces shape and become manifest in mainstream media products. On the surface, it attacked racism. It taught Whites, like Mr. Morgan, the young man at the Town Hall meeting with President Clinton whom we quoted in chapter 1, to see Blacks and Whites as equals. Yet Whites also interpreted the success and assimilation of Bill Cosby's television family as confirming the disappearance of racial discrimination; the show abetted denial.[31]

How might we explain the most prevalent media content, the material that, like the *Cosby* show, attains sufficiently wide distribution to influence public sentiments? Five closely woven forces interact to determine which messages obtain extensive and repeated distribution—and thus social and political force—and which remain either unexpressed or marginalized in obscure media channels. These forces act simultaneously on every media production, which means just about every message we might analyze is over-determined: it has several simultaneous explanations. Briefly, the kinds of messages that receive wide distribution are shaped by

- the mainstream culture, which influences
- the creative needs and limitations and professional norms of individual media personnel and their organizations, which respond to
- the evolving economics of media industries, as shaped by new technology, global market competition, and government policy decisions,
- by political elites seeking to manipulate media content (both news and entertainment), and
- by the changing national and international economic structure and the requirements of its healthy growth.

We have already detailed our understanding of the mainstream culture, the widely shared mental constructs that shape individuals' responses to the other four forces, which we now explore. We shall return to this five-factor model repeatedly throughout the book in order to explain the racial patterns we find in news, entertainment, and advertising.

Media Personnel and Organizations

Bad intentions are not the problem. Media do not produce their messages because executives or other personnel seek to promote racial antipathy. Rather the problematic material arises most importantly from the interaction of the dominant culture with the market pressures on the organizations where media workers are trying to get ahead in their careers. Individuals do this within limitations set by their own creativity, intelligence, boldness, communication skills, and other qualities that affect both the ideas they come up with and their reception by colleagues and superiors. These are shaped, too, by professional norms that guide behavior and judgment, often without clear awareness on the part of the media workers subject to them.[32] Also, just like the largest portion of the audience, the mostly White males who manage media organizations are themselves steeped in the tacit assumptions of a dominant culture that retains vestiges of prejudice. Assumptions of essential racial difference and hierarchy lurk within the culture, and their presence sets up a vicious circle of reinforcement between suppliers and consumers.

Journalists' choices of stories and the specific aspects to report depend upon their congruence with dominant professional norms and organizational routines. Take the pattern of showing so many Blacks in stories of crime. The idea of an in-depth report on the upbringing and experiences of even one criminal defendant, let alone on most of them, would strike most journalists as inappropriate. Culture intersects with elite discourse and journalists' orientations to render such stories politically suspect; they might appear liberal to many conservative viewers, because delving into the context of crime as a way of explaining it may seem to be a way to morally excuse it. Implying that individuals are not fully in control of their destinies, that society as a whole bears some responsibility for social problems, also insults the conservative worldview.[33] In this way such stories would violate journalists' own internalized canons of objectivity and likely call forth elite pressure, even outrage. Attending carefully to language use so that the word *black* would not be used so much in all its many negative combinations ("blackmail" and the like) is even more beyond the journalistic pale.

As to the racialized pattern of expertise in network news, journalists identify legitimate sources by using certain fixed criteria that emphasize institutional connections.[34] Professional norms demand that journalists choose conventionally credible sources, as certified by their rank and affiliation with the best-known institutions, and their ability to influence those institutions' decisions.[35] Sourcing patterns will therefore reflect the larger social structure, which renders African Americans small minorities in the most credible elite institutions. There are simply not very many Black voices to be found in the places where reporters habitually go for expertise. The tendency of reporters to return time and again to the same sources—in part out of habit, in part out of the news organization's need to economize—compounds the problem. Similarly, illustrating welfare with a Black face, as the networks and newsmagazines do frequently and disproportionately,[36] also reflects unthinking habit and ready physical access from downtown news bureaus to the Black poor. Replay such decisions night after night and you get a racial patterning that arises as a by-product of an industrial culture and process, not as a consequence of hiring racist reporters and producers.

Market Demands

The patterns of media messages and media voids that we identify are what economists call "externalities." They are the by-products of more or less rational profit seeking behavior by media organizations facing intense and increasing economic competition for the positive attention of White-dominated mass audiences. This aggregation of individuals has been socialized into the mainstream culture. Media workers seek to make money for their organizations and advance their own careers. That means they must stay vigilantly attuned to the presumed tastes of their target audiences. These creators operate in a professional culture and organizational milieu that transmits lessons about what attracts and sells, what upsets and repels. Ratings and market research increasingly inform decisions, whether about news coverage or entertainment plots.

Before recent changes in the media marketplace set in, news outlets may have been more inclined to run longer, probing reports on domestic racial policy despite any danger of political pressure or audience boredom. But apart from the best newspapers, longer analytical pieces became far less common as market pressures led to more "entertaining" network news and national newsmagazines. Whether on racial matters or a score of others, there was just less room for probing journalism in the highly competitive mass media industry.

In this ratings-driven atmosphere, because media production is almost always a team effort, media personnel must constantly defend their ideas and contributions to their similarly conditioned and pressured colleagues. Thus reporters come to understand, seemingly intuitively, what news is, what a "good picture" looks like on television or on page one, and television show producers come to know which cast choices and plot lines "work" and which do not.[37] In the United States, such decisions include all kinds of assumptions about race, some conscious and some unconscious. They also include commercial factors that have nothing directly to do with race at all.

When it comes to news stories, the decision to play the rape of an upperclass White jogger in Central Park on network news and ignore the simultaneous, similarly brutal attack on a Black slum dweller is not consciously racial. Nor is the decision to lead the local news with detailed footage of a manacled Black gang leader being marched through the police station, while not even showing the face of a White slumlord whose building code violations led to a deadly fire. The landlord has a lawyer and he is not in police custody, so he can keep himself off screen. Police can force the gang leader to make himself available to the cameras for "perp walks" (defendants shown walking while in custody). News organizations crave these as "good TV"— the images add vividness to crime stories and help audiences to visualize the villains in the nightly morality plays, and that maximizes ratings.

As they train and constrain their workers, media organizations themselves experience changing pressures to which they must adapt. New technology, such as direct broadcast satellite, VCRs, and personal computers alter the shape of market competition in ways that have implications for media messages. Deregulating cable and other policy decisions were undertaken to expand the number of national television networks, both broadcast and cable, which radically altered the marketplace. In response to growing competition and declining ratings, network news tended during the 1990s toward broadcasting increasingly nonpolitical, celebrity-oriented and entertaining or sensationalized stories. As we saw, that trend had implications for racial images. Blacks appeared less often than they once did in network news as serious participants in the political arena, more often as players in the sports arena and on stage or screen. No racial intent lurked behind the rise in network news appearances of Blacks in the roles with which Whites have long been most comfortable (athletes and entertainers); White athletes and entertainers were also making the news shows more often. But such entertaining stories about Whites do not reinforce stereotypes about their "race" as they do for Blacks. At the minimum, the news media's focus on Blacks as entertainers and athletes registers a lost opportunity for Whites to learn more important things about African Americans than that they can sing a song or dunk a basketball.

Political Pressure

Race in America is highly politicized, so it should come as no surprise that the decisionmaking of media personnel in the area is also affected by organized and anticipated political pressure. Omi and Winant write of elites pursuing competitive "racial projects" that seek to define race and racial identity in ways that advance larger policy aims and score political or economic gains.[38] They carry out such projects most obviously through news but also through entertainment media. Purely selfish individual interests do not necessarily motivate these projects; elites may seek them because they believe in their morality. The projects take two basic forms. One is content provision: speeches, proposals, think tank reports, public relations campaigns, and other communications designed to reinforce or change the perceptions and preferences of the mass public and other elites. The other is pressure to take a show off the air or prevent publication of a particular news report.

Consider affirmative action as an example of the part played by the media in racial projects, and of all the forces operating in the model. As we shall show in chapter 7, for motives that included both electoral success and a particular vision of social morality,[39] many leaders in the mid-1990s sought to place a critique of affirmative action high on the public agenda. Politicians began attacking the policy, the media publicized the assault, and news reports imposed a Black–White racial frame (as opposed to, say, a gender frame) on the dispute. The media thus helped this racial project along.

Media also have an independent effect of their own on the ideas and pressures political actors advance. The needs of media organizations shape what they are willing and able to transmit and thus how they respond to pressure and manipulation. The attack on affirmative action attained heightened visibility because it played into media needs for simple, symbolic, dramatic conflict.[40]

Chapter Four

The Economy

The operation of the economy strongly influences what our political leaders say and the particular racial projects they mount. In recent decades, the key development has been the rise of global interdependence. The mobility of capital and labor, and the accompanying consolidation of many large corporations from Disney/ABC to Exxon/Mobil Oil, have dampened wage growth for lesser-skilled workers. Income and wealth inequality generally grew.[41] Despite a booming stock market and great increases in total hours worked by household members, average family incomes during the last quarter of the century increased at a glacial pace compared to rates during the previous twenty-five years. Growing anxiety accompanied lowered expectations of stable, let alone lifetime, employment. Global markets were placing ever-mounting pressure on U.S. corporations to keep costs down and employment rosters flexible.

How does all this affect the production of racial meanings in the media? Diffuse White anxiety, anger, and alienation over economic inequality and vulnerability, and the apparent inability of government to address these concerns had two effects. First, they bolstered Whites' susceptibility to anti-Black political appeals.[42] Without a sophisticated understanding of such topics as labor economics, class mobility patterns, and public finance, the potential salience and apparent reasonableness of coded racial claims about wasteful welfare spending, high taxes, and threatening crime grew.

Second, White anxiety encouraged certain elites to mount an active racial project scapegoating Blacks (and, in some cases, other out-groups like immigrants).[43] Here capital punishment and longer prison terms were cases in point. Whatever the effect of death penalties and stricter sentencing on Black crime rates, the crucial impacts of global competition, economic growth, and other such forces on employment opportunities and thus crime cannot easily be controlled or even discussed. And the mainstream culture provides such a plentiful stock of myths, symbols, and homilies about individual responsibility. In this context, it made sense for some political leaders to craft a racial project emphasizing capital punishment and longer sentences, along with cutting welfare, affirmative action, and related policies that disproportionately affect Blacks—remedies conveniently congruent with some of the most vivid images on the nightly news.

From the other side, defending higher government expenditures or taxes explicitly in order to help poor minorities or attacking the notion of incarceration as a panacea for crime became politically risky. It is no accident that Bill Clinton was the first Democrat to win reelection to the presidency since Franklin Roosevelt. By acceding to welfare cutbacks, increased jail terms and police expenditures, the death penalty, and similar positions not previously identified with his party, he disarmed what had been some of the most effective weapons in conservatives' arsenals.

Conclusion

It is beyond our mission here to elaborate more detailed explanations of the origins of the media's racial images. The key point is that *there is nothing in "reality" that compels the presentations of African Americans that the media offer.* What we see and do not see reflects a combination of forces that, with alteration, could result in different representations that are no less defensible. The images are not arbitrary; as we have suggested, they can be understood as products of an interaction of predictable forces. But they do have a kind of arbitrariness in their relation to race. The news does not usually reflect any conscious effort by journalists to cultivate their audiences' accurate understanding of racial matters. Rather, the news embodies the effects of tacitly obeying norms and following cultural patterns of which journalists are only imperfectly aware, and of responding to pressures from elites and markets which news organizations are disinclined to challenge.

We cannot overlook the implications of these inadvertent racial patterns for Whites steeped in mainstream culture, especially for those tending toward racial animosity. The presences and absences of Blacks in key roles and situations create implicit racial comparisons. These construct a sense of the prototypical Black person that fits with *anti-Black stereotypes* readily served up by the culture. The omissions, along with the different subjects emphasized in stories depicting Blacks and Whites, imply exaggerated, fundamental differences between the two groups. They connote that membership in the category of Black persons reliably predicts that an individual will possess disfavored traits and behave improperly. Even if these intimations trace partially to racial differences in social behavior and role, in America they carry ideologically potent and damaging cultural connotations. With these meditations as prelude and backdrop, we turn to a more finely grained analysis of television news, this time at the local level.

5 Violence, Stereotypes, and African Americans in the News

MONG TELEVISION's most salient and frequent concerns are crime and violence. A steady drumbeat of frightening information and images dominates television news, and of course crime drama is a staple of television entertainment. In this chapter we investigate the *racial* skew in televised nonfictional violence. We focus on the most popular single news genre, local television news, emphasizing case studies from Chicago, the third largest U.S. city, an ethnically diverse metropolitan area reasonably representative of the urban markets in which most Americans reside. Not only does local news depict life in America as pervaded by violence and danger; this genre also heightens Whites' tendency to link these threats to Blacks. Although television as a whole and even local news also carries many messages that affirm the social value and racial equality of African Americans, crime reporting fashions a hierarchical racial divide that stereotypes Blacks and associates them with the wrong, dangerous side of the cultural continuum. Glaring racial disparities seem to freeze Blacks' liminal cultural status in place. Even the positive material, in the absence of a larger cultural and factual context, may reinforce negative emotions among ambivalent Whites.

The impact of nonfictional televised violence has received less attention than violent entertainment.[1] Yet the slogan "If it bleeds, it leads" registers the assumption that violence sells news, not just entertainment. Local news shows frequently broadcast more vivid images of violence than "entertainment"—*real* blood, smashed windows, loaded guns, bodies on stretchers. Television news often portrays an urban America nearly out of control: night after night the news overflows with victims and perpetrators of violence. The specifically racial dimensions to the violent news also received little scholarly attention until the 1990s, when studies of Chicago, Los Angeles, Philadelphia, and other markets across the nation began documenting the racial tilt in the crime and violence that pervades local television news.[2]

Statistics do show starkly disproportionate crime rates among Blacks, given their population proportion of about 12 percent. The FBI estimated that 41 percent of those arrested for violent crimes in 1997 were Black (and 57 percent White); 32 percent of those arrested for property crimes were Black.[3] Highlighting the media's ability to construct realities that do not necessarily accord with official statistics and other factual data, public perceptions exaggerate the actual racial disproportion. Sniderman, Tetlock, and Piazza's "Poverty and Politics" survey found a plurality of respondents estimating that 60 percent "of all people arrested for violent crimes in the United States last year . . . were Black," over 40 percent higher than the actual proportion of 43 percent.[4] Local news, with its typically heavy focus on urban crime, may have some responsibility for this exaggerated perception.[5]

This chapter concentrates on violent content broadcast by Chicago's local news (6 P.M. and 9 or 10 P.M.). Whether local news there resembles that in other cities is open to question, of course, but research elsewhere (cited above) has found similar racial contrasts.[6] We analyzed one sample of ten weeks' programming that appeared during 1993–94 on the major local broadcast channels. The book's website contains the coding instructions employed for this study.[7] When comparable we also report the results of a content analysis of Chicago's local news during 1990–91.[8] Data on Chicago's two main dailies, the *Chicago Tribune* and *Chicago Sun-Times*, yield useful comparisons, as did data on infotainment shows like *Cops*.[9]

Despite scholarly emphasis on network news, "[l]ocal TV news is viewed more favorably and consumed by more people than any other news source. Fully 72 percent of Americans watch local news regularly." In comparison, 56 percent read a daily paper regularly, and 41 percent watch network television news.[10] In many markets, especially in the East and Midwest, local news garners higher ratings than network news. Moreover, local news and its racial messages arise close to home, and as suggested by our Indianapolis interviews in chapter 2, help to shape the audience's emotional and cognitive responses to community conditions in a way that the more distant national news may not. Local television appears to be a particularly important news medium in Chicago, where it draws about twice as many viewers as the network evening news shows—fully half the television households in the Chicago area tune their televisions to the late local news on the average night.[11] It is safe to say that Chicago households share few if any other cultural experiences quite as regularly or widely as watching the local news.

Chapter Five

The Violent World of Local News

We defined violence as any threat or experience of physical harm to humans, and found its images pervasive. The most frequent types of violence depicted were accidents, fires, or explosions that killed or injured; murder; child abuse; and other forms of gun violence. Every story that included any of the incidents defined as violent was coded. Local news averaged nearly seven violent items per show, taking up nearly eight minutes.[12] Approximately 58 percent of the violent items concerned serious criminal violence,[13] and 22 percent of these violent items (n = 245) depicted murders. Other researchers have found a similar emphasis on violence in local television news, one that fails to match several measures of "reality," including an enormously disproportionate emphasis on murder as compared with other violent crimes.[14] Actual on-screen violence occurred relatively infrequently (in 13 percent of items). Most often, the aftermath, the victim, or the alleged perpetrator of violence appeared.[15]

Although depictions of violence itself appeared on only a small fraction of the shows, we should not underestimate the degree to which news (and tabloid infotainment) features blood, gore, and other frightening or sensational visual images. Nearly 13 percent of the stories showed visuals of bloodied or injured persons and 6 percent conveyed sounds of suffering; about 16 percent showed damaged property, and the same number featured flashing-light-bedecked police vehicles or other symbols of police emergency. The sense of urgency and threat that these visuals may convey, combined with the verbal texts describing a variety of dangerous persons and events, constructs the world as hazardous and full of risk.

Compounding that image is another element of the programming that the study revealed: the scarcity of reports on systematic attempts to control all this violence. This category includes government or private groups acting, for example, to reduce crime by a neighborhood patrol system, community policing innovation, or arson prevention program. Only about 5 percent of the stories included any reference to control programs. In other words, about 95 percent of the violent stories included no message that any organized body was attempting systematically to suppress violent behavior, let alone to deal with the underlying sources of violence. This may help explain why viewing violent programming apparently leads audiences to exaggerate the possibility that they themselves will fall victim to crime and violence and to overestimate the degree of criminal victimization in society at large.[16]

Racial Subtexts of Crime News

Having described the pervasive environment of televised violence we now turn to the racial subtext of Chicago's local news, the way it closely links Blacks to all these dangers. Looking first at race of alleged perpetrators, we find approximately an equal number of Blacks and Whites (173 versus 179). At one level this equivalence seems reasonable, since Blacks do commit crime far in excess of their population proportions. At another, however, representing Blacks far more often in criminal roles than Whites effectively makes them into symbols of threat. A related signal arises from the portrayal of victims. By a 1.5:1 (241 to 160) ratio, White victims outnumbered Blacks in news reports—even though Blacks in Chicago and most core cities are more likely to be victimized. Another way of comparing news of victimization is length of time devoted to the story: the average story featuring Black victims was 106 seconds long; those featuring White victims, 185 seconds long. Using total story time as a measure, the ratio of time spent on White victims to that on Blacks exceeded 3:1.

This pattern has been remarked on many times, and it probably involves class biases and journalistic norms. The media almost always pay far more attention to a murder victim on Park Avenue than to one on 125th Street. Sadly, a Black murder victim in a Harlem tenement conforms to expectations, so is less newsworthy than a White corpse in a midtown penthouse. The resulting emphases profoundly imply that White life is more valuable than Black.

Racial representation on television actually does not appear to match crime statistics, with local news overrepresenting Black perpetrators, underrepresenting Black victims, and overrepresenting White victims.[17] However, we do not wish to emphasize "inaccuracy" since representing reality turns out to be a conceptual and practical minefield. Even if the proportion of Black victims and criminals were to reflect defensibly "accurate" readings of actual crime patterns, *in the absence of contextual explanations*, the heavy prominence of a racial minority in these stories of violence may worsen negative stereotyping. Additionally, relying upon crime statistics accepts constructions of social reality that we should regard skeptically. Comparing news to official crime data neglects subtleties in defining violence and in categorizing it as criminal—or as newsworthy. Slumlords whose neglect of heat and sanitation codes causes children to become sick, police who harass minority youth without probable cause, banks that refuse to lend to credit-worthy individuals based on race, and apathetic teachers of non-White students all commit a serious kind of crime if not violence against people, a sort not reported in official statistics of crime or in most newscasts.

The research literature strongly suggests that televised violence promotes anxiety and hostility in audiences. The racial subtexts raise the possibility that televisual violence could be focusing those anxieties and hostilities, among Whites, most intensely on Black persons.[18] This possibility is bolstered as we turn to the data on visual and aural portrayals of crimes allegedly committed by Blacks and Whites.

Based on a pilot study,[19] we identified a series of significant images in crime stories that might connote racial differences. The pilot research found a tendency for Blacks accused of crimes to be portrayed as individuals less than Whites—that is, to be lumped together without distinct identities and laden with negative associations. The Black–White differences discussed all reach statistical significance at a $p < 0.05$ level unless otherwise noted, lending confidence that the differences in portrayals are not merely due to chance.

Mug shots make their subjects look guilty. Rarely flattering, the tell-tale gridlines behind the face or the combined portrayal in front and profile shots yield an impression of guilt based on hundreds or thousands of previous, intertextual memories of the image in news and fiction. We found in the 1993–94 sample that stories about Blacks were four times more likely to include mug shots (though the actual numbers were small: eight for Blacks, two for Whites).[20]

Extending the finding of a more differentiated, individualized image for White defendants, the data show that local news shows were more likely to provide an on-screen name for Whites accused of violence than for Blacks (or Latinos). In the 1993–94 sample, 47 percent of Whites accused received a visualization that included their name printed on screen, compared to 26 percent of Blacks. A similar contrast emerged from the 1990–91 sample, where 49 percent of Black but 65 percent of White defendants were named.[21] The presence of the accused's name provides a sense of his or her individual identity. Its absence may suggest that individual identity does not matter, that the accused is part of a single undifferentiated group of violent offenders: just another Black criminal—not much new or noteworthy there. The lower frequency of providing the accused's name tends to efface the differences among individual Blacks. Through such implications of homogeneity, the texts may suggest that the people less often named differ from the dominant group, who are more worthy of naming, more possessed of individual identities.

Another difference that points in the same direction is presentation under the physical control of police officers: being handcuffed, grasped, or restrained by an officer. The news presented Blacks in physical custody more than twice as much as Whites. In the 1993–94 sample, 38 percent of Blacks compared with 15 percent of Whites were so depicted; Blacks comprised fully two-thirds of all persons shown in physical control even though they were less than half of all accused perpetrators depicted. In the 1990–91 sample the numbers were almost identical (38 percent for Blacks,18 percent for Whites); all these differences are significant at $p < 0.01$. Such images attach a heightened degree of threat to Blacks, who seem to require physical control or restraint twice as much as Whites. Night after night the parade of Blacks in the literal clutches of police authority far more than White defendants sends a series of threatening images that insinuate fundamental differences between races.

In the earlier sample we also coded how any defendant shown in motion video was dressed. The Blacks were more likely to be shown in street or jail clothing than Whites (54 percent versus 31 percent), and the finding was highly significant statistically. This is not surprising, given the apparent differences in social class of the Black and White defendants in the news. Still, the depictions again attach symbols of greater threat to the Blacks accused than to the Whites. The importance of clothing as a cue in this regard is well known to defense attorneys, who dress up their clients for court appearances to make them appear less threatening to judges and juries (and cameras).

One possible explanation for these findings is that Blacks commit disproportionately more violent crimes, in which case the nature of the allegations would cause the pattern of negative stereotyping: perhaps the news simply reflects the fact that Black defendants on average *are* more threatening than Whites. However, as we hinted, "accuracy" in this sense is only partially relevant. Without context, the information conjured up by the differential racial images implicitly endorses mistaken assumptions about the relative behavioral tendencies and values of the two racial groups. Even if the reason for any racial differences in news images is that Blacks tend to commit more violent crimes than Whites, it would remain true that the divergent images are conveyed without much explanation. Lacking context, the messages provide grist for unreasoned stereotyping and negative emotions toward Blacks.

Just as important, when we looked only at those accused of crimes associated with violence, the differences persisted, albeit in some instances at a lower level of statistical significance.[22] And similar contrasts show up in the research on local news in other cities that we have cited. Blacks in the news tend to look different from and more dangerous than Whites even when they commit similar crimes.

Explanations

It is tempting but ultimately misleading to lay this pattern at the door of racist or White-dominated news organizations where people of color are underrepresented. Structural forces have far more bearing on the nature of news images than the racial identifications of the personnel. For one thing, Blacks now constitute 10 percent of news employees in local television news and other minorities constitute 8 percent, although the top slot, news director, remains overwhelmingly White; in newspapers, analogous figures are roughly similar.[23]

The difference in providing the accused's name is the one practice most likely linked to unconscious racial prejudice. We can think of no reason to account for the inability of news programs to place a name on screen for Blacks as much as for Whites. The difference may well reside in prototypical thinking: the dangerous Black male is such a familiar type that news workers don't even think to name the individual. This interpretation should not be pushed too far. Large numbers of still photos of Blacks did contain a name label while many of Whites did not; but the prevailing pattern fits with the framing of Blacks as the lesser race.

For the other contrasts in Black–White portrayals, interactions of social structure with news organizations' needs and limitations provide the best explanations. There is an inadvertent class bias in local television news. Put simply, television favors middle- or upper-class persons when they appear in the news, because they have the skills and resources to manipulate its production practices. Thus many of the accused violent Whites in the Chicago news reports were alleged organized crime figures who had money. They could afford bail, good legal representation, and advice on handling the press. Since they were not in jail, these individuals naturally appeared less often in scenes of physical custody, and they could dress more formally. With the ability to hire articulate lawyers and to set up interviews, they were also more likely to receive helpful pro-defense soundbites. Moreover, informants in the industry have told us that police are more protective of the privacy of White or higher-status defendants. Police appear more likely to let stations know they have a "perp walk" scheduled so a station can get footage for its news reports when they have a low-status minority member in custody.

To counter this pattern, journalists would have to understand the class bias and take steps to counteract it. But such overt intervention in the construction of the subject's image—suggesting Black lawbreakers put on business suits, or asking police to uncuff and allow a Black defendant to walk freely for the news camera—would be impractical, and would be viewed by editors as staging the news or editorializing. In the absence of such steps, crime stories— assuming Winant is correct in assuming that most Americans are constantly and highly aware of race[24]—convey scarier images of Blacks than Whites.

It turns out there was another pattern to the exertion of police authority in Chicago's local news. In the 1990–91 sample, we assessed the race of police officials who were quoted on screen about the alleged lawbreaker. Blacks accused of crimes were frequently discussed by White police officers, or by both Black and White police officers in the same story. On the other hand, Whites accused of crimes were almost always discussed *only* by police who were also White. When the accused was White, 95 percent of the time the race of any officer(s) given a soundbite was White. The race of officer(s) commenting on accused African Americans was Black 32 percent of the time. The difference is highly significant statistically. A kind of symbolic segregation of police authority pervaded Chicago's local news. Blacks were shown frequently in what might be called the verbal custody of Whites, but the opposite rarely held. Symbolically this pattern could imply that Blacks are not trusted (and perhaps should not be trusted) to exert police authority over White persons. This situation was almost certainly not the result of journalistic choice. Rather it reproduced the residential segregation of Chicago and the practices of the police force in assigning police of different races to specific neighborhoods. But whatever the underlying social structures, the pattern of broadcast images—the implicit comparison of racial groups, trust, and competence—remains.

There is another angle to all the reporting of violence that could in theory help to counteract the relatively negative images of African Americans. Most of the crime stories contained information about people on the right side of the law: police officers and other government officials, or good Samaritans. If Blacks receive attention in these roles it could help to balance or at least complicate the criminal impressions. However, when we looked in the 1993–94 sample at the race of government officials in violent stories, chiefly law enforcement officers, the segregation of authority by race was striking. Whites formed the large majority of racially identifiable persons handling the violence. In another telling racial statistic, we also probed the race of any "helpers" or Samaritans depicted in the programs. These were defined as people at the scene of violence who have no official capacity but have helped victims and officials cope with it—a person on the street who called authorities or rescued someone from a burning building, for example. Relatively few stories showed helpers, but of those shown, most again were White:[25]

Race	Officials	Helpers
Black	7.8%	13.2%
	(n = 26)	(n = 13)
White	92.2%	86.8%
	(n = 309)	(n = 85)

Blacks acting alone[26] formed a tiny fraction of officials shown (and solitary Asians and Latinos were virtually invisible in this role). One explanation of the images is that Whites may well dominate powerful and therefore newsworthy positions in law enforcement agencies. But, looking more broadly at racial representation, the ratio of White officials to Black officials in local news stories is 12:1 (309 to 26), even though Blacks comprise closer to 35 percent of law enforcement personnel in Chicago.[27] Measuring in seconds reinforces this point: 2,352 seconds were devoted to stories featuring Black officials and 65,124 seconds to Whites, for a ratio of 28:1. Whites constituted the overwhelming majority of racially identifiable individuals in positive social roles. Again using time as a measure, stories featuring Black helpers received a total of 1,890 seconds while those including White helpers received 27,084, for a White–Black helper story ratio of about 14:1.

The Paradox of Black On-Air Personnel

There is one other kind of authoritative figure appearing in the news, though not of the governmental variety: the journalists themselves. In

Chicago and many urban areas, Black anchors and correspondents are a common sight. What do White viewers behold when they tune into these programs? From impressionistic perusal of local news in stations around the country, encompassing thirty-six markets,[28] it appears Black anchors and reporters' spoke from the same perspective as White; there was no difference in their reporting, which is precisely what their job descriptions and professional roles demanded. Voicing a Black perspective would have meant defining the problems covered in the news—such as violent crime—in ways that might be endorsed by a majority of African Americans but only by a minority of Whites. This is not to suggest a radical racial divide in political perspectives, but there are differences: although Blacks may fear crime as much or more than Whites, their interpretations of crime's causes and cures are, on average, different. Those distinctions could construct a different narrative on crime involving Blacks, one focusing more on discrimination as a cause.[29] The Black journalists did not offer this perspective.

Black anchors may be especially significant to formation of White impressions. Anchors in local news may provide the images of authoritative Blacks most frequently encountered by many Whites, who typically live in largely segregated neighborhoods and work for White bosses. The images of Blacks exerting influence over information flow in local news embody the racial ambivalence, and the change, in the dominant culture, for those images carry two simultaneous, implicit messages. On one level, Black anchors demonstrate that African Americans are capable of behaving according to, and reporting from the perspective of, the majority group's values. But on another level, the innocuous Black anchors may also reinforce Whites' impatience with the threatening or demanding Blacks who appear so frequently in the news itself. The anchors' very presence suggests that if Blacks just keep quiet and work hard, the system will indeed allow them to progress, even to earn more money than most Whites. Publicity about anchors' often-exorbitant salaries confirms this. Showing Blacks whose ascribed and achieved traits situate them comparatively close to the desirable side of the ideal trait continuum (chapter 2), particularly in such prestigious and apparently influential public roles, implies that Blacks are not inherently inferior or socially undesirable. Yet the image that undermines old-fashioned racism may promote the denial component of racial animosity.

Beyond this, viewing local news featuring a Black anchor can symbolically affirm for White viewers that they are themselves without racial animus. Whites who feel animosity or worse toward Blacks may even experience an unconscious attraction to local news because its racial messages help confirm their sentiments, while its presentation, in part by Blacks, allows them to deny they have any racist tendencies. Watching the news may protect Whites from confronting their own racial anxieties. Having Black anchors and reporters deliver crime and other stories that may reinforce animosity could allow Whites to think in schematic ways that embody racial animosity without even recognizing their sentiments as racially charged. After all, Blacks themselves provided the information.

Packaging subtly antagonistic images of Blacks as racially neutral information may have great political significance, and not only because of any direct impact of the media on viewers. The benign guise of the images may authorize Whites to voice coded or oblique anti-Black feelings in personal conversation. Hearing such ideas openly expressed may further legitimize and spread the notions, in a kind of reversal of Noelle-Neumann's "spiral of silence."[30] In this case, it is a spiral of voicing: the more people hear racial animosity obliquely expressed, say as anger at crime, the freer they feel to voice similar sentiments, and thus yet more people will hear those views. Meanwhile, the racially charged nature of the perceptions and sentiments remain camouflaged—the unacknowledged racial chameleon—and thus do not threaten Whites' moral self-images.[31]

Comparison to Chicago Newspapers

We cannot expect television to ignore the violent crime and other bad news that continues to plague Chicago and most other urban areas, even during periods when the rate of crime is declining (such as the 1990s).[32] But the depictions of violence by local newspapers offer a revealing contrast. Their coverage was explored during the 1993–94 sample period. Stories that led the television news often received just a few paragraphs on the inside pages of the daily papers. That result suggests other options for covering violence than those dominating local television. While it might be unrealistic to demand that local stations or advertisers sacrifice audience ratings to advance the social good, this study offers evidence that other profit-oriented (print) media manage to handle violence somewhat differently. Nor do newspapers ignore or play down violence; it is a violent world and newspapers convey that reality too.

For ten days out of the sample period, we explored how and whether the *Chicago Tribune* and the *Chicago Sun-Times* covered the stories that made the

10 P.M. local television news on a randomly selected major network affiliate. News judgment showed substantial overlap, as both newspapers covered many of the stories that made the television news. The television news reported sixty-nine violent stories during the ten-day subsample.[33] The *Tribune* reported thirty-four of them; the *Sun-Times*, forty. The *Tribune* was subjected to a more detailed analysis that determined exactly what violent stories it covered and how it presented them. The newspaper profile was perhaps not as different from television as one might expect. The largest distinction is that television expended much more attention on accidents, fires, and explosions than the newspaper—not surprising given the visual appeal of such mishaps. The *Tribune*, which devoted a significant portion of its space to international news, also reported on armed conflict and rebellion in other nations to a much greater degree than local television news.

But it is noteworthy that the *Tribune* did report a lot of violence during this sample period, averaging sixteen violent items per issue. A more precise measure can be gleaned from counting the number of words reported in stories that depicted violence. The average number of words appearing in each issue's stories about violence was 7,767. This total far exceeded the words uttered in an entire half-hour news program. If correspondents speak at about 130 words per minute in a typical newscast, the *Tribune* figure would equal about sixty minutes of television news narration—a solid hour of violence, the equivalent of three full half-hour news shows (when commercials are added in).

What was strikingly different about this print outlet compared with television, of course, was the format of presentation. The *Tribune* had no illustrations at all for 78 percent of its violent stories (n = 127). The paper pictured victims eleven times and accused perpetrators twelve times, so about 14 percent of the stories came with such illustrations. In the case of television, 34 percent of stories showed pictures of victims or perpetrators. Only 3 percent of newspaper stories but fully 23 percent on television showed the aftermath of violence. One important implication of this difference is that newspaper readers normally do not know the race of any perpetrators and victims. Racial sentiments are thus less likely to be implicated by the newspaper's reporting. Another significant difference was that 14 percent of the *Tribune* stories mentioned a systematic government or private effort to control the causes of violence, more than twice the proportion of television stories (6 percent).

Finally, many of the stories that television covered were reported in the *Tribune* but deemphasized by their placement on the inside pages. In the nature of television news, every item is akin to a page one story: if you are watching the show you will be exposed to the story. Readers scan newspapers, and we know that stories not on page one are far less likely to be noticed and read by readers than those on the front page. Placement of stories inside the paper also conveys a message that the events lack urgency and social importance; this connotation may help reduce the salience and emotional potency of stories whose content might otherwise be alarming or provoke hostility.

Compared to television, the *Tribune*, by reporting in a less emotionally vivid mode, appeared to portray a somewhat less threatening or out-of-control world. Violence in newspapers appeared to give less attention to telegenic but often uncontrollable disasters like fires, floods, and explosions; offered visual illustrations in only a fraction of its stories; described violence mostly in words; rarely identified the race of people involved; rarely illustrated the upsetting aftermath of violence; more frequently described organized efforts to control violence; and deemphasized violence through placement of most stories about local occurrences inside the paper.

There are reasons for the contrast that illuminate the somewhat different configuration of forces acting within and upon television news versus newspapers. *Tribune* advertisers are generally seeking a more upscale audience, and regular newspaper readers are more educated and affluent than the average local news viewer. Local television news, as we saw from the ratings, is one of the last bastions of the truly mass audience, with its least-common-denominator approach to content and advertising. If Chicago had a sensational tabloid newspaper like the *New York Post,* the contrast to television might not have been as stark. In other words, local television news is more akin to a sensational tabloid than a newspaper—except that the audience size of local television news is far greater than that of any tabloid.

Conclusion

We recognize that what we found in Chicago may not hold in all particulars for all large cities. Research in other markets that we have already cited does suggest considerable similarity across the United States. But the racial disparities discussed here may be greater in some locations, smaller in others. And of course the news is a moving target. Themes and formats are fads that come and go; a trend to downplay violence could emerge, especially if crime rates continue decreasing into the twenty-first century, which in turn would reduce the negative racial messages. Thus we do not mean to proclaim that the research reported here is the final word. But it does stand as an important example for theoretical purposes, even if limited to Chicago (and Los Angeles and Philadelphia, also intensively studied) during the first half of the 1990s. The findings show how the news business can unintentionally produce subtle images that may *stimulate negative emotions*. And, given urban demographics and common news practices, it is likely that divisive racial signals of the type found in this study do characterize many of America's local news operations.

The racial stereotyping of Blacks encouraged by the images and implicit comparisons to Whites on local news reduces the latter's empathy and heightens animosity, as demonstrated empirically by several experimental studies.[34] To the extent local television news thereby undermines the fragile foundations of racial comity, it could reduce apparent and real responsiveness of White-dominated society to the needs of poor minorities, especially Blacks. The result, in turn, is continued employment discrimination and government unresponsiveness to the urban job loss and economic dislocation that has so traumatized the inner city[35]—and consequent breeding of crime.

We recognize that speculating about effects of television is a risky business. Some White suburbanites may interpret the images of crime and violence in other ways. The messages may, for example, evoke in some Whites compassion and involvement in ameliorative efforts; among many others, the messages may have no impact at all. The same general point about the unpredictability of reactions could be made with respect to other subgroups in the audience. We have dealt with these complications in chapter 2, where we saw the range of roles mediated communication plays in Whites' racial reasoning. That said, we would argue that the patterns we (and others cited) have found in local television news at minimum do much less to encourage racial comity than they might.

Why does television take this path? One reason for the growth of televised violence on programs ostensibly designed to inform as well as entertain is that competition for audiences has intensified. Technology and government policy spurred the competition. By the end of the century, three-fourths of the nation's households had connected to a multichannel cable or satellite television service. Local news producers' decisions to feature violence reflect their presumption that it helps them cope with the competition. The ability of local news to draw ratings that often surpass those of the network news programs seems to support that belief. Moreover, much evidence does suggest a public whose attention is captured most readily by violence and human interest. According to the Pew Research Center, the ten stories of 1998 in which the public voiced the most interest were: the Jonesboro, Arkansas school shooting (news coverage followed closely by 49 percent of respondents); the Oregon high school shooting (46 percent); the U.S. Capitol shooting (45 percent); military strikes against Iraq (44 percent); military strikes in Sudan and Afghanistan (44 percent); outcome of elections (42 percent); unseasonable weather (39 percent); nationwide heat wave (38 percent); conflict with Iraq and UN weapons inspectors (36 percent); and Clinton / Lewinsky (as of early September 1998, 36 percent).[36] Such figures can only heighten the pressures on those running news organizations to keep the news simple and, perhaps, sensational.

Another part of the explanation is elite activity. With persistent public fear, political elites have an incentive to stoke the fires of anxiety, reinforcing attention from audiences and journalists. Although it is rarely as blatant as George Bush's 1988 anti-Black appeal carried via the William "Willie" Horton and prison furlough advertisements,[37] raising the crime issue stimulates in many Whites' minds an image of dangerous Blacks.[38] The effectiveness of such campaign tactics rests upon prototypical thinking that comports with dominant images on local news. Here we have a good example of how technological developments, market forces, and policy decisions, none directly related to race, interact with elite incentives to shape racial images.

The creators of the news also play a role here. The power of the stereotyped associations of Blacks and lawlessness in journalists' own thinking is perhaps most graphically revealed by coverage of the Los Angeles civil disturbances of 1992. Despite the fact that this was a thoroughly integrated uprising in which the majority of those arrested were Latino, and quite a few were Anglo, media depictions heavily emphasized and often equated Blacks as "rioters."[39] It should hardly be surprising that journalists themselves incorporate stereotyped racial schemas in their thinking, which are reflected in the images they produce. The power of stereotypes to guide information processing is noted by Devine, who found that "even for subjects who honestly report having no negative prejudices against Blacks, activation of stereotypes can have automatic effects that if not consciously monitored produce effects that resemble prejudiced responses."[40] The schema of associative links around the concept of urban unrest or "riots" has at its core the concept "Black people," because the largest civil disturbances in American history have generally involved Blacks (sometimes in conflict with Whites, to be sure). Most decisionmakers in news organizations are old enough to vividly remember televised images of the 1960s' Black urban uprisings. These events established their race-linked notions of what a riot is. In a similar way, unfortunately, the news workers' decisions to suffuse so much of the news with images of Black crime and violence may reinforce the current White audience's tendencies to develop schematic associations (or stereotypes) linking African Americans closely with crime and violence. As Gandy observes, "very subtle cues can evoke or activate a structured set of stereotypic images or impressions, [and] increase the potential influence that mass media or other communicators may have on the production of racism."[41]

Changing all this, whether among White journalists or White audiences, is no easy task. Thinking stereotypically is not only an easy habit to fall into, it is a normal way of thinking; in essence, stereotypes are schemas, short-cut mechanisms for processing what would otherwise be an overload of information. Gandy reminds us that stereotypes are very sticky. Overturning them "involves a substantial commitment and resolve on the part of the individual, and it may require the rebuilding of a large part of the individual's cognitive structure because of the multiple links that a particular racial stereotype may have within that structure."[42] Most Whites may have little motivation to make such a commitment. Even if they wanted to rid themselves of the habits of using racial stereotypes, Whites would get little help from television news.

6 Benign Neglect in the Poverty of the News

CRIME NEWS ON TELEVISION depicts African Americans in ways that make group members appear more threatening, less sympathetic than Whites. This pattern places Blacks closer to the dangerous / polluting pole of the ideal trait continuum (chapter 2). But even crime stories themselves do not speak in one voice, since they frequently include images of African American victims who at least potentially might evoke White compassion. Furthermore, crime reports arise within a larger stream of mediated material on Blacks. Thus it would be a mistake to assess the effects of crime reporting in isolation from the rest of the news (and entertainment and advertising). In this chapter we consider news coverage of poverty.

Fear of poverty rests at the very core of the American culture—the "American dream" is precisely the hope of rising from rags to riches. Poverty is also closely associated with African Americans. Media images of Black poverty are by no means wholly negative. Yet we will see in this chapter that on balance they record and reinforce the cultural liminality of Blacks. The media offer those who are not poor, especially Whites, little guidance in reconciling the conflicting emotions toward poverty embedded within American culture, with its simultaneously sympathetic and impatient assumption that America offers the promise of escape from poverty to all who work hard. In fact, the constant reminders of Black poverty, in the absence of equally frequent discussions of its causes, perpetuate the denial of structural barriers that is so central to racial animosity.

Although it is a truism that poverty breeds crime and violence, television news seldom addresses poverty and its causes or consequences explicitly. Rather, it makes an implicit "argument" about poverty, mostly by showing visual images of its symptoms and employing verbal shorthand. Between 1981 and 1986, the average network ran about eleven stories on poverty each year.[1] In 1997, a search for the word *poverty* in the transcripts of a full year of ABC's *World News* suggested a slight drop by the late 1990s. ABC's nightly news program ran eight stories that mentioned poverty explicitly and made its conditions, causes, or solutions a central topic. Others mentioned poverty purely in passing, as in coverage of Mother Teresa's funeral in India where stories noted she had worked with the poverty-stricken masses. Some stories made poverty the topic of light-hearted features, including a report on how the U.S. movie industry was claiming poverty and another on Japanese businessmen who took vows of poverty to become monks.

Yet despite the paucity of explicit stories, we found that television news conveys a lot about poverty. *Visual images of poverty's symptoms* do appear frequently, on the networks and on local television news. The finding suggests that the way television most frequently constructs the public's understanding of such social problems as poverty, and perhaps of race relations more generally, may largely be implicit and visual. By barraging White audiences with unexplained images of poverty among Blacks—a poverty that potentially imposes burdens on the prototypical American, a member of a White middle class family—television implicitly creates symbolic boundaries between people coded according to skin color. This chapter suggests that it is through *absences* of information, implicit comparisons, and visual images that television helps to frame not just poverty but much of America's racial reality and the politics that arise from it.

Based on three ten-day sample periods for the months of January, February, and March 1990, the chapter analyzes broadcasts of the late local news on the ABC, CBS, and NBC network affiliate stations in Chicago, on WGN (the leading independent station, now part of the WB network), and the network evening news programs of ABC, CBS, and NBC.[2] A total of 239 stories were selected for analysis because they mentioned at least one symptom of poverty and linked it explicitly or (most often) implicitly to poverty.[3] Additional data are cited from the 1993–94 sample of Chicago local news shows discussed in chapter 5 and from Chicago and national sample surveys. As suggested by the aforementioned paucity in appearances of the word *poverty* on ABC during 1997, there is little reason to believe explicit attention to poverty had increased by the late 1990s.[4]

The Implicit Discourse of Television News

Only a small minority of stories in the sample period used the words *poverty* or *poor*, or concerned themselves directly with poverty itself, defined here as *the lack of sufficient income and wealth to ensure against physical suffering or to provide clear paths to stable prosperity.*[5] The bulk of television stories cover poverty by mentioning symptoms that are widely associated with it. The stories connect the symptoms to poverty by employing visual images or verbal stereotypes. In most stories, the association of the symptom with poverty is connotative—the visual codes or verbal stereotypes merely suggest that poverty is involved. Thus, for example, in a story that portrayed the murder of a little girl, allegedly by her mother, viewers learned the crime was committed in an "abandoned building" in a "drug-infested neighborhood," by somebody with a history of mental illness. The report associated one poverty symptom, violent crime, with others (drug abuse, mental illness), and linked them to poverty connotatively by showing pictures of blighted buildings and identifying the neighborhood as Chicago's South Side. This is typical of the image clusters that repeatedly appear, signaling that the narratives involve poor people. The image clusters convey information by drawing on the audience's stored assumptions and prototypical categories, their information-processing schemas. Television communicates much of its information about poverty by its repetition of such image clusters.

Poverty as Threat or Suffering

The poverty symptoms shown on television news divide naturally into two broad categories: those that involve behavior threatening to the nonpoor community as well as the poor, and those that involve suffering of the poor. By far, the single manifestation of poverty mentioned most frequently was violent crime. About 40 percent (n = 147) of all the symptoms depicted poverty as a source of threats from the poor in the form of crime, drugs, and gangs, whereas 60 percent (n = 226) showed poverty in a variety of forms of suffering.[6]

Many of these stories depicted the poor as the victims of the threatening behavior, so that the crime / drugs / gangs stories may generate both fear *and* pity among audiences. Yet the stories of suffering, too, are dual-edged. The conditions that victimize the poor imply solutions that raise taxes, heighten guilt, or otherwise impose costs on the nonpoor, potentially stimulating animosity. The unresolved tension between the responses of fear or resentment on the one hand and compassion on the other is central to the linkage between media content and racial comity, and broader democratic theory concerns, which we discuss later.

The news in our sample period sparingly mentioned hunger, homelessness, low housing quality, unemployment, and welfare dependence. The most common specific symptoms in news of poverty as suffering were racial discrimination and problems of health and health care. Local and national news programs differed in the degree to which they concentrated on poverty as threat or as suffering. Each network news show focused substantially less on threat than its Chicago local affiliate.

Explicit Acknowledgment of Poverty

Poverty itself was not a frequent subject of television news, which rarely mentioned the simple lack of money as the core component of poverty. Those without a tacit understanding of U.S. culture who looked in on television news might think that the bad thing about poverty is not that the poor lack money, and thus mobility and choice. Rather, they might infer that, inexplicably, some people choose to live in deteriorated neighborhoods where they frequently either commit or become victims of crime, or have trouble receiving health care and finding adequate schools.

Just four stories in our sample directly documented the extent of poverty in terms of wealth and income distribution. Ironically, given the predominance of the visual on television, in those four instances of explicit attention to poverty as an experience of insufficient income and wealth, onscreen images were among the least stimulating—usually just the anchorperson reciting data. Perhaps journalists considered another report documenting poverty old and relatively dull news, meriting only perfunctory treatment. As noted below, before an issue becomes a prominent continuing story, elites must usually promote a name and frame for it. And in the early 1990s, elites had not been saying much about poverty directly for over twenty years.

Implicit Linkages to Poverty Symptoms

Most stories combined one or more of the poverty symptoms with visual images or verbal stereotypes. Image clusters constituted the most frequent "argument" that television news made about poverty. The dominant visual images appearing in stories that mentioned poverty conditions (appendix table A.6) were Black persons in organized activities like marches, meetings, or church worship; Black persons milling around on the street or in other unorganized activities, usually pictured along with police officers; urban blight—boarded up buildings, trash on the streets, and the like; or Black community leaders or politicians talking to a group. The other way of linking symptoms to poverty employed verbal signals: stereotypes of geographic locations, telling the audience that the story took place "on the [Chicago] South Side" or in a "tough neighborhood"; metaphors (as in "times are still tough" or "his life hit bottom"); and of course explicit assertions connecting low income or the lack of money with poverty symptoms.[7]

Different pictures accompanied different manifestations of poverty. Violent crime and drug abuse were the symptoms accompanied by the densest cluster of visual images, with stories including more than one type of visual—mostly of Blacks marching or milling, of neighborhood blight, or of Black leaders. If visual cues give television its particular power,[8] the most densely illustrated problems may make the deepest impression on audiences—the symptoms that audiences tend to think of when the idea of poverty comes up. If so, the image-laden coverage of violent crime and drug abuse could, by equating poverty most memorably with threat, reduce sympathy to the poor. This possibility may be heightened by the absence of blight images in stories on discrimination and economic suffering, which could evoke viewer sympathy. The only on-screen images for discrimination stories were marching, Black leaders, and milling. For economic suffering, only marching illustrated the stories. Ironically, then, television news failed to illustrate the dismal, decayed landscape of poverty in some of the stories with the greatest potential to evoke sympathy.

The rarity of overt linkages between poverty and the symptoms mentioned can be illustrated by showing how explicit verbal references are heavily outweighed by implicit visual references. Among the 373 symptom mentions, there were 54 explicit mentions of poverty or lacking money, but 491 implicit visual signals (such as blight or marching Blacks).[9] On average, then, each poverty symptom was accompanied by 0.15 explicit mentions of poverty (54/373) and 1.32 visual allusions (491/373), illustrating the dominance of implicit visual discourse.

Meanwhile, another content study, described in the previous chapter, illustrates the way images of poverty as *threat* especially dominate local news. The research conducted during late 1993 and early 1994, sampling 164 local news programs, found an average of about 60 percent of the news hole in Chicago devoted to violence, that is, threatened or actual physical harm to humans. The bulk of the violence reported was criminal violence and a quarter of all reported violence concerned murder; most of the rest involved fires in poor neighborhoods and accidents. Much of this coverage also contained such codes for poverty as Black persons milling at the scene and references to geographical stereotypes like the "South Side." This second, extensive sample again indicates the domination of implicit and visual discourse on poverty, especially in local television news.

Newspaper Coverage: Difference, Similarity, Deficiency

Television news was compared to coverage of the same stories in Chicago's two major daily newspapers for the same period.[10] In most cases, stories covered by at least one television station were also reported by at least one newspaper. Among the poverty-related stories appearing on television that one might reasonably expect Chicago papers to cover,[11] the *Tribune* ignored only seven, the *Sun-Times* ignored ten.[12]

In reporting many poverty symptoms, newspaper discourse appeared just as implicit as television news—and presumably equally difficult to interpret as involving poverty. In fact, for some of the stories, one might argue television news was superior at promoting awareness of poverty precisely because it provided visual cues that at least suggest a link to poverty. For example, television and newspapers closely covered a controversy over Chicago's then-Deputy Mayor for Education. One of her children attended a private school in posh suburban Winnetka even though her job was to improve Chicago's public schools and enhance confidence in them. Television news provided its typical visual cues suggesting a relationship between this controversy and the particular interest of poor people in a better school system. Newspaper coverage generally lacked such signals.

The dearth of visual linkages in newspapers[13] could have both positive and negative impacts on public awareness of poverty and sympathy toward the poor. On the one hand, crime is usually emphasized less in newspapers than on television, generally appearing in short stories well inside the paper. Too, the very visual deficits of newspaper coverage may reduce the potency of poverty-as-threat (crime, drug, and gang) stories. While television news footage usually shows the race of the accused, newspaper stories often lack pictures, and generally do not identify those accused of crimes by race in the text. The experience of reading about a crime in newspapers, rather than seeing it reported on television, might have less potential to stimulate Whites' racial fear—and antagonism or indifference toward the poor (equated with Blacks).

On the other hand, in poverty-as-suffering stories, the same absence of visual cues reduces the ability of the newspaper reader to recognize that the story may have something to do with the poor. In the type of story where the symptoms covered are inherently more likely to evoke sympathy, newspapers may be less likely to promote compassion for the poor than television.

In many cases, looking only at the verbal text, the amount and nature of the information in the two media are surprisingly similar. For example, most newspaper coverage of Martin Luther King Day did not deal any more directly than television with the policy agenda King espoused or with King's underlying goal of reducing poverty among Blacks. Only in one column on the editorial page did one newspaper offer information on the substance of King's program that transcended the hackneyed material television provided (snippets of the "I Have a Dream" speech, church choirs singing and swaying).

Although the information conveyed on television and in newspapers is often quite similar (and similarly limited), in one respect television conformed to the conventional wisdom that sees it as less informative than print. Television was usually sketchier than newspapers on stories directly involving a proposal to deal with the symptoms of poverty. Commercial television news is not generally a medium for policy analysis. Thus, for example, each of the network news programs covered a federal commission's recommendation to provide virtually all Americans with medical insurance. While ABC and NBC explicitly mentioned the impact on the poor, CBS only implied it; and each program only devoted about two minutes to the story— hardly enough for detail. The newspaper coverage provided many more words and much more thorough information, including positive and negative evaluations of its specific provisions.

Implications

This chapter emphasizes media content data. We shall offer some small empirical evidence for their effects, but mainly we rely upon logical extrapolation and push the data vigorously in order to delineate the kinds of effects that media *may* have on public policy and politics in the area of poverty. This section deliberately raises questions it cannot answer, possibilities it cannot confirm. The paucity of research in this area warrants, even mandates, such an approach.

There is a difference between being aware of poverty's symptoms and judging poverty a problem that merits pressing attention from government and society. Television's reliance upon visual symbols and geographic stereotypes to suggest the involvement of the poor focuses attention more on the symptoms of poverty than on poverty—the lack of money—itself. Consider reporting on the closing of the Michael Reese Hospital's trauma center on Chicago's South Side. If the news had explicitly asserted that the poor were somewhat more likely to die from traumatic injuries than the middle class because of the hospital's closing (and the underlying problem of insufficient government funding), it might have heightened awareness of a poverty-linked policy problem. But most stories tended only to imply a connection to poverty via geographic and visual cues. Thus while the story clearly sympathized with those deprived of timely trauma care, given the implicit nature of the discourse, it did not make clear that the deprivation fell most heavily upon the poor.[14]

Stories with visuals transfer little new information by themselves.[15] Coherent verbal narrative must combine with visuals that help explain the text for effective learning of new material to occur. The scarcity of verbal discussion reflects and may reinforce the low priority of poverty on the public agenda. In contrast, by using vivid visual illustration and compelling language, television news has been able to promote urgent government concern for such dilemmas as the drug problem. The very fact that stories about specific conditions arising from drug abuse appear repeatedly packaged with a familiar label like "the drug problem" enhances the likelihood of serious notice in the policy process. (Many drug stories themselves show poverty symptoms, but as we have seen, without explicitly mentioning poverty.)

Only indirectly does television news suggest, for example, that racial discrimination might have something to do with poverty, which in turn might help explain all the crime reported on the same shows. The connections are suggested mainly by the way stories on prejudice often include the same kind of visual images as stories on crime (and on failed health care, inadequate housing, and the rest). Beyond the common visual links, there is little in the news to draw poverty symptoms together as interrelated causes and consequences. Lacking much exposure to poverty as a continuing, multifaceted *social* problem, audience members may find it easier to see poverty as an essentially personal condition susceptible of wholly *individual* cures. Research has revealed that when television stories frame poverty as a "general outcome, responsibility for poverty is assigned to society-at-large; when news presentations frame poverty as a particular instance of a poor person, responsibility is assigned to the individual."[16] The latter type of story, which predominates in network news, generated less sympathetic responses in experimental subjects.

More generally, television's visuals construct "poverty" as nearly synonymous with "Black," and surveys show Whites typically accept this picture,[17] even though poverty is not the lot of most Black persons and more Whites are poor than Black.[18] Visual and geographic cues suggest poverty is overwhelmingly concentrated among Blacks, so much so that merely showing Black persons on the screen may connote the involvement of poor people to many audience members. In this sense news images encourage the sense of the prototypical Black as poor and the prototypical poor person as Black. As we saw in chapter 2 in our review of the Indianapolis data, even people who know the statistics on race and poverty can nonetheless find themselves thinking of the two concepts almost interchangeably.[19]

Further bolstering the equation of Blacks and poverty, racial discrimination was the most frequently mentioned symptom of poverty in the suffering category. Yet reports rarely explained how racism might cause poverty. For example, the ten television stories on Martin Luther King Day all lionized the "slain civil rights leader," but in the vaguest terms. Not one story, for example, assessed current government policy as it might relate to King's goals. The coverage usually depicted these as fuzzy objectives like "brotherhood" or making people "free at last." The King stories denounced racism without explaining exactly why it is bad. They even implied that racism is a thing of the past. The stories tell us we celebrate King because he inspired passage of the civil rights laws that put an end to government-sanctioned racism. Use of grainy black and white film of 1960s civil rights protests compounds the impression that all this discrimination was over and done with long ago.

Research by Iyengar and by Gilens suggests both that perceptions of race and poverty are intertwined for White respondents, and that this is encouraged by television. They also find Whites more likely to hold Blacks than Whites who are poor responsible for their own poverty, revealing strong *denial*.[20] Beyond these studies we have little evidence about the impacts of televisual discourse on poverty beliefs. In an effort to begin filling the gap, we analyzed data from a representative sample survey of Chicago area Whites. It shows significant associations between their poverty and racial attitudes and their media habits. A scale was formed on the basis of respondents' answers to three questions tapping sympathy for the Black poor:

1. Most Blacks who receive money from welfare programs could get along without it if they tried. (52.5 percent agree strongly or agree)
2. On the average, Blacks have worse jobs, income, and housing than Whites. Do you think these differences are because most Blacks have less in-born ability to learn? (10.9 percent responded "Yes")
3. On the average, Blacks have worse jobs, income, and housing than Whites. Do you think these differences are because most Blacks just don't have the motivation or will power to pull themselves up out of poverty? (45.3 percent said "Yes")

These are close relatives to the denial scale analyzed for Indianapolis residents (chapter 2), but they focus more particularly on poverty.

Our suspicion is that qualities of television news documented here, by abetting denial, reduce the understanding needed for enhanced racial comity. Statistical analysis, shown in appendix table A.7, reveals that reliance on television news over radio or print is in fact independently associated with lower sympathy among White Chicagoans toward poor Blacks. The statistical impact of television reliance is about as strong as that of religion and ideology; only education has a noticeably stronger relationship. It is possible that television viewers are predisposed toward less commiseration with the poor, rather than that relying on television suppresses such feelings. But the effect does hold up even with ideological and party identification held constant, strengthening the indication that television watching has an independent influence. The findings are far from definitive, but they do mesh with television's poverty coverage and with associations between racial attitudes and television news exposure reported by others.[21]

Television and the Democratic Politics of Poverty

Television, with all its visual power, cannot set or alter the policy agenda on its own. Elites create an explicit verbal agenda, via their actions and words, that allows a news item or issue to develop into a continuing story penetrating public consciousness (like the drug problem).[22] Only if government elites begin talking once again about the symptoms of poverty in explicit, detailed, and repeated terms as a "poverty problem," leading to proposals for new policy initiatives, will television news feature many explicit stories about poverty. Without elites' guidance and production of newsworthy events that focus attention on poverty, neither television nor print news has much ability to redirect public discourse. Thus in one sense the dominance of the "televisual" seems to have had little impact on the distribution of power in the political process.

But in another sense, the properties of television news may alter the nature and degree of public participation in racial politics, and even affect elites' rhetorical and behavioral options. The implicit and inadvertent "argument" that daily television news constructs about poverty as a social and policy problem closely matches the public's cognitive confusion and emotional ambivalence about poverty. Lacking a consistent thread explaining how threat and suffering are connected to each other, and to a set of causes and potential solutions, the audience is left with no way of resolving any contradictory tugs between fear and sympathy. We saw this kind of ambivalence graphically illustrated by the conflicted musings in our interviews in Indianapolis.

Television offers little insight to those many nonpoor citizens who, like our ambivalent Indianapolis informants, might want to understand how to protect their own legitimate, material self-interest in a safe community, lower taxes, and the like yet still advance what we might call their "moral self-interest" in helping the poor. This is not television's fault, at least as long as it operates within the constraints of conventional practice, elite pressure, market incentives, and the rest. Failing a wholesale reorientation of the profession and of news organizations, it will remain the responsibility of political elites to educate. But few politicians in recent times have seen political advantage in speaking sympathetically about the poor—they have judged that votes reside in speaking about short-run material self interest of the (White) middle class.

One cannot blame politicians for seeking votes where they exist. Yet by doing so, politicians inadvertently bolster television news's consigning of the poverty problem to the realm of the vague and the implicit. The political climate is self-reinforcing: political leaders fail to talk about poverty, a dearth in television coverage results, so the public fails to see poverty as a pressing issue. And that discourages politicians still more from speaking explicitly about it. The word *poverty* itself seems to us to encode a somewhat sympathetic reading of its symptoms. It implies the perspective of the poor themselves. Instead of using this word much, elites invoke oblique references like "welfare," "crime," and "underclass."[23] These words point to the poor from the perspective of the powerful and bring to mind the burden and threat they may pose rather than the suffering they may endure. So the near banishment of the word *poverty* from public discourse may not only reflect but help to shape the political force field that surrounds government decisionmakers.

If television's image-dominated and implicit discourse is self-reinforcing, it becomes difficult for elites to promote issues and solutions that do not fit television's production needs and limitations; and it becomes easy and rational for elites to champion what does fit. Thus is the substance of the nation's policy discourse affected by the economic and technological requirements of a specific industry, commercial television,[24] in ways difficult to reconcile with traditional theories of democratic representation.

Conclusion

The manner in which poverty is covered by mainstream news media may unintentionally affect racial animosity. By neglecting to explain racial discrimination and other structural sources of Black poverty, the news not only abets tendencies to engage in *denial*. The imagery of television news also suggests poverty is concentrated among Blacks, so much so that merely showing a Black person on the screen appears to be a code for the involvement of poor people. The concepts of "Black person" and "poverty" are so thoroughly intertwined in television news that many Whites' perceptions of poverty are difficult to disentangle from their thinking about African Americans. Television helps to construct a widespread sense of the prototypical Black as a poor person (and quite likely, a criminal one). This symbolic rendering distorts the economic and social diversity among African Americans, signaling the homogeneity of the out-group while underlining the salience of Black–White group differences (since we all know the prototypical White American is not poor). More generally the kind of policy reporting highlighted in this case, which is perhaps characteristic of other areas, provides the nonpoor with little basis for contextual reasoning or for elevating poverty or other issues disproportionately affecting African Americans to the agenda for systematic, open-minded government attention. And as already suggested, the news provides White viewers scant foundation for reconciling the conflicting sentiments about poverty in American culture that— through the equation of Blacks and poverty—spill over onto African Americans and help lock them into liminality.

Television certainly possesses considerable positive potential as a force for racial reconciliation, especially if its ability to combine compelling visuals and narratives could be coupled with revitalized elite discourse on poverty and other policy issues. But in actual operation, television seems mainly to reduce the ability of political leaders to address such costly and complex issues as poverty insofar as it heightens the White public's anxiety, impatience, and cynicism. Nor is it easy for middle class Whites to discover from the media their long-term economic interests in reducing the many costs of poverty. Instead, poverty seems a complex of fearsome symptoms having little or no solution, posing no direct relationship to the lives and interests of middle-class viewers beyond the potential of physical threat and fiscal burden that seems to wear a largely Black face.

And it is a great irony that many of the stories that contribute to the on-going racialized narrative of poverty are themselves reported by persons of color and especially Blacks. Our interest is not merely in the irony but in the political meaning it may have for some. The presence of Blacks exerting power in the media provides one of the more potent indicators that Whites can find to bolster their denial that racism still impedes the lives of African Americans. The puzzle of poverty that television news implicitly narrates just about every day is this: how can so many African Americans remain poor (and turn to crime) if the American dream is now as open to them as to everyone else? The lurking answer is the suspicion of Blacks' moral or intellectual inferiority.

7 Affirming Discord

NLIKE POVERTY, the subject of little explicit discourse in the media during the 1990s, affirmative action received heavy print and broadcast coverage. Arguably, affirmative action was *the* site of ideological battle over race in America for the last quarter of the twentieth century. It is largely through debates on affirmative action that contenders have struggled to frame the condition of African Americans and ways of enhancing it. Of course other battlegrounds—including taxation, school vouchers, and capital punishment—implicated Black–White relations. But, as important as these have been, we submit that affirmative action is the one in which the causes, moral status, and remedies (i.e., the frames) for the status of African Americans in the United States were most directly engaged. The touchstone status of affirmative action was reflected in our Indianapolis interviews (chapter 2). In this chapter, using affirmative action as a case study, we ask whether reporting of policy issues involving problems experienced disproportionately by African Americans encourages Whites to see themselves as *sharing group interests with each other in opposition to the interests of Blacks.* Or does coverage intimate that those problems might well belong to the society as a whole?

Roughly speaking, on the one side of the issue are those adhering to what we might call the "individual responsibility" frame, on the other are supporters of the "collective responsibility" frame. In the middle are the majority torn between the two positions. The individual responsibility frame asserts that since discrimination is at most a sporadic, minor impediment that is readily controlled, the main activity of government should be to ensure economic growth. Interventions that undermine efficient resource allocation and investment can only harm prospects for minority progress, while heightening racial antagonism.[1] The collective responsibility frame assumes that individual Blacks (and perhaps other group members, including women) encounter pervasive discrimination that is not easily detected or controlled. Affirmative action is necessary to counter current discrimination and the structural legacies of past mistreatment. This frame sees affirmative action as having achieved notable successes at minimal cost.[2]

According to much of the media coverage, affirmative action sparked a popular uprising[3] during the mid-1990s, an intense outcry of opposition from White Americans based on their perceptions of the policy's injustices and failures—a vigorous affirmation of the individual responsibility frame. *Newsweek* (3 April 1995) ran a cover showing a Black fist and White fist pushing against each other under the headline "Race and Rage," and in another issue (13 February 1995) proclaimed that affirmative action "could dominate the 1996 election year." On the *NBC Nightly News* (19 July 1995), Tom Brokaw said, "Affirmative action: two words that can start an argument just about anywhere in America. . . . We'll be hearing a lot more about this in the months leading to the 1996 election." Such depictions of intense racial conflict suffused the media's constructions of the politics surrounding affirmative action, and doubly misled. First, they did not describe the actual, more complicated state of public opinion, insofar as journalists, politicians, and the rest of us can know it through the imperfect mechanism of sample surveys. Second, they misrepresented the conflict of interest created by affirmative action policies, which does not arise exclusively or even mainly between Whites and African Americans, and which may not exist at all in the long term.

The media depictions had significant political implications; survey data suggest that the media constitute the most important single source of information about affirmative action for Whites.[4] But the impacts, if any, upon politics were likely far more circuitous than we might normally expect. Beneath the information overtly depicting the policy's merits and drawbacks, the sort that can be gauged by conventional content analysis (and journalists' own professional self-critiques), was another and more important layer of meaning, the frame beneath the frame. This one suggested that a fundamental conflict of interest separates racially grouped Whites and Blacks. It is the perception of just such clashing group interests that figure prominently in our model of racial animosity (table 2.1) and have been identified as a key source of Whites' resentment.[5]

White Americans have a range of beliefs and feelings potentially relevant to affirmative action—an ambivalence and complexity generally missing from media coverage.[6] To take just one example of a positive marker, White Americans expressed substantial support for Retired General Colin Powell, an

African American, to become president. A *Time*/CNN poll in June 1995 asked respondents: "Do you have a favorable or unfavorable impression of the following people?" Colin Powell received the highest favorable rating (56 percent) and lowest unfavorable (10 percent) of any political figure (*Time*, 10 July 1995, p. 24). Another CNN poll asked how Powell's position on affirmative action ("he says he does not believe in quotas but supports continuing many affirmative action programs") would affect people's support for him; 37 percent said it would make them more likely to vote for him and 32 percent said it would make no difference; just 27 percent said less likely. It is difficult to square these sentiments with an insistence that Whites are primarily anti-affirmative action bigots. Rather, many are of two minds, or hold opinions too complicated to be summarized by conventional surveys—or headline writers.

One more word: Making our case here does not imply an unqualified endorsement of affirmative action. Specific implementations of the policy have exhibited serious shortcomings, and some have imposed unfair losses on individual Whites. This chapter provides an analysis of the media's version of affirmative action, not an *apologia* for all programs categorized under that rubric.

Overall Slant and Theme of Affirmative Action News

The news media were sampled by selecting via computer search all items that mentioned "affirmative action." These were then filtered to exclude items that offered only passing reference to the policy. Inclusion required that a majority of paragraphs discuss affirmative action. Quantitative content analytical data were generated, but qualitative analysis of the text and visual images proved more important for getting at the framing of news about affirmative action. The sampling covered all items in *Newsweek* and *Time* on news events between 1 January 1995 and 21 July 1995; transcripts of all stories shown on ABC's *World News* during the same period; and, also during that period, a random sample of half the stories about affirmative action on the CBS and NBC evening news programs.[7] The ending date of 21 July was selected because of two climactic events in the debate: a highly anticipated and highly publicized speech by President Clinton (19 July) announcing his new affirmative action policy, and the meetings of the University of California regents (20–21 July) where the body abolished affirmative action in admissions and hiring. A less detailed exploration of coverage in the late 1990s is also discussed.

Chapter Seven

The quantitative analysis coded every assertion in the newsmagazines and the network coverage that expressed an evaluation of affirmative action, a total of 278. (Details on the content analysis can be found on the book's website. Coding was performed by an author and a trained student, with average intercoder reliability at 0.89.) The slant of the different media diverged substantially. Newsmagazines tilted against affirmative action by a ratio of about 3:1, with *Time* slightly less negative than *Newsweek*. All three network news programs, on the other hand, came out at almost exactly a 1:1 ratio. (Content data are available in previous publications[8] or on the book's website.)

The analysis also recorded 217 expressions in the magazines and network coverage of *reasons* for opposing or endorsing affirmative action. Taking the newsmagazines and television coverage together, these balanced quite evenly between supportive and oppositional reasons, dividing into eight categories. The most common oppositional considerations were that affirmative action constitutes *reverse discrimination* (25 percent of all reasons) and that it violates *meritocratic values* (11.5 percent). Prominent on the supportive front were claims that *discrimination remains a problem* (21 percent) and that affirmative action *achieves its important objectives* (19 percent). At this level, the media seemed to do a reasonably good job on the issue. While the newsmagazines energetically attacked affirmative action, the networks offered a balanced depiction of the policy, with favorable and opposing reasons about equally distributed. The quantitative content analysis thus suggests that the information environment was rich enough to enable elites and the mass public to reason through the issue.

However, the quantitative counts do not clarify the deeper signals embedded in the texts. Research suggests that merely counting the number of times the media air a claim can distort an understanding of its likely reception.[9] Not only frequency of repetition, but the vividness, freshness, and distinctiveness of images all affect their impact,[10] as do context and the material that does *not* appear. In ways both subtle and obvious, the media highlighted material propounding the theme of high-intensity emotional conflict of interest between mutually antagonistic Whites and African Americans.

Framing Opinion on Affirmative Action

Public opinion toward something as vague and protean as affirmative action cannot easily be gauged. News texts, survey questions, and public discourse alike suffer from severe terminological imprecision. Discussion of affirmative action tended randomly to select, omit, and combine busing, racially motivated electoral districts, contract set asides, college recruiting, college admissions, government employment regulations, and private hiring and promotion programs. Given the uncertainty about what exactly is meant by "affirmative action," poll questions can yield deceptive results. Still, sample surveys offer mountains of evidence contradicting the media frame.

Journalists, it seems, built their frame on claims by elite sources with an interest in promoting the impression of White arousal, a goal that meshed nicely with reporters' constant search for conflict and drama. In fact, journalists appeared to confuse *elite rhetoric* with the *average citizen's preferences and priorities*. It is clear that some of the most important political leaders who set the media agenda—especially presidential hopefuls—turned more actively hostile to affirmative action in 1995. It is far from clear that their views reflected the sentiments of ordinary White Americans.

A *Newsweek* column by Joe Klein (13 February 1995) contained two of many media assertions that affirmative action had become an enormous political issue, a source of intense White emotion and opposition. *Newsweek* highlighted this view in large print: "A NEWSWEEK columnist says we may be hurtling toward the most sensitive point in race relations since the 1960s" is the article's subhead. "California's effort to end racial preference is just the first step—the issue could dominate the 1996 election year" was the large-print caption on the picture of University of California Regent Ward Connerly and his wife. Connerly, an African American, led the effort to rescind affirmative action at the university. Underneath the picture were the words, "I want to be judged by the quality of my work," implying that those covered by affirmative action programs are not. At the same time, Klein asserted (without evidence) that emotions ran high among Blacks: "The reaction of the Black community [to abolition of affirmative action] is likely to be cold fury, incendiary rhetoric—and a deep sense of despair." An equal opportunity pessimist, he then wrote that "[t]he response from White America is likely to be a disingenuous and slightly smarmy call for a 'colorblind society.' "

Supporting the interpretation that Klein confused the opinions of ordinary citizens with those of elites, in the two sentences about "reaction of the Black community" and "response from White America" he actually referred to leadership elements, not the average individual (who does not speak in "rhetoric" or engage in "smarmy calls"). Equating elites' strategically chosen rhetorical positions with the general public's opinions can lead journalists and their audiences, both mass and elite, to underestimate the zone of potential compromise.[11]

Even if they are deeply flawed, sample surveys offer the only reliable data journalists or scholars have about aggregate public sentiments toward policy issues. The sentiments of Whites as recorded in the surveys are both more complex and more favorably inclined toward affirmative action than the public positions staked out by most political leaders. Four separate surveys in mid-1995, around the time coverage peaked, revealed evidence of widespread support for the principle of affirmative action. In a *Los Angeles Times* poll (1995), 21 percent favored affirmative action that "uses quotas," 50 percent favored affirmative action "without quotas" and 20 percent "oppose[d] affirmative action altogether." This result implies that affirmative action with or without quotas was favored by 71 percent. On this question, even White men were 61 percent in favor of affirmative action (White women, 76 percent) when we combine the "without" and "with" quota categories. Surveys by ABC/ *Washington Post* (March), NBC/ *Wall Street Journal* (July–August), and CNN/ *USA Today* (July, right after President Clinton's speech) all found 70 percent of respondents favoring either affirmative action as then practiced or with reforms. These three, and the rest of the surveys discussed in this section come from archives of the Roper Center P.O.L.L. database at the University of Connecticut.

Every poll taken in 1995 and stored in the P.O.L.L. archive that offers a reform alternative revealed about two-thirds of respondents favoring continuation of affirmative action as is or with reforms. Further, similar questions asked about affirmative action without quotas (in "business," "employment," or "industry") in 1982, 1988, and 1990 found virtually identical percentages. The most comprehensive review of survey data concludes that *Whites' attitudes on affirmative action remained virtually unchanged between 1965 and 1995,* despite journalists' and politicians' frequent claims of a massive shift in the mid-1990s.[12]

The polls did show that a majority opposed "quotas" or "preferences." Thus the *Los Angeles Times* poll of March 1995 that found 71 percent support for the principle of affirmative action also asked if "qualified minorities should receive *preference* over equally qualified Whites" (emphasis added). On this question it found 72 percent of all respondents opposed, 78 percent of Whites—and also 50 percent of Blacks. These results and others[13] suggest not only widespread antagonism toward "preference" programs, but also that many African Americans share the antipathy. Blacks and Whites seem to occupy more similar moral worlds than the news media implied. We should not leap from polling data showing support of affirmative action programs without quotas or preferences to a presumption that every member of the majority would approve any one reformed affirmative action policy. We do not have a definitive sense of the public's opinions on what is actually a diverse range of policy solutions. In addition, Whites may mask their true sentiments when responding to interviewers' probes on affirmative action. In their review of poll data, Steeh and Krysan found, as suggested here, that the average public stance fell "somewhere between color blindness on the one hand and preferences on the other."[14] This book's website displays additional data that support this reading.

At the same time, polling evidence reveals considerable contradiction, uncertainty, or ambivalence. For example, the respondents to one survey both endorsed a referendum *repealing* affirmative action (by a slim margin) and favored another referendum *maintaining* affirmative action (by a larger margin). Whites consider anti-White discrimination a bigger problem than anti-Black, but also seem to accept affirmative action as a remedy for the latter. The instabilities within and across representative samples suggest we cannot infer much about the details of public thinking from conventional surveys, a point bolstered by the Indianapolis interviews reported in chapter 2 that revealed something of Whites' internal conflicts.

We can, however, combine the poll data to reach a reasonable synthesis: A variety of surveys variously worded revealed general support for the principle. They also showed a widespread perception that current applications entail some undesirable costs or practices. Distinguishing among affirmative action programs, Bobo and Kluegel argue specifically that Whites tend to support "opportunity-enhancing" affirmative action policies while opposing "preferential" ones.[15] These strands are congruent with a majority of White Americans wanting to "mend" but not "end" affirmative action, to use the phrase President Clinton invoked in his 1995 speech.

The favorable majority might not have been as robust as the polling data suggest, but at the minimum, the best available empirical evidence lends little support to the pessimistic image painted in the news. Rather, polls consistently suggested a significant reservoir of sympathy and support among Whites for redressive public policies, even if other, less friendly sentiments coexisted. We cannot determine which has been *the* true reading of the

White public's opinion toward affirmative action. In all likelihood, depending on circumstances and stimuli,[16] Whites can genuinely feel both sympathy and antipathy.

In any case, the failure of the issue to catch on in the 1996 election campaign despite the expectations of many pundits and politicians suggests White Americans were much less exercised over the issue than the news media depicted. That leads to another misleading element in media framing of public opinion—the portrayal of intense White arousal over this issue. Beyond the fizzling of the issue in 1996, survey data suggest that Whites and Blacks have long considered it a low priority issue. The best evidence suggests it was not bubbling at the surface of a seething White America's political consciousness in the 1990s. Nor were African Americans obsessing about affirmative action. Although it may have been the most vexing specific issue when interviewers raised the matter of race relations (as we did in Indianapolis), it apparently did not rise to the surface spontaneously as a major problem facing the country among either group.

Thus an NBC/ *Wall Street Journal* poll (March 1995) asked about legislative priorities; affirmative action came in last, far behind the other six issues on which respondents were queried. Another asked an open-ended question: "Is there any one issue that you care about that would make you vote against a candidate for president?" Affirmative action ranked near the bottom, named by just 1 percent. An April 1996 poll asking about issues people would "like to hear discussed by the candidates running for president" had a similar outcome. And none of the frequent polls that ask about the "most important problem facing the country" and recorded in the comprehensive Roper Center database from 1985 through 1996 showed "affirmative action" named as a top priority by more than 1 percent. (One poll in 1987 found 2 percent mentioning "affirmative action/civil rights.") Since about 12 percent of a representative national survey should be made up of African Americans, this figure reveals that hardly any Whites *or* Blacks during these years considered affirmative action a top-priority issue. (If, say, just one-fourth of Blacks named affirmative action as their top issue, that alone would be enough to push the total national figure to about 3 percent.)

Bolstering the misleading depictions of public opinion were the mirror images in sentiments expressed by identifiably Black and White sources in news reports. Seventy-two percent of affirmative action evaluations voiced by Blacks in our sample of news coverage were positive, whereas 71 percent of those uttered by Whites were negative. Separating out ordinary citizens from elite sources (experts or political leaders) makes the division starker. Ordinary "persons in the street" who were Black endorsed affirmative action by a margin of fourteen to two; ordinary Whites opposed it by twenty-eight to four. The coverage also cited general "public opinion" sixteen times—every single instance in opposition to affirmative action, despite all the surveys revealing substantial support.

By creating the notion that an angry White majority was fed up with affirmative action, the media might well have discouraged White politicians from publicly defending the policy.[17] To justify it in this media-constructed environment could have made a politician seem unresponsive, even arrogant. Perhaps this is one reason that none of the twelve network stories on Clinton's affirmative action speech or the California regents' decision showed a White political leader other than the president endorsing affirmative action. That absence, along with the presence of so many White opponents, portrayed a deepening racial polarization, again despite surveys revealing considerable common ground.

Framing Conflict

Beyond characterizations of public opinion, the media had much to say on the policy of affirmative action itself. Here too the coverage misled. The most prominent elements of the text—the headlines, the visuals, the highlighted quotes, and the journalists' narrative emphases—framed the policy dispute as a zero-sum conflict of interest between Whites and Blacks, in which only one group could win and one must lose. Although the spotlight occasionally fell on others, the emphasis, especially in visuals and in quoting of sources, was on Blacks as beneficiaries, who purportedly gain at the direct expense of Whites. Since the majority of immediate beneficiaries of affirmative action have apparently been White women,[18] the central clash might have been drawn along the gender rather than racial divide. Furthermore, the policy does not necessarily create zero-sum conflict of interest.

Television networks and newsmagazines framed affirmative action not merely as a site of clashing interests but as specifically a Black–White fissure. Thus a *CBS Evening News* story of 12 June 1995 that called affirmative action "deeply divisive" also distinguished (in a quote from *Newsweek*'s Joe Klein) two camps on the issue: "Jesse Jackson and African Americans" on the one hand, and "the rest of the country" on the other. The *Newsweek* cover story (3 April 1995) carrying the headline "RACE AND RAGE" and the image of Black and White fists colliding offered two subheads: "AFFIRMATIVE ACTION" and "When Preferences Work—And Don't." Inside the magazine the headline "Race and Rage" appeared again to introduce the lead story, alongside a large picture of a demonstration that emphasized a Black woman yelling.

The text was by no means wholly misleading nor completely hostile to affirmative action. In some ways, this *Newsweek* issue mirrored the ambivalence of public sentiment even as it reinforced the impression of negative emotion coursing through the body politic. The lead story clarified important distinctions among different types of affirmative action programs (recruiting, goals and timetables, quotas). The coverage offered some useful case studies of affirmative action programs, and provided space to the Black sociologist William Julius Wilson and to a Black *Newsweek* editor, Ellis Cose, supporting affirmative action. But this came in a section headed "Battleground Chicago/Report from the Front: How racial preferences really work—or don't." The headline (like the cover) ignored the very distinctions just mentioned, by categorizing all policies as "preferences." By focusing only on *racial* (and particularly *Black*) affirmative action, and employing the war metaphor, using some of the most vivid message components it can deploy, *Newsweek* imposed a core theme of racial conflict. Sniderman and colleagues find through surveys and experiments that the way affirmative action is framed heavily shapes Whites' reactions to it, and framing the policy as "preferences" for Blacks and against Whites evokes (quite unsurprisingly) many Whites' hostility.[19]

Newsweek's lead piece said:

> Never far from the surface of politics, race is rising with raging force in the presidential campaign now beginning. A quarter century ago the issue was busing. In 1988 it was crime. . . . But the most profound fight—the one tapping deepest into the emotions of everyday American life—is over affirmative action. . . .When is it fair to discriminate on the basis of race or gender? Louder than before, Americans seem to be saying, "Never."

Although the paragraph mentioned gender, it identified the issue "rising with raging force" as one of "race." Tellingly and unthinkingly, it equated "Americans" with Whites. It misstated the unanimity and intensity with which Whites allegedly rejected affirmative action. And it implied that affirmative action inherently discriminates, that Whites lose when Blacks win. All in all, the American community as imagined at the heart of this coverage is one of Whites standing at the barricades against Black interlopers.

The coverage also conveyed impressions of Black–White confrontation through its choice of sources. Fully 74 percent of sources (188 of 253) for evaluative statements in our larger sample of news were African American or White, only 5 percent (13) were Asian or Hispanic-Americans. (The rest of the evaluations cited general public opinion sources or were unattributed.) Although women are perhaps the major beneficiaries of affirmative action, opinions of women as a group were never cited, another telling indicator of the Black–White framing.

The visual dimension of coverage also depicted a largely Black–White confrontation. Of the twenty-six stories in the NBC/CBS sample, twenty-three illustrated the debate by showing predominantly or exclusively Black persons as beneficiaries or defenders of the programs; only three stories prominently featured non-Black beneficiaries. Eight stories showed pro-affirmative action demonstrations, all but one predominantly Black,[20] and three stories showed Black persons shouting at a White person.

One story presented a seemingly supportive view of affirmative action that arguably subverted it. This story contributed to the positive side of the ledger in the conventional quantitative content analysis reported earlier, and thus provides a good example of how such analysis can mask subtleties. This CBS report (31 May 1995) quoted the (Black) secretary of the army saying the army "refuses to simply order promotion boards to select a higher percentage of Blacks." Rather, he said, "We will not force it artificially. When it happens, every soldier, every officer who views those promotions will say 'Yes, that was a fair thing.' " Thus he implied that other affirmative action programs are artificial and unfair, because they "simply order" more Blacks to be promoted. The story defended this particular affirmative action program and thus suggests that not all affirmative action is bad. But even as it supported this one policy, the story implied that most other versions of affirmative action do "prefer" Blacks (and only Blacks), discriminate against Whites, and violate what is otherwise an inviolate principle of meritocracy.

By way of lauding the program, the story included a White soldier saying, "It doesn't matter what color you are," or, as the correspondent reported, "race is irrelevant." Yet the central purpose of the army's program is to detect and encourage Blacks and members of other underrepresented groups. Race is not irrelevant. More sophisticated journalism might have room to admit the paradoxes of affirmative action policy—such as its need to practice race, ethnic, or gender consciousness in order ultimately to minimize it—rather than simplifying in ways that may undermine Whites' understanding of the intellectual and moral case for the programs. Given this kind of putatively sympathetic coverage of an affirmative action program, and the framing of the issue in mostly Black–White terms, perhaps it is not surprising that Steeh and Krysan find White public opinion "most negative when [survey] questions about the policy mention Blacks as the only beneficiaries."[21]

Well beyond the 1995 sample period, media coverage continued in a similar vein. Predictions that affirmative action would dominate politics based on overheated portrayals of White outrage did fade by the late 1990s, as nothing of the sort happened. What remained in the media, though, was the presumption that Whites, in irreconcilable conflict with Blacks, opposed the policies. As an example of the Black–White framing, consider the eleven substantive stories about affirmative action that appeared on *CBS Evening News* during 1997 and 1998.[22] Of these reports, six framed the story heavily or exclusively in Black–White terms. Three stories pitted Black interests arrayed along with Latinos against Whites, though Black examples and sources predominated. Just one story emphasized Latinos versus Whites (and in one the frame was ambiguous).

Beyond the Black–White frame, another continuing theme was the zero-sum racial game. When two White students filed a lawsuit charging they failed to gain admission to the University of Michigan because they were "racially discriminated against," NBC's story (3 December 1997) detailed the students' impressive academic and extracurricular achievements. It offered no hint that nonracial forces might have been at play, overlooking how alumni relationships, parental wealth, connections and donations, geographic diversity, and athletic skill have long helped some Whites to gain admission over other Whites (and Blacks) with stronger test scores, grades, and extracurriculars.

Reporters know this. Almost all went to college themselves. But somehow this doesn't inform much of their coverage. Consider *Newsweek*'s (5 April 1999) cover story on the "college admissions game." It includes a profile of a guidance counselor at Maret, a "prestigious private school," who lobbies "admissions officers from Amherst to Yale." He works from April into the summer to "nudge" his students off the waiting list onto the acceptance roster. The writer does not frame this as a story on affirmative action. Yet since this counselor is one of many at prep schools across the country who work similarly with the best colleges, this is a large-scale preference program for upper-middle-class and upper-class Whites. Its size may even dwarf whatever "preferential" pro-Black admissions preference programs still exist. This failure to frame White preferences as such suggests that affirmative action coverage, despite adhering to journalistic norms, has consistently misled Americans.

The effect of the emphasis on alleged "reverse" discrimination (and neglect of pro-White discrimination) is suggested by surveys finding a two-thirds majority of Whites appear to believe that discrimination against them and in favor of Blacks is a problem.[23] Empirical studies suggest otherwise.[24] Steeh and Krysan attribute the perception that Blacks frequently take jobs from Whites to "the negative character of our current public discourse. . . ."[25] Presumably they mean to indict the media, but they might also point to the defects of survey research. Because of selective wording of questions and a narrow range of specific opinions measured, Whites cannot express their ambivalence directly through most poll results. Instead scholarly observers must tease apart seemingly incongruous responses to reveal the genuinely mixed feelings, as we did in our interviews. The sentiments revealed should not be entirely unexpected, given that American political culture itself has never reconciled its simultaneous commitments to both egalitarianism and individual freedom. But this kind of complexity in public sentiment rarely fits conventional news formats and reports.

The deeper inaccuracy of such reporting is that the costs and benefits of affirmative action flow across ethnic and gender lines. Even in strictly short-run individualistic and material terms, every White person is either a woman who potentially or actually benefits from affirmative action or a man with close female relatives (wives, daughters, mothers) who may benefit. That fact illustrates the difficulty of figuring out exactly which racial groups receive benefits and which suffer harms in the short run. In the longer run, affirmative action could help distribute human capital to its most valued uses, thereby making all of society better off. The debate over this policy could quite accurately be considered one among people who share fundamental moral values *and* long-run economic interests.

These points do not gainsay serious problems and understandable criticisms of many programs that have risen under the banner of affirmative action. Among these are special college admissions treatment for children of immigrant groups that have not faced systematic discrimination; contract set-asides for ostensible minority firms actually owned by Whites; and racially gerrymandered congressional districting that may ironically have increased representation of the forces most antagonistic to affirmative action. There is no doubt that affirmative action, like all laudable principles, can in practice yield perverse or unintended consequences. For that very reason, debate and deliberation over this policy would benefit from more rationality, terminological and conceptual precision, empathy, and goodwill. It would be naïve to expect any political process to be dominated by these qualities, of course, but it may not be entirely unreasonable to hope the news media might refrain from undermining them.

Conclusion

Media influence transcends the meaning of the words used to attack or defend policy in the area of race. The deeper connotations of the conflict-exaggerating, simplistic coverage of affirmative action told audiences that Blacks and Whites may hold fundamentally incompatible values and interests, sharing only a tenuous cultural bond. Such material can support the idea that racial boundaries and distinctions are inherently meaningful as it imagines a community in which Blacks are the outsiders and Whites the authentic members. Although research shows considerable overlap in values held by both groups,[26] media have pounded in the lesson of fundamental *difference,* bolstering the argument that racial identity determines and distinguishes Blacks' political behavior, interests, and values from those of Whites.[27] When out-group members seem to possess fundamentally different traits, it becomes difficult for in-group members to trust and empathize with them. And that feeds a downward spiral: members of the out-group recognize the dominant group's distrust and the media's signals of exclusion; the out-group's own sense of trust and goodwill erodes, their suspicion and resentment mount. Such conditions make for hostile communication in public spaces—which further feeds each side's negative emotions.

A widespread perception that people of other races are trustworthy and possess goodwill and understanding encourages White Americans to express their more positive sentiments—to move toward the racial comity end of the spectrum. On the other hand, low interracial social capital,[28] marked by a general feeling among Whites that they cannot trust or understand

Blacks (and vice versa), encourages a pinched, anxious, negative response—and such animosity heightens the salience in this case of anti-affirmative action considerations. As our interviews in Indianapolis suggested, such negative predilections exist alongside the positive ones, awaiting entrance into working memory and attaining active expression when stimulated.

Affirmative action exemplifies how the media's conventional practice of seeking out and dramatizing conflict may have consequences beyond merely leaving audiences uninformed or distracted. Whatever polls on affirmative action itself show, the coverage may have heightened political rejection and, with it, negative emotion (unmeasured by standard surveys)—in other words, undermined racial comity. Yet it might reasonably be asked: if the media coverage had any impact beyond the elite stratum, why did public opinion data remain generally supportive? After all, the media's often confident predictions in 1995 that affirmative action would become a major (even *the* major) political issue of 1996 did not prove valid. That might suggest that all the signals we analyze here had little effect. One explanation would be that people find their own meanings and challenge the ones that seem to dominate the news.[29] Significant numbers of White audience members could be reframing the media coverage of affirmative action, rejecting the version that emphasizes a zero-sum Black–White clash.

The more politically pertinent and illuminating interpretation, however, seems to be that ambivalence is the crux of White public sentiment. The White public can be cued by stimuli in the communication environment to respond favorably and empathetically to specific applications of the affirmative action principle. And where political communication cues the more negative considerations stored in their belief systems, Whites may respond antagonistically. Although the attempt to generate White votes in 1996 by attacking affirmative action did not seem to work in the presidential race, the tactic apparently helped in passing referenda banning the policy in California state government activities, and in Seattle (1998). However, national public opinion seems to have been stable. Responses in a late 1997 *New York Times* poll are quite similar to those in 1995, described previously. In this one, 67 percent of respondents favored continuing affirmative action as is or reforming it.[30]

Sources of Media Depictions

What forces can explain the less-than-ideal contributions of media to this critical policy debate? Why were news organizations so accommodating to one side's frame (individual responsibility) while limiting the other (collective responsibility) largely to pro forma mentions? For one thing, White journalists themselves may be one of the groups most hostile to affirmative action, which has been aggressively practiced in many newsrooms for decades. Given the extraordinary level of competition for the most desirable jobs in the news industry, any policy that seems to pose impediments will be particularly irksome. In addition, journalists are no less prey than other mortals to scapegoating and rationalization. Many newsrooms no doubt have seen cases where manifestly less-qualified Blacks or other non-Whites (or women) were hired or promoted. It is easy for Whites to fall into the cultural habit of noticing and resenting the non-White beneficiaries. Somehow, they overlook the cases of nepotism, personal favoritism, and other deviations from pure merit—or simple mistakes by management—in hiring or promoting Whites who failed to excel.

In addition, it is psychologically comforting for White professionals in a competitive environment to rationalize their own failures to win promotions or raises by pointing to unfair competition from non-Whites. (Interestingly, there seems to be far less resentment of affirmative action for women, both in public opinion surveys and among journalists; we cannot tell whether this reflects underlying racial animosity, recognition that everyone is related to women who might benefit, or something else.)

Other familiar features of media operation help explain the coverage of affirmative action. Beyond the value news producers place on finding and magnifying conflict is the dependence on elite sources and the tendency to favor, at least in some respects, the elites who seem the most powerful and popular.[31] There seems little doubt that, as in the case of poverty, media framing and elite discourse reinforced each other. Few White leaders were willing to praise the policy publicly during the 1990s. The less presence and energy their views had in the media, the more political courage it took for individual White politicians to speak up favorably—let alone to construct a coherent, compelling argument that defended affirmative action. All the momentum was on the side of opponents.

Opponents had the traditional culture going for them too—the core American values of individualism, independence, free market meritocracy, and the like. Affirmative action had to draw on less-fashionable values like compassion and historical understanding (of past and continued flaws in the market for merit)—notions far less supported by well-funded activist think tanks, talk show hosts, and other opinion leaders. In addition, as we noted in our initial discussion of the five forces that shape media outputs (chapter 4), operation of the economy seems critical in this case. The widespread sense of economic insecurity especially apparent during the first half of the 1990s created fertile ground for leaders seeking to displace White attention from more intractable structural problems by scapegoating and creating symbolically potent enemies of the community.[32] The relative prosperity of the decade's latter half may have dampened economic anxiety sufficiently to make scapegoating, at least on the particular issue of affirmative action, less attractive to elites. But that could change.

Hemmed in by interactions of elite pressures, cultural resonances, and the state of the economy, the journalists might well argue they had no practical means of performing in ways more nurturing of social capital and effective deliberation. And indeed, the failure of conventional journalistic practice to yield genuinely balanced and accurate coverage provides a clear example of the racial chameleon at work. Media signals that reflect and possibly stimulate racial animosity arise unbidden and unnoticed as journalists follow their professional rules in constructing reality. This meant a public discourse that neglected many important contextual questions: How bad is continuing discrimination against Blacks, women, and others? What are the benefits to all of society in prying open opportunities for those subject to discrimination, and what is the scope and distribution of real costs? Which specific affirmative action programs have been abused, and how should they be reformed? How many deviations from pure merit are countenanced already, for reasons besides affirmative action—how many alumni children receive preferential college admissions, how many well-paying summer jobs or entry positions go to the offspring of the well-connected? Monica Lewinsky got her history-making White House job not because she was one of the most intelligent, well-educated, and promising young people vying for the handful of coveted White House internships, but because her parents knew a Democratic Party bigwig. This was hardly an exceptional departure from standard practice. In her home state, for example, many of the University of California regents and politicians who opposed affirmative action intervened—hundreds of times—to secure favored admissions treatment for children of associates and patrons. Most of these beneficiaries were White and affluent.[33]

Of course, knowing more context will not necessarily lead to an American consensus in the new millennium. But wide recognition of some basic facts could push things in a positive direction. Think what it might mean if every White person fully grasped that American society continues to feature, as it has for centuries, a variety of "preferences" for Whites—and if minority members saw that Whites are not in a rage of unswerving opposition to affirmative action. A narrative that consistently included such information would bolster racial comity, enhancing the possibility that Whites might reconcile their conflicted feelings about affirmative action by seeing the shared group interests more clearly. Given what we know about the media's ways, however, the absence of such a narrative was predictable—and sadly emblematic of the media's inadvertent promotion of racial conflict and political rejection.

8 Black Power

AVING SEEN how media practices increased impressions of Black–White conflict over affirmative action, the signature racialized media issue of the 1990s, in this chapter we turn to routine mass media portrayals of Black leadership and power. Our goal is to fathom the extent to which news coverage might inadvertently strengthen Whites' "fear of being controlled by others,"[1] as Schuman et al. put it. We ask how news may foster misperceptions and even demonization of Black politics, set limits on White understanding, and thus contribute to animosity. To this end we look at representations of Black political activity and leadership in local and national news, with particular reference to the two Black activists most publicized during the 1990s: the Reverend Jesse Jackson and Minister Louis Farrakhan. We find that network news operations, without racial intent or awareness, cast black political activity as alien and threatening.

Conflict-Seeking and National Black Politics

We begin with an extended case study that demonstrates in concentrated form the consequences of common television news practices, most particularly conflict-seeking, the search for iconic visuals, the perceived need to convey simplified versions of events and actors, and the plain desire to save money and time. The conflict-seeking norm is a well-documented criterion of newsworthiness, as is television's need for visuals and its simplification bias.[2] All of these revolve around the goal of appealing to audiences, constructing drama for gaining their continuing interest, and thereby generating profit. The media's take on Jackson and Farrakhan also reflect, it must be said, the limited imaginations and the shortcut thinking endemic among too many creators of television news, along with the threatened reactions of the White political establishment. These forces behind the news interacted with the unique dynamics of Black politics during Jesse Jackson's two presidential campaigns. They undermined his admittedly limited chances to win the Democratic nomination. More importantly, they associated assertive

Black leadership such as Jackson's with the threats to Whites embodied in Farrakhan's race-baiting, anti-Semitic rhetoric—this in spite of the fact that Jackson's "rainbow" campaign sought explicitly to build an alliance of working-class and middle-class Blacks, Whites, and others. Here we see how seemingly innocuous news practices can alter the balance of Black political power and derail healthy, multiracial coalition politics.

Bennett and Lawrence's concept of "news icon" helps explain how the needs of television news for narrative simplicity and drama may override the requirements of a more subtle and complex story. A news icon is a dramatic event or image dropped into a news narrative that purports to give visible shape to a larger truth. Bennett and Lawrence distinguish icons from other news images by their power to survive long beyond the moment of their birth.[3] For example, George Bush's illness into the lap of the Japanese prime minister at a state dinner came to symbolize a chronically weakened U.S. economy and appeared repeatedly in the *New York Times* and *Los Angeles Times* as evidence of American economic decline long after the Japanese economy had itself gone into serious recession.[4]

For this case we analyzed national news coverage on the three major networks of Jackson's presidential campaigns during the 1984 and 1988 primary seasons, and additional television coverage of Louis Farrakhan between and after these years. Before we examine the reports we first need to set a context for interpreting the assumptions of journalists as they covered these events.

During the 1980s and 1990s, the news media openly worried about the rise of Louis Farrakhan's influence among African Americans, in part reflecting simplifying White assumptions of a monolithic Black public opinion.[5] The evidence points in another direction. For example, a 1994 CNN/ *USA Today* national poll of Black adults asked how well an African American leader or organization represented their views. The results appear in table 8.1. Here we see that in 1994 Jesse Jackson and the NAACP were by far the most representative of a spectrum of African American opinion.[6] Without gangsta rappers in the list, Louis Farrakhan and the Nation of Islam would have placed last, judged even less representative and perhaps more extreme than Clarence Thomas. Moreover, Louis Farrakhan was unknown to nearly a quarter of the respondents, second in obscurity only to Colin Powell just before his ascent to media attention in the 1995–96 presidential nomination season. Incidentally, it is noteworthy that despite his relatively frequent ap-

Table 8.1 Who Best Represents African American Opinion, 1994 (figures are percentages)

	Very Well	Somewhat	Little	Not at All	Never Heard of	DK / Refused
Jesse Jackson	40	35	12	11	0	1
NAACP	37	34	15	10	1	3
African Americans in Congress	29	32	15	7	7	11
Colin Powell	26	21	9	6	31	9
Clarence Thomas	16	24	17	27	5	11
Ben Chavis	11	21	16	21	14	17
Louis Farrakhan	11	22	15	28	22	2
Nation of Islam	10	19	19	32	11	10
"Gangsta" rappers	5	8	16	53	14	3

Source: CNN/ *USA Today*, 23 August 1994, survey of Black adults.

pearances as a high official on network news during the Reagan, Bush, and early Clinton administrations, Powell was the least known of all the Black leadership in this poll of African Americans. It may not be entirely accidental that this same man was the most attractive Black leader by far to Whites.

Our case study begins with an off-the-record conversation in January 1984 between Jesse Jackson and two Black reporters in which Jackson made disparaging references to Jews ("Hymies") and New York City ("Hymie-town"). Present at the meeting was Milton Coleman, a Black reporter for the *Washington Post,* who later revealed the comments to a colleague writing a story on Jackson's foreign policy. The remarks soon surfaced in the press and heightened media sensitivity to Jackson's association with Louis Farrakhan, leader of the Nation of Islam. This association crystallized an enduring news icon that highlighted Jackson's apparent anti-Semitism.[7]

Meanwhile Farrakhan took advantage of national publicity to advance his agenda for Black separatism. He had endorsed Jackson's candidacy (prior to that point he had avoided conventional politics) and for a few months was active in his campaign, using the Nation of Islam as a forum for his endorsement. Jackson appeared at several Nation of Islam rallies and on one occasion was videotaped embracing Farrakhan at the podium. The embrace and the "Hymie" affair led to a series of escalating diatribes that repeatedly linked Farrakhan's inflammatory rhetoric to Jackson and to Blacks in general. In February, Farrakhan made a speech in which he set the rhetorical grounds for assuming Black solidarity, an assumption the media transformed into a news icon that would repeatedly pit Blacks against Jews: "I say to the Jewish people, who may not like our brother, it is not Jesse Jackson you are attacking. When you attack him, you are attacking the millions who are lining up with him. You're attacking all of us. . . . Why dislike us? Why attack our champion? Why hurl stones at him? It's our champion. If you harm this brother, what do you think we should do about it?" (CBS, 26 February 1984.)

Jackson waffled on whether he had made the "Hymie" remarks and did not immediately disavow Farrakhan's statement. For a brief time he accused some Jewish organizations of hounding his campaign. Then, two weeks after the reports first surfaced, Jackson admitted having made the remarks and publicly apologized to a Jewish group in a Manchester, New Hampshire synagogue. The national news media did not seem to accept Jackson's apology as genuine, however. In one story on his admission and apology, for example, a replay of the Farrakhan speech warning Jews followed Jackson's remarks (ABC, 27 February 1984). The media had a story of a candidate's verbal gaffe and his alleged hypocrisy—prime material for campaign news. The clash between two minority groups, linked with a presidential candidate who was running against racism but apparently exhibiting prejudice himself, as shown by his consorting with the anti-White extremist Farrakhan—all this propelled a small feeding frenzy.[8]

Following the scent also led television news to scramble important political distinctions between city and national politics during the 1984 New York primary. Much of the coverage emanated from New York City, where Mayor Ed Koch was planning his campaign for reelection. Jackson's widespread appeal among New York's Black voters and his association with Farrakhan provided Koch with an issue that divided Blacks from Koch's bases of support among Jews, conservative Whites, and recent immigrants; a history of bitter conflicts had weakened the city's coalition of Blacks and Jews.[9] By stepping into the national news spotlight, Koch reinforced the associative metaphor by recalling Jackson's visit to the Middle East in 1979 and his meeting with Yasir Arafat. Typical of this was a story broadcast on NBC on 3 April 1984 in which Koch indignantly rejected Jackson's candidacy: "Jesse Jackson . . . has embraced a murderer, someone who wants to destroy the Jewish people in the state of Israel." His remarks were followed by photos of Jackson's embracing greeting of Arafat, an echo of his embrace of Farrakhan.

News conventions of objectivity call for an exploration of both sides of an issue. The use of a news icon, however, weakens the effect of such a "ritual" of objectivity.[10] For example, the story of his 1979 meeting with Arafat included Jackson's rejoinder that an embrace was as customary in the Middle East as removing one's shoes upon entering a house in Japan. In this and various other stories on Jackson's apparent anti-Semitism, expert observers and Jackson himself sometimes offered contrasting views that challenged some of the facts or interpretations upon which the news icon were based. But these were unable to overcome the icon's compelling attraction. It resurfaced in other contexts as an axiomatic truth, free of qualification or question, especially when the time pressures of primary campaign news coverage could not accommodate challenging commentary. Here the iconic embrace reemerged, strengthened by additional exemplars it had collected in the interim.

For example, the "Hymietown" controversy reemerged during the New York primary in early April 1984, when Farrakhan threatened to kill the *Washington Post* reporter Milton Coleman for betraying Jackson ("a fitting punishment for such dogs"). In this story NBC reported that Jackson had "moved to deal with the threat of one of his supporters." These periodic analyses of Jesse Jackson's relationship with Farrakhan included video footage of the two in the signal embrace at a Nation of Islam podium. An over-the-shoulder still from the footage often introduced these stories. In this example the reporter provided a thumbnail sketch of Farrakhan's role in Jackson's campaign: his intervention in the release of an American pilot from Syria and provision of security to Jackson by Farrakhan's security detail, the Fruit of Islam, before Secret Service protection began. Jackson was in this and other reports called upon to free himself from Farrakhan's embrace, but also was reported to have repeatedly refused to do so (NBC, 3 April 1984)— while being shown over and over quite literally in his arms.

A week later Farrakhan disingenuously denied having made the threat on Coleman's life. Once again the graphic image of the embrace appeared and the reporter introduced Farrakhan as "one of Jesse Jackson's key supporters" (NBC, 11 April 1984). This claim came despite Farrakhan's low standing among Blacks and the miniscule size of his organization. These associations dogged Jackson through five months of the primary season that year, appearing in nineteen major stories, as shown in appendix table A.8.

The irony in this is that during the 1984 primary season, television news self-consciously reflected on its "soft" coverage of the Jackson campaign. In a story broadcast during the New York primary, for example, a *Chicago*

Tribune reporter claimed that "[t]here's a double standard. He's a different kind of candidate because there's a consensus that he can't be elected president so they don't put him to a tougher standard like Mondale or Hart" (CBS, 4 April 1984).

Most telling in this coverage were the media's implicit assumptions about Black politics and how these created a drag on the Jackson candidacy. Much of the 1984 coverage implicitly and explicitly tied Jackson's fortunes to a solid Black vote. Similar stereotypes of political homogeneity and a framing of Black candidacies in racial conflict terms have been documented in Chicago mayoral races[11] and in congressional elections.[12] This assumption of a unified Black mind may reflect the White journalists' unconscious tendency to think of out-group members as far more homogeneous than their own, manifestly diverse in-group. The insistence upon disavowal of Farrakhan's remarks suggested a Black solidarity analogous to a polluting contagion: Farrakhan's anti-Semitism transmitted to Jesse Jackson by virtue of the embrace, whose welcome by the Black electorate pointed to its extremism or anti-Semitism. By accepting the logic of Farrakhan's message of Black solidarity (and its implicit message of Black gain at White expense), the news created a false political dilemma. As early as the New Hampshire primary, television commentators warned that Jackson's flirtation with Farrakhan threatened to split the Democratic coalition, in which Blacks and Jews play pivotal roles—an ill omen for the November election (ABC, 27 February 1984).

By the middle of the primary season this logic had infiltrated conventional political analysis. For example, during the Pennsylvania primary an ABC commentator opined that if "[Mondale or Hart] attack a Black leader, they could lose Black votes. If they don't they could lose Jewish votes" (9 April 1984). At the end of the campaign, just before the Democratic convention, Brit Hume of ABC argued that Jackson's failure to disavow Farrakhan "the man" put Mondale into a political dilemma. Mondale now had to disavow Jackson so that his embrace of Farrakhan would not infect Mondale and his chances against Reagan. The problem again: lose Black votes or lose Jewish votes.

The power of the news icon had overcome reality, indicated most dramatically by a CBS / *New York Times* poll taken just prior to the Democratic convention. It revealed that *Black voters actually preferred Mondale over Jackson* 53 percent to 31 percent, and only 5 percent said they would defect from the party if Jackson refused to support Mondale (CBS, 10 July 1984). Moreover, Jackson won significant proportions of the White (and Jewish) vote in many primaries. By this time, however, Farrakhan's media reputation had been established and would continue to dog Jackson, driven by the self-sustaining logic of a presumed Black solidarity. Despite the close of the 1984 political season, Jackson would not slip away from this media-reinforced association. Farrakhan's ascent to public attention, itself abetted by the media, would keep the issue alive until the 1988 campaign when it was refreshed, with no intervening events to warrant it.

Farrakhan's own independent media career took off in 1985 when he made a series of speeches to Black audiences around the United States. In five of the six major stories on Farrakhan that year, Jesse Jackson was either mentioned or shown in his embrace. The absence of a frenetic political campaign drew more thoughtful analytical pieces on Farrakhan's significance, but the logic of the icon continued to attract other exemplars of anti-Semitism. On 3 March 1985, for example, a CBS analysis of the divisions between Blacks and Jews specified as its causes the meeting of the Black former ambassador to the United Nations, Andrew Young, with the Palestinian Liberation Organization (PLO), Jackson with PLO head Arafat, and Farrakhan with Jackson, likened again to the spread of a political infection. Later that year Farrakhan met with Libyan leader Moammar Khadaffi, and thus absorbed yet another infecting agent which he would pass on to Jackson during the 1988 campaign.

Typical of these off-year analytical pieces on Farrakhan's significance and appeal was an NBC story of his October 4 speech to an audience in Madison Square Garden (all three networks had similar take-outs on the speech the following day). The report depicted Farrakhan as "more popular than ever" with Blacks, though the correspondent provided no evidence of this except for the fragmentary comments of two attendees. These suggested that Farrakhan's appeal had little to do with ideology, political agenda, or specific belief but rather with his defiance: "He has a lot of guts, and that's what we need, somebody with guts." In the report Harvard professor Alvin Poussaint explained the basis of Farrakhan's appeal as vicarious identification with a Black willing to stand up to Whites (NBC, 7 October 1985).

The report cast a favorable light on Farrakhan's separatist strategy by differentiating the "constructive" parts of his message from his demagoguery. Farrakhan's message was, however, doubly inviting to a species of racism: "Look beloved, *you* contribute to the White man's racism. *You* contribute to their calling you *nigger* and thinking you're an inferior person, because you don't do anything in the way of *producing.*" Farrakhan extolled Black self-sufficiency and thereby simultaneously fed denial, relieved Whites and White institutions of responsibility for economic conditions in Black communities and, by virtue of his baiting of Whites in general and Jews specifically, provided cover for White racism. To the extent that the news media magnified his political influence among African American citizens, Farrakhan's coverage conflated legitimate political issues—such as affirmative action—with marginal and even extremist views.

The 1988 Democratic primary season brought a new Jesse Jackson strategy but the same news icon, which by then had encompassed a trio of villains: Arafat, Farrakhan, and Castro. Between primary seasons television news sustained Jackson's connection to Farrakhan by repeated references to his 1984 campaign. For example, an extended analysis of Jackson's campaign began with a poll showing 25 percent of Democrats supporting him. "This time," the commentator said, "there would be no pictures of Castro, Arafat, and Farrakhan," as each was dutifully pictured with Jackson in the story. The remainder of the analysis depicted several analysts alarmed at Jackson's widening appeal, especially among White working-class Democrats; "publicly [Democratic leaders] welcome him, but privately there is worry" (ABC, 30 July 1987).

Two weeks later a CBS report called attention to Jackson's new "white bread" appeal in contrast to his earlier "embrace of Farrakhan, cozy chats with Arafat, and meetings with Castro" (14 August 1987). Despite Jackson's conscious attempt to refashion his image, the news media continued to lace their coverage of the 1988 campaign with the imagery of his 1984 embrace of Farrakhan and radical politics, albeit at a slower pace, as illustrated in appendix table A.9.

Despite the negative media associations, commentators once again attributed Jackson's rise in popularity to reverse racism, as if journalists were treating him gently, in a tacit form of affirmative action. One story quoted Ben Wattenberg that the absence of media criticism of Jackson's radical politics had led to his "surprising surge" in popularity (NBC, 11 March 1988). This took place just prior to Jackson's reversal in Wisconsin in early April and another punishing campaign in New York, where Mayor Koch once again received a national media forum for his repeated claims that Jackson was a liar and his advice to voters that they would be "crazy" to vote for him.[13]

Farrakhan's repeated association with Jesse Jackson—himself an iconic representation of Black political aspirations—led to a marked rise in Farrakhan's national media visibility. The percentage of news time devoted to Farrakhan and the Nation of Islam as compared to other Black political organizations—NAACP, Urban League, CORE, SCLC, and the Rainbow Coalition—rose dramatically in this period. In 1984, for example, Louis Farrakhan was the focus in over 68 percent of major news stories dealing with Black political activity, and in 1985 in over half the stories. In fact, the media frequently discussed the political significance of Farrakhan's politics in the mid-1980s, articulating his philosophy and characterizing him as a driving political force among Blacks. In 1984 and 1985, *over half* the time devoted to stories about Black leaders and organizations on the network evening news concentrated on Farrakhan. As media devoted much of their attention to Farrakhan's politics, the discourse about Black politics shifted accordingly to anger, division, anti-Semitism, and separatism. For example, analysis of the evening network news on American Jews during this same 1984–94 time period (140 stories) reveals about two-thirds concerned with anti-Jewish prejudice. Of these, nearly 55 percent centered on Black anti-Semitism, much of it thematically linked to Louis Farrakhan and his symbolic representation of Black politics in general. If one knew nothing of the political world except that represented on national newscasts, one would have gotten the impression of growing Black separatism fueled by a fresh and politically significant wave of Black anti-Semitism.[14]

The proportion of news time spent on Farrakhan and its substantial focus on anti-Jewish attitudes suggested a growth of anti-Semitism among Blacks in general. This was facilitated by misperceptions of Black politics (shared by Whites in general) and the tendency of media to personify group identity in the person of single individuals.[15] By exaggerating the political significance of Louis Farrakhan for Blacks, calling repeated attention to his association with Jesse Jackson, and elevating the importance of the racially symbolic respects of Jackson's candidacy over the bread-and-butter issues on which he tried to run, television news set in motion a political dynamic that depleted comity between Blacks and Jews and thus weakened what historically has been the most reliable and productive political link between Blacks and Whites. Additionally, by highlighting the New York model of failing Black–Jewish coalition politics, the national media generalized from the most divisive local example, overlooking the quiet success of the coalition in other cities, such as Chicago[16] and Los Angeles.[17]

Most importantly, the news media provided a marginal political figure with a national forum and thereby enhanced his political credibility and apparent power. Prior to his piggyback ride on the shoulders of Jackson's candidacy in 1984 to increase his own political standing, Farrakhan could attract only handfuls of listeners to his speeches. By 1985 Farrakhan could draw audiences of ten thousand or more[18] and by 1995 had sufficient credibility and standing to draw a highly publicized gathering of Blacks to Washington, D.C.—the Million Man March—that well exceeded the numbers in Martin Luther King Jr.'s 1963 March on Washington. Although the national media were not the sole cause of Farrakhan's rise to power, they inflated his true significance among Blacks, undermining the bases for interracial comity not only among Jews but also among Whites frightened by a new menacing face of Black politics.

Putnam argues that "virtuous cycles" based on mutual trust do not require an idealized view of partners in political coalition; nor are they doomed to falter on differences of interest. They depend, rather, on mutual respect and realistic appraisals of what each partner brings to the political relationship. The exchanges that follow build long-term trust and encourage development of further virtuous cycles that help build stable political community.[19] The coverage documented here depicted and perhaps contributed to a vicious cycle of finger pointing and recrimination that depleted racial comity between otherwise natural political allies, fragmented an important segment of the liberal coalition, and handicapped the development of effective Black leadership.

A news icon of the type examined here misinterprets and magnifies the significance of incidents that give shape to latent fears and suspicions born of segregated lives and misunderstanding, and thus constructs a plausible reality that changes the structure of political opportunity. Not unlike the way media fascination with flamboyance and conflict drew individuals attracted to those qualities into the New Left—the Yippies—and thus derailed the long-term political strategies of the more serious-minded in the movement of the 1960s,[20] the news media riveted their attention on Black separatist politics long enough to open a window of opportunity for a skillful political figure like Louis Farrakhan. Conventional news practices magnified the significance of his standing in Black public opinion and thereby undermined the legitimacy and visibility of its actual political strivings.

The repeated use of the Jackson–Farrakhan icon reflects a confluence of forces mentioned at the outset of this section. Those who fabricate television news seek visuals—preferably readily recognizable, symbolic ones—that can condense a set of emotional meanings and pump up the drama. Assuming, perhaps correctly, that the audience is neither well informed nor paying close attention, news producers also work with, and perhaps themselves have, highly simplified understandings that will easily gain viewers' recognition and comprehension. Once they find a visual symbol like the Jackson–Farrakhan embrace, it is hard for television news personnel to let it out of their clutches. Beyond stimulating the audience's recognition, repeated use saves money—no need to send a camera crew for a new visual when the file footage is such "good television." The creators of the news programs reveal here not only attention to the bottom line, but also, perhaps, a deficit of creative thinking about how they represent Black political activity—or indeed any political activity.

Finally, as in previous chapters, we would point to the constraining and conditioning influence of elite discourse on portrayals of news subjects. Throughout a career in elective politics that began in 1984, at least until he became personal minister to the Clinton family in 1998, Jesse Jackson was feared and derided by his own party's establishment. At the same time, he was a useful symbol of threatening Black power for conservatives like Republican senator Jesse Helms of North Carolina, who featured Jackson in campaign literature aimed at the racist vote. Farrakhan, of course, was even more useful on this score. When a figure enjoys very little support at the elite level, it becomes easier for journalists to express their negative evaluations,[21] whether it be a Jackson or Farrakhan or, at the other extreme, a David Duke (former KKK leader and perennial Republican candidate in Louisiana). Here again, several factors merge to overdetermine the production of mediated images that may have implications for race relations.

Black Politics in Local News

But is Jesse Jackson a unique case? If we look more broadly at media representations of Blacks in politics, would we find a different story? In this section we show normal practices and implicit comparisons that made the treatment of Jackson understandable and predictable. Using our Chicago sample, we looked at stories of Blacks and Whites participating in politics and found Black activists often pleading the narrow interests of the Black community, with White leaders much more frequently representing the broader community. News about Blacks who acted politically may have conveyed the notion that they spoke and behaved more than Whites to advance "special interests" against the public interest. Comparing the portrayals of White and Black leaders provides an excellent demonstration of the ways the news constructs implicit, inadvertently racial contrasts. None of the signals conveyed is overt. Rather, the meanings arise in the juxtaposition of Whites habitually pictured in one way and Blacks in another. We do acknowledge that this analysis is limited to one city for one brief time period, so we advance the findings as suggestive of the kinds of subtle, alienating racial distinctions that news may draw—not as a definitive discovery of a universal media tendency. However, coverage of the putatively Black issue of affirmative action (chapter 7) and of Jackson and Farrakhan fit into familiarly congruent patterns. They lend further support to the possibility that media practices do little to build Whites' understanding or acceptance of Black political power, which is vital to racial comity.

Using the 1990–91 Chicago local news sample, we examined every story that concerned public policy and coded each soundbite for the race of the spokesperson and whether they criticized, defended, or made recommendations for action by government or public officials (we dropped those exclusively focused on campaign details or events).[22] We then determined the justification for each utterance. Each explicit or implicit claim that the government was violating or should be serving an interest comprised such a warrant. The four possible justifications included public interest (452 assertions), ethnic self-interest (180), general interest in corruption-free government (181), and "special" interests not associated with race, such as gay and lesbian people (49).[23]

Fully one-third of the time that audiences heard Blacks endorsing or criticizing a government action, those spokespersons argued for the specific interests of Black persons. By contrast, of those assertions made by Whites, about 5 percent were specifically targeted for Whites. Thus, when Blacks made political statements on television they were six times more likely than Whites to be arguing for the specific interests of their group.

An even greater imbalance exists at the level of motivation: White political spokespersons endorsed government service of Blacks' interests thirty-eight times. This means that Whites in politics defended Blacks' interests more often than they overtly defended the interests of their own group (which they did twenty-eight times). On the other hand, only one Black spokesperson defended the notion that government should serve Whites' interests. Television audiences were likely to get the impression that Blacks demand a lot from government and receive considerable support from Whites in that quest, but then fail to reciprocate. At the same time, Blacks in politics appear more selfish, less moved by the public interest. Most of the time that Whites spoke about government action, they defended it in terms of the public or larger community interest. The ratio of public interest to ethnic self-interest assertions for Whites was 10:1 (278 to 28), favoring the public interest.[24] In comparison, for the Blacks the same ratio was about 1:1 (64 to 66). For every public interest claim, Blacks uttered a self-interested demand. In the implicit comparison, then, Whites appeared ten times more public spirited and politically altruistic in their balance of concerns than Blacks.

It is important to remember that these measures tap public rhetoric, not politicians' actual goals or thoughts. Political actors frequently rationalize selfish demands in terms of the public interest. The assumption here, though, is that overt assertions, not the hidden agendas of speakers, shape audience perceptions. In this realm of image and rhetoric, Blacks are portrayed in ways unlikely to engender expansive political feelings among Whites. Rather, the picture connotes a political system in which one group mostly identifies with and seeks a broader social good, while another, the outsiders, strive, often stridently, for their own good with little regard for others. The implication of zero-sum conflict is embedded in such a portrait, as is a sense that Blacks may not truly belong to the larger community.

Now it may well be that Black activists and elites do treat Chicago politics as a zero-sum game in which any gain for Whites is a loss for Blacks. Perhaps most of the time Black political leaders do speak up largely or exclusively for Black interests; many theories of representation would endorse just such narrowly focused behavior. In fact, legislative districting designed to augment Black chances for election assumes that such representatives would voice the interests of Blacks more energetically than those of other groups, yielding both symbolic and concrete benefits. In this sense, the media images could be considered "accurate."

But they omit the structural causes of the Blacks' self-interested quest and the key contextual fact that the White halo is merely an ironic reflection of White privilege. To protect those benefits, White politicians need only defend the status quo, in general terms by invoking "the public interest," or in terms of nonracial values such as meritocracy or low taxes. In fact, White politicians frequently demand and receive special subsidies that disproportionately benefit Whites, like mortgage tax deductions, pork barrel construction projects, and defense plant contracts. White politicians also enact subsidies limited largely to the wealthy, such as maintaining the mortgage deduction for vacation homes.[25] Were media to treat class cleavages with the kind of attention and symbolic drama they devote to race, such policies could conceivably displace some racial animosity. In any event, to serve their ethnic group, White politicians need not use an overt rhetoric of White power; they need not mention power—or Whiteness—at all.

Representation of Black Leadership in National News

Beyond the highlighted, iconic leaders (Jackson and Farrakhan), how do the national media treat the rest of the Black leadership? The ABC news transcript data—for which we have three year-long samples—provide an opportunity to probe the larger scope of and context for Black political discourse.[26] Appendix table A.10 lists all the names of a selected group of Black leaders mentioned by ABC news in at least three different stories during the same twelve-month sample period (1990–91) used in chapter 4. Leaders mentioned only one or two times are grouped together in the table as "all others."[27]

The two Black leaders who received the most attention were the ones who generated the most negative controversy, Supreme Court nominee and Justice Clarence Thomas was mentioned in the most stories, followed by former Washington, D.C. mayor Marion Barry. These two men also accounted for slightly over 40 percent of the sound bites. Barry appeared in the news because of drug charges against him, and Thomas because of his Supreme Court nomination and the ensuing controversy over sexual harassment.

On the other hand, the news also covered General Colin Powell and Health and Human Services Secretary Louis Sullivan with some frequency; they appeared as important government leaders, their race irrelevant. Leaving aside the extraordinary Thomas affair, table A.10 shows ninety-seven stories and seventy-one soundbites. Assume ABC provides an average of six news broadcasts per week (during weekends, the nightly news shows are frequently preempted by sports and other programming) for a total of 312 per year. This figure means that, on average, ABC mentioned a prominent Black leader somewhat less than one time every three shows (97 / 312) and conveyed the voice of a leader one time for every four and one-half shows.

We next examined the subject of the stories that mentioned Black leaders. Of the 186 stories, slightly more than half (94) included an accusation that he had committed a crime (including sexual harassment) or a leader's denial of committing a crime. These totals, inflated by the travails of Thomas and Barry, suggest a side effect of standard news values. By granting high priority to dramatic controversy among the powerful and lower priority to ordinary policymaking, the networks ensure that aside from a few institutionally newsworthy officials, any leader who receives concentrated attention is likely to be in some kind of trouble. Since high institutional position and accompanying newsworthiness characterizes hardly any Blacks (during the study period, only Colin Powell, Louis Sullivan, and House Democratic Whip William Gray) but many Whites, network news tends to show White leaders in a positive light vastly more often—both proportionally and absolutely. Here again, as with the matter of political altruism, network news reflects some aspects of reality—there are few Blacks in top federal leadership positions—but distorts other aspects: the typical Black official is not accused of malfeasance.

Establishing yet another disadvantageous Black–White contrast, when Black leaders spoke they often criticized government policy. Not once in the 1990–91 sample did a Black leader praise the government, suggesting that White audiences are exposed to a stream of images in which Black leaders often attack government and rarely support it. By contrast, the norm of balance ensures that most stories that show White leaders criticizing policies will portray other White leaders voicing support. There is, after all, a greater pool from which such balancing voices can be conveniently drawn. The composite image is of nearly unrelieved carping by Black leaders as compared with a more balanced pattern of praise and reproach arising from powerful Whites.

On one level, this implicit comparison may accurately reflect a much greater incidence of complaint among Black political actors than Whites. But the status quo builds in advantages for Whites who, in comparison to Blacks, have less reason to complain. By neglecting this context, the media again make Black political leaders look bad. In noting this we do not mean to suggest that every time a Black leader attacks a government policy reporters should halt the narrative and inject several contextual sentences about the legacy of racism, structural impediments, and White privilege. News conventions make this awkward and impractical. But it is important to recognize that the apparent impossibility of providing regular context may have significant ramifications for Black–White relations.

To establish greater confidence for these findings, consider the data for 1994 and 1997 in appendix table A.11. We searched for the names of *all* one hundred most influential Black leaders identified by *Ebony* magazine. One striking difference between the two years is that the sheer numbers dropped by 50 percent: Black leaders appeared in 137 stories in 1994 and just 68 in 1997, with a concomitant decrease in soundbites from 102 to 51. The drop from 1990–91, when there were 103 sound bites, is particularly noteworthy since the method in 1990–91 recorded a lower number of leaders than we would have obtained if we had searched stories for all one hundred leaders, as in the later two periods.

Even if we omit the Clarence Thomas stories for 1990–91, the later years also show evidence of an overall change in network news practices. In 1994, the persons most mentioned from the *Ebony* list of most influential Black Americans were Michael Jordan, Michael Jackson, and the redoubtable Louis Farrakhan; in 1997 the title went again to Jordan, followed by Bill Cosby. By 1997 only five Black government officials made the list, compared with ten in 1994 and seven in 1990–91. Jesse Jackson and Colin Powell appeared on the roster all three years but the overall drift was toward celebrity and sensation. In both the later years, as earlier, an accusation of crime accompanied a significant percentage of leaders' appearances, and crime was a major topic of stories in which leaders appeared. The same negativity found in the leaders' rhetoric in 1990–91 characterizes their discourse in the later periods: we coded thirty-three instances in which government was criticized and just one of praise during 1994 and 1997 combined.

Is the pattern of images merely a by-product of the networks' more or less accurate representation of the reality of Black America? Yes and no. Scholars have long documented the impossibility of the media's achieving the goal of comprehensive accuracy or objectivity in portraying the world.[28] The scholarly literature shows how professional culture, economic incentives, political pressure, and cognitive limitations among journalists and their audiences ensure that the news offers only partial, selective representations.

Consider the reporting on Marion Barry during 1990–91. The coverage accurately reflected one level of reality: the experience of an unusually scurrilous politician who happened to be Black. But there are effective, conscientious Black mayors toiling all over the country who together attained only a fraction of the network visibility garnered by Barry alone. That the Barry stories comprised a high proportion of all ABC images of Black politicians during the sample year is due to the journalistic emphasis on unusual controversy and drama, not to a reality that the typical Black mayor is, like Barry, a corrupt drug user. So even when they correctly reported Barry's crimes, indictment, and conviction, the networks might have promoted inaccurate cognitions among White audiences who understood this mayor to represent a larger category.

Prototype theory tells us that for the majority group, Blacks in the news may represent or symbolize all Blacks in a way singular Whites do not stand for all Whites. Since prototypes are constructed of unconscious stereotypical traits, the dominant images of Black leadership trade on and feed the familiar impressions of negativity, danger, and corruption. These are all the more compelling for White audience members—especially those who have limited personal contact or hostile predispositions toward Blacks—since the news presents itself as a representative sample of the world's events. The human tendency toward prejudiced stereotyping is of course not the media's responsibility, but that disposition means many White audience members may over time combine individually accurate news images of Blacks into a schema antagonistic to Black political activity. This would hold especially when the leaders most frequently, recognizably, and vividly depicted—like Jackson, Farrakhan, and Thomas—are associated with symbols and stereotypes likely to call up old White fears.

Conclusion

Every mediated communication possesses a range of potential readings. The news texts that we analyze in the first part of the chapter demonstrate that African Americans can and do exert various forms of power in the United States. Blacks are not always victims or threats. This demonstration in itself marks a radical change over the past thirty years toward a more diverse, socially beneficial (and "accurate") construction of Blacks in the news. Consistent with our thesis that the contours of cultural change in race relations can best be monitored by close and systematic analysis of the mass media's images, in this chapter we have also demonstrated the continuing deficits in the portrayals. The growth in depictions of Blacks acting competently in responsible positions coexists with signals that reinforce the older sense of fundamental racial difference and a newer sense of fundamental political conflict. The studies of Jackson and Farrakhan as embodiments of Black political power, and of affirmative action—frequently depicted as illegitimate preference for a single undeserving out-group—provide perhaps the most vivid examples of this latter tendency. Even though few Whites may draw racist inferences from such portrayals, they could feed the sentiments we discussed in chapter 2: the ambivalence—the uneasy mixture of distance, ignorance, impatience and hesitant, vacillating sympathy—or animosity that still characterizes most Whites.

Current practices may tend to obscure larger truths about the diversity and the many positive contributions of Black persons to the larger national community. It may not be impossible to consider altering the news to make images of Blacks more complicated. Innovations could build on a recognition that single stories involving individual Black persons might be truthful on any given day, yet accumulate over time to construct within many viewers, especially those predisposed by animosity or racism, a distorted impression of Blacks as a social category. A deliberate choice to introduce more complexity and variety in images of African Americans could, on balance, make television news more positive, less likely to arouse White antagonism, precisely by making it more "accurate"—bringing news images more into line with overall African American demographics, values, and lifestyles. But for reasons we discuss later, media organizations seem to feel it would be illegitimate to deliberately reshape Black images in the news.

Finally, we must acknowledge a further turn to the puzzle: Actions taken to ameliorate one misimpression could heighten another. For example, reducing reports of Black crime and victimization could instill among Whites an unwarranted sense of Black progress. Similarly, television's deliberate use of Black experts on non-"Black" issues, while conveying the positive diversity of the Black community, could simultaneously feed the complacency of Whites who insist racial discrimination has ceased. And correcting the implication that Blacks are more demanding of government responsiveness than Whites could lead networks to broadcast soundbites from spurious, unrepresentative Black "leaders."

While there is no easy way out of such dilemmas, they point to the familiar need for context. By routinely providing context, television news could reveal the continued prevalence of discrimination, illuminate the structural forces that make crime attractive in the ghetto, and explain why so many Black political leaders adopt a confrontational style. But complex, nuanced context is difficult for daily news reports to convey on a regular basis. We return to the reasons for this, and possible paths to improvement, in chapter 12. First, we turn to the racial politics of entertainment and advertising.

9 Prime-Time Television: White and Whiter

PRIME-TIME TELEVISION offers a rich store of evidence for judging the state of interracial comity, in part because of the sheer numbers of people who watch the shows broadcast during those hours and because recent changes in technology and Federal Communications Commission (FCC) regulations, one of whose unforeseen consequences is a mediated segregation. In 1998, the top ten shows in Black households were completely different from the top ten in White households. The groups shared only four in common among the top twenty, and among the ten most popular shows for Blacks, none rated higher than 98 among Whites, with most rated between 109 and 119.[1] The division by race is a relatively new phenomenon enabled by the increase in shows targeted specifically (but not exclusively) for Black audiences, the result of the expansion of the television universe by cable and satellite. This has decreased the break-even points for broadcasters and converted minority audiences into an economically attractive target in their own right. The Big Three networks are aware of this division and opt for attracting the largest White audience by appealing to what network executives perceive as their preferences for largely segregated entertainment, although there are some indications that this may be breaking down for the youngest White audiences.[2]

Given these wide disparities in viewing audiences, program content should be a revealing indicator of the way racial boundaries are created and maintained as traditional racial stereotypes and biological racism decline. In this chapter we evaluate the content of the most popular entertainment shows for White audiences. We gauge the quality of interactions between Blacks and Whites and the qualities of Black characters to determine the symptoms of Black and White division, cognitive and cultural.

The Foundations of Racial Comity

In his work on the importance of social capital for achieving economic and political well-being, Putnam identifies a key ingredient to be the presence of horizontal relationships, patterns of communication unfettered by social boundaries imposed either by formal roles or by cultural divides that restrict the opportunity to know someone as an individual. Candor, open debate, and informal interaction outside the workplace encourage real exchange that draws people with opposed positions from ideological extremes to more negotiable middle ground. The specific good created is the lowering of transaction costs imposed by mutual fear and suspicion. Formal hierarchical relationships, in contrast, restrict candor. Organizations regard intimacy as taboo, for example, because it threatens productivity and because it poses risks for superiors and subordinates alike of exposing exploitable weaknesses.[3]

Two avenues are available for overcoming mistrust and fear. The natural intimacy usually found in blood relations or close friendships offers one such path. Indeed, some studies show that the increased empathy that comes with intimacy with even a single member of a stigmatized group can improve attitudes toward the group as a whole.[4] Our interviews of Indianapolis Whites with Black relatives by marriage support this conclusion. In the absence of these deep ties, dense patterns of involvement in horizontal networks such as voluntary associations, clubs, and neighborhood groups offer the other path to overcoming mistrust. Indeed, some argue that individuals from weaker groups often use secrecy, privacy, and deception to resist abuses of power and authority, making them harder for dominant group members to know. Under these circumstances, more informal involvement in multiple sites increases opportunities for communication that develops trust and common ground.[5] In these venues people have an opportunity to see each other as more or less equals rather than as supplicants and benefactors. The key here is extensive interaction in several different settings, not just fleeting contact, for example, in the workplace.

Support for this argument comes from numerous tests of the "group contact" hypothesis that close and sustained contact with members of minority groups promotes positive, tolerant attitudes. Casual interracial contact in work settings alone does not necessarily increase understanding or tolerance, primarily because one or more necessary components for the process—equal status; common goals; intergroup cooperation; and the support of authorities, law, or custom—are likely to be absent.[6] The culprit at the heart of the problem of group mistrust and suspicion is the tendency for people's perceptions to be "theory-driven," relying upon stereotyped generalizations to develop expectations about the prototypical, most representative member of a category.

That tendency toward theory-driven perceptions helps illuminate the significance of White reactions to the successful *Cosby* show. When they quizzed White viewers about their reactions to the show, Jhally and Lewis found that rather than reducing their prejudice, Whites came away from the show with the message that the fictional Huxtable family proved that Blacks *could* make it in American society if they worked hard enough. Unsuccessful Blacks therefore had only themselves to blame.[7] Prototype theory suggests that information on Bill Cosby or Michael Jordan, taken as unrepresentative of their category, is not generalized to the category of Black males. Bill Cosby does not disprove the inferiority of other Blacks; rather he has become irrelevant as a Black exemplar because he has effectively (symbolically) become White. He no longer represents a Black person very well because he does not possess the traits that such people (according to the culture) typically exhibit. These are largely marginal traits—positively as athleticism, musical expression, and sensuality, and negatively as unreasonableness, exaggerated strength, dissonance, disorder, and sexual excess—the inverse of idealized "White" values.

Evidence shows that people use *both* data (real world examples) and prototypes (mental schemas) to represent groups to which they belong, *but only use prototypes* to represent groups to which they do not belong and about which they therefore know less.[8] Just so, for segregation limits opportunities for Whites to meet a wide variety of Blacks. They come to depend on mediated images for cataloging Blacks that tend to generalize traits at the simplified prototypical level, positive and negative.

Media and Cognition

Because of continuing patterns of racial segregation, the media by default become important sources of information for the development and reinforcement of prototypes. Gray has described the media and popular culture as "the cultural and social sites where theoretical abstraction and cultural representation come down to earth, percolating through the imagination of America."[9] These often supply important currents in our political discourse and affect minorities relationships to larger society, and their life chances. Cultivation research demonstrates how expectations and responses may be due mainly to a mediated reality that in the absence of personal experience may be every bit as credible a foundation for belief and even behavior.[10] One study, for example, examined racial attitudes among White students at the University of Wisconsin who had little or no firsthand experience with African Americans. The more that students watched entertainment television, the more likely they were to believe that Blacks were affluent and successful; the more they watched television news, the more likely their belief that Blacks were worse off and deviant.[11] Other research demonstrates how exposure to stereotypic portrayal of Blacks primes Whites to use racial explanations for subsequent, unrelated media portrayals. For example, students primed with material that highlighted the lazy, unintelligent, aggressive, and socially destructive traits of an imaginary Black student were more likely to judge that Rodney King brought his beating by Los Angeles police upon himself by his unresponsiveness and failure to stop when pulled over. Students primed with a counter-stereotype were more likely to say that King had been an innocent victim.[12] Other evidence suggests that the effects of this sort of priming last for some time and that such stimuli are effective even when presented below conscious recognition thresholds.[13]

We believe this theoretical foundation is necessary to understand the significance of the messages we receive from the most dominant form of mass communication and its major content. If steady diets of television entertainment supply and reinforce these prototypes, then we need to determine what is currently on the menu.

Black and White in Prime Time

For our study of prime-time entertainment, we analyzed the patterns of interracial interactions and the qualities of major Black characters in a two-month sample of the most highly rated programs (excepting news and sports) for White audiences, 66 shows in total. The shows were broadcast in April and May 1996, a period that includes the all-important "sweeps" tally when audience viewership data are collected for establishing advertising rates.[14] To the extent these shows depict Black–White relations, they suggest the limits of permissibility and present, for White audiences, the dominant prototypes that both instruct and reflect. If television is an escapist medium, the images ought to define a range of comfortable imagery while revealing the prototypes that register the culture's vision of what is right and proper.

The first analysis explores whether characters are in essentially equal roles or in a formal, hierarchical relationship and the extent to which such relationships limit the kind of exchange necessary for overcoming Whites' simplified perceptions of Blacks. As we pointed out above, these relationships may take either of two roads, that of intimacy or of casual involvement in a variety of informal contexts. Accordingly, two dimensions of the coding scheme include verbal intimacy, the degree of familiarity in the verbal exchanges of the characters, and extra-role involvement, whether the relationship extends beyond the formal demands of the work place. These two and one other—the degree of cooperation coming to a decision—are adapted from a study that charted interracial interactions on television entertainment.[15] We also added the pattern of gender relations, as well as some descriptive features of the characters and time spent on camera. (A coding scheme appears on the book's website, <http://www.raceandmedia.com>.)

To provide some context for judging the significance of the interracial data, we developed two additional data sets. One came from a set of coded interactions between White characters in a random sample of 10 percent of these shows (for a total of 153 interactions). The sub-sample included seven shows: two episodes of *Home Improvement,* and one each of *Boston Common, Mad About You, Frasier, ER,* and *NYPD Blue.* The patterns here are sometimes quite different and are attributable in part to a number of structural features of the shows. With one exception (*Boston Common*), for example, the sitcoms rarely included Black characters.[16] Except for an irregularly recurring character—Jackie Chiles, a send-up of Black criminal attorney Johnnie Cochran—the regular cast of Seinfeld was all-White, as were *Friends* and *Home Improvement.* The White characters on these shows revealed much about their personal lives to each other and the audience; this is of course a principal source of humor. For this reason, we will mainly but not exclusively restrict comparisons to dramatic shows.

For the other data set, we used the same coding scheme on a two-week sample of the ten most popular shows for Black audiences. Broadcast in the late spring of 1998, these included two episodes from each of the following shows: *Cosby, Good News, In the House, Living Single, Malcolm and Eddie, Moesha, Sister, Sister, Smart Guy, Steve Harvey,* and *The Wayans Brothers,* for a total of seventy-six interactions.[17] (Note the absence of a dramatic show in this list; at century's end there had never been a successful drama series primarily about Blacks, though a new series produced by Steven Bochco— *City of Angels*— debuted in 2000.)

One goal of our quantitative analysis of these interactions is to expose unusual counter-examples that stand out from and thus help define what is taken for granted, what ordinarily remains imperceptible. As Hall has pointed out, "The really significant item may not be the one which continually recurs, but one which stands out as an exception from the general pattern—but which is *also* given, in its exceptional context, the greatest weight."[18]

Racial Divides

One finding stands out immediately from looking at the broad patterns in the data: the content of entertainment television reflects a real-life racial divide, constructing a world that limits development of interracial comity using a number of structural and symbolic conventions. For example, table 9.1 reveals that though they represent slightly less than 40 percent of the program time analyzed, dramatic programs account for 76 percent of all Black–White interaction time. This is largely because a significant part of the action in most sitcoms takes place within private homes where television plies close to the shores of segregated reality. Dramatic shows are set within public institutions—police or hospital organizations—where the reality of nonprivate life intrudes on a regular basis and where Blacks and Whites are much more likely to be thrown together. Nevertheless, in shows favored by White audiences, the interchanges between Blacks and Whites are restricted by unequal power relationships: over two-thirds of interracial exchanges are between characters in superior/subordinate roles. In *NYPD Blue*, for example, the majority of interracial scenes are between Arthur Fancy, a Black lieutenant, and his White charges; in *ER* they take place between Peter Benton, a Black resident, and a White intern.

By contrast, just 28 percent of White–White interactions in dramatic shows are between characters in positions of unequal organizational power.

Table 9.1 Power Relationship by Audience and Genre

| Relationship | Interracial Relationships (White Shows) | | White Relationships (White Shows) | | Interracial Relationships (Black Shows) |
	Sitcoms[a]	Dramas[b]	Sitcoms	Dramas	Sitcoms
Peer	68.3%	24.1%	98.9%	72.3%	51.3%
Hierarchical	31.7	75.9	1.1	27.7	48.7

[a]24 percent of total interaction time
[b]76 percent

This is perhaps not unexpected, but what is remarkable and striking is that Blacks now hold the upper hand in these mediated relationships, a finding explored further below.

Organizational hierarchy explains the formal, correct tone of interracial relationships: in over half, verbal exchanges confine themselves to the task at hand and are marked by emotional distance and reserve. This is not to suggest a robot-like conversational mode. Four in ten of such interactions involve spontaneous verbal exchange, joking, and unspoken understanding, but such comparative looseness works within the bounds of the common assignment they share. In only a small fraction (6 percent) of the verbal exchanges do the Black characters reveal much about themselves beyond what they need to discharge their formal responsibilities. In *ER*, for example, Benton, the Black chief resident (played by Eriq LaSalle) holds a barrier of reticence against the often emotional protestations of his White intern.

The greater number of peer interactions between White characters opens up much more space for individuation: 44 percent of the White characters reveal something personal about themselves to set the context for their professional relationships. For example, in contrast to their Black supervisor (played by James McDaniel), the working detectives in *NYPD Blue* regularly allude to their personal relationships—former wives, troubles with current relationships, drinking problems, and the like.

The verbal reserve in interracial scenes is echoed in the restriction of dramatic action to task—catching crooks, healing trauma victims, making a sale. Over eight in ten interactions center on the task at hand. In only 12 percent do the interracial pairs make reference to future or past nonwork activity (going out to eat, attending a party, having a drink, etc.), and in only 3 percent of the interactions does the camera actually follow them into a nonwork setting. Contrast this with the 19 percent of the dramatic interactions in which White characters share their personal lives with each other. In other words, Whites are six times more likely to involve themselves personally than are interracial pairs.

Because dramatic action centers on the resolution of problems, decisionmaking makes up much of the action in these shows. Here is where we find a potential seedbed of comity, as Blacks and Whites work together to consider problems and solutions. Little more than half of cross-racial interaction involves scenes in which the characters make decisions. In these, however, hierarchy preempts negotiation, as the majority—58 percent—are arrived at by the decision of the character in charge. Of the remainder, about a quarter are shared and the rest negotiated. Thus the conventions of authority and hierarchy erode the basis for shared decisionmaking and the potential for expression beyond formal role requirements.

One could argue that it is plausible and reasonable for professionals and workers to confine most of their action and conversation to the task at hand in a workplace setting. Thus one could not attribute this formality strictly to the delicacy of interracial issues. But there is additional evidence for a racial wariness in cross-gender relations. The majority of interracial scenes are between characters of the same sex, about 57 percent. Approximately one-third are between mixed-sex pairs, with about 11 percent in scenes where a Black character addresses two or more mixed-sex Whites. Table 9.2 shows, however, that when the Black character is male, there is a very strong likelihood that the White is male as well. Over 70 percent of cross-racial interactions for Black males are with White males and only two in ten are with White females. The pattern reverses for Black females. Here more than half are with White males.

This pattern holds regardless of the authority held by the Black character: no matter whether in a (formally) superior, equal, or subordinate position, Black females appear in the majority of cross-gender interracial exchanges. The pattern is especially pronounced when the character is in a subordinate position. Among these, nearly seven in ten of Black females speak to White males, but only 11 percent of subordinate Black males speak to White females. While it is true that more than two-thirds of all interracial scenes include Black men, this does not explain why most intergender relations are between Black women and White men. There are, after all, a sub-

Table 9.2 Interracial Relationship by Gender

	Shows Popular with Whites		Shows Popular with Blacks	
	Black Male	*Black Female*	*Black Male*	*Black Female*
White female	21.1%	57.9%	18.2%	38.1%
	(30)	(33)	(10)	(8)
White male	69.7	26.3	78.2	52.4
	(99)	(15)	(43)	(11)
White male and female	9.2	15.8	3.6	9.5
	(13)	(9)	(2)	(2)
Total	100.0%	100.0%	100.0%	100.0%
	(142)	(57)	(55)	(21)

Note: Figures in parentheses represent numbers of cases.

stantial number of White female characters in these shows. Here the remnants of an apparent taboo against Black male / White female couplings may be operating: when Black males speak to a White, it is usually to a White male. Table 9.2 also includes the sample of shows popular with Black audiences. The same pattern is evident as well, though the nearly 3:1 ratio is reduced to about 2:1.

The story lines in these programs do not constrain the development of intimacy among Whites, however. Despite the limitations imposed by format—forty-four-minute dramatic shows that intertwine several developing narratives—intimate relations between White characters of both genders develop as a matter of course, even as hierarchy inhibits intimacy and even casual involvement between races.

Utopian Hierarchy and Distance

Whereas patterns of relationships in the early years of television mirrored American society—Blacks subordinate to Whites—the latest pattern also reveals hierarchy, *but in utopian reversal:* over 70 percent of Black characters have professional or management positions. These are solo roles, however, in which the Black character has few Whites in precisely the same hierarchical position with whom to enjoy peer relationships. In fact, hierarchical patterns account for two-thirds of interracial interactions in the programs popular with Whites. Of these interactions, a little more than four in ten of the superior roles are held by Blacks, about a quarter by Whites, and the rest feature peer relationships.

Strict role-governed behavior raises a barrier to interracial personal involvement. Indeed, as the interpretive analysis below shows, formal roles become so symbolically invested for Black characters that informal relaxation of rules is rare and thus clearly noticeable when it does appear. Although sitcoms loosen these barriers somewhat, they follow the pattern established in dramatic fare, where Blacks are far more heavily represented. Even in the virtually all-White *Friends,* one of the male leads has a Black boss who briefly appears a single time to berate the quality of his work. In *Home Improvement,* the White lead's Black boss also appears once in a longer sequence to pressure him into giving up time with his wife to entertain a visiting client. This reversal of traditional stereotypes reflects the polarizing tendencies of racial prototypes, here the Black characters (on the positive pole) being significantly more industrious, disciplined, and responsible than their irresponsible White charges.

Table 9.3 Interracial Relationship Type by Audience and Genre

	Shows Popular with Whites			Shows Popular with Blacks
	Sitcoms	*Dramas*	*All*	
Black superior to white	24.4%	47.5%	42.7%	13.2
	(10)	(75)	(85)	(10)
Peer	68.3	24.1	33.2	48.7
	(28)	(38)	(66)	(37)
Black subordinate to white	7.3	28.5	24.1	38.2%
	(3)	(45)	(48)	(29)
Percent of total interactions	20.6%	79.4%	100.0%	100.0%
	(41)	(158)	(199)	(76)

Note: Figures in parentheses represent numbers of cases.

Perhaps because comedic devices are less appropriate as modes of distancing, dramatic shows maintain boundaries between Blacks and Whites by using organizational hierarchy. Consider the patterns in table 9.3: Compared to the relatively equal footing of Blacks and Whites in sitcoms, dramatic fare reverses the pattern with three-quarters of the cross-racial interactions between characters in unequal power positions. This is precisely the opposite of White interaction in dramatic shows, where nearly three-quarters are between characters who are essentially peers. In fact, bosses are by definition usually outsiders to the community created within the workplace scenarios. So the image of the Black as boss is a utopian reversal that manages at the same time to keep Blacks outside the community of understanding and interest around which most plots revolve. Consider *NYPD Blue,* for example, where the majority of dramatic action takes place among two female and four male detectives who are comparative equals. These characters know something about each other's private lives—romances, bouts with alcoholism, failed marriages, and the like—which not only weaves the plots together but also permits the audience an insight into their professional work: why they react the way they do to particular criminals, to professional rivals, and of course to each other. The interaction of these characters with their chief is not dictated by distant formality; far from it. But their personal lives rarely intertwine with that of their superior, making their professional relationships with their peers the principal source of personal familiarity.

In *ER,* several Black characters work as doctors and nurses. They make up a miniature hierarchy of superiors and subordinates within the hospital—from a Black female chief surgeon down through the nurses' aides who work in the emergency room. But once again, their relationships to their White counterparts remain within the confines of their professional duties.

In dramatic shows, hierarchy is even more pervasive when gauged by the involvement of star characters: nearly two-thirds of interracial interactions in dramatic action center on these recurring Black characters. In these, about seven of ten Blacks appear in roles superior to Whites. For example, in *NYPD Blue* the majority of interracial interaction is through the Black lieutenant in charge, and in *ER* the Black lead is a head resident whose charge is a White intern. About one-third of interracial relationships in sitcoms suggest or actually depict some involvement beyond the job. In dramatic series, the percentage falls to 11 percent. This meager intimacy results from the formal distancing of hierarchy, but also from making Black dramatic characters significantly more solemn and taciturn than Whites about their jobs and life in general.

As one might expect, hierarchy defeats verbal expression of intimacy, defined here as self-disclosure by the Black character. Formal, role-bound exchanges are the rule in two-thirds of interracial relationships where Blacks appear as superiors to Whites, matched by 60 percent of those in which Blacks are subordinated to Whites. The pattern is the same but even more pronounced for relationships beyond the workplace, the second informal route available for involvement. Data on these interactions are displayed in appendix tables A.12 and A.13. Here over 90 percent of involvement between interracial pairs of unequal power is confined to the task at hand. Among peers (those with equal power), about two-thirds are limited to task.

Well over 90 percent of interracial hierarchical relationships are confined to task performance, no matter whether the Black character is in a superior or a subordinate position. Hierarchy defeats intimacy, whether indicated by self-disclosure or involvement beyond the workplace, whether in interracial pairings or in exchanges between Whites. Put simply, the patterns here show that peer relationships are necessary for full-blooded character development of the sort necessary to go beyond the idealized traits that define social prototypes.

The pattern of polite interracial distance is so prevalent in entertainment television that a counter-example is surprising and refreshing. For example, in one episode of *NYPD Blue,* a Black detective shares information about a corrupt correctional officer with the two male lead detectives,

Sipowicz and Simone. Although the casual friendship is confined to their roles as crime fighters, the emotional effect is striking because of the contrast with the reserve that is so common in the ordinary interactions of the detectives and their Black supervisor. Such is also the case in *ER* where Benton, the Black resident, maintains a chilly distance from the puppy-like enthusiasm of a Waspy intern on the pretext that medical professionalism does not admit any relaxation of formality. In one episode the resident (who has been criticized for his distant bedside manner) holds the hand of an unconscious, dying AIDS patient and begins to weep. This exception stands out because it is so rare; it violates the audience's expectations for the stoic physician.

Prototypes and Boundary Maintenance

Allowing for the restrictions imposed by roles invested with formal authority, there remains a layer of scrupulous responsibility in Black characters that is not explained strictly by dramatic convention nor by the codes of realism. Prototype theory would predict that for the few Black characters who appear in these programs to surmount the tendency of a White audience to reduce their identity to negative stereotypes, they would need to renounce virtually all symbolic traces of Blackness and embody those characteristics associated with White virtue.

In *NYPD Blue*, for example, the characters work within a culture of professional excellence and detachment. In this setting, the Black lieutenant (Fancy) is a picture of repose, calm, and control. Everything goes more or less smoothly. But there is little or no personal interaction between him and the other characters, whose routinely observed private lives outside the workplace reveal weakness and moral lapses. The lieutenant surmounts this merely human stratum where he remains largely opaque, all-knowing, smooth, capable. Recognizing the limitations of a small sample of episodes from each particular show, we consulted an Internet database summary of every story line for this series, a total of 110 shows from its inception in 1993 through 1998.[19] Although the database does not provide the actual script, it includes detailed summaries that reveal the focal characters and the strands of the plot lines. Of these 110 episodes, only eight put the lieutenant at the center of dramatic action where some personal aspect of his life is revealed. Of these, half touch on his home life and half his professional life. Regardless of venue, however, most are founded on the stereotyped themes of dysfunctional Black families and Black drug abuse. One plot involves Fancy's foster son who is returned to his natural mother after she completes a detox program; in another episode aired two years later, the foster child appears again, this time as a suspect charged with possession of a kilo of heroin. (The work-related episodes focus on the racial tensions between Sipowicz and the lieutenant, two shows that involve Fancy's brother, also a policeman, who has racial troubles with his commanding officer, and an episode in which Fancy and his wife are pulled over for having a broken taillight.) In these comparatively rare personal glimpses into Fancy's life, a sympathetic image emerges of a soft-spoken, sacrificing, stolid human being whose professional excellence works tirelessly against an implicit racial gradient. The racism is, however, located in lapsed and weak Whites rather than in the institutions themselves. Fancy is, after all, the man in charge, an exemplar of quiet resolute excellence to be sure, but one somehow distanced and remote, an inevitable product of carrying the weight for a racial category.

In *ER*, the White doctors in general exude an air of insouciance and relaxed confidence, which occasionally leads to lapses of professional responsibility. In one example, the mainly Black emergency staff nurses and paramedics interrupt two White doctors talking about the promotion of a doctor to chief resident to remind them of their duties to a trauma patient. The preppy White intern, who is the Black surgical resident's charge, wanders into the operating theater with a bemusement that belies the fact that he is unprepared for the procedure. In one episode he mistakes throat surgery for chest surgery and is punished by Benton by having to hold up the patient's arm for the duration of the operation. In another episode, Benton has a running argument with the White intern about his arriving late from a vacation. They go outside to get sandwiches. In contrast to Benton's request for a turkey sandwich on wheat bread (no mayo), the intern orders a Polish sausage with cheese. The Black resident's example of restraint and good health is met with casual disdain by his preppy charge. Through all of this the Black surgeon maintains a sullen reserve and a steely professionalism, even as he learns he has been possibly infected with HIV transmitted by a (Black) nurse with whom he has been having an affair. Despite his discipline and hard work, this deviation from the path of White virtue serves as a reminder of his precarious position as a symbolic inversion of the Black prototype. His weeping over the dying AIDS patient foreshadows his own vulnerability to the infection.

Our sample of these popular shows is intended to detect broad patterns across all genres. Nevertheless, when an interesting exception to a pattern surfaces, it is worth teasing out its implications. One such important exception occurred during the 1999 season of *ER* when the Peter Benton character had a romantic fling with a White British doctor played by British actress Alex Kingston. It is noteworthy that *ER* is the only fictional show that makes the top twenty ratings for both Blacks and Whites, a market position that may have eased the producers' decision to break the barrier.

The female doctor is the aggressor in the relationship but Benton resists for a time because of the trouble he anticipates the interracial relationship will bring. He succumbs, however, and the two wind up on camera in bed with each other, a notable and ground-breaking event for prime-time television.[20] The relationship ends, however, because the Benton character decides he needs to devote more of his limited personal time to his deaf, out-of-wedlock son.

In fact, Eriq LaSalle, the actor who plays the role of Benton, insisted to the executive producer and writers that the relationship end because he felt it perpetuated the stereotype of a professional Black man pursuing a White woman. In his view, in his perception of the dominant audience's reactions, it sent the message that a Black man could only have a stable relationship with a White woman, since his character's prior relationships had all ended badly. As LaSalle put it, "We have to take care of the message that we're sending as African Americans . . . that we have the exact same type of exchanges with our mates that we get to see our White counterparts have" (*Washington Post,* 9 April 1999, p. B1). LaSalle also reported on audience reaction to the romance: a flood of angry viewer mail in response not to the romance itself but its demise.

There are several interesting implications in this controversy. One is of course the sensation created by the event, which stands out precisely because of its rarity. Dozens of newspapers published stories on this fictional relationship. A *Guardian* columnist commenting on the relationship's termination noted: "In this respect Britain is different. Half of British-born Caribbean men, a third of Caribbean women and a third of Asian men are in relationships with White partners. . . . Not surprising then that mixed-race relationships in British soaps are commonplace and, if anything, same-race relationships between black characters have in recent times become something of a rarity (*Guardian,* 29 March 1999, Features p. 6).

The *ER* plot line is also noteworthy for its precedent-setting example that suggests to cautious producers and writers that they do not risk alienating a large prime-time audience by depicting interracial romances. It may be that familiarity with the Benton character had finally overcome the tendencies of many White viewers to racial prototyping. In other words, many Whites may have come to see Benton—recalling our hierarchy of ideal trait attainment—as a normal (not liminal) person, one who happened to be Black, rather than one whose identity derived primarily from racial membership. Still, the White audience's apparent acceptance of Benton may also have depended on the character's perfectionist qualities that rendered him better in most professional respects than the White colleagues in his dramatic midst, a "Whiter-than-White" prototype. In this sense he became similar to Bill Cosby and other supremely successful and rare cases such as Oprah Winfrey and Michael Jordan.

Further study is needed to resolve these competing interpretations. One suggests an extension of the group contact hypothesis, a test of the idea that it may indeed be possible for Whites to enlarge their racial sympathies by attending to compelling fictional programming as in the *Roots* phenomenon of the 1970s. The other suggests another affirmation of prototype theory where the Benton character may have become (symbolically) irrelevant as an example of Black men in the eyes of many in the White audience, as was true for White perceptions of *Cosby*.[21]

So much for audience perceptions. As for the production side of this case, we also interviewed one of the principal writers for the program and for these specific episodes, Dr. Neil Baer. Dr. Baer is noteworthy not only for his medical degree but also for his graduate training in the sociology of culture at Harvard. Believing strongly that even fictional programming influences audiences, he was sensitive to the wider racial meanings of the Benton character and to the large multiracial audience for *ER*. Baer and the other writers substituted the interracial romance for the contentious, interracial professional relationship between Benton and Carter, the preppy intern. Here the writers strove to cast against type, in one program, for example, making a gangbanger White and his victim Black. The intent was to challenge and defy audience expectations and to enlarge their sympathies, though Dr. Baer did not elaborate on this choice beyond commenting that he thought these twists would be "interesting." Similar to our reading of Benton's exquisite discipline and industriousness as a hindrance to the fuller development of his character, Baer regarded Benton's perfectionism as a character flaw that prevented his having a normal life. Nevertheless, Baer continued,

Benton was not exceptional in this regard, for the other doctors' personal lives were disrupted by their work. Perhaps so, but the distinguishing feature of Benton is his steely reserve, sufficient alone for retarding any bonding with his male colleagues. Once again, the exception that makes the normal pattern visible is the one interracial romance. This single but noteworthy case could represent one of those events that may in hindsight prove to be a leading cultural indicator of a significant change in media producers' attitudes and perhaps in the audience. The test is of course its evolution from what is regarded as exceptional and daring to what British audiences regard as normal and barely noteworthy.

Exceptions are always interesting, but more important are the background patterns they reveal. Those patterns show Blacks largely isolated from the White characters by virtue of their superior organizational status, their elevated position enhancing the symbolic qualities of their racial identity. They thus take on the exaggerated attributes of characters similar to those in a morality play or allegory. This is doubly likely in the current political climate where Black failures are attributed less to genetic inferiority and more to individual failures of effort and moral fiber. Inflected as they are with this symbolic freighting, they act less as interesting, complex characters than as inverted prototypes: they incarnate the pure values of the dominant culture in a body and with a skin color usually associated with the opposite. In so doing they fail to develop the qualities that might make them fully dimensional humans like the real-world Whites the majority audience knows.

Conclusion

Hierarchy has multiple functions in entertainment television. It provides symbolic affirmative action that casts Blacks in superior roles that exaggerate their real-life success, even as it erects a formal barrier to cross-racial engagement. But hierarchy is also an inevitable product of changes in White racial attitudes interacting with the political economy of television broadcasting. These create the dynamics that would seem to account for the kinds of Black characters who, by embodying prototypically White traits like discipline, restraint, quiet competence, and industry, seem to reach acceptability in prime-time television.

A convergence of theory and research from a number of disparate fields accounts for the dominant images we find in entertainment television. From prototype theory we learn that prototypes are unconscious embodiments of stereotypical traits that make up a socially constructed category. Thus a "respectable Black," such as Colin Powell or Bill Cosby, is the refinement of a White middle-class prototype, a collection of traits that embody a set of culturally dominant consensual values. On the other hand, Tupac Shakur, Louis Farrakhan, and (the postarrest) O.J. Simpson are prototypes of dangerous Blacks, the embodiment of polar opposite traits. The characteristics embodying respectability are "Whiteness," which may explain why Whites do not regard respectable Blacks as typical of their race. This is confirmed by research on the polarization of perception of members of out-groups—the best are seen as better than the best in the in-group, but the worst are seen as worse than comparable insiders[22]—and by Jhally and Lewis's findings on how Whites' perceptions of Bill Cosby did not change their fundamental views of Blacks in general.[23]

As the rationales of dominance have shifted from those of nature to nurture, it is not surprising that African Americans now appear more frequently in popular dramatic series than in comedies, a reversal from the early decades of television when highly rated series such as *Amos 'n' Andy, Beulah*, and the *Jack Benny Show* featured characters that played upon White beliefs in inherent Black servitude.[24] Current racial ideology, rooted as it is in individual effort, is a humorless project, doubly so, ironically, because of a tendency to restrict public discourse on issues of ethnicity and race to polite but ultimately disengaged exchanges that suppress true feelings. There are exceptions, of course, such as the occasional racial flare-up between Sipowicz and Fancy on *NYPD Blue*. Sipowicz, however, represents a vestige of explicit, White, non-Wasp working-class racism rather than the more prevalent unacknowledged resentment and ambivalence among most Whites.[25] The tacit conspiracy of silence maintains the racial gulf, real and mediated.

While the broad patterns in this study reveal both structural and symbolic impediments to the growth of racial comity, prime-time entertainment does register Black progress up the cultural hierarchy to liminality and, in the best cases, normality. While projecting a well-meaning idealization where Whites report to Blacks may create a small reservoir of good feeling among Blacks and liberal Whites, it also shuts off a comparatively cost-free source of racial comity. It imposes a hierarchical distance on interracial relations that hobbles the enlargement of sympathetic imagination, although we caution that this point draws upon only *ER* and *NYPD Blue*.

Unfortunately, this appears unlikely to change as television executives make programming and casting decisions under growing competitive pressure. Competition initially encouraged the traditional Big Three networks (ABC, CBS, NBC) to cast more Blacks. In part this reflected the disproportionate share of the viewing audience that is Black.[26] Based on their perceptions of a shrinking and increasingly polarized racial market, programming executives are, with few exceptions, targeting more homogeneous audience segments and thus contributing to a more racially segregated culture.[27] Beyond this, the programs targeted especially to Black audiences, mostly farcical sitcoms, may have the unintended consequence of confirming stereotypes for the many Whites who come across them.

Thus market pressures have prodded leaders of the traditional broadcast networks to reach out to increasingly affluent (and therefore) White audiences, whom they perceive as preferring largely segregated entertainment. Consider the remarks of Sandy Grushow, president of 20th Century Fox Television: "I don't think anybody's crying out for integrated shows. By pursuing advertisers and demographics rather than a mass audience, the networks have declared they don't need Blacks in their audience."[28]

Black producers contend that crossover audiences exist for rap music and professional basketball, so the real problem is that of marketing. Ralph Farquhar, producer of *Moesha* and *South Central* argues, "There's crossover if there's an effort to create the exposure. It's a marketing problem. But they don't want to do it. So there's a chitlin circuit on TV."[29] The perception among Black producers is that times have changed, even from the 1980s when the *Cosby* show and its spinoff *A Different World* drew White audiences. The executive producer of *A Different World*, a show that addressed serious social issues, drew this comparison: "There was a kind of freedom that existed then that doesn't exist on the networks now. . . . If I pitched that show today, I'd be laughed out of the room. It's a different time."[30] Economic impetus collided with political duress in early 2000, when the major broadcast networks—faced with the threat of a boycott by the NAACP—agreed to feature more Black actors in prime time. Political pressure will thus continue to operate alongside short-term economic incentive and long-standing cultural habit in shaping network entertainment's racial imagery.

ELEVISION COMMERCIALS are leading cultural indicators. There are no people more expert in a society's cultural values and taboos than those who create television advertisements. And every year, most Americans see many thousands of their products: television commercials lasting from ten to sixty seconds. Although this experience would once have yielded almost no impressions of African Americans, Black persons now appear regularly in commercials playing a variety of roles. The quintessential manifestation of twentieth-century consumer culture once affirmed the racial inferiority of Blacks either through exclusion or demeaning stereotype. By century's end it presented a patina of inclusion and equality. More than news or prime-time entertainment, a summary view of advertising offers seemingly compelling evidence that Blacks have attained cultural parity with Whites.

In our interviews, we found that interpersonal *contact* between members of the two racial groups is a vital force in shaping attitudes and feelings. Contacts of duration, depth, and equality can bring about racial understanding; contacts of the opposite sort have little potential beyond confirming existing fears and stereotypes. And commercials are all about human contact. They typically show people relating to each other in and through the consumption of products. The purpose of these scenarios is to create an emotional bond, a contact and then a connection between characters in the ad and its viewers / consumers. This chapter explores the racial dimensions of contact images in commercials.[1]

As throughout the book, we are not claiming that viewing these images has a massive impact on Whites. But we do believe ads provide uniquely appropriate indicators of the culture's racial heartbeat. In pursuing public notice for its clients' wares, it is possible that advertising agencies, which are nothing if not creative, could be stretching cultural limits, exercising a potential to nudge Whites toward racial comity. Treating Blacks and Whites equivalently, showing them in comfortable contact across and within racial groups, could both reflect and spur such progress. On the other hand, a fear

162

of controversy and a cleaving to the conventional could be leading the agencies to create messages that subtly reinforce the mainstream culture's racial divisions and apprehensions.

As Corner puts it, ads link products in varying degrees of directness with "established forms of goodness."[2] The goal of television advertisers is "value transfer," from the feeling tone of the ad to the product itself. To put a finer point on the concept of "goodness," we again invoke the work of anthropologist Mary Douglas[3] on the concepts of purity and pollution. This research provides theoretical purchase on the deeper cultural strands that may weave a constraining web upon the images of African Americans, even as Blacks attain increasing media prominence. As we have discussed, Blacks hold liminal status, moving in transition along the continuum from contaminated and contained to a more acceptable status. Since the delegitimization of overt racism during the 1950s and 1960s, Blacks seem neither fully rejected nor wholly accepted, neither categorized identically with Whites in a color-blind American community nor universally linked to a rigidly demarcated domain of pollution and danger.

Although the culture has progressed substantially, it still underscores racial categories in many ways, and the very act of categorization establishes an implicit hierarchy, according to Malkki: "Thus, species, type, race, and nation can all be seen in this context as forms of categorical thought which center upon the purity of the categories in question. They, all of them, tend to construct and essentialize difference. But more, such categorical types also operate to naturalize and legitimate inequality. In the most extreme case, the construction of one category may imply the denaturalization and even dehumanization of another."[4]

Does television advertising enact a symbolic spectrum between Whiteness and Blackness, situating Whites, the dominant group, closer to the region of the pure ideal and Blacks to a liminal realm that borders on the polluting and dangerous? Or are members of the two groups depicted equivalently? Do the many images of Blacks in commercials now hint that dividing people into racial categories is incorrect and morally wrong, spurring the groups toward acceptance, even closeness across a racial line finally receding in significance?

Images of contact undermine the validity and challenge the naturalness of racial classification, separation, and hierarchy. As suggested in our examination of prime-time entertainment in chapter 9, the absence of contact sends the opposite message. To measure contact, we look for images connoting closeness and trust among individuals on screen, or between them and the viewer. Thus closeness would be marked by direct physical contact between actors. Trust would be indicated by an investment of authority in a character who communicates with the audience; measures here would focus on the engagement of the actors with the audience, directly as in speaking and indirectly as indicated by the importance of their roles. Measuring the amount of interracial contact, and the degree to which contact *within* each group reaches equal levels for Blacks and Whites, also illuminates how far cultural change with respect to race has progressed. In addition, advertising should reflect any cultural idealization of Whiteness by drawing distinctions among African Americans, treating those of relatively lighter skin tone differently from those who are darker.[5]

Sample and Coding

We analyzed commercials from one week of prime-time programming on ABC and one on the Fox network, along with two weeks on NBC, yielding a total sample of 1,620 codeable ads.[6] No significant differences between these three networks appeared.[7] Eliminating 147 spots with East Asian actors and three where race of the actors could not be identified reduced the sample used in most analyses to 1,470.[8] The sample was designed to measure dominant cultural patterns and to reflect the viewing experience of an audience member tuned to prime-time programming. Thus we analyzed an *ad appearance* rather than an ad. In other words, if a particular spot for, say, Sears appeared five times during the sampled prime-time programming, its images were coded and added to the data set five times. The data do not include 1,470 distinct commercials, but 1,470 appearances of ads since many ran more than once.[9] This sampling method was checked extensively against the alternative of counting each different commercial just once, and the one chosen seemed best.[10]

We assume that prime time is the showcase of mainstream culture, but that advertising might alter as programmers head out toward the niches to address narrower audience tastes. The analysis therefore also encompasses samples of sports programming, MTV, and Black Entertainment Television (BET).[11] These supplements to the main sample allow us to explore exactly how flexible the culture is. To take an obvious example, if the taboo against interracial physical intimacy ever gets violated, we might expect to find the exceptions in cable programming for niche audiences like the youth-oriented MTV or Black-oriented BET rather than in the plain sight of broadcast prime time.

To be coded, a commercial had to depict at least one racially identifiable human character and promote a service or product other than a television program or theatrical feature.[12] Codes for contact among characters included intimate skin contact (a romantic, affectionate, or sexy caressing or nuzzling), as in razor commercials where a woman strokes a man's just-shaved face; speaking on screen to another character of the same race; hugging; or kissing. Contact between characters and the audience was measured by coding the race of characters appearing or speaking first or last on screen; in close-up or as a hand model; speaking to and / or instructing the audience in direct address; or in a manner emphasizing sexuality. A description of the coding protocol appears at <http://www.raceandmedia.com>.[13]

Rising Numbers and Declining Stereotypes

Most previous research has focused on the relative paucity of Black actors in commercials and on stereotypes in the specific representations of African Americans. Our findings indicate a new era. Of the entire 1,620 prime-time ad sample, 952 or 58.8 percent featured only Whites while just fifty-three depicted Blacks alone (3.3 percent). But the full sample of 1,620 did include fully 465 ads featuring both Blacks and Whites (28.7 percent), and 147 more (9.1 percent) with actors of an East Asian facial cast (most of them also showing Whites and / or Blacks), so prime-time television advertisers could reasonably claim to represent a wide swath of America's ethnic diversity. Coding did not yield significant differences in such stereotyping images as performing to music or playing sports. It became apparent after coding the first week of prime-time programming that relatively few ads showing these actions appeared, and when they did, it was usually in integrated scenes. Thus we found overt conventional stereotyping diminished.

Luxuries and the Single-Race Commercial

If advertisements provide unspoken indicators of genuine but obscured cultural truths, we might predict significant contrasts in the precise nature of Blacks' and Whites' appearances, actions and interactions. First, then, we compared all-Black with all-White commercials. We expected the former typically to tout necessities, rather than luxury or fantasy-arousing prod-

Chapter Ten

ucts. The latter usually allude to the realm of ideals and purity, and their texts tend to include more images of contact with the audience or between on-screen characters (such as in romantic perfume commercials). We suspected that Blacks rarely take center stage in commercials where positive value transfer and ideal arousal is the primary pitch; when they star in ads, they usually hawk products with practical value in daily life. It is in ads for products that are luxurious, frivolous, or fantasy-related that positive value transfer may be especially important for advertisers, because they cannot hope to sell the goods simply by giving mundane information about how well it satisfies utilitarian needs. In the 545 commercials for luxury / fantasy products (including perfume, cars, and credit cards), only six featured an all-Black cast—whereas 385 were all-White. This ratio of 64:1 lends support to our suspicion that commercials tend to treat Blacks and Whites differently. The contrast is illustrated in figure 10.1 below. Ads where Blacks' presence is unmistakable—because they are the only people visible—rarely appear when the product is designed to arouse fantasies of the ideal self, the ideal world.[14] Most of the all-Black ads promote items in the necessity category: groceries, household items, food, and drugs. Generally, these are the less-expensive products as well. Nacos and Hritzuk, in their study of print and television ads, found a parallel association between the nature of the product and the presence of all-Black or all-White casts: "Ads that promote expensive merchandise are likely to depict Whites only, while ads offering lower

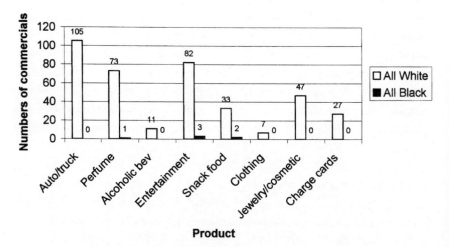

Figure 10.1 All-Black and All-White Luxury and Fantasy Product Ads

cost items are more likely to show models of both races or Blacks only."[15] The data may also be read as indicating that among the total of 952 all-White ads in the sample, 385 or about 40.4 percent touted luxury/fantasy products. This compares with just six ads touting such products among the fifty-three all-Black commercials in the sample, or 11.3 percent.

We discussed in chapter 9 the racial divide in television viewing habits. Networks know the demographic breakdown of their audiences from the ratings data and sell advertising time based on that information. Thus the production processes of programming and advertising are interlaced and driven by demographic information.[16] Most of the programs in our prime-time sample are more or less consciously designed with Whites as the primary (though not exclusive) audience. It is therefore not surprising that we found these patterns in White-targeted programming. There were slight differences in the advertising on programs that featured Black stars, such as *Martin*, bolstering our belief that many advertisers do pay attention to racial representation in commercials and do employ racial targeting.[17] But the more useful data on the possible influence of audience demographics arise from comparing broadcast prime time with cable's BET, which is centrally targeted to African Americans (more on this shortly).

Contact

Next we assessed the images of interpersonal contact in the commercials. We expected the ads to display images of close contact far more frequently for White than Black characters. We predicted that advertisers choose dominant group members as the normal or prototypical representative of people using and extolling products, and use them disproportionately to enact scenes of close contact. This tendency would reflect market pressures and the assumption that the majority prefers seeing other Whites in commercials. Advertisers seem to believe that Whites, at least unconsciously, identify with fellow Whites, and resonate to their on-screen relationships with each other and the touted products.[18]

The data in table 10.1 illustrate how we measured contact through the content analysis. The table displays the total numbers of ads featuring each type of contact, and the percentage these represent as a proportion of all opportunities Blacks and Whites each had to appear in these situations. Whites had 1,417 opportunities: 465 in the integrated ads and 952 in all-White commercials. Blacks received 518 opportunities: 465 in those same integrated

Chapter Ten

Table 10.1 Images of Contact among Blacks and Whites as Proportion of Opportunities in All Ads*

Race of character(s) Shown	Ads that Show Whites	% White of White opty. (n = 1,417)	Ads that show Blacks	% Black of Black opty. (n =518)	W:B Ratio
Speaking to character of same race	209	14.8%	8	1.5%	9.6
Caressing skin	105	7.4	6	1.2	6.4
Hugging	148	10.4	15	2.9	3.6
Kissing	59	4.2	6	1.2	3.6
As hand model	669	47.2	51	9.8	4.8
First on screen	1274	89.9	118	22.8	4.0
Speaking last	723	51.2	78	15.1	3.4
Speaking first	718	50.7	88	17.0	3.0
Last on screen	1340	94.6	191	36.9	2.6
Speaking to audience	478	33.7	75	14.5	2.3
Receiving close-ups	753	53.1	127	24.5	2.2
Instructing audience	389	27.4	67	12.9	2.1
Sexualized	136	9.6	27	5.2	1.8
Total	6,865	Avg. 4.9/ad	830	Avg. 1.6/ad	3.0

Note: All differences between percent Black of Black opportunities and percent White of White opportunities (e.g., between 1.2 percent and 7.4 percent with respect to caressing) are statistically significant beyond p = 0.001, except for sexualization (p = 0.08).

*Opportunities in column 5 are calculated for Blacks as the total of all-Black plus Black–White integrated ads; for Whites in column 3 as the total of all-White plus Black–White integrated ads. Ads in which East Asians appear are omitted.

Black–White ads and 53 in all-Black ads. Overall, Whites had nearly three times more opportunities to be shown in contact with each other or with the audience than Blacks.

The first four rows of table 10.1 display the four measures of characters' contact with each other, within the scenario of the commercial; the rest show the measures we deem to tap closeness of contact with the audience. The bottom row of the table gives a kind of overview of what we'll call "contact images," while suggesting the relative peripherality of Blacks' roles. The 518 ads with Black actors featured an average of 1.6 contact images of African Americans. Yet the 1,417 ads in which Whites appeared included an average of nearly five (4.9) contact images. Thus White characters in commercials were about three times more likely to appear in contact with each other or with viewers than Blacks, even controlling for the larger number of appearances (opportunities) Whites had.

The table lists variables in descending order of the White to Black *appearance ratio*. For example, the first row in the table shows data for speaking to a same-race character. About 14.8 percent of all commercials in which Whites appeared showed one White talking to another; the comparable figure for Blacks conversing with another Black is 1.5 percent. This produces the ratio shown in the last column of the row of 9.6 (14.8 / 1.5), meaning Whites were 9.6 times more likely than Blacks to engage in this form of contact. After controlling for the many more opportunities Whites had, they still appeared almost ten times more often speaking to a same-race character than Blacks.

The appearance ratios shown in table 10.1 indicate that television advertising conveys images suggesting racial separation and hierarchy, though the disparity was greater on some dimensions than others. Images of African Americans in contact with other characters on screen—speaking to other Blacks, caressing skin, kissing, or hugging—are nearly taboo in prime-time commercials judging by the substantial differences from Whites' contact images. Just one ad (for Robitussin) accounted for half of the six times Blacks kissed, and one other kiss appeared in a public service announcement (a subgenre presumably freer of market pressures). It almost goes without saying that commercials eschewed interracial physical contact. But the very fact that we expect this marks the continued power of racial hierarchy and pollution fear. By the end of the twentieth century, to our knowledge no broadcast network television commercial had ever shown a Black adult being caressed or kissed romantically by a White. Readers might think "of course not," but this expectation—alive almost a century and a half after slavery's demise—registers the profound barriers to acceptance of racial intimacy, and thus genuine equality, embedded within the culture.

Besides portraying characters involved with each other, conveying the existence of real connection between on-screen characters, commercials can also establish a kind of contact between the characters and the viewer. Shown in the rows below the bold line in the body of table 10.1, the data here also reveal consistent racial disproportions, though not as great as for contact between characters.

The greatest disparity was in use of hand models. Nearly half of the ads (48.2 percent) featured a hand model, a shot where a hand was the main human feature on the screen. As a percentage of opportunities, White hand models appeared almost five times more than Black. The next rows of the table show that White characters were almost always among the characters shown first and last on the screen—positions likely to register strongly with viewers. Blacks were much less likely to appear in the all-important opening and closing shots, though the disproportion was greater for opening shots. Similarly, Whites had the opportunity to be the first and last characters speaking far more often than Blacks. The aspect of close contact with audiences that showed the least racial disparity was sexualization.[19] Perhaps surprisingly, Blacks were less comparatively disadvantaged on this dimension than on the others. Black actors' sexuality was highlighted in 27 showings, Whites in 136, for an appearance ratio of about 1.8:1.

So far we have emphasized the entire ensemble of 1,470 all-Black, all-White, or Black-White ads. But another revealing comparison might focus on images of Blacks and Whites in the 465 integrated ads, where Blacks' and Whites' opportunities for audience contact are equal.[20] The White:Black appearance ratios change when we isolate the integrated ads, but the outstanding impression is how consistent the disparities, and the limits on Black actors' contacts, appear. Thus, for example, for close-ups, the appearance ratio is 2.4; this compares with a ratio of 2.2 in the full prime-time sample.[21] In other words, to take an example, within integrated commercials where in theory there should be no difference in the frequency of Blacks and Whites receiving close-ups, Whites are more than twice as likely to be featured in this way—and thus to enjoy, we suggest, closer contact with audiences.

Exceptions: Sports, MTV, or BET?

We did not expect the culture as inscribed upon the racial imagery of television commercials to be monolithic. Economic incentives drive advertisers to target increasingly narrow demographic segments,[22] and we expected images to differ accordingly. Thus, we also looked outside the mainstream of prime-time television, suspecting we might find exceptions to the patterns of symbolic separation and hierarchy. In particular, we looked at commercials on the Black-dominated BET cable network and expected them to contrast most markedly with those shown on mass-oriented shows by the major broadcast networks. We also examined ads in more narrowly targeted programs, specifically (male-oriented) football spectacles and (youth-targeted) music videos (MTV), believing they would come down somewhere in between.

With the caveat that the three samples of niche programming are too small to support definitive conclusions, we turn first to sports. African

Americans provide a disproportionate share of the stars in the most highly rated broadcast sports, so it seemed possible that the commercials sandwiching the slices of athletic achievement would provide more equality of images. We found, however, that the commercials promoted virtually the same symbolic distinctions as revealed in the prime-time sample. Close contact between characters was slightly more prevalent than in prime time, though again not enough truly to breach the symbolic barriers. As to connection with audiences, Blacks were about 10 percent more likely to appear in the closer relationship positions with viewers than was true in prime time. The differences with prime time were slight, though consistently in the direction of more intimacy during sports programming. Rather than display all the data, we present in table 10.2 (columns 2 and 3) the data on all-Black commercials promoting luxury or fantasy-linked commodities during the sports broadcasts. Just three commercials out of 115 were all-Black. This is about the same as the proportion in the prime-time sample.

Turning to MTV, Gray[23] has suggested that advertisers targeting the White youth market deliberately employ symbols from the urban Black youth culture. Yet the MTV commercials did not differ radically from the main prime-time sample. Close contact among and between Whites and Blacks runs about the same as in prime time. As displayed in the fourth and fifth columns of table 10.2, the dearth of African Americans in luxury/fantasy product commercials appeared on MTV in about the same degree as on sports and prime time.

With BET we finally discovered significant differences. BET is largely

Table 10.2 Luxury/Fantasy Ads on Sports Programs, MTV, and BET

	Sports		MTV		BET	
Product	Total Luxury Ads	All-Black Luxury Ads	Total Luxury Ads	All-Black Luxury Ads	Total Luxury Ads	All-Black Luxury Ads
Auto/Truck	56	1	1	0	22	1
Perfume	0	0	19	0	5	0
Alcoholic beverage	23	0	9	0	20	11
Entertainment	4	0	29	2	16	4
Snack food	16	1	20	0	19	1
Clothing	3	1	23	0	2	1
Jewelry/Feminine products	0	0	11	0	21	9
Charge cards	13	0	1	0	1	0
Total	115	3	113	2	107	27

controlled by Blacks and reaches an audience that is 89 percent African American.[24] If any television outlet transcends the boundaries and puts Blacks and Whites on more equal footing, it should be BET. This network establishes what is possible but apparently unachieved on the White-owned and White-targeted networks. On the sampled nights, at least, BET ran a substantially higher proportion of all-Black commercials than appeared in the prime-time sample: 44 of the 207 BET ads coded, around 21 percent were all-Black (compared with 3.6 percent of the prime-time sample). All-Black ads ran at a comparatively high rate for luxury or fantasy products also; as columns 6 and 7 of table 10.2 show, around one-fourth of the 107 commercials for these products featured only African American actors. Recall that barely more than 1 percent of such ads in the other samples were all-Black.

Because we expected BET, being aimed at Black audiences, to show the most distinctive commercial images, we analyzed close contact images in the same way as for network prime time. Appendix table A.14 displays the detailed data. On BET, *the rate of contact was about the same for Blacks and Whites;* on ABC, NBC, and Fox, it was, on average, three times greater for Whites. In some dimensions, such as sexualization and speaking to the audience, Blacks enjoyed higher contact on BET than Whites. The contrast with White-dominated, White-targeted broadcast prime time is dramatic.

Interpreting the Data

Arguably, the frequent appearance in prime time of images involving close contact among Whites connotes the existence of social trust within the dominant group, setting up an implicit comparison with Blacks, who received comparatively few such depictions with other Blacks (let alone across racial lines). The difference implies racial separation and hierarchy. Thus, for example, the stark disparity in appearances of caressing, kissing, and hugging among African Americans as compared with Whites suggests advertisers' belief that many in the White audience remain troubled by images of contact with Blacks. A similar indication arises from the relative paucity of Black hand models. Advertisers targeting majority audiences may prefer not to use clearly perceptible Black hands even where a commercial includes both Whites and Blacks using a product, because, consciously or not, they fear the White audience will make associations with pollution and danger. With respect to advertising outside prime time, the results indicate that those who produce and schedule television commercials believe at some level that cultural distinctions run very deep. They suggest that ad agencies assume that predominantly White audiences—even young ones or those simultaneously seeing Blacks in positive (albeit limited) roles, as athletes or musicians—must be served the standard fare of racial imagery. In accordance with their liminal status, African Americans are acceptable in some arenas, some strictly defined roles, but not in others: as exciting gladiators on sporting fields or entertainers on rock stages, yes; as symbolically attractive and thoroughly integrated product hawkers, relatively rarely.[25]

Beyond the data already discussed are both quantitative findings not displayed in the tables and limitations in this study that almost certainly led to an underestimate of the racial disparities. As an example of the first, consider the frequent depictions of White children being hugged (n = 59) and kissed (n = 14), symbolically embraced by the culture as precious. This compared with a paucity of Black children similarly celebrated (n = 4 hugged, none kissed). On the other hand, the considerable presence of sexualized images of Blacks in prime time is both intriguing and illustrative of this study's limitations. The very forbidden, threatening, or mysterious nature of Black sexuality in the White culture may make its use in some ads attractive to advertisers, as long as those images are carefully contained—as long as the portrayal is brief and does not show interracial intimacy. Exoticism is one result of this approach toward using Black models. Thus, where darker models are used in fashion magazines, they are likely to be treated as "exotics, tribal, ethnic, not just regular people," according to the dark-skinned supermodel Iman.[26]

The data suggest that advertisers who target predominantly White audiences find it more palatable to show Blacks being sexy than acting romantic (kissing, caressing) or simply talking with each other. Depicting Blacks kissing, hugging, or speaking to each other may be more humanizing, that is, it may promote more sense of commonality with Whites than highlighting their (allegedly exceptional and thus stereotyping) sexuality. Surprising at first blush, the controlled use of images from the liminal or polluted realms is predictable from Mary Douglas's research, and from the simultaneous exploitation and fear of Black sexuality that has long pervaded White culture.[27] As the impure and dangerous embody the forbidden, they sometimes represent allure and titillation. Group stereotypes often draw upon the temptation of illicit vices: immediate gratification, recklessness, unbridled sensuality. As Douglas points out, "order implies restriction; from all possible materials a limited selection has been made and from all possible relations a limited set had been used. . . . This is why, though we seek to create order, we do not simply condemn disorder. We recognize that it is destructive to existing patterns; also that it has potentiality. It symbolizes both danger and power."[28] These modes of thinking offer dominant and subordinate groups a symbiotic realm that defines forbidden pleasure for the former and a restricted arena for achievement by the latter.

The anxious self-consciousness of advertisers' practices in this area is suggested by the attention within the industry to a single commercial run in a few local markets by Ikea, a Swedish-owned furniture company. According to Bob Garfield, ad reviewer and columnist for *Advertising Age*, this "taboo-buster" of a spot was a "daring . . . advertising breakthrough . . . a departure. . . ."[29] Garfield's year-end review of ads cited this one as the best of the year for its "understated daring. . . ."[30] This enthusiasm arose merely because the ad showed a White man apparently married to a Black woman.

Beyond this, the count of sexual images in the sample is misleading. Our coding method made no distinction in degree of sexualization. The ad showing one shirtless Black weightlifter for half a second in a montage with several other (White) actors was coded, just as was the one displaying four or five White woman in revealing garb for several seconds each. Most sexualization of Black characters was, like the first example, fleeting, frequently accompanied by a depersonalizing or even dehumanizing of the actor. For example, a commercial for Hanes women's underwear failed to depict the face and head of a sexualized Black woman; viewers saw only the briefest partial glimpse of her torso and legs. Yet several White women's pelvic areas and faces appeared in lingering shots.

The BET sample reveals that advertisers can achieve more equal patterns of Black–White images when they target majority Black audiences. On the other hand, taboos on interracial intimacy remain as inviolate on BET as elsewhere, perhaps because they would be just as controversial among Black as White viewers. And the White-dominated culture prevailed even on a network designed for Black audiences; a high proportion of BET ads entirely omitted or gave only peripheral roles to African Americans. Whites predominated in some of the most intimate images on BET commercials, such as hugging, kissing, and hand modeling.

In part, this overrepresentation of Whites even on BET is traceable to the racial political economy of advertising. Because many corporations do not invest in filming separate commercials, they show the same ones on BET as on the White-oriented networks. If Blacks constituted a large enough market for their products, presumably more corporations would invest in all-Black or Black-dominated ads. Furthermore, the type of products BET promotes may help explain the divergence in images of Blacks. The most striking contrasts were the more numerous advertisements for alcoholic drinks and the lower proportion of commercials for financial and information services on BET than in the prime-time sample. The alcohol pitches also contributed most of the sexual images and other signs of same-race contact. There were actually more alcohol ads (twenty) in this two-night sample of BET than in the entire four-week prime-time sample (eighteen). This cultural artifact recapitulated the disproportionate presence of liquor stores and the paucity of banks in African American neighborhoods.[31]

The very fact that there *is* a racial political economy of advertising reflects the kind of implicit yet powerful hierarchical categorizing that Malkki writes about. The patterns of images hint at advertisers' belief that majority group audiences notice and respond to the racial makeup of commercials. In a world without racial hierarchies and boundaries, a truly race-blind world, we might see Blacks receiving as many close-up shots and hand modeling assignments as Whites. We might even see Black hand models in otherwise all-White ads, a phenomenon that did not occur in this sample. Similarly, White audiences might occasionally view an ad montage of ten different characters wandering the aisles of, say, K-Mart, eight of whom were Black and just two White. No such commercial appeared in the sample; the majority of characters in montage ads were always White.[32] In a race-conscious culture, depicting a Black majority would risk suggesting that if White people go to a K-Mart store, they would find most customers there African American and most products appealing mainly to that group. Even where Blacks are admitted into the world of an ad, then, it seems commercials still track the racial inequalities and anxieties of the larger culture.[33] The absence of scenarios featuring Whites and Blacks contacting each other and enjoying products, in which Whites are outnumbered by Blacks, captures the culture's racial disquiet.

It also reflects the advertising industry's own racial segmentation. The industry actually has openly identified, separate ethnic "accounts." For example, *Advertising Age* reported on 7 May 1997, that K-Mart had named "an

agency of record for its estimated $5 million African American account."
The same story noted that a different agency handled K-Mart's "Hispanic
account." Other reports appear throughout this trade magazine, the "bible"
of the industry, registering the assignment of particular agencies to specifically labeled "African American" accounts. That the advertising industry
routinely segregates advertising accounts indicates that racial segmenting—
and thus racially conscious image production—are taken for granted in this
field.[34] The racialized economy of advertising has been documented in radio, whose long-standing and stark racial segmentation may foreshadow the
future of television. In that industry, there exist "no urban / Spanish dictates" and "minority discounts," meaning that many corporations instruct
their ad agencies not to advertise on stations formatted to appeal to Black
("urban") or Latino ("Spanish") audiences, and to demand steep discounts
if they do. The rationales often arise from absurd stereotypes, such as that
"Black people don't eat beef," or "Hispanics don't buy or lease cars."[35]

There are complexities in our own data that we can discuss here only
briefly. For example, using population proportion as the standard for equal
representation, one might argue that some of the findings reveal something
close to racial equivalency. Thus, in table 10.1, we find 718 ads showing a
White speaking first and 88 a Black, for a ratio of about 8:1, fairly close to
population percentages. The dominant culture now clearly signals to unre-
constructed White racists that, like it or not, African Americans are in-
escapable and at least on some levels acceptable members of U.S. society.
Over time the mere presence of blacks in commercials may challenge and
help further to reduce the traditionally racist component of the culture. On
the other hand, the absolute numbers also can be read as showing how even in
integrated ads Blacks play subordinated roles, appearing in intimate relationships less than Whites on every dimension coded. And we believe it is
these implicit comparisons, embedded in the appearance ratios, that cru-
cially reflect and connote racial hierarchy and set boundaries to the inclusiveness of the commercial world. As an example, even controlling for
numbers of appearances, a White is three times more likely than a Black to
appear in the authoritative role of introductory spokesperson. Such implicit
contrasts may naturalize unexamined assumptions of racial hierarchy.[36]

Equally important, our data underestimate the absolute disparities, because the *codes do not count numbers of characters.* In most instances, integrated ads had many more Whites than Blacks. Thus we coded an ad as

including both Blacks and Whites first on screen when the first shot in that commercial showed a group of five Whites and one Black. A commercial that showed six Whites and a Black in close-ups was coded the same as one that depicted a single White and a single Black. Had we been able to count each separate actor in each separate scene (a totally impractical assignment), absolute and relative disparities would have been far greater. The figures given here, therefore, err markedly on the conservative side. In analyzing their data on Black images in print and television advertising, Nacos and Hritzuk discovered similar disparities: "[I]n the vast majority of ads showing members of both racial groups, Whites almost always outnumbered Blacks by far and were more prominently placed. . . . [I]n almost all ads and commercials we coded as depicting Blacks and Whites, only one or two Black and *several* White persons were shown. Had we counted each Black and White person in those ads, the dominance of White faces would be far greater. . . ."[37]

Skin Color

Finally, based on a prime-time subsample, we looked at skin shade among African Americans.[38] Darkness evokes danger and dirt, so that mental associations of the color black and the words *Black person* may be negative among most Whites; certainly the color evokes notions of difference. We therefore assumed that using dark-skinned actors would create real concerns among advertisers. Blacks themselves may have internalized dominant cultural ideals in ways that make their responses to cultural stimuli such as skin color more similar to Whites than might be expected.[39] These conditions would tend to produce an unstable, uneasy compromise: the frequent use of Blacks in advertising, but perhaps under tacit rules about the skin tone as well as numbers, roles, and product associations of Blacks. An implied preference for lightness would predictably follow from the hierarchy of ideal trait attainment as suggested in chapter 3. We therefore expected that in general advertisers would prefer lighter-skinned Black actors, even if unconsciously, particularly for products pitched to audiences' fantasy, luxury, and ideal self-images.

Since lighter skin is empirically associated with higher-status occupation,[40] and high status with attainment of U.S. cultural ideals, we expected Black actors playing characters of higher status or using higher-status or ideal/fantasy products to be lighter skinned than those playing low-status roles. Because women in ads are frequent carriers of symbolic associations to purity, safety, innocence, and beauty—and women's attainment and cultural value are more strictly tied to physical traits than men's—we expected advertisers' preference for light skin to be more pronounced for females than males.[41] Similar reasons led us to suspect a similar premium on lightness of skin for child models. Finally, all-Black ads in this subsample numbered 15 of the 122 ads shown. Given the hypothesized potency of skin color, we expected light-skinned Blacks to predominate in all-Black ads. Where advertisers go out on a cultural limb to employ all-Black casts, producing a commercial whose viewers cannot avoid noticing the Black actor(s), we felt they are especially likely to compensate by using those with lighter skin tones.

Reliability analysis confirmed that the best coding scheme would measure just two shades of definable Black skin color—light and dark.[42] For this study we randomly chose one of the weeks (27 November 1996 through 3 December 1996) of prime-time advertising on NBC. Of the 408 commercials shown, 122 (30 percent) included at least one identifiably Black actor; 107 were integrated, and fifteen had exclusively Black casts. We counted a total of 466 individual Black persons appearing in these 122 commercial showings.

Considering skin color for the sample at large, 44 percent were classed as dark skinned and 56 percent as light skinned. The difference was statistically significant.[43] This finding supports our expectation that a majority of Blacks employed by prime-time advertisers would be light skinned. The data also supported our suspicion that light skin shade would be more common among female actors: the vast majority (75 percent) of them were light skinned, and the preference for light-skinned females held among children too.[44] The expected link between lighter skin shade and luxury/fantasy product advertising did not appear consistently. One reason is that breaking a sample of just 122 commercials and 466 actors into fifteen categories yields small numbers. A larger sample might yield clearer results. Finally, we anticipated finding that commercials featuring only Black actors would include more light- than dark-skinned Blacks. Since light-skinned Blacks outnumbered darker ones overall (56 to 44 percent), the issue is whether this predominance is more pronounced in all-Black than in integrated commercials. This was indeed the case, as the light skinned outnumbered dark skinned by a 4:1 ratio in the all-Black ads, compared with about 1.3:1 in the integrated ones.[45] Though suggestive, we would not make too much of this finding, since there were only fifteen all-Black commercials; more generally, this sensitive but revealing area of skin tone is one that demands further research.

It is possible that the 56–44 percent split in light-skinned versus dark-skinned models parallels the actual distributions of skin tone in the general African American population. However, we suspect that a representative sampling of African Americans would yield a much higher proportion of individuals we would classify as dark skinned than of those falling into the light category.[46] In addition, previous research buttresses the assumption that advertisers are highly color or race conscious.[47] This reflects commercial considerations: in describing the preference for lighter skin shades—not just among Blacks but even among White models when casting the all-important cover—*Vogue* magazine editor Anna Wintour observed that, for fashion magazines, "it is a fact of life that the color of a model's skin (or hair for that matter) dramatically affects newsstand sales."[48]

Those Blacks with lighter skin—appearance closer to the White ideal—have greater opportunity than darker Blacks to earn money by appearing in commercials generally, and in specific types of commercials. This advantage of light skin accrues with particular strength to Black females. Black males (as males of all ethnicities) enjoy a wider latitude of variation in physical traits that can be considered attractive. In addition, the symbolic associations of darkness with exoticism, with strength and danger, can sometimes even be an advantage, depending on the image an advertiser seeks to convey. An obvious example is athletics; African American sports heroes can be dark skinned and still amass hefty advertising fees.[49] But in the main, the data indicate that advertising reproduces the racial hierarchy and liminal status of African Americans rather well. The culture awards Blacks provisional acceptability, with a preference for those whose physical features place them closer to the White end of the ideal trait spectrum. That cultural bias translates into greater upward mobility and easier social acceptance for African Americans with lighter skin. In this way advertising inscribes economic value as it ascribes cultural value to lightness of skin.

Conclusion

At one time the color hierarchy was so pronounced that even light-skinned Blacks were virtually absent from commercials. But the culture has been undergoing transition since the 1950s. As a sensitive barometer of cultural change, advertising indicates how far the transformation had progressed by the end of the century. Euro-Americans were seeing Afro-Americans in a high proportion of commercials. Good intentions, political pressure, and market forces have yielded real progress, making African Americans more visible in advertising. This reflects and bolsters a culture that disapproves of traditional racism, with its strict racial isolation and genetic inferiority. However, Blacks were not randomly distributed in commercials, as they would be if the transition to colorblindness had been achieved. No longer relegated to invisibility or exiled to a primitive realm of pollution and danger, Blacks' racial category nevertheless still matters. Black actors do not have the same opportunities as White actors in television commercials, and this both mirrors and reinforces the liminal status of Blacks in majority culture. The findings reveal the racial chasm still bisecting American culture, the distinctive messages about the two races still put forth by a genre exquisitely sensitive to the majority's anxieties. The results also support the validity of anthropological observations on the ways a society's dominant culture distinguishes between in-group and out-group members. And they closely track the underlying racial content of prime-time television discussed in the previous chapter.[50]

The images we find do not arise from individuals deliberately setting out to sustain racism, but from normal institutional processes. Decisions on racial casting are rooted especially in the assumption that Whites react negatively to commercials that have "too many" Blacks. Advertisers usually choose actors with the goal of appealing to a predominantly White target audience. They frequently decide to represent Blacks on screen, but virtually always outnumbered by Whites, a pattern that reenacts racial categorization and preference. The inevitable by-product of these choices is to lower the frequency of images that show Blacks caressing skin, talking to audiences, talking to other African Americans, and so forth. The decision to include only one Black (or no Blacks) in a commercial is simultaneously a decision that ensures fewer images of Blacks in close contact with each other, with White characters, and with audiences.

When they want such concepts as "fantasy vacation," "luxurious," "cute baby," "warm family scene," or "sexy romantic couple" to animate an ad, most sponsors and their advertising agencies automatically think White. Those who craft commercials probably do not recognize the subtle but pervasive way their products may inadvertently perpetuate the traditional racial pecking order. Even if they did, advertisers may be correct to assume that consistently associating Blacks with luxury products, allowing African Americans to dominate Whites in numbers and roles, or showing Blacks as intimately as Whites could undermine the appeal of many products. If so, change may come slowly to this aspect of commercial culture, where Blacks' status may remain in the limbo of cultural liminality.

⓫ Race at the Movies

CONTINUING OUR EMPHASIS on the liminal status of African Americans, and the resulting ambivalence among White producers and consumers of cultural products that feature Blacks, this chapter examines the elements of progress and the continued racial divide in mainstream movies. We find something like parity between Whites and Blacks in sheer visibility: Black actors, especially males, now commonly take major and minor roles in expensive productions and box office blockbusters. Unlike advertising, where—celebrity exceptions aside—tokenism reigns, movies often highlight African American characters; Hollywood has arguably done more to integrate Blacks into productions than any other mass medium. Yet exclusion of minority actors from certain roles and actions persists. The racial differences mark non-Whites, insinuating a racial hierarchy and a need to limit interracial contact. We conclude our comprehensive exploration of mass media with movies not only because they represent the most inclusive genre, but because they embody and summarize most of the book's themes.

Background

The literature on representations of Blacks in film is, perhaps unsurprisingly, largely critical. Images of Black males and females[1] receive criticism not merely for calling upon stereotypes of irresponsible and irrepressible Black sexuality and criminality, but for presenting one-dimensional characters who lack the rounded complexity of real people. In our terms, these critics are charging that by applying distinctive, stereotyped traits, movies make Blacks appear less individuated, more homogeneous. Whites already know that the members of their group come in all moral and intellectual shapes and sizes. They know much less about Blacks, and the critics suggest that film reinforces Whites' ignorance of Blacks' variety and humanity.

Critics have also dissected the regressive themes in most of the major Hollywood films that feature Blacks as stars or co-stars, notably the Black–

White (male) buddy films popular from the 1980s into the 1990s.[2] Examples include *48 Hours* and *Lethal Weapon,* both of which scored well at the box office and spawned sequels. These and many other films subordinated the Black characters who, laden with stereotypical qualities, become helpers to the White leading man who holds them in "protective custody."[3] Other scholarship critiques the heavy concentration of movies on the "Black criminal milieu,"[4] noting among other things the apparently close relationship between the fictional portrayals and the negative images of African Americans arising from television news and tabloid "infotainment" stories on crime. As it conveys information about African Americans' putative flaws, such content also participates in the preexisting White discourse of blame and denial that undermines racial comity.

In order to develop and perhaps qualify these insights, this chapter probes the top earning films of 1996, those that earned $25 million or more at the box office in the United States, excluding animated films or movies with largely nonhuman casts.[5] We begin with a qualitative analysis of race in the three highest-earning films with White-dominated casts in which a Black was one of the top two male protagonists: *Independence Day, A Time to Kill,* and *Jerry Maguire.* We also assess reviews of these movies, treating them as a kind of cultural sensitivity gauge. Then we move on to a quantitative content analysis. The story is mixed: heartening progress combined with indications of continued subtle stereotyping and distancing or exclusion of African Americans—patterns, incidentally, that are compounded when it comes to Latinos and Asians by sheer neglect.

Complexity in Ethnic Representations on Film

The three 1996 films that earned the most at the box office while employing majority-White casts *and* a Black as a central protagonist conveyed prominent and arguably quite positive images of Black persons. As such, these films provide useful examples of the mixed racial messages that Hollywood produces. This analysis sets the stage for the more data-intensive discussions later on.

The first setting for multiple meanings was *Independence Day,* the highest-grossing film of 1996 (over $308 million in domestic box office revenues) and one of the biggest hits of all time. Will Smith, as Captain Steve Hiller, was not only the top-ranked cast member, he was unambiguously heroic. Yet this film also takes frequent refuge in classic ethnic stereotypes to gain laughs or audience recognition. Thus Randy Quaid plays a drunken Latino pilot whose alcoholic stupor is supposed to be funny, although he later sobers up and re-deems himself. A nerdy, brilliant Jewish scientist (Jeff Goldblum) is hectored for comic relief by his Yiddish-accented, over-protective father, though the scientist too becomes a hero. Minor characters shown reacting to the scary alien ship landings feature an array of ethnic stereotypes: chattering Arabs; a Black street person holding a liquor bottle (along with a White companion); a hysterical gay and apparently Jewish man with an intrusive mother ("Ma, head for Aunt Esther's!" he screams over the phone); Black and seemingly Latino kids playing basketball in an inner-city neighborhood with rap music blaring. In scene after scene we see Black faces in the background of busy war rooms, meeting rooms, and the like, while White experts occupy center stage. Black–White conversations almost all involve hierarchical relationships with the White in charge of critical decisions and the direction of the plot.

Perhaps most noticeable on close analysis is that although the film does endow Steve with many heroic traits, he continues to be marked by stereo-typically negative "Black" traits as well. Despite his presumed college edu-cation (as an Air Force officer) he still speaks in ghetto slang. Thus he says to an alien he captures: "You got me out here draggin' your heavy ass . . . with your dreadlocks stickin' out of my parachute. . . . You come down here with a (sic) attitude." Along with the Jewish scientist and the president, Steve saves the world, but they and other Whites devise the plans; Steve's contri-bution is physical skill and bravery.

On the personal side, Steve is committed to a monogamous relationship, but lives with a woman to whom he's not married. A stripper, Jasmine Dubrow (played by Viveca Fox) has a child by another man. Even though in-volved with an Air Force officer and living a middle-class lifestyle, she appar-ently has no occupational options beyond trading on her sexuality. Her intellectual capacity appears impaired: she fails to grasp the seriousness of the alien ships hovering all over the world, even the one over her own neigh-borhood. After complaining about Steve's having to go on active duty to deal with an alien menace she barely notices, she continues on to her job, appar-ently unperturbed, with little concern about her child's fate—despite seeing her neighbors furiously packing and heading for the hills. Later, however, like all the main characters, she transcends her limitations and becomes heroic in her own way. The data analysis will show that the implicit deroga-tion of Black woman here is not exceptional.

A Time to Kill provides our next repository of complex images. This film attempts to evoke White empathy with the Black experience of racism. Yet the heroics and the suffering that occupy the bulk of the film's time are those of the White stars, not the Black actors. And in its world, racism consists of flaws within individual bigots, curable through White paternalism, not Black organization or self-help.

The two White racists who brutalize a young Black girl and animate the plot are wholly evil, snarling and stupid, unlike any human most of us would admit to knowing—but one that most of us recognize as the stereotyped rural, drunken, uneducated White Southern bigot. The father of the girl, Carl Lee Hailey, played by Samuel L. Jackson, kills the two criminals before they can come to trial, and the story revolves around his own trial for murder.

Matthew McConaughey plays attorney Jake Brigance, the White savior of the film who represents the defendant. After Carl Lee shoots the villains, we see a little blond girl, Jake's daughter, in tight close-up; this is apparently intended to stimulate empathy in the White audience, to show how the majority of those implicitly addressed by the film would feel if their own little girl were attacked. Just to make the equation clear, Jake's wife (Ashley Judd) asks, "Isn't she the sweetest thing?" to which Jake responds, "When I look at her I can't help thinking about Tonya" (the Black girl).

Although the plot emerges from the crime committed against Carl Lee's daughter and then by him, the movie spends the bulk of its time on the White protagonists. Carl Lee and his family have just a small fraction of the dialogue that Jake and his family do. The audience spends far more time mulling the injuries and suffering of the White stars, who are repeatedly threatened and attacked for courageously standing up to bigotry; it sees much less of the difficulties experienced by the Black characters. Reinforcing this reading, we coded the close-up shots accorded the top-billed characters. Close-ups are a mechanism for "focalization," for concentrating the audience's attention and identification.[6] We found that costar Sandra Bullock, playing an apprentice lawyer, received almost twice as many as Jackson—and McConaughey four times as many.

Here we see how the political economy of mainstream movie production, built around the star system, affects the ideological message of character and dialogue. To have focalized the film through the Black family's experiences, to have expended the bulk of the dialogue and close-ups on Samuel L. Jackson and other (essentially unknown) Black actors, would have transformed this film's market position. For studio executives, it would have gone from being a potential (and actual) blockbuster to a niche-market movie likely appealing mainly to African Americans.

As it is, arguably, the movie simultaneously conveys an image of racial hierarchy as it attacks old-fashioned violent racism. When it subordinates the Hailey family's suffering to that of Jake and his family and friends in order to secure the involvement of the dominant audience, the film signals that White pain is more important, more interesting, more meaningful. The choice to focus so heavily upon the Whites reflects (recalling our multiple determinant theory) the mainstream culture and the market at work on the filmmakers, and therefore on the audience. Moreover, by focusing on absurdly overdrawn, frothing-at-the-mouth Klansmen, the movie implies that organized hate crime looms among the largest and most fearsome problems created by racism. Like other movies and television shows made in the 1990s but rooted in the ethos of the pre-civil rights South, including television's *I'll Fly Away* and the film *Mississippi Burning,* this approach provides White audiences a basis for complacency or denial by directing attention away from current manifestations and effects of racism.

Perhaps as an unrecognized outgrowth of this perspective, the film stands against organized political action by ethnic groups. Reflecting a strong chord in late-century elite discourse and news media themes, the movie assumes a cynically antipolitical stance, assuming that every side in political action deserves equal condemnation. It portrays a Black minister from the NAACP who marched with Dr. Martin Luther King as a corrupt self-seeker trying to exploit a situation for his own benefit. The minister tells Carl Lee he should hire an NAACP-sponsored lawyer who has sensitivity to the "needs of the movement." The organizers raise funds ostensibly to support Carl Lee and his family, but use it to line the coffers of the NAACP and Carl Lee's own crooked minister. Carl Lee refuses the NAACP's offer of help, condemns their political agenda, and chooses the White lawyer over affiliation with an organized effort by African Americans. The moral of this story is that individual cooperation, apolitical and ad hoc, provides the only real path to racial reconciliation. Collective organization and action are either corrupt or dangerous. However one feels about this position, it is clear that this "entertainment" vehicle, like so many, does take a covert political (and antipolitical) stance.

Finally, consider *Jerry Maguire,* starring Tom Cruise and Cuba Gooding Jr. (who won an Oscar for best supporting actor). The nature of the main characters and their relationships, the subtle blend of traditional stereotypes with a promotion of interracial friendship, testify to a complex racial text. On the one hand, the movie shows a burgeoning closeness between a White and a Black man, one in which each depends on the insights and understanding of the other. Theirs is not the merely professional relationship of polite distance that characterizes many of the interracial friendships we saw on prime-time television. On the other hand, playing a sports agent, Cruise, the eponymous White man, does the intellectual heavy lifting. Although his client, an African American football player client named Rod Tidwell (Gooding) and Rod's Black wife Marcee both possess a college education (she majored in business), they cannot succeed financially; they are powerless without their agent's economic wisdom. The chief advice Jerry gives Rod is to act less cynically egotistical about the game of football and to submerge his anger at inferior treatment by the White owner. Jerry instructs Rod to curb his selfish emotions and his barely controlled instincts, attributes shown in several scenes of Rod dancing, yelling, and browbeating Jerry. (One gave rise to a briefly famous catchphrase, "Show me the money," which Rod humiliatingly forces Jerry to chant responsively with him.)

Rod—who against stereotype shares a deeply committed monogamous intimacy with his spouse—does teach Jerry how to relate better to his wife, Dorothy. Yet Rod and Marcee, despite their college degrees, speak in ungrammatical street slang, and she habitually uses vulgar profanity in ways a mainstream movie would rarely if ever show a wealthy, educated White female character doing. The contrast between the aggressive, abrasive Marcee and Jerry's docile, worshipful Dorothy constructs a hierarchy of racial desirability, at least for most White male audiences. Furthering the stereotypes, a sportscaster describes Rod's childhood as encompassing "your father who left the family on Christmas eve, the mother who cleaned the steps of a prison to make your tuition." In this way the film gives Rod an irresponsible Black father and long-suffering, cleaning-lady mother who sweated to pay his tuition. By making Rod the rare (if not unique) NFL star who excelled in football at a major college program without receiving a scholarship, the movie sacrifices realism to connect with the stereotypes.

Movie Reviews as Maps of Hollywood Consciousness

In our multifactor model of the forces that produce messages shaping racial comity, we suggested that a complicated interaction arises between market pressures and the mass culture that affects the thinking of producers and consumers of media messages. At the same time, political pressures from elites seeking political gain operate on this industry as on all others. And the economy connects to trends and themes in Hollywood films as to political discourse: bad or unstable economic times seem to produce different types of films than those from prosperous epochs. Mainstream Hollywood films—the ones produced and marketed in hopes of earning tens or hundreds of millions of dollars in profit—are expensive, high-risk investments in which the force of the market is obvious if not overwhelming.[7] Yet those who make films are also creators with something to say, however trivial, derivative, or dumb it may sometimes be.

We believe film reviews may provide an indicator of the play of these market and cultural forces through the racial images of films. Reviews are critical to the marketing of modern Hollywood films. Though they cannot make or break movies, they can help create a positive or negative "buzz" around a film, especially in the big cities where first-weekend ticket sales can determine a movie's fate. When movies "open big," studios tend to invest more in advertising and ensure distribution to more theaters. Reviews can augment this all-important opening reception. Perhaps this is why film companies spend lavishly to influence reviewers with special screenings, receptions, access to star interviews, conveniently packaged press materials, and junkets. The judgment of the review does not have to be positive to help. A review that labels a picture implausible and ultraviolent may, especially if it praises the special effects and sound track, help sell the film to its target audience. Whether they give a film thumbs up or thumbs down, reviews help to set a context, a series of expectations that tell audience members what a film is about, what pleasures or annoyances it promises.

Given their central role in the marketing of film, we decided to test the sensitivity of reviews to the racial subtexts that we detected in the three movies. How many reviewers picked up on the racial stereotypes and other political content? If the people who look at movies for a living either fail to notice such material, or find it unworthy of comment, we can hardly expect the average White viewer to notice them. Such a void in the text of reviews would buttress the insensitivity of the White audience to the negative stereotyping, racial hierarchy, and distancing. The institution of reviewing would be a component in a Hollywood machine that perpetuates, however unintentionally, racial alienation. On the other hand, if reviewers do discern and discuss the problematic material, it would indicate racial sensitivity among these cultural arbiters. Reviewers could even be leading forces in reshaping Whites audiences' sensibilities, tastes, and ultimately market demand.

Political pressure may be the least obvious of the forces at work here. But what elites say and don't say in part reflects the global political economy; the "national mood" they both set and amplify seems to affect what Hollywood produces. The cover story on *Independence Day* that appeared in *Time* articulates the linkage of political zeitgeist and film production: " 'The U.S. is desperately in search of an enemy,' says Paul Verhoeven, who has directed some stunning sci-fi (*RoboCop, Total Recall*). . . . 'The communists were the enemy, and the Nazis before them, but now that wonderful enemy everyone can fight has been lost. Alien sci-fi films give us a terrifying enemy that's politically correct. They're bad. They're evil. And they're not even human.' "[8]

Alien villains do not bring to mind any politically controversial, real-life enemies of ordinary people. In turn, we speculate, perhaps reviewers unknowingly attune themselves to elite discourse in deciding what in the movies they regard as relevant, timely, and acceptable to observe. If most reviewers failed to comment on the ethnic stereotyping and hierarchy in some of the year's hits, it may be because elites in 1996 were not saying much about racial equality and discrimination. If anything, as we saw in the chapter on affirmative action, the word in the mid-1990s was that Whites were tired of organized political demands among Blacks and other minority groups. In that political environment, criticizing racially tinged images might have seemed uninteresting or excessively "politically correct," that is, unfashionably and punctiliously liberal. Reviewers, like the filmmakers themselves, must worry about pleasing their audiences and bosses.

We culled reviews from the "major paper" collection in the Lexis-Nexis database[9] and from *Time* and *Newsweek*. We found a total of thirty-nine reviews of *A Time to Kill* and forty-three each of *Independence Day* and *Jerry Maguire*. First we searched for the occurrence of the words *Black, African American, race,* and *stereotype.* There were no references to ethnic stereotypes in any of the reviews of *A Time to Kill* or *Maguire.* Three of the reviews did gently chide *Independence Day.* Only the *New York Times* expressly noted the ethnic stereotyping, criticizing "*one* obnoxious, regrettable ethnic stereotype"—not of Blacks but of the Jewish father (emphasis added). The *San Francisco Chronicle* mentioned "slightly overstated stereotypes" and *Time* wryly noted that "an ensemble cast fleshes out the stereotypes," but reviewers in these instances did not make clear the ethnic offensiveness involved. (Three reviewers also mentioned the antigay stereo-typing.) Most film reviewers did not even discuss the ethnic stereotypes, and the three who did barely identified them. Their tone was never condemna-tory or even particularly critical so much as ironic. No reviews of *Indepen-dence Day* alluded to the racial subtexts, just one mentioned the word *Black* (in describing Will Smith's character), and none mentioned "race" or "racism" (except in talking about the "human race" or "alien race").

As for noticing the issues around Black–White contact, the reviews of *Jerry Maguire* managed almost entirely to avoid them. The words *race* or *racism* never appeared in any review. Just one review mentioned the word *Black*, in describing Rod Tidwell (Cuba Gooding Jr.), and in quoting his line "I love Black people" as funny: "Moments like these will bring down the house" (*Washington Post* review). To its credit, at least this review mentioned that the film occasionally alludes to Black–White doings, but the critic found its use of identity politics funny. Viewers saw a Black man repeatedly cavort-ing around in uncomfortable resemblance to the cake-walking, dancing "coon" stereotype of old[10] as he chanted phrases like "I love Black people."

Lost in the laughs may have been the irony of this line: Rod is never shown loving anyone but himself and his immediate family; he never evinces any solidarity with other African Americans. In any case, the notion that an audience composed largely of Whites can innocently laugh at such an image disturbingly denies the serious issues underlying the choices about Black identity confronting wealthy African Americans. DeMott has written about the falsely comforting, denial-abetting assumptions of interracial comfort and friendship that infuse some films and television shows—Rod's "I love Black people" proclamation, with its supposition that we can all laugh together at race, provides a prime example.[11]

It is not as if the troubling allusions to race relations in *Jerry Maguire* are buried very deeply. When Rod decides to stick with Jerry as his agent (rely-ing, like Carl Lee in *A Time to Kill* and Steve in *Independence Day* on White expertise), Rod's brother derides him: "An African-American man running with a little ball, working for White owners and White agents. It's the iconog-raphy of racism. . . ." Here the screenwriters tweak the intellectual critics of race, sports, and culture. In so doing, arguably, they trivialize the criticisms. The script even includes an observation on the image of Blacks in film and the market demands of African American audiences! During a dinner scene, Marcee says, "So I go to see a so-called "Black" film the other day. . . .

Twenty minutes of coming attractions. All Black films, all violent, I'm talking about brothers shooting brothers, Wesley Snipes with guns the size of our house, killing, blood flowing, cars crashing . . . blood blood blood blood. Is this all they think we want to see? Come on! I enjoyed *Schindler's List*. Give me a little credit. . . ."

But Marcee's behavior may rob her of such credit. She often acts as if barely in control of her emotions and uses vulgarities freely. For example, while watching his father make a great play on television, their son, Tyson, dances around and says to his family members "That's my motherfucker!" Marcee grabs him and admonishes: "Why don't you be the first man in your family not to say that word? And then we'll let you live." Several stereotypes are bound up in this little colloquy. It's difficult to imagine the filmmakers having the cute White kid in this film (Dorothy's son) say such a thing. Tyson's antics recall the pickaninny stereotype, the Black child as rascally comic relief.[12] The fact that Tyson swears is an implicit indictment of his parents and other relatives—of this Black family's values. And indeed, before threatening Tyson only half-jokingly with physical punishment, the mother says all the men in the family speak in this off-putting fashion. Of course viewers of the film know that this indictment marks the foul-mouthed Marcee as hypocritical. When responding to stingy contract offers, she says, "Please remove your dick from my ass!" and "You're gonna reject this shitty contract. You're gonna play out your existing shitty contract and go be a free agent next year and the hell with Arizona. . . ." The use of profane language by unexpected characters serves to distance and differentiate Blacks in many movies.

None of the reviewers in major newspapers explore this hardly subtle racial subtext. This may be an index to the discomfort in the wider culture at confronting the complexities of racial alienation and stereotyping head on—unless, perhaps, it is murderous old-fashioned racism in the South, the sort tackled and denounced in *A Time to Kill*. Reviewers of *A Time to Kill*, of course, could hardly miss the racial content of the film. Three noticed its overwhelming focus on the White characters' perspective to the neglect of the Blacks' (e.g., Roger Ebert in the *Chicago Sun-Times*, 24 July 1996). Two did point out the film's exclusive concern with a kind of racism that holds less significance in the lives of most Blacks and Whites lives than most other contemporary forms of discrimination. But even with this text to work on, most reviewers passed over the problematic racial themes.

Although movie reviewers are not academic film theorists and their readers are not cinema studies majors, it is surprising how little attention reviews paid to racial images in movies that featured African American stars and often commented directly on Black–White relations. For the reasons we have suggested, reviewers may fail to notice these messages or believe them to be inappropriate material for commentary. Either way, the absence of more sensitivity in reviewing may be both symptom and cause of problematic movie images.[13]

In suggesting this we do not mean to imply that if only reviewers would demand it, Hollywood would suddenly start disgorging a steady stream of positive message movies. We know Samuel Goldwyn spoke for most of his industry when he said he'd use a Western Union telegram (not his movies) if he wanted to send a message. Action dramas, sci-fi extravaganzas, and farcical comedies will remain Hollywood staples. We only wish to suggest that reviewers' failure to discuss the gratuitous and unconscious racial material provides a useful indicator of the mainstream culture's concerns—and obliviousness. We turn now to our broader samples.

Cast Analysis

To see whether people of color are obtaining not merely visibility but also centrality in the influential characterizations of Hollywood, we analyzed the race or ethnicity of the top ten cast members, as determined by official cast listings,[14] in the sixty-three films grossing more than $25 million during 1996.[15] The films are listed in appendix table A.16. This analysis is a tougher undertaking than may at first appear. Many films center their action on four or five speaking parts. Even an actor listed sixth or seventh in the credits may appear on screen for just a few minutes and have only a handful of lines; in some cases this made it difficult for us even to determine the names of actors in a film, let alone their ethnicity. At the same time, this very problem demonstrates why mere visibility in films cannot be equated with having a noticeable or memorable role that might influence audience perceptions.

Whites continue to dominate the casts of mainstream films: 496 of the 630 actors were White, 106 were Black, and 28 were Asian, Latino, or other. Nineteen of the films listed exclusively White actors in the top ten cast positions; six listed exclusively Black; and one exclusively Asian. That left thirty-seven integrated films with at least one non-White among the top ten billings.

Although not our primary concern, we do want to note before moving on to look closely at African American images that no movies featured a majority Latino cast and only one was majority Asian. The latter was *Rumble in the Bronx*, a karate film starring martial artist Jackie Chan. This is of course the prototypical role for Asian male stars. In the other films where they did appear in the top ten cast rank, the Asian actors played cursory parts, often as assistants appearing on screen only briefly.[16] Most Latinos, also featured rarely, were confined to negative or menial roles.[17]

In twelve of the sixty-three top movies of 1996, at least one Black person had a starring (i.e., top three billing) role. And Black males were represented somewhere in the top ten cast ranking for slightly over half of all the films— albeit when they star in films, the plots usually focus on sports, crime, or violence.[18] There is a marked gender disparity in treatment of Black actors: Black females receive most of their starring roles in movies with mostly Black casts that cater to Black audiences.[19] Just 27 percent of the films listed a Black female as a top ten cast member, about half the rate for Black males. Over half (seventeen of thirty-three) of the Black women appearing in top ten positions did so in just four films—those with essentially all-Black casts. These were *The Preacher's Wife, Set It Off, Waiting to Exhale,* and *A Thin Line Between Love and Hate.*[20] For men these four films provided twenty-three of the seventy-three appearances in the top ten cast positions.

Black males received top billing in seven films, three of them majority-White: Will Smith in *Independence Day,* Denzel Washington in *Courage Under Fire,* and Sinbad in *First Kid.* The fact that three White-dominated and majority-aimed films could star Black persons and earn solid (in the case of *Independence Day,* spectacular) returns at the box office marks real progress. These films were not about race and their stars' racial identity was incidental to the stories. Although some might criticize the films for just that reason— saying that the dominance of White actors and perspectives effaces the Black identity of the Black stars—there is surely a positive function to showing African Americans as just plain people.[21]

When we calculated the average cast rank of each group (which could theoretically run from 1, the highest-billed actor, to 10), we found that Blacks and Whites were not as far apart as one might expect. Black males ranked about as high as White males, although Black females ranked lower in the integrated films than White females.[22]

Another way of looking at the cast rankings is through the lens of money. Is there a relationship between the number of Black actors in the top ten and

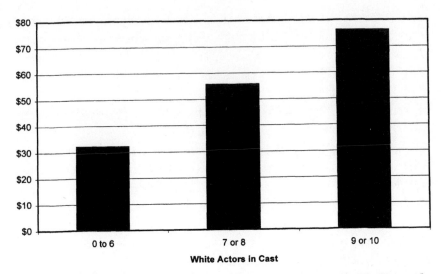

Figure 11.1 White Casting and Average Box Office Gross, Excepting Two Blockbusters*
Note: The relationship between number of White actors in top ten cast ranks and box office earnings in millions of dollars. Numbers of films with 0 to 6 White actors in top ten: 7; with 7 or 8 White actors: 21; with 9 or 10 White actors: 33.
* Omitted are the two blockbusters *The Nutty Professor* and *Spacejam*. The sixty-one included films are all those earning over $25 million at the box office in 1996 that featured human casts.

the box office returns? Omitting the two exceptional cases—*Nutty Professor* and *Spacejam*, fantasy films loaded with special effects and starring respectively the most popular "crossover" Black comedian in movie history and the most popular basketball player in history—we find an apparent "tipping point." In examining residential integration, scholars have discovered that a majority of Whites can accept as many as about 25 percent Blacks in a neighborhood or school (or at least say they can). But around 30 percent we reach a tipping point when Whites are scared off.[23] Perhaps it is only coincidental, but as figure 11.1 shows, once the number of Whites in the top cast reaches 70 percent, the average box office gross nearly doubles; and with nearly all-White films (those with nine or ten Whites in the top ten), there is another jump up in revenues. We shall return to this implicit political economy of racial images in film.

Occupation and Role Analysis

The films provided a narrow range of roles for most Blacks. Only one arguably portrayed a Black male character in a starring role of complexity and subtlety, Denzel Washington in *Courage Under Fire*. Playing a lieutenant colonel who happened to be African American, Washington was depicted as both admirable and flawed. Audiences got to know him more intimately in his authentic humanity than is usually the case with Black characters in entertainment (including prime-time television, with its distanced, idealized star Black characters).

The most frequently shown occupations among the 106 characters played by Black actors were military and police (twenty-two); blue collar or service workers (eighteen); and athletes (ten). Of the six characters portrayed as owning businesses, *all appeared in the same four essentially all-Black films mentioned earlier* (*Thin Line, Preacher, Set It Off, Waiting*) and four of five (nonowner) business executives are in the same films.[24] This does suggest a benefit of films that serve the niche minority audience: even if seen by relatively few Whites, these films do challenge some stereotypes. On the other hand, the occupational data also show the failure of mainstream film fully to integrate Blacks into a wide range of roles.[25] Incidentally, every one of the five minority characters whose role was coded as "criminal" was a Latino. That no top-ten-ranked cast member was a Black (or White) criminal suggests that making Latinos the bad guys may expose filmmakers to less danger of criticism for stereotyping than would their choosing Blacks.

Behavior of Minority and White Characters in Film

We analyzed behavior on four dimensions that initial observation suggested might distinguish Black and White characters in these major releases. Our thinking was shaped in part by our findings in television news, entertainment, and advertising:

1. We expected that Blacks might be depicted as more violent and more in need of restraint by responsible authorities than White characters, on average. We counted whether characters committed acts of physical violence and how often they were physically restrained, handcuffed, or in jail. Readers may recall our finding that Blacks are more likely to be shown restrained in local news programs, and we were curious to see whether the same fearsome image of the Black male is repeated in film.

2. An age-old stereotype of Blacks is hypersexuality. There were some indications in our investigation of television advertising that Black sexuality was indeed more exploited, for males if not females. We assessed in-

stances of characters having sex in bed or without clothes and being otherwise sexualized versus instances of hugging / kissing, caressing, and uttering "I love you" not in bed or naked. The idea was to test whether Blacks, more than Whites, are pictured as purely sex-oriented rather than interested also in close human relationship and nurturing intimacy in which sexuality is secondary.

3. Pilot study and the close analysis of the three films discussed earlier showed an apparent tendency for African American characters to use language differently from Whites. Language use is a potent cultural and social marker of status and acceptability, and Black characters seemed disproportionately likely to utter street profanities and to speak nonstandard English, even when their characters' social class and education would predict otherwise. In assessing profanity, we counted only strong vulgarity (e.g., "motherfucker"), not standard cursing ("damn").

4. Despite the success of a handful of Black actors (mostly males) at achieving stardom in mainstream movies, tokenism of the sort present in advertising continues to be practiced in Hollywood. A pilot study indicated a disproportionate use of African Americans in roles where they might have speaking lines yet play no part in advancing the story. By practicing tokenism, moviemakers can include minority cast members without truly incorporating them into the narratives. Based on the pilot study, we looked specifically for Blacks occupying entry guard or security agent positions. These are functionaries who speak but have no important impact on the plot.

This portion of the study is based on analysis of the top twenty-five movies of 1996–97 (excluding animation films), listed in appendix table A.16. It was impossible to test every possible dimension of behavior, and we recognize that unmeasured elements of behavior might not show racial differences, or might even show more negative White images than Black. We submit this evidence as an effort to offer quantifiable and systematic evidence of Black–White differences in movies. We do not represent the findings as definitive, but as exemplars of the kind of detailed content analysis necessary to penetrate to the deep, subtle level at which most racial image-making in the media now operates.

Eleven elements of the narratives were coded. To be coded, characters had to utter at least one full sentence, have their names mentioned in the movie dialogue, or somehow help forward the story line. If a nameless character appearing in one or two scenes had lines like "Hi," and "Yeah," their behavior was not coded. Where characters did meet this standard, their behavior was coded for actions that we thought might distinguish Black and White actors. The movies were coded by two graduate students.[26]

In figures 11.2 and 11.3, the percentages should be interpreted as the proportion of the ethnic/gender group shown in the specified guise. The differences in the size of the bars in figure 11.3 illustrate especially graphically the contrasts in portrayals of Black females and White females. Contrasts for Black males and White males are illustrated by a similar bar graph in figure 11.2. For those who want the details, numerical data for both genders are displayed in appendix table A.17. The first row in that table shows the numbers of characters of each group who qualified by being named, speaking a sentence, and/or advancing the plot. Looking only at this row, we see that 240 White characters met this standard, and thirty-six Black. African Americans achieved considerable visibility in the films, although it is also clear that males predominate over females.[27]

The rest of appendix table A.17 provides the data to test our initial ex-

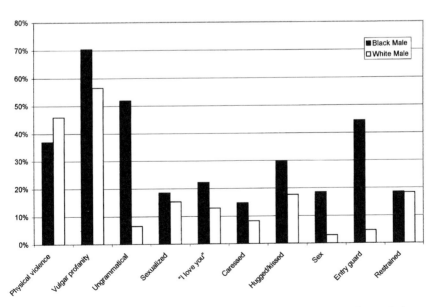

Figure 11.2 Percentages of Black and White Male Characters Shown in Different Guises

198

Chapter Eleven

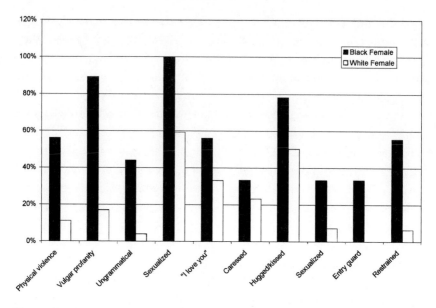

Figure 11.3 Percentages of Black and White Female Characters Shown in Different Guises

pectations by comparing percentages of characters in the different ethnic and gender groups that engages in each of the coded behaviors. Thus under Black male, for "Physical violence," the numbers "10" and "37 percent" appear. This means that ten of the twenty-seven named Black male characters committed physical violence. That number represents 37 percent of the twenty-seven Black males. By comparison, 46 percent of the 170 named White males acted violently. Looking specifically at images of violence and restraint, a gender difference emerges. When it came to portrayal as violent or requiring incarceration or restraint, at least in the top 1996 Hollywood films, on average Black males did not seem more violently inclined than White. However, Black females were markedly more violent than White, in percentage terms five times more so. And they were nine times more likely to be shown in conditions of restraint—55 percent of Black female characters versus 6 percent of White females. This finding accords with other results discussed below that suggest that movies portray Black females as less civilized than their White counterparts, less obedient to societal norms usually followed by women.

The second postulate was that Blacks would be disproportionately associated with an implicitly animal or biological sexuality and less so with more romantic and sensitive versions of affection and intimacy. Again there is partial support, again with special respect with Black females. Depictions in scenes showing partial nudity or emphasizing sexual stimulation of other characters (and presumably the audience) are equivalent for Black and White males, but not for females. Every Black woman was sexualized; although White women were far more likely to be depicted in this guise than White men, they were far less sexualized than Black females. Thus arguably, traditional gender roles, the use of women as sexual objects, continues in Hollywood's top films—but especially so for Black women.

As for actually portraying sexual acts, both Black males and females were much more likely to have sex than their White counterparts. Based on our admittedly limited sample, this finding suggests that Hollywood depicts Blacks as more sexually driven on average than Whites, perhaps because filmmakers assume audiences expect this of Black characters. This tracks with a general conclusion that Black characters are more likely on average to violate what might be thought of as middle-class conventions of sobriety and restraint. We can speculate that some Whites' perceptions of Blacks as lacking in middle-class virtues, as lazy and unwilling to work hard for success, may receive fortification from the subtle contrasts in movie characterizations. Such perceptions were evident in our own interviews and in national survey data. Black characters seem more likely on average to seek and receive immediate physical gratification. White audiences know from the news that Black women in particular bear children out of wedlock at comparatively high rates, reinforcing such impressions. We can conclude nothing definitive, but the differences are *consistently* in the direction of greater Black sexuality.

On the other hand, looking at depictions of characters in nonsexual intimacy, measured by uttering the phrase "I love you" or engaging in nonsexual hugging, kissing, and caressing, differences between Blacks and Whites are not consistent. If anything, Blacks are shown to be more affectionate than Whites. This image could counteract, at least in part, the implications of all the sexualization. In this sample, as in the advertising study, no instances of interracial sexuality or nonsexual intimacy occurred.[28]

Turning now to language use, we suggested that Blacks would engage in significantly more profanity and ungrammatical speech than Whites. The pertinent data from appendix table A.17 reveal striking contrasts. Black males were more profane than White males, though a majority of both used profanity in this sample of movies. All but one of the Black females swore, 89 percent, compared with 17 percent of White females. The disparities in grammatical usage were even greater—in fact barely any White characters spoke ungrammatically compared with around half the Blacks. Part of this finding may be due to Blacks tending to portray less-educated characters. Still, as already noted, we found examples of Blacks with high education using ungrammatical, perhaps stereotypically "ghetto" speaking styles. And even if occupational differences partially explain the differences in language use, this pattern nonetheless constructs African Americans as occupying a different, quite separate cultural universe from Euro-Americans. Filmmakers may believe audiences, Black as well as White, expect African American characters to speak in certain ways and would not relate to them as typically, recognizably "Black" if they spoke differently. At the same time, this difference in symbolic behavior depicts Blacks as possibly less restrained, less governed by middle-class conventionality, which parallels the disproportionate sexuality attributed to Blacks.[29]

Our final expectation concerned the depiction of Blacks in menial roles. Movies show cab drivers, cashiers, clerks, street vendors, and so forth in profusion, but they are rarely given lines to speak, let alone a name. That is why we chose to look specifically at entry and security guards, which preliminary study revealed as a frequent assignment for African American actors. Society depends upon security guards, trusts them, and thus there is a positive component to the image of a minority person in that position. On the other hand, casting a Black in this role smacks of tokenism: it earns a filmmaker credit for ethnic diversity without affecting the overall plot development or marketing appeal. In any case, the hypothesis was strongly confirmed: fully fifteen of the twenty-three guards shown in the sampled films were Black.

As in prime-time television, interracial intimacy was missing from most films. Only work or professional relationships developed across racial lines.[30] Again, romance across racial boundaries was absent,[31] even when film conventions would otherwise lead one to expect it. Thus in several major studio productions of the 1990s, a Black male with legal authority assists or works closely with a vulnerable White woman. Examples include Samuel L. Jackson's relationship to Geena Davis in *The Long Kiss Goodnight*, Morgan Freeman's to Ashley Judd in *Kiss the Girls*, Denzel Washington's to Julia Roberts in *The Pelican Brief*, and Wesley Snipes's with Diane Lane in *Murder at 1600*. All chastely avoided romance. The presence of Black men as competent professionals with trusting relationships to White women does mark an important advance, but the absence of romance between the leading man and woman where a thousand White movies have inserted it exemplifies the enduring racial distance. These examples of Blacks' continuing cultural liminality provide a fitting note on which to conclude.

Conclusion

As we said at the outset, film is an intricate site of cultural expression about race. By combining qualitative examples with quantitative methods for analyzing content usually applied only to news, this chapter attempts to capture the complicated flavor of race images in Hollywood's most popular movies. Hollywood has improved its contributions to race relations significantly over the past thirty years. But the dominant movie images of Blacks still create voids where White viewers might *potentially* find more consistent challenges and correctives. Different kinds of movies could nurture the more positive side of Whites' ambivalent ledgers, their empathy, hope, and yearning for connection. We do not mean to suggest that having big-budget movies with African Americans as "positive role models" and heroes of complexity would by itself significantly alter race relations. Rather, the scarcity of such films records as it contributes to the persistence of misunderstanding, stereotypes, and animosity.

We recognize the complicated task that the film industry faces. Part of the reason for the movie images of Blacks lay in the way stereotypical movie representations interact with human perception. In a sense, each member of the ethnic group bears the burden of representing his or her entire category. For some film viewers, if a character conforms in any way to negative stereotypes, that is what they will notice and remember; they will disregard any nonstereotypical qualities the same character demonstrates.[32]

There may be no easy solution to this conundrum. Market pressures loom even larger in the realm of movies than in journalism. It may be unrealistic to expect films aiming for the widest possible audience—the kind that constituted our sample—to be much different from what they are. Movies with more complicated and varied representations of minorities do get made, but they generally do not break through the $25 million ceiling set for the sample. Often marketed as if they will only appeal to a minority audience, such movies can become victims of studio executives' unimaginative, self-fulfilling prophecies. Frank Price, former head of Columbia Pictures, expressed what appears to be an industry consensus when he spoke about *Rosewood*, a serious film concerning a massacre of Blacks, before it went on to do poorly at the box office: "If you're looking at this as a studio executive, you've got [director John] Singleton in the plus column and nearly everything else in the minus column. . . . It's a period piece. It's disturbing. And to cross over, Whites will have to plunk down $7.50 to feel heavy guilt."[33] Another studio executive, a vice president of development, observed:

> When I'm in a meeting about a big film, if the script doesn't call for a black or minority character, it really doesn't cross our minds to put somebody black in it. It's not racism, though I'm sure that's what everyone wants to call it. But all-white movies sell. There's no blacks in 'Saving Private Ryan' or 'There's Something About Mary,' and they sold at the box office. So there's not a lot of incentive to make changes. It's wrong, but that's the reality. [34]

Perhaps the studio bosses are correct; maybe films featuring too serious a Black subject or too many Black actors can only appeal to minority audiences. If so, the economics dictates another vicious circle: low projected revenues from a limited audience dictates lower spending on production and marketing, which yields lower audience appeal—and lower revenues.[35]

Yet surveys suggest that Blacks and Latinos may make up about one-third of the movie-going audience.[36] This points to another problem: the vicious circle may be compounded by restricted demand for serious, nuanced movies among all ethnic groups. Just because a minority group faces serious problems in the United States does not mean its members will have more somber tastes at the box office than the majority group. In recent years, a series of thoughtful and provocative films about the African American experience, such as *Rosewood* and *Get on the Bus*, have done poorly at the box office even among Blacks. At the same time, pure entertainment fare like *Booty Call* and *Set It Off* generated major financial returns, largely from African Americans.[37] Whites usually spend the largest share of their ticket money on less-challenging entertainment as well. If indeed minority groups have similar entertainment preferences to the dominant group, then serious films may never attain the distribution and influence we might like.

Ironically, an element of cultural commonality between ethnic minority and majority groups—shared taste for light entertainment—may work to reinforce *perceptions* of cultural difference by creating market pressures that discourage filmmakers from giving minorities wider-ranging roles in mass-appeal movies. But at least in the current environment, Blacks (though not Asians or Latinos) regularly star in mass-oriented films. Moreover, serious niche-market films featuring minority perspectives do get made and seen, although mostly by minority group members. To improve this situation will require interest and cooperation from audiences, not just from the film industry.[38]

In this regard, the experience of *The Preacher's Wife* may be dolefully instructive. Patrick Goldstein writes that this film was a kind of "great White hope" for Hollywood.[39] Made by the highly successful Disney studio with the largest budget ever for an all-Black picture (over $60 million), *Preacher's Wife* was directed by proven box-office winner Penny Marshall (a White woman) and starred two African Americans of established stature among Whites and Blacks, Denzel Washington and Whitney Houston. Disney "carefully positioned *The Preacher's Wife* as a cozy family film promoting the universal themes of romance and redemption" and the studio was "determined to make the film appear as safe as milk." Disney boosted the film's chances with "a heavily promoted Houston soundtrack." With *Preacher's Wife* the hope was to challenge the prevailing belief in Hollywood that "films without White stars still attract only Black audiences."[40]

Before the movie was released, *Time* quoted Whitney Houston herself as saying "What's so alien about us? I don't understand why there's such a big thing about all-Black casts. I've seen movies with all-White casts. . . . It's a movie. Either you like it or you don't."[41] In the end, *Preacher's Wife* wound up grossing $31 million at the box office, less than *A Thin Line Between Love and Hate* or *Set It Off*, farces targeted more narrowly to Black audiences. These figures suggest that very few Whites went to see *Preacher's Wife* despite all that it had going for it—and not all that many African Americans. The market has sent a strong message to the film studios: making a big budget, all-Black film is a risky proposition indeed.[42]

A simple survey of the top box-office hits of 1999 reveals continuity with 1996. Four of the top twenty-five movies (excluding three animated features) showcase a Black man in a starring role (top-three billing). All are one-dimensional characters in gimmicky, violent movies (*The Matrix, Wild Wild West, Entrapment*, and *Deep Blue Sea*). Lawrence Fishbourne plays a rebel, Will Smith a hired gun, Ving Rhames a crooked FBI man, and Samuel L. Jackson a brilliant entrepreneur who is also adept at fighting genetically engineered, vicious sharks. None of the top twenty-five films starred a Black woman. A film starring another Black man, *Blue Streak*, with Martin Lawrence as a jewel thief, ranked twenty-sixth at the box office in these calculations. *Life*, an integrated comedy starring Eddie Murphy, Martin Lawrence, and Obba Babatunde as convicts, was the highest-ranking film (thirty-first) in which Blacks occupied all three top roles. The top movie with an essentially all-Black cast—and the highest-earning feature with a Black woman in a starring role—was *The Best Man* ($33.8 million, in fifty-third place). Resembling *The Preacher's Wife* in its attempt to deal with contemporary African American life in a realistic and nuanced way, *The Best Man* once again confirmed the maxim that films with mostly Black casts that do not feature violence (or Eddie Murphy) cannot earn more than about $40 million.

Demographics increasingly create market pressures for inclusiveness. Projections indicate that by 2010 one-third of the U.S. population will be non-White; by 2030, there may not be a majority racial or ethnic group (i.e., Whites will constitute less than 50 percent and no other group will make up more than 50 percent).[43] Since Blacks and Latinos already constitute a disproportionate share of the box office audience, the influence of minority tastes on Hollywood—already felt in the frequent casting of Black males (such as Wesley Snipes and Will Smith during the 1990s) in action films for young male audiences—will grow. Beyond this, a large portion of Hollywood's revenues, in some cases more than half, arises from *foreign* markets. The majority of the world is non-White, many nations' audiences are non-White, and ethnic and racial inclusiveness should only facilitate profitability in many overseas markets.[44] Indeed, as the movie and video production industries in foreign countries grow and become more competitive with the now-dominant American industry, it may make rational business sense for Hollywood to attend more carefully to non-White audiences. In this way, there is the potential for the externalities of Hollywood profit-seeking to turn more positive. The path to highest profits might lead through even greater ethnic diversity, and that could spill over into casting Blacks and other minorities in a greater variety of roles and films. Some of them are bound to offer (like *Courage Under Fire*) the kinds of nuanced images of genuine humanity that might contribute to racial comity—understanding in place of denial and rejection, acceptance in place of fear and stereotype.

12 Reflecting on the End of Racial Representation

THE SENTIMENTS, relationships, and communication signs we have documented emerge from a long cultural tradition in the United States. They also arise from an inherent human tendency to form group identities. In writing a book exploring the media's role in all this we do not mean unduly to emphasize their culpability. We have sought a better understanding of how media may unintentionally reinforce the negative tendencies in racial group dynamics, even as they also contribute to positive movement in some respects. We have employed the media as a kind of leading indicator, a barometer of cultural change and variability in the arena of race. In this chapter we summarize our findings and their possible significance and suggest a new goal (or end) for media operations in the realm of race: encouraging audiences and media producers alike to become more critically self-aware as they deal with the culture's racial signals. Such activity would serve not only the social interest in racial comity, but the media's long-term economic interests as well. And it would set the stage for an eventual cessation—an end in the other sense—to color consciousness, for arrival at the time, however far off,[1] when "race" no longer holds meaning for media producers and their audiences.

Benedict Anderson's work on "imagined communities" helps explain the cultural-cognitive process that draws the lines between groups. All community is imagined; as Anderson shows, this was true hundreds of years ago when the earliest mass media, by creating common information space, enabled collective group consciousness to transcend geographic space and become national identity.[2] Today, the same processes operate: common identification is shaped by mediated images of who constitutes one's own people and nation. It stands to reason that Blacks' media images will be critical in determining the degree to which African Americans are imagined by White Americans (and even by themselves) to be part of the community.

Chapter Twelve

Liminality and Ambivalence

The typical White's racial attitudes and the dominant cultural tendencies by the end of the twentieth century had moved significantly beyond old-fashioned racism. Even in south central Indiana, a place where the KKK once held considerable sway, only a minority seem to harbor deep racial animosity and only a small percentage of these profess beliefs in inherent Black inferiority. We have attempted to capture this altered cultural status by using the concept of *liminality* to describe Blacks' *transition* from rejection toward acceptance. The mixture of media images, and of White beliefs, hopes, and fears about Blacks registers the liminality. As we have said, the media operate both as barometer of cultural integration and as potential accelerator either to cohesion or to further cultural separation and political conflict—or perhaps to both.

Racism has its origins in the ideology that justified domestic repression, domination, and enslavement. Although such rationales are now anathema to respectable society, the cultural residues anachronistically remain, detached from their former political ends. Thus while formal legal restraints upon Black progress are absent, the culture still accepts or promotes voluntary behavior such as living in racially segregated communities and marrying within color lines, rejuvenating the artificial distinction of race, which continues to impose burdens upon both groups.

It is true nevertheless that a growing number of Black Americans have entered the middle class and a few have provided highly visible symbols of extraordinary success. The success stories validate the culturally venerated *qualities* (hard work, restraint, discipline) that elevated these exceptional African Americans. The implicit argument is that such qualities are all Blacks need. Those who do not succeed are therefore responsible for falling back upon a subculture regarded by many Whites as replete with moral pollution. As powerful evidence of this moral / cultural argument, consider that the celebrated African American successes have yet to defeat the powerful cultural forces that limit media portrayal of intermarriage between Blacks and Whites. Yet this, after all, is the *sine qua non* resolution to the problem of race. Nearly four hundred years after Blacks and Whites began living together in America, cultural taboos against interracial romance and sexuality remained strong enough that no major Hollywood film by century's end had yet paired first-rank Black and White stars as a maturely sexual, long-term couple. In the hundreds of romantic dramas and comedies of the last third of the twentieth century, not one featured a star of the magnitude of Demi Moore, Michelle Pfeiffer, Julia Roberts, or Susan Sarandon opposite a Black male lead.[3] When interracial relationships were featured, on-screen sexuality was virtually always toned down. Program producers and advertisers apparently believe that prime-time television is not ready for such a relationship either. This will change eventually, but any boundary crossings will remain for some time noteworthy, daring exceptions.

Beyond failing to vanquish the old cultural line-drawing and hierarchies, the highly visible but exceptional successes create the very condition we call "liminality." The predominant imagery of Blacks on television oscillates between the supremely gifted, virtuous, and successful and the corrupt, criminal, and dangerous (with some Black athletes a bit of both), much more so than it does with Whites. There is little in the way of the merely ordinary, those examples that fail to register a blip on a cultural radar screen calibrated to detect only the extremes. Marianne, the twenty-six-year-old White female we introduced in chapter 2 who went to an integrated Florida high school, put it this way:

> I can't remember when the last time was that I heard even so much as a Good Samaritan story on the news. And they *have* to be out there! I mean they have to be out there. There have to be more Black people in America that we can view as the public, than athletes and drug dealers. I mean, what's in the middle? What's in the middle of athletes and drug dealers? People! Normal people who are moms and dads and husbands and wives, and grandmas and grandpas and kids! Why do we never see anything about them? I mean they don't focus on good White people either. The news doesn't focus on good people period, which I hate watching the news; it's not a good thing. (Laughs.) But I just think that the only thing the media portrays to us as America—whether America is White or Black, about Black people, is athletes and drug dealers. And there's never anyone in between.

Marianne's comments, even if exaggerated, underscore the unforeseen consequences of practices that create the bipolar representations of Black prototypes in the media, the saints or sinners syndrome.[4] These images reproduce the culture's ambivalence, helping to explain the cognitive dissonance among many Whites, who admire a few individual Blacks representing spectacular achievement. These same Whites still cannot accept Blacks as equal in the face of continuing social dislocation and pathology, often represented with the face of menace and complaining anger. Having no way to sort out these opposed perceptions, many Whites predictably feel conflicted about remedial policies—and even about the moral way to regard Blacks. Should they be chastised, upbraided, disciplined, looked down upon? Or should they be understood, loved, protected, accepted as one of our own?

The media's limited portrayals of Black success hold a distant second place to the more common portrayals of turmoil and inadequacy. The result is a pastiche that generally fails to bolster sympathetic Whites' favorable attitudes, let alone to challenge racists or move ambivalent Whites toward comity. As an example, the evidence in chapter 7 suggests that the climate of opinion created by the media and political elites arguably launched a spiral of silence, whereby the actual opinion majority, which was favorable in principle to affirmative action, might have felt overwhelmed by a perceived hostile majority. Meanwhile the background patterns of Black–White interactions in media entertainment typically enact social distance and suggest that the groups operate in distinct moral universes, with implicitly opposed interests. There are, of course, instructive exceptions. One is the friendship of Mel Gibson and Danny Glover in four *Lethal Weapon* movies; another is that portrayed in *Jerry Maguire*. Though laudable, these movies do showcase the White actor, the (far) bigger star, who serves as the focal point of the plot and intellectual driver of its problem solving.[5]

Note that although we have distinguished between news, entertainment, and advertising, there is little reason to believe that such distinctions significantly shape people's responses. The *overall patterns* of images and information establish the mental associations, the schemas used to process the social world. The most relevant differentiation is not between genres but between different patterns of communicated information and the prototypes they construct.[6] Whether in news or any other mediated communication, these patterns involve the overt associations between concepts, the repeated joint appearances. An example in news stories would be prisoners needing restraint and African American males; in movies, unrestrained profanity and Black females. Relevant patterns also include those linkages that the text does *not* encourage, because the concepts rarely appear together, such as technical expertise and African Americans.

The frequent pairing of social pathology (crime, cheating, violence, low self-discipline) and unpopular policy (welfare, affirmative action "preferences") with Blacks helps sustain the largely unconscious linkages that guide information processing. The experimental evidence demonstrates these linkages help ratify the White fear and rejection that act as a drag on support for ameliorative race policy in the public sphere and reinforce the separations in the private. The ignorance bred of private separation then makes Whites more susceptible to simplifying, partial media messages, a process fairly described as a vicious cycle.

In what way do media images cast Blacks outside the common identity (community)? How might they tend to tip ambivalent Whites in the direction of racial animosity, toward feelings that increase susceptibility to anti-Black political appeals? And in what ways do they fail to supply material that might prod those with animosity toward ambivalence and even comity? We now summarize our findings and their theoretical foundations.

Summary of Findings

The news presents a face of Black disruption, of criminal victimizing and victimization, that compares unfavorably with Whites. Such depictions may increase Whites' fear of entering Black neighborhoods, as it reduces their sympathy for Blacks—who are in fact far more afflicted by violence and crime than most Whites. In our Indianapolis interviews, only those who had prolonged personal contact with Blacks in arenas beyond the workplace failed to make comments that touched on the deep-seated fears and anxieties attached to Blacks as a social category. Ambivalent Whites spontaneously associated Blacks with poverty and welfare cheating, even where their lived experiences taught otherwise. The respondents expressed parallel frustration with Black leaders perceived as opportunistic and whining (Jesse Jackson), extremist (Louis Farrakhan), or corrupt (Marion Barry)—neglecting the many White politicians who match those descriptions. As suggested by our own audience research and that of others, such thinking finds nourishment, if not its origin, in images and implicit comparisons constructed in the news.[7]

Affirmative action was one issue that brought negative emotions to the surface. Few Whites in our interviews had anything positive to say about it, regarding such policies as fundamentally unfair. (Those on the lower end of the denial scale, however, were much less likely to reveal negative feelings.) The issue was vivid and salient in their minds, despite its being mainly beyond the realm of personal experience and thus of their self-interest. As a "wedge issue" it elicited the most corrosive feelings of racial animosity among respondents who were unaware that affirmative action had actually been more of a boon to women than to Blacks. Only one respondent spontaneously connected the mistreatment of the two groups. The salience of the issue to our Indianapolis sample (if not to the national samples asked to name "the most important problem facing the country," noted in chapter 7)[8] reflects the intense media coverage framing it in Black and White. That unlabeled preference programs have long benefited athletes and the children of (overwhelmingly White) college benefactors and alumni went almost totally unmentioned in media narratives. When asked directly about this less publicized stripe of affirmative action, virtually all in our Indianapolis interview sample agreed that it too unfairly violated meritocracy. Although this opinion was not accompanied by the visceral reaction aroused by pro-Black affirmative action, it does demonstrate the potential ameliorating influence of context. By deliberately raising the example of alumni and athlete preference in college admissions, we provided a context to reframe affirmative action, and our interviewees' reactions altered, softened. This suggests to us that were media to provide context, they could encourage similar movement away from animosity, back at least to ambivalence if not to comity.

In the less obviously political realms of entertainment and advertising, the pattern is one of disengagement, separation, and exaggeration. Cable's broadening of the television spectrum has created niche markets for which producers have crafted shows that obey market necessity by establishing product differentiation—a kind of cultural segregation. This inevitably leads to the heightening of racial distinction and significance, if not by appealing to cultural stereotyping than by the loading up of symbolic weight. The few Blacks who appear on programs favored by Whites carry the burden of racial distinction that, based on the evidence, is individually laudable but disengaged from the lives of the White characters. As one of our more media-savvy respondents observed on her impressions of interracial dramatic action, "In some situations they are definitely in competition with each other. In other situations I think that they are—I don't know. I can't say that they're friends, because in just thinking of what is on those two shows [*Chicago Hope, ER*], they don't hang out. They don't go places together; they don't talk on the phone after work; they don't hang out. They don't have anything to do with each other in life. They work together and that's about it."

Film is more racially progressive than television in some respects, due largely to its different political economy. Movies require fewer viewers to achieve profitability, and (presumably more tolerant) young persons and non-Whites make up disproportionate shares of the target audience. In addition, its creators appear to be more homogeneously liberal than is true of those in other media industry segments. This is quite an irony, given the right's overwhelming concentration on the alleged liberal bias of the news media, which have done little to promote left-leaning racial policy since the civil rights bills were passed in the mid-1960s.[9] Still, Hollywood limits the roles of Black characters and reinforces some cultural stereotypes (Black female aggression, ungrammatical language). Like television, it also usually skirts interracial intimacy. The distancing subtly evident in entertainment is reflected in the carefully crafted television ads that make racial distinctions in how they depict luxury products and display Black intimacy. These exclusions leave latent traces of the unconscious cultural judgment that drive them, of the dangers White producers still feel when scripting and casting ads, the most prevalent and most heavily invested media messages. The cautions of the marketplace do not emerge from a void; they reveal the cultural anxieties and background assumptions of their White investors.

But mediated communication is a moving target. At the turn of the twenty-first century, this industry was undergoing revolutionary transformation. Patterns documented here will change and exceptions to our generalizations will arise, as the new century and the new configuration of mediated communication take shape. As suggested by Dr. Benton's romantic liaison with a White female physician on *ER*, content previously taboo will begin to appear and the patterns we found entrenched may dissipate.

Theoretical Implications

The exceptional and unsettled cultural status of Black Americans interacts with the other factors in our model—the ordinary practices and continuing needs of media organizations and personnel, economic change in the industry, pressure from elites, and a globalizing economy. These interactions yield the unintended social and political communications we have explored throughout the book. We now point to their theoretical implications, and then illuminate possible paths to improvement.

For news it is clear that conventions of objectivity, the relatively simple techniques used to ensure balance and avoid bias, are not up to the task of covering issues in a racialized culture. For example, we found that the standard media rules employed to avoid bias—to ensure balanced communications that don't favor one side over another in a dispute—fail to banish the problem. Media coverage inadvertently boosted the individual responsibility position on the affirmative action issue, and local news implicitly promoted Whites' racialized fears of crime; the latter demonstrably increases Whites' hostility to the political and other interests of Blacks.[10] The visual nature of poverty coverage in the news, the paucity of explicit propositional discourse, also illustrates television's unbalanced if unpremeditated intervention in shaping elite and mass responses to a policy issue. These sorts of bias are not the ones conventionally defined as such by journalists, but they are no less significant for that.

Other media practices also interact with race to produce unintended consequences. The journalistic norm of seeking dramatic appeal in social conflict—a practice scholars have long viewed as problematic for democratic citizenship[11]—affects other realms of political communication as well. For example, in chapters 7 and 8, we saw how narratives that subordinated issue substance to political conflict and process yielded reporting that may have undermined racial comity. The emotional potency of an affirmative action narrative depicting the issue (misleadingly) as one holding White self-interest hostage to Black advancement found its target in our Indianapolis sample. The interview respondents similarly reacted to portrayals of complaining and inflammatory Black ministers. As the evidence shows in chapter 8, the dramatic visual icon depicting Jesse Jackson in Louis Farrakhan's embrace, and its implied assertions of an increasingly solid and extremist Black vote (uniformly contradicted by opinion polls), traded on the search for sensationalism. Unwittingly this provided a window of political opportunity for Farrakhan who drew larger and larger audiences as his media coverage increased. This scenario was reminiscent of the way the media's conflict-seeking heightened visibility for the flamboyant and militant wings of the New Left in the 1960s, to the detriment of wider public understanding and acceptance of the antiwar movement's policy analyses and recommendations.[12]

At a broader level, the evidence points to the need for refinement in theories regarding the nature of mediated political information. We must conceptualize the media's potential political influence to include implicit judgments and comparisons, and combinations of presences and voids. Audiences and media producers alike make comparisons to other messages and to more direct experience. This means measuring what is in the text alone does not clarify its political nature and potential impacts. Consider how in chapter 4 we found a scarcity of Black experts and dominance of expertise by Whites in network news, and in chapter 8 we saw White politicians depicted as far more altruistic and less demanding of largesse from the community treasury than Black. Such material sets up contrasts that in themselves are meaningful and possibly relevant to racial sentiments.

Relatedly, not only news and its overtly political content but the more covert politics of entertainment and advertising affect schematic thinking about race and about other matters of political import. As we pointed out earlier, audiences do not necessarily catalog their experience by the markers of market or academic specialty but draw implicit contrasts from their entire range of cultural experience. The limited scope of expression and representation by Black characters in movies enters the schema system right alongside the dearth of Black expertise in the news. The absence of close interracial social contact in prime-time entertainment parallels a similar absence in advertising and in most news reports. Though these voids are caused in part by actual social patterns, we have shown that such media images often fail to reflect other, equally significant aspects of the real world—or to *explain* the valid but disturbing and racially coded aspects of society that they do convey.

Our findings demonstrate that using simple measures of media exposure fail to reveal the potential power of the mediated material, which may arise from a single vivid prototype or exemplar, or perhaps from what is *not* in the news. Similarly, if any impact comes from *past* experience of media images as they interact with other cultural sources, then assessing only current exposure is bound to underestimate the media's influence. Thus seeing lots of images of (apparently) altruistic White politicians talking about the public interest is a major component of the overall mediated communication that establishes the invidious comparison to Black politicians, who seem self-seeking. It may take just a few exposures to apparently selfish, querulous Black leaders to implant the negative comparison after seeing all those images of White politicians, especially in light of White audiences' inherent favorability toward in-group members.

Representing Race

One could argue that news may have negative impacts merely as an inadvertent if unfortunate by-product of accurately conveying "realities," say, that Black leaders actually are, after all, more prone to demand overtly group-based government assistance. But as we have seen throughout, these facts arise out of complicated contexts that help explain disparities without invidiously disparaging African Americans. They are susceptible to serious misinterpretation by Whites raised in a culture with a long history and continuing residue of racist suspicion. In covering stories about Black individuals, journalists may not merely be representing a single newsworthy event in which a Black happens to take part. Journalists may also be selecting exemplars or prototypes that represent the category "Blacks" and get compared to Whites' images of themselves. Each in a series of news stories may be defensibly accurate, yet the combination may yield false cognitions within audiences. If "accurate" news reports yield inaccurate inferences, then we have a serious conundrum to which the response "We can't help it, we're just reporting the facts" is insufficient.

Here seems to lie the crux of the representation problem, at least for news: Is the journalist's responsibility limited to creating an accurate verbal and visual record in the news text, or does it encompass stimulating an accurate mental representation in the audience's minds? The first goal is problematic enough: there are always happenings and interpretations that might legitimately merit coverage yet fail to survive the filter of the newsmaking process. But beyond is the even harder task of encouraging accurate understanding among audience members. Presumably the justification of professional news creeds is to ensure that audiences can grasp something like truth—and cease adhering to verifiable untruths, such as the notion that Blacks commit over 60 percent of the violent crimes in the United States or soak up a huge proportion of the federal budget. Accuracy for its own sake, without concern for audience understanding, hardly seems a legitimate end for journalism.[13]

We fully understand, of course, the controversial nature of our suggestion that identifiable or determinate truths or realities exist for audiences to understand. Anybody writing about commercial culture at the end of the twentieth century could hardly miss all the arguments for the contingent nature of truth and for the social construction of reality. We do not wish to contest those points as a general matter. Nor do we deny that undisputed facts, even if we could agree on them, would still admit of a multitude of possible interpretations. What we are suggesting is that (1) there are facts relevant to race relations, such as crime statistics and welfare budgets, that are widely available; (2) it is better for American society if those facts are known as such by its members (with the caveat that experts and empirical studies can be wrong); and (3) where facts or their interpretation are in dispute, as is generally the case with race, an explicit, self-critical awareness on the part of communicators and audiences of what is at stake is better than unmindful acceptance or close-minded rejection.

If we were to restrict our concern to textual accuracy, we would run into serious conceptual and normative problems. Consider some of the important research that we have previously cited. Gilens finds overrepresentation of Blacks in images of poverty, and Gilliam et al. and Romer et al. find that local television news overrepresents Black perpetrators and underrepresents Blacks as victims in crime stories.[14] Such findings raise questions about the usefulness of numerical proportionality as a criterion for assessing accuracy. Do we want news to cover Black males accused of crime in proportion to their actual percentage of all crime perpetrators (which masks differences in arrest and conviction rates)—or of all convicts? What about type of crime: should portrayals be proportional too, so that the "right" number of Black and White males are shown as rapists, gang members, organized crime hit men, extortionists, and the rest? Is the proper gauge the percentage of Black males shown as criminals compared with the percentage of Black males shown as noncriminals? Should national data form the basis for setting up the racial representations, or should they reflect only local conditions? Exactly why should one be preferred over the other?

Assuming these questions were answered, how could the news adjust itself to the chosen standard? News events do not necessarily flow in consistent fashion to allow, say, covering a few extra White gang members in February to balance an overrepresentation of Blacks during January. If no White gang members are arrested in February there will be no way to achieve the balance. If we decided the standard should be that the majority of Black males shown in news not be criminals, we would be demanding a radical change in news values. And the list of objections could go on. Clearly the problems are magnified if we turn to representations in advertising or entertainment, which do not even claim or aim to depict "reality."

Even if we had clear answers to the media issues, we know people tend to disregard counter-stereotypical or counter-schematic information. This is apparently true even in many cases where a person recognizes the existence of misleading stereotypes.[15] It takes active, self-critical awareness and discipline to counteract schematic tendencies in one's own thinking,[16] which most audience members have neither the motivation nor the skills to accomplish, especially on a subject as perplexing as race.

As an example, returning to our interviews, a very well-educated seventy-year-old man who had run a factory in Indianapolis made this observation on the reasons for continuing Black disadvantage:

> Well I think that they are largely environmental having to do with education being, I think, inferior in general. Blacks are not as well educated. Obviously the social pressures that they face that we don't in general. In terms of job placement and advance and the ability to get any job they want. It's more difficult for them. And there are obstacles, obviously, all along the way, mostly from the social and cultural environment, in which they live. Poverty has a lot to do with it. In general they are not as well off economically as Whites, and we know that the better off you start off economically, the more apt you are to do well. So I think there are a lot of reasons. A lot of them are attitudinal. A lot of them I think are that Blacks, for a number of reasons, are perhaps don't appear as motivated as one would hope. But a lot of that again relates to the fact that their social environment makes it a lot more unlikely that they're going to be motivated to get ahead.

Yet even this sophisticated and informed man expressed racial animosity, claiming that Black workers in his factory had used race as an excuse to extract a variety of concessions: "Whenever there was any disciplinary action taken against a Black, we were almost invariably faced with EEOC [Equal Employment Opportunity Commission] charges or something like that. That we felt were unwarranted. And in fact I think without exception even when they went to the EEOC, in no case were we found guilty of discrimination on the basis of race. But it never kept them from raising these actions against us." Although not inconceivable, it seems unlikely that almost every Black person disciplined at this factory actually did play the race card with the EEOC. More likely, the few times this happened were highly salient for a man not used to having his authority challenged, a man raised in a culture that makes racial identity noteworthy and meaningful.[17] He blamed what he regarded as the liberal-leaning media for encouraging Black aggressiveness: "I think the media in general supports the legislation that has encouraged this demand mode."

What Is to Be Done?

Theoretical inquiry in the social sciences always rests upon a foundation of normative goals. Our empirical and analytical questions emerge from the issues that our values guide us to consider important. Our own normative ends for mediated communication in the life of a democratic community include the following:

1. Providing accurate representation of knowable facts (like the size of the Black population and the welfare budget).

2. Seeking to create dominant frames in the audience's minds that are rooted in such facts, or at least in consciously chosen and openly announced value commitments; that is, selecting and highlighting and therefore popularizing understandings of social problems, causes, and remedies based on what we know, not what we fear or unmindfully assume.

3. Providing self-critical material that offers context and clarifies the causes of the images that appear. In this mode, the news would report that Black crime rates are much higher than White, but that racial difference disappears if we control for employment status. They would show former Washington, D.C. Mayor Marion Barry to be a miscreant, while acknowledging that they paid so much attention to him because his story was sensational, not because that story offered any basis for generalizing about Black mayors. In such ways the news would continually remind audiences of the inadequacies and inevitable partiality of mediated communications.

It may be too much to ask the news media to analyze and potentially undermine their own credibility. Virtually every book ever written about them has called for news stories to provide more context, but to little avail—for reasons well understood by scholars.[18] Entertainment and advertising executives have even less responsibility or ability to clarify America's world of race, although, as we have suggested, some movies and television shows may occasionally do a better job at this than most news outlets.

In response to this conundrum we would *encourage critical audience awareness and public deliberation over media effects on America's racial culture.* The novelty of our suggestion is that we call for government and foundations to fund a systematic effort to make culture industry practices themselves integral to the public issue agenda, not isolated within a specialized professional and academic dialogue. We urge systematic monitoring of media output on race matters and a public debate on these productions, akin to the long-standing, government and foundation-subsidized discussions and investigations of media violence.

The parallels to media violence are instructive. Although the public's choices in the media marketplace might indicate their desire for violent, uninformative media content, polls suggest Americans are concerned about the social effects of their own viewing behavior. Surveys have found that over 50 percent of the public support some form of government regulation to limit violence on television, and 82 percent believe television programming is too violent.[19] Perhaps responding to such sentiment, Congress included in the Telecommunications Act of 1996 a requirement that a "V" chip be installed in newly manufactured television sets, providing some parental control over receipt of violent shows. Evidence suggests that the public would welcome restraints on the negative by-products of their own media consumption habits.[20]

We believe that the images of race embedded within much media content are as problematic for society as the images of violence. Thus there is both reason and precedent for a major monitoring program. It would provide the basis for informed cultural debate among reflective audiences and media personnel. Argument—even the vigorous, loud variety—tends to pull disputants in from ideological extremes and frozen misunderstandings, or at the least stimulates communication.[21] The very process of making the implicit culture explicit and debating its effects on ourselves would engage the members of the two racial groups with each other and ultimately, we think, enhance mutual trust and understanding. Such discourse could build social capital, the kind of trust and empathy across group lines that is the essence of racial comity.

Understanding can also be assisted if Blacks for their part can see how White fear, rejection, denial, and even stereotyping do not constitute proof of irremediable racism. There may be less malignant explanations, as Patterson argues with particular eloquence.[22] And as we have suggested, a racially prejudiced position on one dimension does not a racist make. A stance of mutual understanding and seeking for more benign explanations does not mean Blacks or Whites of goodwill must tolerate politicians' opportunistic manipulation of racial animosity and ignorance, as in the "Willie" Horton advertisement, or deliberate distortion of the racial stakes in affirmative action. On the contrary, this fuller understanding provides the intellectual and ethical basis to denounce such behavior for the moral bankruptcy it evinces—moral denunciations, by the way, glaringly absent from elite discourse on those particular matters.

Perhaps these issues are moot; perhaps no amount of mediated counterexample to stereotype, no length of cultural argument, no enlargement of

Blacks' own empathy with Whites, would suffice. It may be that Whites need to understand better their prejudices and misunderstandings, and the ways these are reflected and perpetuated by mediated communication, before dialogue would do much good. But progress has to start somewhere, and here is the opening we see: our work suggests that some White persons may fear, dislike, even think Blacks fundamentally different and inferior, yet still, out of self-interest or moral self-examination or ambivalence, support government policies to help. Such policies could themselves decrease inequality and nurture a sense of common purpose and success. A virtuous spiral might ensue, in which Blacks start seeming less foreign and threatening, which encourages more personal association and openness to positive media messages, corrects misapprehensions, fills in knowledge gaps—builds the necessary trust and understanding for expanding political and economic success. At the very least, the ongoing interracial dialogue we propose would highlight the social costs of the opposite trend, the common interest in terminating vicious cycles of suspicion and animosity.

Although our own emphases tend to obscure the point, we believe some of the most important prior studies offer considerable if unrecognized support to our reading. Kinder and Sanders, in stressing the role of racial resentment, and Sniderman and Piazza in their emphasis on the anger generated by affirmative action, make too little of the very large portion of unexplained variance in racial policy attitudes that they discover.[23] Kinder and Sanders find that racial resentment explains about 10 percent to 35 percent of the variation in Whites' policy stands. This suggests the bulk of opinion is unrestrained by the resentment. That does not mean Whites' displeasure is unimportant; it may even be decisive to particular elections or other political outcomes. But it does suggest the potential for change. Sometimes support for good policy can precede good intentions—especially if encouraged by communication media. Furthermore, what comes through, especially from Kinder and Sanders' research, is the surprising failure of "rational self-interest" to make much difference to individuals' racial policy positions. For example, Whites' employment and economic status has little impact upon their attitudes toward affirmative action; nor does having children in school significantly affect their opinions about busing. One thing that makes media imagery so important is that it likely fills the vacuum left by the failure of material self-interest calculations significantly to shape Whites' policy attitudes.[24]

Merelman suggests that the most desirable form of intergroup mass communication is syncretism, a union of perspectives in which dominants accept some of the subordinates' "cultural projections" (or racial projects) and vice versa.[25] Content that melds group views and opens up new, synthetic perspectives has been rare. Yet this is what is necessary for media to facilitate racial comity, and the potential malleability of many Whites' beliefs suggests the possibility that such material might have an impact. This may hold especially for younger Whites. It seems possible that generational replacement could accomplish what past mediated exemplars and relationships have not. The youth culture of the 1990s as epitomized by popular music, MTV, and youth-targeted movies and television shows, seems less fearful, more positively attracted to syncretic expressions.[26] And as we have noted, even as *ER* and *Ally McBeal* were gingerly testing the fictional boundaries, in the real world interracial dating and marriage—embodiments of syncretic interpersonal communication—were increasing as a new millennium began. For older generations, however, self-conscious awareness and conversation on the racial meanings and implications of mediated communication constitute the form of syncretism with the most potential to promote racial comity.

In this light, the media's mission must be to provide a context that will encourage and allow audiences to engage in interpretation and active challenge of assumptions and stereotypes. The ultimate objective should be serving the interest of genuine autonomous thinking by an audience not unknowingly bound into one discourse and prevented from thinking through another. Seeking such an end could allow journalism to enhance racial understanding not only directly but indirectly by promoting a more critical, analytical frame of mind among media audiences.

The goal of journalism's professional credos, presumably to give audiences a chance to decide for themselves on the truth and implications of a reported matter—to serve audiences' intellectual autonomy—may be better promoted by self-consciously shaping the stories with what might be called *editorial objectivity*. That is, news organizations could make a commitment to provide an explicit, self-critical, and intellectually honest assessment of the political and social import of the reported matter. Thus when they cover yet another ghetto crime, local news shows could disrupt the conventional narrative flow and discuss expressly the dangers such reports pose of reinforcing racially damaging myths. Correspondents could put a human face on the defendants and victims, ordinary people who suddenly find themselves subjects of the news. This angle, we submit, could produce compelling, ratings-boosting material, aside from its social benefits.

To counter the documented tendency of so many Whites to think through negative stereotypes, reporters could note that crime rates of employed Black and White adults are the same. If it seems redundant to restate this mantra every time they report Black crime, consider how many times reporters employed such introductory phrases as "O.J. Simpson, the former football star charged in the slaying of his former wife Nicole," or "President Clinton, who stands accused of lying about his relationship with Monica Lewinsky, a former White House intern," as if many Americans after the first day or two did not know who these people were.

The mass-oriented news media do not provide this kind of contextualized reporting, and argue they cannot. Though citing various factors, they usually emphasize that the business interests of media trump civic interests. They would lose audiences and advertisers with the kind of reporting critics want, which is in any case too expensive to mount. Not to mention the problem already cited: normative standards are unclear, and thus perhaps impossible to meet in any consistent way. Yet even though perfection is unattainable, the difficulties do not excuse the media from trying to improve.

Turning from news to entertainment, normative and practical difficulties are no less profound. Nor is entertainment all that different from news in its political sense. The excellent documentary *Color Adjustment* reveals that producers of almost all the successful shows that featured Blacks prominently, from *Julia* and *I Spy*, pioneers of integrated entertainment in the 1960s, on through *Roots* and *Good Times* in the 1970s and *Cosby* in the 1980s, were highly self-conscious of their political and opinion impacts.[27] We documented similar self awareness on *ER* in the 1990s. These programs were, in other words, quite clearly not *just* entertainment but also consciously produced political communications whose creators anticipated reactions from elites and activists as well as advertisers and audiences. This shows if nothing else how politicized race relations are. Even producers for seemingly escapist entertainment cannot write roles, create situations, or cast Black actors without consciousness of race, and this market reality records Blacks' liminal status and strained relationships with Whites.

In the same way that careful consideration raises true perplexities for any attempt to prescribe the proper course for journalism, in the area of entertainment we also must ask ourselves hard questions. What images and conditions of Blacks, who inescapably represent their race to Whites in this culture, would we *like* to see on television and in film? Does a *Cosby* show enhance the bases for racial comity in its challenge to stereotyping? Or is it somehow comforting to Whites, implicitly casting blame on all Blacks who don't "fit in" quite as perfectly as the Huxtables? *ER* denies old prejudice by depicting a superbly competent and conscientious Black surgeon. Nonetheless, does *ER* also undermine comity by suggesting that Dr. Benton treats Black patients differently from White—even if that is both a realistic reflection of our race-conscious society and a legitimate dramatic device? There is no easy way out of the dilemma of reinforcing White complacency by making the entertaining Blacks such purified exemplars of White cultural ideals that, like the Cosby family or Dr. Benton on *ER*, they seem (by their disruption of Whites' normal mental associations) "not really Black."[28]

Here again the first step is self-conscious awareness on the part of audiences and media workers alike as to what meanings and implicit comparisons are embedded, and how they may reflect and reinforce unfortunate thoughts, negative emotions, or unthinking assumptions. We do not think it too much to ask that movie producers at least consider the possibility that they could make money, even blockbusters, with Blacks cast against type or in more truly egalitarian relationships. At a minimum, we would hope a monitoring project that documents the limited roles, behaviors, and attributes available to Black as compared with White actors could alter audiences' awareness of the subtle signals emanating from Hollywood's dream factory.

The same holds for prime-time television entertainment, where audience segmentation and "narrowcasting" was by century's end yielding a degree of cultural resegregation: programs targeted to Blacks quite separately from those aimed at Whites, with vast racial disparities in ratings a sad barometer of social division. Indeed, the 1990s saw a parallel movement toward more segregated public schools.[29] And of course segmentation is the very basis of advertising. The producers of ads might argue they have the least creative leeway of any media outlet to reshape outputs on promise of some indirect benefits to racial harmony. Advertisers have to keep audiences comfortable to gain goodwill and move products. Here again, even if it would not spur change, monitoring could reveal to all the potential implications for racial understanding of business as usual in this industry. As noted in chapter 10, standard practices at century's end included openly announced ethnic and racial separation and labeling of advertising accounts, and outright discrimination against Black-owned or targeted radio stations.

In response to monitoring, how might media organizations fulfill a higher calling? No longer should news workers rest satisfied with a formulaic balance in their verbal narratives. And the potential effects (in more technical terms, the negative externalities) of profit-driven advertising and entertainment call for an overhaul in these industries' formulae as well. We propose that journalists and even entertainment and advertising personnel use monitoring to take continuous stock of the cumulative effect their individual reports and programs might have on race relations. We suggest media workers make the connections first in their own minds, and then in their texts, between yesterday and today, between visuals and verbal messages. We thus call for a new form of comprehensive narration. This may require new types of news editors and entertainment producers who look for patterns over time in media products, scouting for exclusions, inaccurate connotations, and misleading comparisons or juxtapositions. At the same time, they should seek to supply media narratives that provide a context allowing audiences to engage in more active interpretation and challenge of unthinking assumptions.

Is this utopian? Perhaps, but fortunately, we need not rest our call to media improvement on an appeal to altruism or social responsibility alone. Market pressures will likely drive policy departures as *mass* media and their advertiser clients search for ways to distinguish themselves and remain valuable. The mass media face competition from individually customized news and entertainment vehicles delivered via broadband information networks. And they confront the need to satisfy increasingly diverse audiences both domestically and globally. What *mass* media have to offer in competition with the narrow-gauged, individualized new media forms is context and narrative coherence. To stay competitive, news media seeking mass audiences will sell their credibility as information integrators, master narrators of the data and opinion cacophony that might otherwise overwhelm (or totally isolate) citizens. Entertainment and advertising producers, though driven to specialized narrowcasting, will nonetheless still find that integrative, broadly appealing products are the best way to advance their careers.[30] Any television or movie company would far rather have a single *ER, Titanic,* or *Independence Day* than five small successes, for reasons ranging from sheer return on investment to prestige and fame to stock market valuations. Attaining this goal will require increasing and more continuous sensitivity to diverse ethnic sensibilities on the part of mass-oriented media organizations.

Beyond this is the interest mass media possess in racial comity itself. Social alienation threatens their long-term profitability. One product of a low sense of community, of decreasingly common interests across group boundaries, we believe, is declining inclination among audiences to spend time with news media.[31] Conditions of high alienation and cynicism about society's collective ability to solve problems through democratic deliberation and political action reduce the size and attentiveness of news audiences.

As for entertainment, a shrinking mass audience watching in an increasingly sour frame of mind will render commercial time less valuable to advertisers, many of them mass marketers (ranging from Wal-Mart and Sears to GM and Ford to McDonalds and Pizza Hut) who do *not* seek narrow-niche audiences. Alienation from the larger community may drive yet further cultural segmentation, diminishing profitability of those mass media productions and advertisers seeking the largest audiences. In any case, deteriorating social trust diminishes the overall financial wealth of society;[32] this reduces the money consumers have to spend on HBO, movie tickets, cars—all products, media and nonmedia—as it lessens the profitability of advertising.

The same reasoning holds if we assume that mass media will be largely replaced in the new millennium (not merely supplemented) by niche media perhaps targeted down to the level of the individual. If the media system does indeed move toward supplying tailor-made news, information, entertainment, and advertising via broadband digital connections to every home, opportunities for many Americans to experience syncretic learning and challenges to stereotype and misunderstanding may diminish. Market incentives may push in that direction, but in the long run it is not a prescription for a healthy economy or communication industry. A distrusting, anxious society of individuals sharing thoughts and feelings only with like-minded individuals, where communication across group boundaries becomes even more exceptional than it has been, is a society likely to become poorer, not to mention less democratic.[33] So again, there is at least some reason to hope that enlightened media executives will see that promoting intergroup understanding can serve the longer-term interests of their enterprises. But, alas, short-term market pressures may push more compellingly in the opposite direction.

All this said, we must acknowledge the considerable degree of uncertainty that remains in our understanding of media products, their reception, their social implications—and the ideal direction they might take if all were as we wished. Yet it seems reasonable to assume that mediated images of race do mirror and help to shape the culture that spawns racial understanding and misunderstanding. Any move toward racial representation that is more socially responsible, and that may even be more profitable, is a move worth making.

Appendix

Data Tables

Table A.1 Items Constituting the Racial Denial Scale

	Indianapolis				National Surveys			
	Strongly Agree (%)	Agree Some (%)	Disagree (%)	Strongly Disagree (%)	Strongly Agree (%)	Agree Some (%)	Disagree (%)	Strongly Disagree (%)
1. Irish, Italians, Jewish and many other minorities overcame prejudice and worked their way up. Blacks should do the same without any special favors.	32.2	44.6	18.2	5.0	31.2	44.9	16.0	7.9
2. Most Blacks who are on welfare programs could get a job if they really tried.	35.0	42.8	16.9	5.3	25.4	35.3	18.7	6.5
3. If Blacks would only try harder they could be just as well off as Whites.	17.5	40.7	25.6	16.3	23.9	41.6	21.8	12.7
4. Black neighborhoods tend to be run down because Blacks simply don't take care of their property.	17.0	33.2	29.0	20.7		42.0		
5. A history of slavery and being discriminated against has created conditions that make it difficult for Black people to work their way up.	15.2	35.7	22.5	26.6	22.3	40.0	23.3	14.3

Sources: Question 1: NES, 1992; NES, 1986; 3, NES, 1992; 4, Race & Politics Survey, 1986. Sniderman and Piazza (1993) report only percentage agree responses; 5, NES, 1992.
Note: the percentages are calculated from a base that excludes the middle "neither agree nor disagree" category.

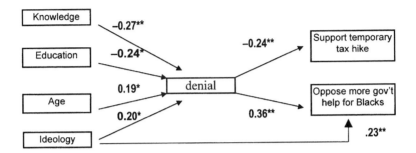

Figure A.1 Causes and Consequences of Racial Denial
Note: Figures are partial correlations (Pearson's r).
**p < .001; *p < .01

Table A.2 Characteristics of the Survey
and Interview Groups

	Survey *(N = 251)*	*Interviews* *(N = 25)*
Age	43.9	52.2
Education	14.3	14.2
Income		
< $15K	6.9%	4.0%
15–25K	17.4	8.0
26–50K	27.1	32.0
51–75K	21.9	20.0
76–100K	9.7	20.0
> $100K	10.9	8.0
Ideology		
Liberal	14.7%	8.0%
Moderate	48.1	32.0
Conservative	37.2	60.0
Denial		
Low	15.4%	12.0%
Moderate	53.0	60.0
High	31.6	28.0
Average	8.8	9.0

230

Appendix

Table A.3 Mentions of "Black" in ABC *World News*: Story Categories*

	1990-91			1997		
Topics	Number of Stories	Percent of All Stories	Percent of Stories Excluding Nonracial Uses	Number of Stories	Percent of All Stories	Percent of Stories Excluding Nonracial Uses
South Africa	102	34.0	36.4	4	2.2	3.6
Victimage/Vulnerability	76	25.3	27.1	21	11.5	19.1
Politics	37	12.3	13.2	4	2.2	3.6
Crime	22	7.3	7.9	26	14.2	23.6
Nonracial use	20	6.7		73	39.9	
Antidiscrimination policies	16	5.3	5.7	17	9.3	15.4
Other	11	3.7	3.9	17	9.3	15.4
Human interest	8	2.7	2.9	9	4.9	8.2
Sports	6	2.0	2.1	10	5.5	9.1
Africa	2	0.7	0.7	2	1.1	1.8
Total	300	100	100	183	100	100

Source: ABC *World News Tonight* (including *World News Saturday* and *World News Sunday*) transcripts, January–June 1990 and July–December 1991; January–December 1997.
*Includes two stories that mentioned "African American" in 1997, without mentioning the word *Black*.

Table A.4 Story Topics Mentioning Blacks, ABC *World News*, July–December 1997

Topic Categories	U.S. Story Topics	Non-U.S. Story Topics
Crime	Aberdeen Army base rapes Murder victim helpful to all, brown, Black, White Geronimo Pratt released after 27 years in prison Racist murders of Blacks by Army Pvt. Burmeister (n = 2) O.J. Simpson civil trial (n = 6) Beating/rape of young Black girl Beating of young Black boy Murder trial of accused in murder of rabbinical student after racial unrest Controversy over D.A.'s remark that Black jurors are undesirable Ennis Cosby murder suspect Militia targets Blacks, Asians, Hispanics Sexual harassment by Black man in Army (n = 2)	Murder of Black in London Blacks and Whites disappointed and fearful; crime up since Mandela took office in South Africa
Victimage and vulnerability	Report on church burning Teen pregnancy	South Africa Truth Commission

(continued)

Table A.4 (*Continued*)

Topic Categories	U.S. Story Topics	Non-U.S. Story Topics
	Schools now more segregated	Anti-Somali racism
	Black women more prone to breast cancer (n = 2)	among Canadian
	U.S. 50 years ago when Jackie Robinson	troops
	joined Dodgers	
	Discrimination and fear in Matteson, Illinois	
	Fuzzy Zoeller anti-Black remarks about Tiger	
	Woods	
	Death of William Brennan, antiracist Justice	
	Death of Rudolph Bing, antiracist opera director	
	Promise Keeper group is against racism	
	Racist slave posters withdrawn from auction	
	Inner city kids prone to asthma	
Human interest	Paul Freeman, Black conductor	
	One rich White kid compared to one poor Black	
	kid, both going to college	
Statistics	Blacks suffer more heart disease	
	Hispanics will outnumber Blacks in 2050	
	Black admissions to University of California law	
	schools way down	
	Black unemployment down, but still in double	
	digits	
Sports	Larry Doby, first Black in American League	
	baseball	
	Jackie Robinson anniversary (n = 2)	
	Tiger Woods first Black to win Masters tournament	
	(n = 2)	
	Latrell Sprewell denies racial component in attack	
	on coach	
Antidiscrimi-	Critique of Clinton's race policies	
nation policies	Split on affirmative action between Black former	
	government official William Coleman and his	
	daughter	
	Clinton's kick-off speech for Race Initiative	
	Multicultural focus for Race Initiative	
	Affirmative action in law schools; one Black's	
	success	
	Backlash against affirmative action in Michigan	
	Anti-affirmative action referenda (n = 2)	
Other	Ebonics controversy	Hillary Clinton visits
	White CEO who helps rebuild burned	South Africa
	Black churches	
	Controversy over Black actor playing Jesus	
	Howard Stern mentions jokes about Blacks	
	Sojourner Truth should be in Suffrage Memorial	
	Poll of Blacks and Whites on racial	
	discrimination	

Table A.5 1997 Black Soundbites: Topics and Roles

Topic	Professional, Expert	Law, Legal	Government Official	Blue Collar	Community Activist	Person on Street	Other	Total
Crime	1	4	10		1	5	3	24
Human interest	6	2				13	2	23
Court proceedings/ Government hearings	2				2	7	1	12
Sports/Entertainment			5				6	11
Discrimination	1		2	3	1	1	2	10
Disasters/Rescues/ Weather events			1			3	1	5
Deaths, Anniversaries, Memorials			1			2		3
Science/Technology				1		2		3
Health/Smoking						1	1	2
Economics			1					1
Foreign affairs						1		1
Electoral politics								0
Other	4	6	2			1	3	16
Totals	14	12	22	4	4	36	19	111

Table A.6 Dominant Visual Images of Poverty

Image	Percentage of Poverty Symptom Stories (n = 239) Including Image	Number of Stories Including Image
Black persons marching	62.3	149
Black persons milling	56.5	135
Urban blight	56.1	134
Black leaders speaking	30.1	73

Table A.7 Whites' Attitudes Toward Race and Poverty as Function of Media Use

Dependent variable: three-item scale on poverty as individual Blacks' fault
Significant independent variables[a]

Education	-0.18^b	
		(-7.9)
Religion	-0.18^b	
		(-3.6)
Television reliance for news	0.18^b	
		(3.4)
Ideology	-0.11^b	
		(-3.3)
Local news station watched most frequently	0.27^c	
		(2.6)
Adjusted R^2	0.20	
F	28.4^b	

Note: Entries are unstandardized regression coefficients; numbers in parentheses are t-statistics.

Notes on variables in equation: Regression of White Chicagoans' attitudes on the poverty-related attitude scale measured from the 1991 Chicago Area Study Project, a random survey of the Chicago metropolitan area conducted by the Northwestern University Survey Laboratory. White respondents' answers to questions designed to tap their feelings toward Blacks were subjected to factor analysis indicating that two basic dimensions were tapped by the questions. Based on the factor analysis, answers were added into scales. The scale used as the dependent variable generated a Cronbach's reliability alpha of 0.56, a relatively low reliability score that indicates the scale should be treated with some caution. However, the factor analysis did strongly support the surmise that the questions tapped two distinct dimensions. Please note the following explanations of independent variables.

Ideology is ideological self-identification from 1 (extreme liberal) to 7 (extreme conservative); Education is years of schooling; Local news is number of days per week respondent reports watching early and late local news (scores ranged from 0 to 14); TV watching is how many hours per day respondent reports watching TV; Party identification, with codes 1 for Democrat, 2 for Independent, and 3 for Republican; Gender is coded 0 for female, 1 for male; TV reliance is source of most political information, with 1 for heaviest reliance on newspapers or magazines, 2 for heaviest reliance on radio; and 3 for heaviest reliance on local or network TV news; Religion is coded 1 for Catholic, 2 for Protestant, 3 for Jewish, and 4 for no religion (18 sample members citing other religions were excluded); Station is coded so that habitual watchers of WLS (ABC affiliate and highest rated) for local news are coded 1 and all others coded 0; Age in years.

[a]Other independent variables entered but not shown because their effects do not reach statistical significance: frequency of watching local TV news, party identification, gender, and age.

[b]$p \leq 0.001$.

[c]$p < 0.01$.

Appendix

Table A.8 National News Coverage of Jesse Jackson, 1984 Primary Season

Date	Network	Story	Use of News Icon
2/26	CBS, NBC	Jackson in trouble for his anti-Semitic remarks; Farrakhan comes to his defense	Farrakhan embrace at podium; Farrakhan as enthusiastic supporter
2/27	CBS	Ethnic slurs and strain on Black–Jewish coalition	Embrace of Arafat
4/3	NBC	Farrakhan (top Jackson supporter) threat on Milton Coleman	Shoulder graphic*; Farrakhan embrace at podium
4/4	CBS	Threat on Coleman by Farrakhan; media soft on Jackson campaign	Farrakhan influential Jackson supporter
5/1	CBS	Farrakhan registers to vote; calls Hitler great man	Farrakhan embrace at podium
5/1	NBC	Civil Rights Commission asks Jackson to repudiate Farrakhan support	Shoulder graphic
5/22	NBC	Analysis of Farrakhan's threats on critics	Farrakhan actively supports Jackson
6/5	NBC	Retrospective on primaries	Jackson's refusal to disavow Farrakhan support; Farrakhan embrace at podium
6/28	CBS, NBC, ABC	Farrakhan, Jackson supporter, calls Judaism a dirty religion	Footage of Jackson at a Farrakhan speech
6/29	NBC	Jackson arrives from Cuba with freed prisoners.	Embrace of Arafat (photo); Farrakhan embrace at podium
7/2	ABC	Jackson and Mondale at NAACP convention	Farrakhan embrace at podium
7/3	CBS, ABC	Mondale and Jackson settle differences	Farrakhan's message disavowed
7/7	CBS	Jewish vote not taken for granted by Democrats	Farrakhan embrace at podium
7/10	CBS	Poll shows Blacks prefer Mondale to Jackson, 53% to 31%; analysis of Jackson campaign	Farrakhan embrace at podium; experts for and against embrace
7/30	ABC	Farrakhan at Washington Press Club	Farrakhan as supporter of Jackson; Farrakhan embrace at podium

*A corner graphic showing a still of Jackson and Farrakhan and Jackson embracing.

Data Tables

Table A.9 National News Coverage of Jesse Jackson, 1988 Primary Season

Date	Network	Story	Metaphor
6/25/87	NBC	Analysis of Jackson's new image	Farrakhan as millstone in 1984
7/30	ABC	Growing support among working-class Democrats for Jackson; fear among party regulars	Closeness to Arafat, Farrakhan, Castro
8/14	CBS	Jackson changing his direction to front-running middle-of-the-roader	Coziness with Arafat, arm in arm with Farrakhan, stroll with Castro
9/7	ABC	Jackson announces for president (profile)	Past relationship to Farrakhan; Farra-khan embrace at podium
3/3/88	NBC	Super Tuesday, uneasiness about Jackson's candidacy; lingering doubts about growing power	Farrakhan embrace at podium
3/11	NBC	Jackson on a primary roll; fear that he will be candidate. Reverse racism explains rise to power	Association with radical Arab states, Castro, Farrakhan
3/28	ABC	Democratic leaders in awe, fear Jackson breakout	Farrakhan embrace at podium
4/9	NBC	Jackson vs. Ed Koch; Jackson poison to Jews	Farrakhan embrace at podium
4/10	ABC	Jackson in New York primary	Reference to embrace of Arafat; Farrakhan embrace at podium
4/11	NBC, ABC	NY primary and Israel	Farrakhan embrace at podium
4/12	CBS	Jewish vote	Embrace of Arafat
4/17	NBC	Friction between Jackson and NY Jews	Jewish boy in Brooklyn remembers Jackson embracing Farrakhan

Table A.10 Stories Mentioning and Quoting Top Black Leaders, ABC *World News* 1990–91

Leaders	Stories		Soundbites	
Clarence Thomas	89	(47.8)	32	(31.1)
Marion Barry	23	(12.3)	10	(9.7)
Louis Sullivan	14	(7.5)	14	(13.6)
Jesse Jackson	14	(7.5)	6	(5.8)
Colin Powell	7	(3.8)	3	(2.9)
David Dinkins	6	(3.2)	7	(6.8)
Benjamin Hooks	6	(3.2)	7	(6.8)
Douglas Wilder	5	(2.4)	5	(4.8)
William Gray	3	(1.6)	3	(2.9)
All others	19	(10.2)	16	(15.5)
Total	186	(100.0)	103	(100.0)

Note: Figures in parentheses are percentages.

Table A.11 Mentions of "100 Most Influential Black Americans," ABC *World News*, 1994 and 1997

	1994			1997		
	Stories	Soundbites	Subject or Story Linked to Crime	Stories	Soundbites	Subject or Story Linked to Crime
Dennis Archer, Detroit mayor	3	2	1			
Carol Mosley Braun, U.S. Senate				3	6	0
Ronald Brown, U.S. Commerce Secretary	7	3	0	3	0	2
William Campbell, Atlanta mayor				3	3	2
Benjamin Chavis, Director, NAACP	5	10	2			
Bill Cosby, entertainer				7	0	5
Joycelyn Elders, U.S. Surgeon General	7	5	2			
Mike Espy, U.S. Agriculture Secretary	6	3	5			
Louis Farrakhan, Nation of Islam	10	15	2	4	2	2
Rev. Jesse Jackson	7	6	2	6	12	1
Michael Jackson, entertainer	10	0	6			
Earvin "Magic" Johnson, NBA player	5	3	0			
Michael Jordan, NBA player	15	5	0	11	3	1
John Lewis, U.S. House of Rep.	4	3	2			
Carrie Meek, U.S. House of Rep.	3	3	0			
Kweisi Mfume, U.S. House of Rep. 1994 Head, NAACP 1997	8	9	1	3	4	1
Hazel O'Leary, U.S. Energy Secretary	3	9	0			
Gen. Colin Powell	6	2	0	4	2	0
Charles Rangel, U.S. House of Rep.	4	3	1			
Franklin Raines, Director, OMB				3	3	0
Clarence Thomas, U.S. Supreme Ct.	6	0	1			
Togo West, Army Secretary				4	0	
Oprah Winfrey, entertainer	4	2	0			2
Total all others	28	21	2	13	23	15
Grand total	137	102	27	64	58	31

Sources: ABC 1994 and 1997 *World News* transcripts: search for stories mentioning 100 most influential Black Americans named in *Ebony* magazine in May 1993 or May 1994. Total number of persons on list in one or both years: 114. For 1997 data, search for those named to top 100 list in *Ebony* in May 1996 or May 1997. Total number of persons on list in one or both years: 112. Leaders listed in table were named three or more times.

Data Tables

Table A.12 Verbal Intimacy by Interaction Type

	Black Superior		Peer		Black Subordinate	
Formal	67.1%	(57)	33.3%	(22)	60.4%	(29)
Casual	31.8	(27)	50.0	(33)	37.5	(18)
Self-revealing	1.2	(1)	16.7	(11)	2.1	(1)
Total	100.0%	(85)	100.0%	(66)	100.0%	(48)

Note: Figures in parentheses represent numbers of cases.

Table A.13 Extra-Role Involvement by Interaction Type

	Black Superior		Peer		Black Subordinate	
Role-governed	91.8%	(78)	68.2%	(45)	93.8%	(45)
Indirect involvement	7.1	(6)	22.7	(15)	6.2	(3)
Direct involvement	1.2	(1)	16.7	(6)	0	(0)
Total	100.0%	(85)	100.0%	(66)	100.0%	(48)

Note: Figures in parentheses represent numbers of cases.

Table A.14 Images of Contact among Blacks and Whites in BET Commercials

Race of Character Shown:	Whites in BET Ads as percentage of White Opportunities (n = 110)		Blacks in BET Ads as percentage of Black Opportunities (n = 148)		W:B Ratio
	n	%	n	%	
Kissing	8	5.4%	3	2.7%	2.0
Caressing skin	22	14.9	13	11.8	1.3
Hugging	21	14.2	17	15.4	0.9
Speaking to character of same race	18	12.2	17	15.4	0.8
As hand model	81	54.7	40	36.4	1.5
Speaking last	96	64.9	52	47.3	1.4
Last on screen	128	86.5	84	76.4	1.1
First on screen	124	83.8	82	74.6	1.1
Receiving close-ups	106	71.6	76	69.1	1.0
Speaking first	57	38.5	43	39.1	1.0
Instructing audience	28	18.9	31	28.2	0.7
Speaking to audience	39	26.4	43	39.1	0.7
Sexualized	12	8.1	20	18.2	0.4
Total	888	Avg. 6.0/ad	631	Avg. 5.7/ad	1.0

Table A.15 Comparison of Single Ad to Ad Showing Samples

Products Advertised	Single Ad Sample		Multiple Showing Sample	
	Frequency	*%*	*Frequency*	*%*
Alcoholic beverages	2	0.8	5	1.2
Appliances	8	3.1	10	2.5
Auto repair, gas	1	0.4	4	1
Cars and trucks	19	7.5	27	6.6
Clothing	2	0.8	3	0.7
Communication and information	13	5.1	18	4.4
Credit/Charge cards	5	2.0	12	2.9
Department and furniture store	43	16.9	75	18.4
Drugs	27	10.6	36	8.8
Entertainment	16	6.3	20	4.9
Entertainment appliances	9	3.5	13	3.2
Fast food	20	7.9	52	12.8
Feminine products	17	6.7	25	6.1
Financial	4	1.6	4	1
Grocery	27	10.6	47	11.5
Household goods	6	2.4	6	1.5
Perfumes	12	4.7	15	3.7
PSA	9	3.5	13	3.2
Snack food	8	3.1	16	3.9
Other	6	2.4	6	1.5
Total	254	100	407	100
Racial Composition				
All Black	11	4.3	17	4.2
All White	156	61.4	245	60.2
White and Black	61	24.0	100	24.5
East Asian included[a]	26	10.3	45	11.1
Skin Touch[b]				
All Black	1	5.9	1	3.3
All White	16	94.1	29	96.7
Speak Other Character				
All Black	0	0	0	0
All White	39	86.7	73	87.9
Black/White	5	11.1	10	12.0
Sexualization				
Blacks only	1	2.7	2	4.5
Whites only	29	78.4	34	77.3
Black/White	7	18.9	8	18.6

[a]Including one race unknown.

[b]All comparisons including and below skin touch are based on commercials including Blacks only, Whites only, or Blacks and Whites only; those including East Asians excluded. Figures for ABC only.

Data Tables

Table A.16 Top-Earning Movies During Calendar 1996

Ranking	Film	Box Office Gross
1	*Independence Day*	$306,155,579
2	*Twister*	$241,721,524
3	*Mission: Impossible*	$180,981,866
4	*The Rock*	$134,069,511
5	*The Nutty Professor*	$128,814,019
6	*Ransom*	$125,810,051
7	*The Birdcage*	$124,060,553
8	*101 Dalmatians*	$109,686,011
9	*A Time to Kill*	$108,766,007
10	*Phenomenon*	$104,464,977
11	*The First Wives Club*	$103,708,261
12	*Eraser*	$101,295,562
*		
14	*Star Trek: First Contact*	$86,249,815
15	*Space Jam*	$83,038,821
16	*Mr. Holland's Opus*	$82,569,971
17	*Broken Arrow*	$70,770,147
18	*Jerry Maguire*	$65,675,817
19	*The Cable Guy*	$60,240,295
20	*Courage Under Fire*	$59,031,057
21	*Jack*	$58,478,604
22	*12 Monkeys*	$56,988,975
23	*Executive Decision*	$56,679,192
24	*Primal Fear*	$56,116,183
25	*Jingle All the Way*	$54,460,867
26	*Tin Cup*	$53,888,896

Note: These figures are for the twenty-five films included in the analysis of behavior. Note that the original top seventy list of films consisted of those grossing $25 million (during calendar 1996 at the U.S. box office), reduced to sixty-three by exclusions of animated and animal films. (From <www.mrshowbiz.com.>) This means a few films that might have made the list with both years' receipts included did not because they did not earn $25 million during calendar 1996. The other films that earned more than $25 million in calendar 1996 and are included in the analysis of cast rankings include: *Sleepers, Dragonheart, Up Close and Personal, Jumanji, Shakespeare's Romeo and Juliet, Grumpier Old Men, The Mirror Has Two Faces, Dead Man Walking, Sense and Sensibility, Happy Gilmore, The Ghost and the Darkness, Michael, The Truth About Cats and Dogs, A Thin Line Between Love and Hate, Set It Off, Waiting to Exhale, Matilda, Striptease, Heat, Rumble in the Bronx, Eddie, The Preacher's Wife, Sargent Bilko, Leaving Las Vegas, Mars Attacks!, Spy Hard, Eye for an Eye, Father of the Bride, Part II, Harriet the Spy, First Kid, Daylight, From Dusk Till Dawn, Down Periscope, That Thing You Do, Escape from L.A.,* and *Kingpin.*
*Rank 13 occupied by *The Hunchback of Notre Dame*, an animated film.

Appendix

Table A.17 Percentages of Each Ethnic/Gender Category Shown as Specified

	Black Male	White Male	Black Female	White Female
Total "named" characters	27	170	9	70
	(100)	(100)	(100)	(100)
Physical violence	10	78	5	8
	(37)	(46)	(56)	(11)
Vulgar profanity	19	96	8	12
	(70)	(56)	(89)	(17)
Ungrammatical	14	11	4	3
	(52)	(6)	(44)	(4)
Sexualized	5	26	9	41
	(18)	(15)	(100)	(59)
"I love you"	6	22	5	23
	(22)	(13)	(56)	(33)
Caressed	4	14	3	16
	(15)	(8)	(33)	(23)
Hugged/kissed	8	30	7	35
	(30)	(43)	(78)	(50)
Sex	5	5	3	5
	(18)	(3)	(33)	(7)
Entry guard	12	8	3	0
	(44)	(5)	(33)	(0)
Restrained	5	31	5	4
	(18)	(18)	(55)	(6)

Note: Entries show the numbers of "named" characters in each situation and the percentages (in parentheses) they represent of all "named" characters of that gender and race.

N o t e s

Preface

1. E.g., Edsall and Edsall 1991; Carmines and Stimson 1989; Kinder and Sears 1996.
2. For works on other groups see Dines and Humez 1995; Subervi-Velez 1994; Hamamoto 1992; Weston 1996.
3. Winant 1994.

Chapter One

1. Kinder and Sanders 1996, 272; Winant 1994; Gabriel 1998; Delgado and Stepanic 1997.
2. Hacker 1992; Wilson 1996.
3. Massey and Denton 1993.
4. Bogle 1989.
5. Exactly what "Whiteness" means or how to "correctly" classify a person as White are important issues but beyond our scope here. Delgado and Stepanic (1997) show that there is no determinative way of defining Whiteness. Instead of venturing further into this area, we simply note that we consider as White those people defined as such by the U.S. Census. According to those criteria, Whites remained the majority racial group at century's end, though they almost certainly will not remain so one hundred years hence. We also leave aside questions about distinguishing race from ethnicity. In ordinary language as well as Census practice, race classifies according to physical traits, primarily skin shade, although the Census classification "Hispanic" conflates race and ethnicity. The confusion about this matter is reflected in the Census Bureau's reports. In December 1998 it listed the following classifications in its report entitled "Resident Population of the United States: Estimates, by Sex, Race, and Hispanic Origin, with Median Age." Notice in this title that "Hispanic Origin" becomes its own classification system alongside race and sex.

- White
- Black
- American Indian, Eskimo, and Aleut
- Asian and Pacific Islander
- Hispanic origin (of any race)
- White, not Hispanic
- Black, not Hispanic
- American Indian, Eskimo, and Aleut, not Hispanic
- Asian and Pacific Islander, not Hispanic

Without denying the significance of these perplexities, we do not think it necessary to delve into them for our purposes. Most people know who is White and who is Black in America, and it is that consciousness that constitutes our subject.

6. See Hartmann and Husband 1974; Dates and Barlow 1990; Fiske 1994; Campbell 1995; Merelman 1995; Gandy 1998.

7. See Delli Carpini and Williams 2000; Hickey 1998.

8. Schuman et al. 1998.

9. Cf. Herbst 1993.

10. Since racial distinctions are heavily cultural if not arbitrary, we must acknowledge that even in writing about and especially in coding media texts in terms of race and attributes like skin color, we face the danger of perpetuating the very distinctions we want to overcome. This is unavoidable, however, and we can develop critique and understanding with the simultaneous knowledge that sorting people into "races" based on skin color is neither scientifically real nor morally desirable. We are writing about how people come to classify themselves and others into categories called "race," not about which race people "really" are.

11. See Fiske and Taylor 1991; Iyengar and McGuire 1993.

12. Kerner Commission 1968.

13. Page and Shapiro 1992.

14. Putnam 1993; Fukuyama 1995; Kawachi et al. 1997.

15. Iyengar and Kinder 1987; Page and Shapiro 1992; Bartels 1993.

Chapter Two

1. See, e.g., Morrison and Lacour 1997; Feagin and Vera 1995; Hacker 1992; Edsall and Edsall 1991.

2. Patterson 1997; Thernstrom and Thernstrom 1997.

3. Sniderman and Piazza 1993; Kinder and Sanders 1996; Hurwitz and Peffley 1998.

4. Gaertner and Dovidio 1986.

5. Cf. Goldberg 1993.

6. Wilson 1996; Massey and Denton 1993; Ricks 1998.

7. Wilson 1996.

8. See especially Schuman et al. 1998; Kinder and Sanders 1996.

9. Gaertner and Dovidio 1986; Kinder and Sanders 1996; Sears et al. 1997; Hurwitz and Peffley 1998.

10. Cf. Carmines and Layman 1998, 129; Kinder and Sanders 1996, chap. 9; Jamieson 1992; Edsall and Edsall 1991.

11. As Raymond Franklin (1993, 90) observes, "The underclass is the first step in a process by which Whites derive an 'understanding' about all Black people." See Gans 1995; on stereotype-confirming behavior by some Blacks as responses to inequality, see Mercer and Julien 1994, 138; Hall 1997, 263; cf. Patterson 1997.

12. See Wachtel 1999 on Whites' "indifference" and its ameliorability.

13. Cf. Schuman et al. 1998; Kinder and Sanders 1996; Sears et al. 1997.

14. Schuman et al. 1998.

15. Garrow 1978.
16. Kinder and Sanders 1996.
17. A reliability analysis yielded an alpha of 0.71.
18. The discussion is based on the following OLS regression model:

	B	SE B	Beta	T	Sig T
Constant	10.5	1.4		7.4	.0000
Knowledge	−1.26	.32	−.27	−4.0	.0001
Education	−.32	.09	−.24	−3.5	.0006
Age	.04	.01	.19	2.9	.005
Ideology	.91	.31	.2	2.9	.004
Multiple R	.48				
R^2	.23				
Std error	2.8				

Knowledge is a three-point index based on the accuracy of the respondent's answers to two questions: the percentage of the U.S. population that is Black and the percentage of the federal budget spent on welfare. Education is years of schooling. Age is as of last birthday. Ideology is self-designation as liberal, moderate, and conservative and coded as one through three, respectively.

19. Though as Kinder and Sanders (1996) and Schuman et al. (1998) find, individualism can be used as cover for racial prejudice.

20. Correlation r = 0.14, p = 0.03. Note that in this and succeeding chapters we sometimes use the measure Pearson's "r," the most commonly used measure of the strength of a correlation. It can run from 0.0 to 1.0; the higher this number, the stronger the association between two variables. If a negative sign precedes the number, it means the two variables are inversely related: the higher the score on one, the lower on the other. The "p" refers to the probability that a finding is due to chance. Generally, social scientists have confidence in associations with a "p" of 0.05 or less, meaning that there are fewer than five chances in a hundred that the results are traceable to chance.

21. Nadeau and Niemi 1993.
22. Cf. Gilens 1999.
23. See Jencks 1992 on the poorly understood, partial success of poverty programs. In our own sample, we did assess media impact and found just one statistically significant effect. The number of hours of entertainment television respondents watched in a week (not shown in appendix figure A.1) had a small but noticeable negative influence on support for the tax increase. This could be misleading, since the less educated spend more time in front of the television, as do the more conservative respondents in the sample. Once these influences are removed statistically, however, television watching exerts its own influence: r = −0.16, p < 0.001. This could suggest that contact with entertainment television on balance reduces racial comity (note also the parallel findings of Armstrong, Nuendorf, and Brentar 1992), but we suspected that media images have more subtle influences than can be measured by standardized survey questions. This is

why we turned to face-to-face, conversational interviews, and devote the rest of the chapter to them.

24. Quoted in Ferguson and Rogers 1998, 163.

25. Herbst (1993) discusses the need for more varied indicators of public opinion; cf. Entman and Herbst 2000.

26. Kahneman, Slovic, and Tversky 1982.

27. Fiske and Taylor 1991.

28. Kinder and Sanders 1996.

29. Gilens 1999, 114, 128.

30. Pettigrew 1998.

31. Sigelman and Welch 1993; Ellison and Powers 1994.

32. Many White suburbs even *outside the South* enforced restrictive covenants that contractually prevented homeowners from reselling their houses to Black persons. Many of these owners received federally subsidized FHA and VA mortgages. These federal agencies accepted and even promoted racist covenants (Brodkin 1999, 44–50). All homeowners, but Whites disproportionately, were eligible for the enormous housing subsidy distributed by the mortgage interest tax deduction.

33. Cf. Patterson 1997, 75.

34. Lakoff 1996.

35. Cf. the "cultivation" theory of Gerbner, Morgan, and Signorielli 1994.

36. Kaniss 1991.

Chapter Three

1. Schuman et al. 1998, 7; see also ibid., 112–13, 154, 306–7.

2. Even the data on principles are equivocal. They show, for instance, that White discomfort over half or majority Black representation in schools or neighborhoods is high: only half of Whites say they would accept a majority Black school (Schuman et al. 1998, 120, 139–53; cf. Farley et al. 1994). Social desirability inflates responses to such questions; real world experience with White flight suggests a far lower actual comfort level.

3. Schuman et al. 1998, 327. Of course many observers would argue that the path toward true equality does not encompass costly government programs or affirmative action, and that failing to support such remedies is not a sign of racial animosity (e.g., Sniderman and Piazza 1993; Thernstrom and Thernstrom 1997). Rather, they would say, the many costs of such programs clearly outweigh any benefits to African Americans and the nation as a whole. Obviously, we cannot settle disputes over the desirability of government activism and affirmative action here. As suggested in the text, we emphatically do not equate conservative stands on public policy with racism. But a positive correlation between conservatism and racism has emerged in most studies, and there is a logical reason. Conservatism tends to deny the need for government action and tends to hold individuals responsible for their fate (Lakoff 1996). Conservatives' deep belief in the ability of individuals to succeed through disciplined work in a free market may predispose them to deny market failures like racial discrimination. This point helps explain findings that where conservatives believe an individual *has* been victimized by overt

discrimination, they often endorse government policies or other forms of help for that person (Sniderman and Piazza 1993).

4. See especially Feagin and Vera 1995.

5. Schuman et al. 1998, 156–57.

6. Ibid., 166.

7. Ibid., 167.

8. Ibid., 276.

9. Ibid., 46–47; see also Feagin and Sikes 1994; Cose 1993; Massey and Denton 1993; Wilson 1996; Ricks 1998.

10. See Reeves 1997; Frymer 1999.

11. Schuman et al. 1998, 315.

12. Tajfel 1982.

13. Sidanius and Pratto 1993.

14. Fiske and Taylor 1991, 98.

15. Gilens 1999; Gilliam and Iyengar 1998; Peffley and Hurwitz 1998.

16. Entman 1993.

17. Schuman et al. 1998.

18. Douglas 1970.

19. Douglas 1970; cf. Malkki 1995.

20. Turner 1967; Malkki 1995.

21. Malkki 1995, 7.

22. See Kochman 1981.

23. See Patterson 1997.

24. Cose 1993; Hochschild 1995.

25. Jamieson 1992; Kinder and Sanders 1996, 247; Mendelberg 1997.

26. *Time* illustrated the same phenomenon. Crowd scenes on covers (painted by artists) had anonymous Blacks, and in one case *Time*'s cover pictured a doctor named Keith Black, an African American, to illustrate its story on medical innovators. Representing medical researchers (rather than Americans) in general, this choice usefully challenged stereotyped expectations. However, the point remains that despite good conscious intentions, when thinking the concept "prototypical *American individual*" the editors unconsciously choose a White. Commercial thinking may also play a role: magazine publishers claim that covers picturing Blacks (presumably excepting such cultural heroes as Jordan and Winfrey) sell significantly fewer copies on the newsstand than those showing Whites. The *Newsweek* of 6 September 1999 showed a White girl prominently in the foreground, two other children in soft-focus background; it is included in the count of ten White exemplars appearing in the magazine as described in the text.

27. See Rosch 1981; Lakoff 1987.

28. Rothbart and John 1993.

29. Tajfel 1982.

30. Rothbart and John 1993, 38; see Wetherell and Potter 1992, 38.

31. Rothbart and John 1993, 40.

32. Ibid., 43–44 (emphasis added). Also see Pettigrew 1979.

33. Patterson 1997, 45–48.
34. Ibid., 195.
35. Dowden and Robinson 1993.
36. Kluegel and Bobo 1993; also Iyengar 1991.
37. Patterson 1997, 28, 38.
38. Ibid., 41.
39. Kinder and Sanders 1996, 275.
40. We avoid the thickets of the debate between those who insist on the nearly infinite potential readings of media texts and those who believe in the impact of a text's preferred meanings. What we are saying is that, by taking large samples in an area of discourse over time, one can see patterns that quantitatively predominate in texts and, in part reflecting this dominance, match up well with patterns of thinking among the largest groups of audience members. This does not deny the presence of alternative readings and subcultural currents that contest prevailing views. But it does assume that, absent a way to organize these alternative views into a coherent political or social force, it is the dominant patterns that merit the most attention, for they are the ones that best help explain and drive social and political relations. Cf. Budd, Entman, and Steinman 1990.
41. See, e.g., Fiske and Taylor 1991; Iyengar and McGuire 1993.
42. Entman 1989.
43. See Kawakami, Dion, and Dovidio 1998.
44. Pieterse 1992; Marx 1998.

Chapter Four

1. We share the assumption of most social theorists that cultural forces and other constraints outside individuals' control heavily shape their subjectivities. We do not mean to imply that people freely and consciously paint their portraits of the world from an unlimited palette. They do enjoy some degrees of freedom, which vary according to education, wealth, social class, and many other variables.
2. Fiske and Taylor 1991, 391.
3. Fiske and Taylor 1991.
4. Rosch 1981; cf. Lakoff 1987.
5. Lakoff 1987, 41.
6. Fiske and Taylor 1991, 109.
7. Cose 1993, 48; cf. Feagin and Sikes 1994.
8. Cf. Patterson 1997, 63.
9. The 1997 videotape data were collected for inclusion in *Media and Reconciliation*, commissioned by the President's Initiative on Race (Entman et al. 1998). More details on the coding protocol can be found in the report, which is posted on this book's website. The data were gathered and analyzed under Entman's supervision and the report chapter was co-written with Debra Burns Melican and Irma Munoz, then students at Harvard's Kennedy School of Government. Judith Gaddie also contributed significantly to the analysis and coding of the data.
10. The 1990 tapes are from January, February, and March. The first transcript sam-

ple encompasses January 1990 to June 1990 and July 1991 to December 1991; the second, calendar year 1997. The 1990–91 dates are staggered in order to obtain a full year period that excludes the highly unusual news event that dominated television between August 1990 and March 1991, the war against Iraq.

11. Transcripts are machine readable, allowing much more efficient and accurate analysis of verbal text than is possible by looking at tapes. In addition, obtaining tapes of an entire year of network news is prohibitively expensive. Thus we chose transcript analysis for methodological and practical reasons.

12. Ethnic groups were treated as "represented" in the 1997 research if one or more persons clearly identifiable as a member (1) caused or clearly helped to cause the newsworthy event, or (2) were centrally involved in the story by being shown in three or more medium or close-up shots, or (3) had at least one soundbite. The event causation criterion in (1) was not difficult to apply; most news stories make the causal agents behind the event depicted quite clear. Stories may include other people, but they are usually observing, commenting, or reacting. In addition, when a Black fulfilled that first criterion he or she usually fulfilled the second or third as well. Stories with Black representation could be coded as "Blacks only," "mixed—Black and White," or "mixed—White and more than one minority," depending on who actually spoke, who appeared on the screen in medium or close-up shots, and who caused the reported event. For 1997, the sample included foreign stories, and the amount of news amounted to 32.5 hours encompassing nine hundred items. Because non-Black minorities were included in the 1997 study, comparability with the 1990 sample is not complete.

Twenty-five percent of the broadcasts were double-coded in order to determine coder reliability for the 1997 sample. Using the Brennan-Prediger (1981) formula (correcting for chance coder agreements), it was determined that the average reliability figure was 89 percent. All but one of the reliability figures was over 82 percent; five were over 90 percent; the low figure was 79 percent for ethnic representation—which was of course our key variable. However, presumably the same subjective ambiguities that lowered the reliability here would likely be experienced by actual viewing audiences. Where one coder missed the brief appearance of, say, an African American which the other caught, the likelihood is that many in the actual audience also did not notice that appearance. In the main, the disparities between White and non-White percentages discovered are large enough that this amount of error is tolerable. In addition, there is no reason to think the errors are anything but random.

For the 1990 sample, inclusion criteria were slightly different: either Blacks had to clearly cause or help cause the reported event or be centrally involved. For this sample that meant that Blacks (not including anchors or reporters) appeared at least three times in medium or close-up shots *and* spoke on camera twice or more. That selection process produced a sample of 138 stories involving Blacks, lasting a total of 267.5 minutes. As a proportion of the total news hole (1,980 minutes) in the sample, this represented approximately 13.5 percent, not an insignificant amount. In this sample, stories about Blacks in other countries were *not* counted, on the assumption that their activities are not directly relevant to attitudes and issues in the United States; for the most part, this meant excluding coverage of South Africa. Details on the South Africa findings can be found in Entman 1994a, as can more information about the coding.

13. Although it is not our focus here, it is worth noting again that most of the stories featuring Asians or Latinos concerned people and events in Asia or Latin America (88 percent and 52 percent, respectively). These reports did not feature Asian Americans or Latino Americans, whereas the bulk of stories featuring Whites alone concerned domestic (United States) matters. Network news appears largely to bypass the experiences and contributions of these two groups, though not of African Americans.

14. Lakoff 1987.

15. Gandy (1998, 47–48) notes that even cultures of dark-skinned peoples make this connection of blackness with evil and danger.

16. This label has been endorsed by Patterson (1997).

17. The first category, crime, includes violent and drug crime, political corruption, and sexual harassment. The politics category encompasses Black politicians running for political office, Black judges being considered for nomination, Black officials acting out their official duties, or Black leaders/activists/groups (not running for or holding office) petitioning, marching, protesting, making political demands or accusations of racism. The victims category includes occurrences of natural or social misfortune such as fire, or of bad government programs, poverty, bad schools, bad health care, and the like; Blacks as victims of racial tensions; and implications of being victims such as discussions of nongovernmental social programs for poor or inner cities, and Blacks doing things to improve their lives. Human interest stories are features that depict Blacks as central characters; these are stories in which Blacks are not criminals or victims or making political commentary. The statistics category covers reports that recite statistics about conditions of Blacks or comparing Blacks to Whites. "Antidiscrimination policy" is the code for stories on government policies or court rulings (also statements, speeches, and opinions) on civil rights, discrimination, affirmative action, or other racial issues

18. Similar findings are recorded in Nacos and Hritzuk 1998, 32.

19. See Graber 1996b and Cook 1997 for summaries.

20. We studied three randomly chosen sample months in 1997 from ABC's *World News* (April 4 to May 2, July 21 to August 18, and November 14 to December 14), using the same coding protocol as for Blacks. Latinos were identified from last names certified as such by Irma Munoz, a member of the coding team originally from Mexico, or from explicit verbal designations within the stories.

21. Rothbart and John 1993, 40.

22. Following these selection criteria means that we detected almost every appearance of Black experts during the sample period. The only exceptions would be stories in which one Black expert had a single soundbite.

23. This estimate comes from extrapolating: Whites were quoted ninety-four times in just the 13.5 percent of the 1,980 minutes that featured Blacks centrally and were thus included in this subsample. Assuming Whites spoke at least as often in the other 86.5 percent of the news hole yields 705 soundbites.

24. Entman et al. 1998, 26–55.

25. The data can be found in Entman et al. 1998, 40. We would note, however, that though NBC showed the fewest Black reporters, at 14 percent of all stories it had the highest representation of Blacks in the news of the three networks.

26. See Hurwitz and Peffley 1998; Gilliam et al. 1996; Edsall and Edsall 1991; Russell 1998; Valentino 1999.

27. On crime rates: Jencks 1992, 185–89. On arrest rates: Morris 1993; Hacker 1992, chap. 11.

28. Wilson 1996, 22.

29. Patterson 1997; U.S. Department of Justice 1998, table 4.10.

30. Omi and Winant 1994.

31. Cf. Jhally and Lewis 1992; Budd and Steinman 1992.

32. Tuchman 1978.

33. Lakoff 1996.

34. Tuchman 1978; Gans 1979; Paletz and Entman 1981.

35. Entman and Page 1994.

36. Gilens 1999.

37. On news: Tuchman 1978; Gans 1979. On prime-time entertainment: Gitlin 1983.

38. Omi and Winant 1994.

39. Cf. Lakoff 1996.

40. Entman 1989.

41. Galbraith 1998, chap. 1.

42. Cf. Edsall and Edsall 1991; Hacker 1992; Kinder and Sanders 1996.

43. Edsall and Edsall 1991; Domke, McCoy, and Torres 1999.

Chapter Five

1. See, however, Lafayette 1994; Gerbner, Morgan, and Signorielli 1994; Comstock and Paik 1991.

2. The emphasis of local news on violence is demonstrated in numerous studies around the country. See, e.g., Kaniss 1991; Campbell 1995; Klite, Bardwell, and Salzman 1997; Romer et al. 1997; Gilliam et al. 1996; Rosensteil, Gottlieb, and Brady 1998. The racial element specifically is discussed in Entman 1990a; Peffley, Shields, and Williams 1996; Gilens 1996; Trotter 1990). Supplementing news shows are the syndicated tabloid "infotainment" shows. Content analyses of such programs as *Cops* find violent crime overrepresented and Black and Latino suspects "more likely than White criminal suspects to be the recipient of unarmed physical aggression by police officers" (Oliver 1994, 179). See also Grabe 1999.

3. FBI 1998, 240.

4. Survey described in Sniderman, Brody, and Tetlock 1991.

5. Romer et al. 1997; Gilliam et al. 1996.

6. Somewhat different results, based on different coding methods, were found for New York City by Nacos and Hritzuk 1998.

7. The sampling period ran from 6 December 1993 through 13 February 1994—a

total of ten weeks that generated 164 coded news broadcasts. During this time, early and late evening local news shows were taped on a random rotating basis, with an emphasis on the three highest-rated stations (the network affiliates of ABC, CBS, and NBC: Channel 7-WLS, Channel 2-WBBM, and Channel 5-WMAQ) but also including the 9 P.M. news reports of the two major independent stations, Channel 9-WGN and Channel 32-WFLD, an affiliate of the Fox network. The local news programs broke down as follows: forty-two on WBBM (Channel 2); sixteen on WFLD (Channel 32); fifty-three on WMAQ(Channel 5); forty-two on WLS (Channel 7); and eleven on WGN (Channel 9). WFLD and WGN did not broadcast an early local news show; both broadcast one hour of news at 9 P.M. For comparability to the other local news programs, which ran thirty minutes from 10:00 to 10:30, the WGN and WFLD shows coded were sometimes the earlier half hour (9:00 to 9:30) and sometimes the later (9:30 to 10:00). Fewer of these shows were coded than for the three major network affiliates (WBBM (CBS), WMAQ (NBC), and WLS (ABC)), because the latter enjoy the overwhelming share of the audience.

Coding was done by Entman and by several graduate students trained and carefully monitored by him. In recoding by the author of a sample of the programs already coded by a graduate student, high intercoder reliability was shown, averaging approximately 90 percent. Reliability in selecting items as codeable (i.e., as containing violence) was 94 percent. Most disagreements consisted of failures to code fleeting appearances of visual symbols of violence or of officials or helpers.

8. Entman 1992a.

9. Tabloid shows generate significant audiences that in some markets approach those attained by one or more network news shows. Sixty-two more programs coded during the 1993–94 study period consisted of a random rotating sample of these "infotainment" shows. They combine interviews, reenactments, and documentary footage to construct stories of real events that are deliberately paced and packaged to maximize entertainment value. In general, although levels of violence varied significantly across shows, the racially differentiated images found in local news was similar in these shows (Entman 1994b; cf. Grabe 1999; Oliver 1994).

10. Pew Research Center 1997; cf. Trigoboff 1998.

11. During the period just before the study began, for example, the Nielsen ratings for those network affiliates' late news were 17.0 for WLS, 13.3 for WBBM, and 16.8 for WMAQ, meaning 47.1 percent of television households in the Chicago metropolitan area had their sets tuned to one of those channels at 10:00 P.M. The ratings for WGN and WFLD news were substantially lower, although not insignificant. Some households may watch both WGN at 9:00 and another station at 10:00, so that the actual percentage of households watching the late news may be slightly under 50 percent.

12. The total of 1,134 items, when divided by the 164 different news broadcasts in the main study, yields an average of nearly seven violent stories per show. The average local news program included 476 seconds, about eight minutes, of stories about violence. Note that violent incidents reported within the sports segment of the program were excluded, even though many of the sports segments featured a brawl of some sort. This was

based on an assumption that such violence may not have the same effects as that taking place in the "real world," away from the athletic arena where bloody confrontation is somewhat artificial and contained. Others, including most prominently George Gerbner and colleagues, have argued that all violent incidents should be treated as equivalent. Further probing into the nature and effects of violence in sports reporting is merited, but beyond the mission of this chapter.

13. These consisted of stories about armed robbery; beating, physical assault, fights; bombing or arson fire or attempts; child abuse (physical attack, neglect, sexual abuse); drug dealing; murder (one suicide coded here); negligent action or inaction endangering life and limb (e.g., faulty school bus or airplane maintenance); nonfatal shooting or gun violence generally; other seriously injurious violent attack (requiring hospital treatment) including stabbing, hit and run by car, poisoning, and rape or attempted rape.

14. Romer et al. 1997; Gilliam et al. 1996; Klite, Bardwell, and Salzman 1997; Campbell 1995; Kaniss 1991.

15. In 23, 20, and 15 percent of items, respectively. Coders were instructed that if more than one type of violent image appeared, they should select the lowest number code (most severe image) that applied. If on-screen violence appeared, for example, victims might also have been shown, but the code entered would be for the on-screen violence.

16. Gerbner, Mowlana, and Nordenstreng 1993; Hamilton 1997.

17. Romer et al. 1997; Romer, Jamieson, and de Coteau 1998; Gilliam et al. 1996. This pattern may be found in international news also, as African victims of ethnic war obtain less attention than European. See Myers, Klak, and Koehl 1996.

18. For experimental evidence, see Peffley, Shields, and Williams 1996; Gilliam et al. 1996; Oliver 1999; cf. Price 1989; Mendelberg 1997; Valentino 1999.

19. Entman 1990b.

20. In the 1990–91 sample the difference was not statistically significant.

21. Entman 1992a, 350; difference significant at p = 0.09.

22. Ibid., 354–55.

23. On television: Stone 1997; on newspapers: Voakes 1997.

24. Winant 1994.

25. Another five officials and two helpers were identified as Latino; none in either category were Asian.

26. The table does not record instances in which more than one person of the same or different races were shown as helpers or officials.

27. In 1997 there were 8,485 White police officers, 3,404 Black, and 1,388 Hispanic in the city of Chicago, according to the Chicago Police Department's *Annual Report 1997*. Since the bulk of crime news stories come out of the city, the Chicago statistics are most relevant for our purpose. Although most suburbs and their police forces are largely White, some have large minority populations and police force representation.

28. Entman 1990b.

29. On the difference in perception by Whites and Blacks of continuing discrimination, see Hochschild 1995; Schuman et al. 1998; Verhovek 1997.

30. Noelle-Neumann 1993.

31. See Dovidio and Gaertner 1986 and McConahay 1986 on ambivalence and aversive racism; see also Sears 1988; Sears et al. 1997.

32. See, e.g., Witkin 1998.

33. The dates were 8, 14, 17, 23, and 29 December 1993; 6, 15, and 20 January 1994; and 8 and 13 February 1994.

34. Iyengar 1991; Gilliam et al. 1996; Peffley, Hurwitz, and Sniderman 1997.

35. Wilson 1996.

36. Pew Research Center 1998.

37. Jamieson 1992; Mendelberg 1997.

38. Gilens 1999; Peffley, Hurwitz, and Sniderman 1997.

39. Gandy 1998, 173; Hunt 1997; Smith 1994.

40. Devine 1989, 12.

41. Gandy 1998, 55.

42. Ibid., 55.

Chapter Six

1. According to Iyengar 1991.

2. The sample periods in 1990 are 10–14 January, 21–25 January, 6–10 February, 16–20 February, 1–5 March, and 26–30 March. For the period totaling thirty days, 210 broadcasts were theoretically available, but several were preempted by athletic events, and in other cases the taping machines malfunctioned, yielding a database of 197 shows. There is no indication that having the excluded shows in the sample would in any way alter the conclusions of the study.

3. Full details on selecting and coding stories appear in Entman 1990b. An excerpt is provided in the book's website.

4. In the early going of the 2000 presidential campaign, during 1999, several candidates, including Vice President Albert Gore and Governor George W. Bush, joined President Clinton in making poverty an explicit issue for government attention. Any long-term effects of this attention could not be predicted.

5. A more precise definition, such as "having income levels at or under the government's official poverty rate for a family of four," cannot be used. Television news does not calibrate its uses of concepts like poverty. Except in four stories that actually describe statistical studies of poverty, none of the coverage uses specific income or wealth figures.

6. A more detailed breakdown of the 373 symptoms of poverty depicted is as follows:

Threat:

Violent crime	18.8%
Drug abuse / dealing	10.7%
General crime	5.9%
Gangs	4.0%

Suffering:

Discrimination, racism, police brutality	13.4%
Physical, mental health problems	11.5%

Economic problems, unemployment	9.7%
Housing, homelessness	6.4%
Education, childcare	6.2%
Need for power, protest	4.3%
Child abuse, family breakdown	2.9%
Explicit mention of poverty / poor	2.7%
Hunger, transportation problems	2.6%
Welfare	0.8%

7. Geographical stereotypes appeared in 65.3 percent (156) of stories mentioning poverty symptoms; metaphors in 18 percent (43); and explicit linkages to poverty in 22.6 percent (54).

8. Graber 1990.

9. The symptom did not have to be included right along with poverty to count as an explicit linkage. That is, any explicit mention of the condition of being poor, anywhere in a story that mentions a poverty symptom, qualified as an explicit linkage. The same conservative coding practices were followed in coding implicit linkages.

10. Actually, to ensure that deadline differences did not skew the results, the newspapers were checked for periods including one day before and one day after the periods sampled on television. For example, newspapers for the period 28 February through 6 March were sampled for the comparison to the television coverage broadcast during the period 1 March through 5 March.

11. This comparison excludes those feature and background stories appearing in the national media that did not have a clear local news peg. For example, network news stories on Lee Trevino, hard times in a small North Dakota town, and AIDS among poor women were not counted. In addition, many stories were covered on more than one day and / or on more than one station, so the total number of specific story topics is considerably lower than the total number of stories—for example, there were ten different stories on the four stations concerning Martin Luther King Day. The newspapers only had to publish one story each to be counted as having covered the same story—not ten stories each.

12. Most of the stories involved crime and drugs, about which there is no dearth of information on television, so the omissions seem inconsequential.

13. In a few cases, there were photographs featuring the same cues as those appearing on the television screen, such as a crowd of Black persons and police on the street.

14. Note, however, that *60 Minutes* and other news forms not analyzed here might have different, more powerful impacts. Indeed, "fictional" television and movies may well treat homelessness, racial injustice, and the like with more frequency, complexity, and sympathetic detail than most news stories. We touch upon these possibilities in chapters 9 and 11.

15. Neuman, Just, and Crigler 1992.

16. Iyengar 1991, 19.

17. Gilens 1999, 137–38.

18. Thernstrom and Thernstrom (1997, 233) note that 26 percent of Black families had incomes below the poverty line in 1995 compared with 9 percent of White families; cf. Jencks 1991.

19. On automatic stereotyping, see also Kakawami, Dion, and Dovidio 1998.

20. Iyengar 1991; Gilens 1999.

21. Gilliam et al. 1996; Gilens 1999.

22. Cf. Entman 1989 on the need for repetition by elites.

23. Gans 1995.

24. Cf. Altheide 1991.

Chapter Seven

1. Sniderman and Piazza 1993, 236; Thernstrom and Thernstrom 1997.

2. E.g., Bowen and Bok 1998; Edley 1996; Guinier 1998.

3. Cf. Page 1996.

4. Patterson 1997, 149.

5. E.g., Kinder and Sanders 1996.

6. Alvarez and Brehm (1997) maintain Whites are uncertain, not ambivalent. They measure uncertainty by a two-item index of level of general political information (number of Supreme Court justices and maximum number of presidential terms). This measure taps the specified concept of uncertainty quite indirectly. Research needs to measure uncertainty *about affirmative action and related matters*—for instance, how much anti-Black discrimination still exists, how much Whites suffer from implementations of affirmative action, how effective past affirmative action programs have been. Even well-informed people have a high level of uncertainty about such matters because many have been inadequately measured and studied, and the empirical studies that do exist have been underpublicized. Ambivalence and a qualified support appear to describe the opinion data best, with sentiments also fed by the uncertainty that afflicts most observers.

7. Resource limitations required limiting the study to this sampling of network outlets. Because all ABC transcripts were available without charge, and taped excerpts of network news from the Vanderbilt Television News Archives were costly, the analysis of both verbal and visual content was based on a representative sample of affirmative action stories on CBS and NBC. Analysis of ABC was confined to the verbal text.

8. See Entman 1997 or Entman 1998 for tables displaying the content data.

9. Greenberg 1988; Shrum 1996.

10. Shrum 1996; Shedler and Manis 1986.

11. Cf. Patterson 1997, chap. 5.

12. Steeh and Krysan 1996.

13. Ibid., 144–45; also see, on common ground in polls, Seib and Davidson 1994.

14. Steeh and Krysan 1996, 128; cf. also Kuklinski et al. 1997.

15. Bobo and Kluegel 1993.

16. Cf. Zaller 1992.

17. Cf. Patterson 1997, chap. 5.

18. This does not imply that affirmative action and other policies have eliminated discrimination against women either. See U.S. Federal Glass Ceiling Commission 1995.

19. Sniderman et al. 1993.

20. The reason for this might be that almost all demonstrations for affirmative action were in fact predominantly Black. There is no way to verify this possibility. In any case, by using images of racially coded demonstrations so often to illustrate the coverage, the media exaggerated the degree of racial conflict within the citizenry.

21. Steeh and Krysan 1996, 138.

22. A total of twenty-four stories were recorded on Lexis-Nexis as having mentioned the words *affirmative action* on the CBS *Evening News* for this period. Thirteen of these were routine reports by anchorpersons under one hundred words; eleven were longer stories by correspondents, the subject of the analysis.

23. Steeh and Krysan 1996, 139; Entman 1998.

24. Blumrosen 1995; cf. Sturm and Guinier 1996, for an exhaustive study of affirmative action complexities.

25. Steeh and Krysan 1996, 140.

26. Sniderman and Piazza 1993; Seib and Davidson 1994; Hochschild 1995; Feagin and Vera 1995; Wilson 1996.

27. The O.J. Simpson case probably best exemplified the racial gulf in the 1990s (Hunt 1999; Fiske 1994), but it would be a mistake to generalize from it. There is undoubtedly an ideological chasm here rooted in vastly and systematically differing histories and personal experiences. Blacks have long experienced harsh treatment by police authority because of their race and been treated more harshly by the criminal justice system. That particular disagreement does not logically or empirically predict similarly stark disagreements in all other policy domains.

28. Putnam 1993; Fukuyama 1995. We regard the concept of social capital as a useful metaphor for psychological feelings of community and solidarity, of shared subjectivity, among members of different ascriptive groups. We do not mean to suggest it is quantifiable in the same way as economic capital, nor does using the concept imply acceptance of Putnam's entire argument. For critiques see Norris 1996; Tarrow 1996; and Bennett 1998.

29. E.g., Gamson 1992; Neuman, Just, and Crigler 1992.

30. An indirect indication of media influence may reside in surveys, including the 1997 *New York Times* poll mentioned in the text (Verhovek 1997) and the Sniderman and Piazza 1991 study *Race and Politics*. Both find substantial gulfs in sentiments toward preferential affirmative action programs between those with high school or less education and the college educated. White persons of higher educational attainment oppose the programs more even though no more objectively affected (or potentially affected) by affirmative action than those of lower attainment. The gulf may reflect the difference in attentiveness to the elite discourse in the media among the two groups. The better educated could be more attuned to media, more likely then to imbibe the dominant slant, which was, as we have argued, against "preference" programs. However, more data would be needed to make that case definitively.

31. Entman 1989; Entman and Page 1994.
32. Cf. Edelman 1988.
33. Frammolino, Gladstone, and Wallace 1996.

Chapter Eight

1. Schuman et al. 1998, 315.
2. Bennett 1996; Entman 1989.
3. Bennett and Lawrence 1995.
4. Dahl and Bennett 1995.
5. See Reed 1993; Dawson 1994.
6. Ben Chavis may have enjoyed similarly high levels of support, but he had at the time of the poll just been ousted as the executive director of the NAACP for spending tens of thousands of dollars of the group's money for an of out-of-court settlement with a woman who had accused him of job discrimination and sexual harassment.
7. See Broh 1987.
8. Sabato 1991.
9. Mollenkopf 1995.
10. Tuchman 1978.
11. Ettema 1990.
12. Reeves 1997.
13. Dates of these 1988 broadcasts: NBC, 6 April; NBC and ABC, 9 April; NBC and ABC, 11 April; NBC and ABC, 17 April.
14. A comparison of three data sets drawn from three national studies of anti-Semitism conducted in 1964 (NORC), 1981 (Yankelovich, Skelly, and White), and 1992 (Martilla and Kiley) reveals a long-term *drop* of anti-Semitism among Blacks and Whites, steepest between 1964 and 1981 and then a further but lesser drop between 1981 and 1992. For example, dividing respondents into three groupings based on their agreement with a set of anti-Semitic statements, about 40 percent of Whites fell into the highly anti-Semitic group in 1964 as compared to 14 percent in 1992. Among Blacks the percentages were 53 percent and 33 percent, respectively. Because Blacks began at higher levels of anti-Semitism and did not drop as far as Whites, this increased the relative distance between the two groups. Nevertheless, there was no sign of increase in extreme Black anti-Semitism between 1981 and 1992. However, the groups defined as moderately anti-Semitic increased slightly among *both* Blacks and Whites between 1981 and 1992.
15. Gitlin 1980.
16. Ettema (1990) reports one case of a Black–Jewish controversy in Chicago in 1988 that stayed in the news for a brief time.
17. Sonenshein 1993.
18. Gates 1996.
19. Putnam 1993.
20. Gitlin 1980.

21. Entman 1989.

22. Blacks spoke about government policy in 146 stories, making a total of 200 coded assertions; Whites spoke in 339 stories for a total of 523 times. Individuals or spokespersons for groups representing other ethnic interest groups, or for groups representing a mixture of ethnics, made up most of the rest of the 862 total assertions relevant to policy issues. For a few assertions, race could not be determined.

23. For example, a claim was coded as "public interest" if the person endorsed a policy on the grounds it would "serve the people of Chicago." An ethnic self-interest claim would be something like: "It's time Mayor Daley stopped cutting aid to hospitals serving the Black community." A corruption-related claim would be: "The city's restaurant inspectors frequently ask for bribes." And other special interests might be endorsed by a person who said: "The city government ignores the needs of the gay community."

24. Most of these instances involved a person defending the interests not explicitly of the "White community"; there was little invocation even of the term *White,* a finding that would not surprise those who research "White studies," who find that Whites are generally not conscious of their racial identities or racial privileges as such (Delgado and Stepanic 1997). Rather, we recorded references to interests such those of "the suburbs" or "the North Shore" (i.e., affluent northern suburbs of Chicago) or "the middle class" as code words for "White." On the other hand, references to "inner city" and the like were coded as equivalent to Black. However, though "White" was rarely invoked as a racial category to which government should respond, "Black" was, and this is another contrast that makes Blacks seem especially demanding.

25. We recognize that determining the ultimate beneficiaries of subsidies or any government program is complicated; middle-class realtors and working-class caretakers may also benefit from the tax deductibility of vacation homes. But our larger point about the media's general neglect of conflicts in class interests and emphasis on racial friction remains valid.

26. The procedure for identifying the leaders to code was as follows. In a pilot study we first searched the ABC transcripts for twenty-two weeks in 1990 and 1991 for all names on *Ebony* magazine's 1990 and 1991 lists of the "100 Most Influential Blacks in America." Of these people, twenty had speaking appearances on ABC. The final analysis searched for all appearances of these twenty names in the 1990–91 sample. The three hundred ABC stories that mentioned the word *Black* or its synonyms within the year-long 1990–91 sample (discussed in chapter 4) were *also* searched for these twenty names and for any other identifiably Black leader. This means that only those twenty Black leaders found in the pilot sample could be coded in the final sample, unless leaders appeared in one of the three hundred stories mentioning the word *Black* or synonyms. The 1990–91 study may therefore miss some mentions of Black leaders. However, random checking suggests that few mentions of Black leaders were overlooked because their appearances (with the exception of Colin Powell and Louis Sullivan) were generally linked to their race (and thus with the mention of the word *Black*), and because the pilot did select most of the nation's most prominent Black leaders. This issue does not arise in the later

two periods, 1994 and 1997, where we searched for all one hundred names in the year's *Ebony* list.

27. These leaders are: Tom Bradley, Sharon Pratt-Dixon, Joseph Lowery, Ron Brown, John Conyers, Ronald Dellums, Charles Rangel, Craig Washington, Coretta Scott King, Nelson Rivers, Sidney Barthelemy, and Harvey Gantt—all mayors, members of Congress, or heads of civil rights organizations.

28. Tuchman 1978; Gans 1979; Bennett 1996; Entman 1989.

Chapter Nine

1. BBDO 1998.
2. Cf. Sterngold 1998 with Haas 1998.
3. Putnam 1993, 174.
4. Batson et al. 1997
5. Parks 1982, 91.
6. Pettigrew 1998; see Sigelman and Welch 1993; Ellison and Powers 1994.
7. Jhally and Lewis 1992.
8. Fiske and Taylor 1991, 116.
9. Gray 1995, 35.
10. Gerbner and Gross 1976; Shrum 1996.
11. Armstrong, Neuendorf, and Brentar 1992.
12. Power, Murphy, and Coover 1996.
13. Fiske and Taylor 1991, 258–59; cf. Devine 1989. The distinctions between stereotypes and prototypes can be clarified as follows: whereas prototypes name *specific cases* taken to represent a whole category, stereotypes define the *distinguishing traits* the culture records as characterizing the most representative members of a category. Prototypes are implicit; stereotypes explicit. If asked to name a typical bird, most people say robin or sparrow—specific cases—without thinking through why they do. They answer in terms of unconscious prototypes. Only if you then ask what makes a robin a typical bird, will they realize and be able to dredge up a list of stereotypical traits: they are small, fly, make pretty sounds, live free of domestication, and so forth. Thus the "bird" schema stores links to these concepts, and the wide diffusion of this schema in the society determines and records the culturally shared view of robins as prototypically representative birds. This does not preclude an understanding that other less typical cases like chickens may still fit into the category.

What distinguishes stereotypes and prototypes most clearly is that stereotypes are subjects of overt public discussion and critique and thus perhaps exert less power than the more subtle—indeed in ordinary language unnamed—prototypes. The public critique centers precisely on denying that the stereotypical trait is representative, the claim that although the real world may contain examples of the stereotyped character, the person exhibiting those traits is atypical. On the other hand, individuals may see and judge specific members of a group as "typical examples," that is, as highly representative or prototypical, without suffering notice or shame—or even self-awareness. These unmindful schemas organize "an enormous amount of our knowledge about categories of things. . . .

We constantly draw inferences on the basis of that kind of knowledge. And we do it so regularly and automatically that we are rarely aware that we are doing it." Lakoff 1987, 86.

14. The shows are as follows: eight episodes each of *ER* and *NYPD Blue;* eight each of *Frasier, Friends, Home Improvement,* and *Seinfeld;* six of *Caroline in the City;* four of *Boston Common* and *Mad About You;* and three of *Single Guy.*

15. Weigel, Kim, and Frost 1995.

16. Although in the top 10 during the sample period, this program lasted only one season. It featured a White man who had a platonic relationship with a Black woman; she advised him on his romantic travails with other women.

17. A second coder was trained (but not informed of the intent of the study) and given a random sample of 20 percent of the interactions. Reliability coefficients (Kappas) for the content analysis were as follows: gender of character 1.0; gender relationship 0.90; character type 0.82; role played 0.94; relationship type 0.87; task dependency 0.93; decisionmaking 0.84; verbal intimacy 0.81; extra-role involvement 0.88.

18. Hall 1975, 15.

19. The plot summaries come from an Internet site, <http://epguides.com/ NYPDBlue>, that goes into fine detail on plot, cast members, and key production personnel. We recognize the potential reliability problem in using what is essentially an unofficial, voluntary Internet site for research data, but a number of unrelated factors bolster its credibility. First, the author has kept a meticulous record of every single minor character in each episode (even those uncredited), as well as of the writers and directors and air date. In addition, we checked the accuracy of the plot summaries of the eight episodes analyzed, and also those of a number of subsequent episodes. These were both accurate and complete. We have little reason to doubt the accuracy of the data for the other episodes, especially data on the presence of a major star as a principal character in any of the episodes.

20. Interracial romances have occurred from time to time on the afternoon soaps and one also occurred on *Ally McBeal* in 1999.

21. Jhally and Lewis 1992.

22. Fiske and Taylor 1991, 135–36.

23. Jhally and Lewis 1992; cf. Rothbart and John 1993 and Gandy 1998 on the stickiness of stereotypes.

24. Dates 1993, 268.

25. See Kinder and Sanders 1996; Schuman et al. 1998.

26. See Ofori 1999, 3, who cites Nielsen ratings indicating the average American household has the television on 50.24 hours a week; the average Hispanic household 56.17 and African American, 69.49. Ofori's data also suggest, however, that advertisers are unwilling to pay as much to reach Black as White audiences, at least when it comes to radio, *irrespective of their income levels.*

27. Cf. Turow 1997; Sterngold 1998.

28. Quoted in Sterngold 1998.

29. Quoted in ibid.

30. Quoted in ibid.

Chapter Ten

1. Previous research on images of Blacks in advertising include Bristor, Lee, and Hunt 1995; Dates 1993; DeMott 1995; Elliot 1995; Kern-Foxworth 1994; O'Barr 1994; Pieterse 1992; Seiter 1995; Wilkes and Valencia 1989; Wonsek 1992; Zinkhan, Qualls, and Biswas 1990. On Black–White relationships in television entertainment, see Weigel, Kim, and Frost 1995. On the place of advertising in motivating consumption, see Budd, Craig, and Steinman 1999.

2. Corner 1995, 117–18.

3. Douglas 1970.

4. Malkki 1995, 257.

5. One dimension we do not cover is the sound track. Our impression is that voice-over narration and music in commercials more frequently highlight African Americans than do visual images, at least in some product categories. If so, it would add an interesting wrinkle to the findings here without altering their basic thrust. We cannot, however, follow that thread further in this study.

6. We deliberately chose Fox because it originally targeted African American and other "urban" audiences. It might be expected to run commercials that are less White-dominated than the other three networks. ABC and NBC were chosen randomly from the Big Three. The initial sample of ads was taped from broadcast affiliates in Raleigh-Durham, N.C.; to check for possible influence of this southern location, we analyzed a fourth week of prime time emanating from the NBC affiliate in Los Angeles. As always, more extensive sampling would have been desirable, and more research is needed for refinement and verification. But the present data set appears to be the most extensive and the content analysis the most detailed yet undertaken in the study of race and television advertising.

7. One difference not germane to this research was that the week of Los Angeles prime time included significantly more commercials that featured East Asians (fifty-two, compared with ninety-five in the other three weeks combined). This is probably a straightforward result of the large population of East Asian ethnic groups in Southern California.

8. Several other ads had racially ambiguous actors in certain codeable categories; they received a special code and are excluded from the analyses where they come up. Arguably, appearances by such actors are theoretically significant. Occupying the border-lands between Black, White, Latino, and Asian, the models might well have been chosen precisely because sponsors felt viewers would project their own preferred ethnic identity onto them. We might expect to see more of these actors in commercials in the future as the population of the United States becomes more multiethnic. For now, however, the overwhelming majority of actors in commercials are racially identifiable. We exclude the data on Asians to make analysis clearer; including them in the tabulations would not change results in any significant way. Other research (Entman et al. 1998; Lee 1998) suggests that East Asians are generally underrepresented and often stereotyped in mass media products; also see chapter 11 (on movies).

9. This sampling method seemed best since it captures the image patterns as they flow to viewers who become more likely to register commercials the more they are repeated. Furthermore, weighing a commercial that appears once equally to one appearing fifteen times would provide a misleading map of the images actually embodying the culture (on the importance of repetition to viewer cognition of commercials' visual arguments, see Messaris 1997). As we show below, analysis of a one-week subsample revealed no significant difference when each distinct ad was counted just once. Moreover, differentiating ads for the same products can be a daunting task. Many commercials include a montage of scenes that may change slightly—by the inclusion or exclusion of just one or two scenes—from showing to showing. It is not clear whether these should count as the same ad or different ones. Given the strong theoretical reason to sample as we did, we saw little reason to limit the included commercials to one appearance each.

10. As noted in the text, the samples analyzed here are based on ad *showings,* meaning that if the same commercial appeared ten times during a sample week, it was coded and entered into the data set ten times. In this note we assess the impact of composing the sample by counting just one of each commercial shown. We randomly chose ABC prime time for the week of 3–10 December 1995, representing about one-fourth of the total prime-time sample, for the test.

We decided to count commercials as distinct if they contained at least 50 percent new scenes not previously appearing in the sponsor's ads that week. So if a Sears ad showed eighteen scenes, eleven of which had appeared in a commercial already shown, this one was not counted again. If, however, an eighteen-scene ad contained only five that had already appeared, it was counted as a new commercial and coded. In other cases, of course, the identical commercial was shown repeatedly and it was easy to eliminate all but one of them from this test sample.

Appendix table A.15 presents comparisons of the product representation, overall racial composition, and a few representative content attributes for the week of ad showings (n = 407), the basis for the discussion in the main text, and for the week counting each separate commercial only once (n = 254). The two samples differ only slightly in overall results. The first breakdown shows the products featured. The differences in percentages composing the two samples reveal that department and furniture stores and fast food outlets were most likely to run the same ads repeatedly. Racial composition was virtually identical. As a proportion of the total ad *showings,* all-White ads were 60.2 percent, compared with 61.4 percent of the single-ad sample; Black–White integrated ads made up 24 percent of the former, compared with 24.5 percent of the latter. As to specific content, again the differences are minimal. The variables of skin touching, speaking to other characters, and sexualization, shown in the table, are typical.

We conclude that sampling method probably made no difference to the findings discussed in the text. However, we continue to believe that using ad *showings* as the basis for this sort of research makes the most sense because our interest (the dependent variable) is the flow of cultural signals to audiences. If the focus had been on describing the universe of television commercials, a single-ad sampling might have been more appropriate. As it turns out, the data tell us the same thing either way.

11. The sports sample included four football games: a Monday night NFL game (ABC), two Sunday NFL games (Fox and NBC), and the Superbowl (NBC). A total of 265 ads were codeable. We also coded two evening's worth of commercials on youth-oriented MTV (22 October 1996 and 7 December 1996), from 10:00 P.M. to 2:00 A.M. for a total of 165 commercials during the eight-hour period. Finally, we coded eight hours of prime-time and late-evening programming on BET (8:00 P.M. to midnight, 30 October 1996 and 15 December 1996).

12. The scenes of movie and program commercials tend to cut so quickly from one to the next, the relationships, words, and actions of characters are so unclear without the context of the entire film or program, and the sheer numbers of characters appearing are so great that these texts do not fit the coding protocol or methodologies that work for other commercials. It appears unlikely that this subgenre violates the norms practiced in the other television advertisements, but we cannot dismiss that possibility.

13. To conserve space and readers' patience, we offer complete details on coding at the book's website. Coding reliability was established by training two assistants and comparing their independent coding of six hours each (two evenings) of prime-time advertising to that conducted by the first author. Average reliability was 0.90; with correction for chance agreement the figure was about 0.88, using the Brennan-Prediger method (1981). Most disagreements arose over the racial identity of marginal characters, those who appeared fleetingly. If coded as Black, these racially ambiguous characters would shift some of the coding categories from all-White to Black-White. Sometimes coders caught these appearances and considered the actors Black, whereas in other cases they did not note the appearance as that of a Black character. For the most part, however, coders agreed, and most coding categories required straightforward and objective judgments.

14. On luxury and fantasy in ads, see Bonney and Wilson 1983, and Messaris 1997.

15. Nacos and Hritzuk 1998, 22.

16. Turow 1997; Budd, Craig, and Steinman 1999.

17. For example, *Martin* aired on Fox between *The Simpsons* and *Married With Children*. In our sample, *Martin* featured two all-Black ads, whereas the other two shows had none. And *Martin* showed three all-White ads (out of nine commercials), compared with five (of ten) on *Simpsons* and seven (of twelve) on *Married*.

18. For evidence of high sensitivity to racial representations in the advertising industry, see Garfield 1996a and 1996b; Wolverton 1997; Turow 1997; Goldman and Papson 1996.

19. Some of the images coded as sexualization showed intimacy of two characters with each other, but most suggested intimacy only between a single character on the screen and the viewer. Thus the categorization in table 10.1.

20. To conserve space, we do not display the full data table here; it is available at the book's website.

21. Taking the White to Black appearance ratios in the order they appear in table 10.1 (i.e., from speaking to same race character to sexualization), the ratios for the 465 integrated ads are: 8.8; 8.3; 3.7; 5.3; 6.5; 2.8; 5.4; 4.1; 2.9; 3.4; 2.4; 3.2; and 1.6.

22. Turow 1997.

23. Gray 1995, 157.

24. Schlossberg 1993.

25. Testimony to that inference can be found in the business and advertising trade press; see, e.g., Schlossberg 1993; Miller 1992; Wolverton 1997. The latter suggests that Olympic skating champion Kristi Yamaguchi would have enjoyed a much more lucrative endorsement career if she had not been Asian American. Research also strongly implies such sensitivity; see especially Turow 1997 and Goldman and Papson 1996.

26. Spindler 1997.

27. Hooks 1991; Kern-Foxworth 1994; Pieterse 1992.

28. Douglas 1966, 95.

29. Garfield 1996a.

30. Garfield 1996b; also see Wynter 1998 on advertisers' continuing fear of showing interracial physical contact that may offend minority as well as majority group audiences.

31. Cf. Wilson 1996, 44.

32. An occasional fast food ad showed scenes in which Blacks predominated but one or two Whites appeared in the background. This of course reversed the typical practice. We speculate that advertisers assume that White audiences realize McDonalds and Burger King operate outlets in Black neighborhoods, serving an overwhelmingly Black clientele. Thus the scene is not threatening; it is encoded to suggest an inner-city locale where Whites do not normally travel. In any case, these are not montage ads, which show a series of different unrelated persons enjoying the product in rapid succession; not one of the latter genre of ad depicted a Black majority. And Whites experience the ads intertextually: they know from going out to eat in their own largely segregated neighborhoods and from the bulk of fast food commercials (most or all-White) that the clientele will be largely White.

33. Parallel findings for Britain are discussed in Branthwaite and Pierce 1990.

34. In a perceptive review of a Denny's Restaurant commercial that was made to counter unfavorable publicity over the company's loss of racial discrimination lawsuits, Garfield (1997) refers to "the normal level of racial and gender bean counting" in producing commercials. Beyond the "toxic tarot of racial politics" that infuses much of advertising, he also notes that class bias often overlays racial bias in these images, suggesting (in our terms) that advertisers prefer Blacks of high achieved and body traits over those more removed from the cultural ideal.

35. Ofori 1999, 2, 13.

36. Hall 1990.

37. Nacos and Hritzuk 1998, 21–22.

38. This part of the analysis is reported in more detail in Entman and Book 1999. Professor Constance Book of Meredith College inspired the detailed probe into skin color and contributed valuable ideas to the skin color research.

39. See Russell, Wilson, and Hall 1992.

40. Hughes and Hertel 1990; Keith and Herring 1991; Seltzer and Smith 1992.

41. Russell, Wilson, and Hall 1992; Coltrane and Adams 1997.

42. We enlisted thirteen independent student coders (who included Blacks and Whites). They were asked to make a simple categorical judgment: Was the skin color of Blacks in a sample of television commercials "light" or "dark"? Using this system, intercoder reliability (after correcting for chance as recommended by Brennan and Prediger 1981) exceeded 0.90 among the thirteen coders.

43. Statistically significant at $p < 0.01$.

44. Differences with dark skinned statistically significant at $p < 0.01$.

45. Differences statistically significant at $p < 0.05$.

46. Cf. Russell, Wilson, and Hall 1992.

47. Besides works already cited, see on race and advertising Elliot 1995; Seiter 1995; Branthwaite and Pierce 1990; Zinkhan, Qualls, and Biswas 1990.

48. Quoted in Spindler 1997; cf. Turow 1997, 94–95.

49. Hoberman 1997.

50. Cf. Nacos and Hritzuk 1998, 23.

Chapter Eleven

1. Guerrero 1993a; Bogle 1989; Hooks 1992; Jones 1993; Lyman 1990.

2. Guerrero 1993b.

3. Ibid.

4. Pines 1995, 69.

5. Thus, of the top seventy grossing films (over $25 million U.S. box office), we analyzed sixty-three. The films excluded were: *The Hunchback of Notre Dame* (#13); *Toy Story* (#31); *Beavis and Butt-head Do America* (#32); *Muppet Treasure Island* (#43); *Homeward Bound II* (#50); *James and the Giant Peach* (#57); and *The Island of Dr. Moreau* (#59).

6. Shohat and Stam 1994, 205; Branigan 1992.

7. It is also clear that some films are not made purely to maximize profit. Some get produced on small budgets for presumably small absolute returns, though sometimes large percentage earnings. Still others are made for more purely artistic (or egotistical) reasons by filmmakers who feel they have important ideas to express. So we do not mean to suggest that every flick arises from its makers' profit-seeking.

8. Corliss 1996, 58.

9. This comprises most of the major newspapers in the United States, including the *Sacramento Bee, San Francisco Chronicle,* and *Los Angeles Times,* the *Chicago Tribune* and *Sun-Times,* the *Atlanta Journal-Constitution, St. Petersburg Times, Washington Post, USA Today,* the *New York Times,* and the *Boston Globe.*

10. Bogle 1989.

11. Demott 1995; also Bogle 1989, 281–87.

12. Bogle 1989, 7.

13. We understand that stereotypes do have a strong commercial purpose. The film studios want audiences to recognize characters, types, and genres. Audiences do not want to be mystified or, beyond certain generic conventions, surprised—or at least most

film companies believe as much. This is what drives the use of such stereotypes as those found in *Independence Day.* Everybody is familiar with the kvetchy Jewish parent; throwing one in is an easy play for laughs.

14. Several Internet movie databases provided cast and other data: <http://us.imdb.com>, <http://www.tvguide.com>, and <http://moviepeople.hollywood.com>.

15. In constructing the original sample we relied upon figures for calendar 1996. Several films were in release during 1997 as well and their total box office earnings were higher than those for 1996 alone. We use the total box office revenue figures where the specific amounts earned are relevant.

16. B. D. Wong in *Father of the Bride* and Jeff Imada in *Escape from L.A.* are examples.

17. Here is the complete list of occupations of characters played by actors we identified (from last names and biographies) as Latino: not ascertainable: 3; teacher: 1; criminal 5; military: 1; golf caddy 1; stripper 1; bartender 1. Yet Latinos are projected to account for 13.8 percent of the U.S. population in 2010 and 16.3 percent of the population in 2020. Asians are projected at 4.8 percent by 2010. U.S. Bureau of the Census 1997, 9.

18. Examples of such films are *Space Jam, Set It Off,* and *A Thin Line Between Love and Hate.*

19. Black females appeared in seventeen of the sixty-three movies, six of which had majority Black casts.

20. *Set It Off* featured one White; thirty-nine of forty top ten cast members in the films were Black.

21. The other four films starring African American males had mostly Black casts: Eddie Murphy in *The Nutty Professor,* Denzel Washington in the *The Preacher's Wife,* Martin Lawrence in *A Thin Line Between Love and Hate,* and Michael Jordan in *Space Jam.* Black females received top billing in two of the all-Black films, *Waiting to Exhale* and *Set It Off.*

22. Full data can be found in Entman et al. 1998, and on the book's website.

23. Farley et al. 1994; Schuman et al. 1998.

24. The exception is Vanessa Williams who plays an executive who is victimized and needs protection by the apotheosis of great White hopes, Arnold Schwarzenegger, in *Eraser.*

25. We cannot make too much of these data alone. Although many parts were military or police and blue collar or lower-level service workers, we cannot say these choices are necessarily negative or stereotyping. We did not measure the occupational distribution among Whites. It could be that Whites were shown proportionately even more during the sample year in those occupations. Obviously the role distribution is in part a function of the films that earned over $25 million in 1996. Many of the top movies that year happened to involve police and military forces, though not always in dramatic or realistic settings (e.g., police figured prominently in the tense drama *Heat* and the silly comedy *First Kid;* military personnel populated the serious *Courage Under Fire,* the fantasy *Star Trek,* and the farce *Down Periscope*).

26. Charles Merritt and Brian Kenner at the Kennedy School of Government, Harvard University. The analysis of cast ethnicity was performed by three students at Harvard Law School: Simone Boayue, Caryn Kennedy, and Anita Raman. Their hard work on the content analysis was invaluable. More information on the coding protocol can be found in Entman et al. 1998, where data for Latinos and East Asians are also discussed. Reliability tests were carried out on three sample movies: *Jerry Maguire, Courage Under Fire,* and *Ransom.* Overall, coders achieved correspondence for *Jerry Maguire* for eighty of eighty-eight categories (91 percent); equivalent figures for *Ransom* and *Courage* were 92 percent and 95 percent. Given the extensive pretesting and training, this gave us confidence in assigning the task of coding the film texts, which is far more complicated and time consuming than for any news program, to a single coder.

The aspects coded were:

Commit Physical Violence. Physical violence was recorded if a character purposely and directly injured another character. (The character had actually to commit the violence; merely ordering somebody else to be harmed does not count.)

Vulgar Profanity. Profanity defined as use of the more vulgar expletives.

Ungrammatical. Coded if characters spoke improper language (nonstandard English, not merely occasional slang).

Sexualized. "Sexualization" is defined as showing characters scantily clothed in such a way as to invite the sexual interest of both the audience and the other characters within that scene (e.g., in *Independence Day,* Jasmine Dubrow dances in bikini underwear at the strip club.)

"I Love You." The utterance by characters of "I love you" or close synonyms of committed intimacy.

Caressed. Caressing was recorded when one character touched another in a situation that clearly would not lead immediately to sex (e.g., in *A Time to Kill,* Matthew McConaughey's character strokes the cheek of Sandra Bullock's character when she is in the hospital, but they do not embrace or become more physically intimate).

Hugged/Kissed. The number of times a character hugged or kissed another character was recorded, again if the act was not moving toward a sexual encounter (e.g., in *Courage Under Fire,* Denzel Washington's character embraces his wife when he returns home).

Sex. We recorded the number of times a character either engaged in sexual activity on screen, or was clearly implied to have had sex even if not explicitly shown.

Entry Guard/Security Agent. Coding characters whose sole role was to provide protection or guardianship for another character or object.

Physically Restrained, Handcuffed, In Jail. The number of times a character was physically restrained by others, handcuffed or chained, or put in a holding facility was coded (e.g., Samuel Jackson's character in *A Time to Kill* is shown in jail after his arrest for murder).

27. Identifiably Latino actors have a far lesser presence than Blacks; East Asian presence was negligible; see Entman et al. 1998.

28. The findings on sex and intimacy, and all the others, could be a function of the particular films that showed up as top earners in 1996. Part of the explanation for the results lay in the specific movies sampled and roles occupied. In a year where, say, romantic comedies scored bigger at the box office, these data might look quite different, since such films rarely star Blacks and typically feature a lot of nonsexual intimacy. In another year, where action thrillers take all the top spots, sexuality and romance might be less prevalent for both Blacks and Whites. Thus it would not be proper to generalize too broadly from these findings.

29. It might be argued that Blacks in "reality" are less likely to follow White middle-class patterns of communication (Kochman 1981) and public behavior (Patterson 1997). Of course, Hollywood has never exhibited much concern with "accuracy." Again, without getting into unproductive arguments about reality, we want to point out the importance of contextualizing, of explaining fully the reasons and meanings of any difference in behavior that appears linked to race (cf. Shohat and Stam 1994, 203). We would not expect Hollywood film to delve into such matters, of course; but our point is precisely that without doing so, the films participate in the discourse of racial hierarchy and difference. It is also worth noting that studies find African Americans holding social and moral values, including religious beliefs, that are as conservative or even more so than Whites (Hochschild 1995).

30. Even in *The Nutty Professor,* Eddie Murphy's remake of the Jerry Lewis film featuring a predominantly Black cast, Blacks relate to White characters largely within confines of their work roles. *Independence Day* does portray a close relationship that seems to transcend cockpit chatter, between Will Smith and a White pilot, but the latter is a minor character who dies early in the film.

31. In *Waiting to Exhale,* Angela Basset's husband has an affair with a White woman though it is only alluded to, not shown onscreen.

32. Shohat and Stam 1994, 183; cf. Lakoff 1987; Rothbart and John 1993; Devine 1989; Pettigrew 1979.

33. Streisand 1997.

34. Samuels and Leland 1999.

35. Cf. Rhines 1995.

36. Braxton 1997; Gandy 1998, 116.

37. Goldstein 1996.

38. On the production side, the obvious explanation for the findings is lack of presence by minority filmmakers. Blacks comprise under 3 percent of the membership of the Directors Guild of America and of the Writers Guild; membership of the Academy of Motion Picture Arts and Sciences, which awards the Oscar, is about 4 percent (Lambert 1996, 44). As of 1994, only seven movie theaters were owned by African Americans (Rhines 1995).

39. Goldstein 1996; cf. Masters 1996.

40. Goldstein 1996, F1; the rule of thumb in Hollywood is that films with essentially all-Black casts can earn no more than about $40 million (Masters 1996, 73).

41. Masters 1996, 73.

42. The exceptional case is *The Nutty Professor*. Eddie Murphy has probably been the Black movie actor with the most crossover appeal. Moreover, although the film featured more Blacks than Whites, it was integrated and not set in an exclusively Black milieu like *Preacher's Wife*. It was also a pure entertainment, a farce featuring outlandish special effects and tour de force comedic acting by Murphy as compared with the more serious and dramatic subject matter of *Preacher's Wife*. (Bogle [1989, 286] suggests Murphy's most successful films have largely featured him in roles that harken back to the "coon" stereotype, the feckless rascal.) Nonetheless, Murphy's experience does show that a mostly-Black film can attract White audiences with an appealing star and the right formula. When Murphy has made films set in largely Black milieus, however, they have seemingly confirmed the Hollywood rule and had limited box office success (see Guerrero 1993b).

43. U.S. Bureau of the Census 1997.

44. Cf. Lambert 1996, 46.

Chapter Twelve

1. We like to ask our classes if they think that humans a hundred generations from now will still be categorizing themselves and others into "Black people," "White people," "Italian Americans," and the rest. They always acknowledge that eventually, even if it takes a thousand generations, these distinctions will disappear as intermarriage does its inevitable blending of color and ethnic distinctions—and as communication technology renders geographical boundaries less significant to social relations.

2. Anderson 1991.

3. The arguable exception, *Guess Who's Coming to Dinner* (1967), proves the rule. Beyond the extreme chasteness of the couple's on-screen relationship, the Black man (Sidney Poitier) represents a superhuman conglomeration of every cultural ideal except for skin color—a Johns Hopkins doctor, well-spoken, deferential but confident and masculine, extraordinarily handsome by almost any standard. A handful of minor films (in terms of star power, box office receipts, and promotion budgets) such as *Jungle Fever* (1991), *One Night Stand* (1997), and *Some Kind of Hero* (1982) have shown interracial sexuality on screen. None to our knowledge leads ultimately to marriage and children. And given our interest in leading cultural indicators, we believe the most pertinent data arise from the major productions, those on the scale of *Pretty Woman*, *As Good as It Gets*, *Sleepless in Seattle*, *Good Will Hunting*, or *Jerry Maguire*. These are among the 1990s productions that featured romantic relationships and ranked among the 178 movies films that have ever (as of 1999) grossed over $100 million (Internet Movie Database 1999). In fact, not one of these 178 movies highlighted a relationship between a Black male and White female, and just one involved the opposite racial pairing, *The Bodyguard* (1992), in which sex occurred off-screen and the couple did not culminate their relationship with marriage. Ironically, as we have noted, broadcast television—perhaps because required to be mostly suggestive and thus freed from having to fulfill the conventional narrative expectations that obtain in movies (which would entail showing potentially controversial nudity and intense physical and sexual contact between lovers)—seems to have been more daring. Besides *ER*, *Ally McBeal* and some soap operas have featured interracial

romances. But to our knowledge no interracial couple has ever had the starring role on a major network program.

4. Cf. Hall 1997, 229.

5. *Jerry Maguire* could have been called *Rod Tidwell* (Cuba Gooding's football player), but that would have violated truth in advertising as it limited the potential box office take.

6. See, e.g., Ford 1997; McCarthy et al. 1997; Murphy 1998.

7. E.g., Gilens 1999; Gilliam et al. 1996.

8. It seems that Whites do not regard affirmative action as among "the most important problems facing the *country*" (emphasis added), but do feel it among the most important problems of *race relations*.

9. Cf. Garrow 1978.

10. Gilliam et al. 1996.

11. E.g., Entman 1989; Patterson 1993; Bennett 1996; Rojecki 1999.

12. Gitlin 1980.

13. On ultimate goals, see Entman 1989; Commission on Freedom of the Press 1947; Bennett 1996.

14. Gilens 1999; Gilliam et al. 1996; Romer, Jamieson, and Coteau 1998.

15. See Banaji, Hardin, and Rothman 1993.

16. Cf. Gandy 1998.

17. The number of EEOC complaints for racial discrimination brought in fiscal 1998 was 28,820 (EEOC 1998). There is no way this could represent, as implied by generalizing from our informant's claim, almost all instances of workplace discipline affecting minorities. These are surely more numerous. And, since racial discrimination does continue, some portion of these complaints are valid. In fact, the EEOC's actions in 1998 suggest they believed around 32 percent of complaints had validity. And in all likelihood many more victims of discrimination fail to file EEOC complaints than file them. This is not to deny that some minority individuals do take advantage of EEOC mechanisms to retaliate against employers who are not discriminating.

18. Entman 1989; Bennett 1996.

19. Scott 1994, 7.

20. Cf. Hamilton 1997.

21. Cf. Barber 1984.

22. Patterson 1997.

23. Kinder and Sanders 1996; Sniderman and Piazza 1993.

24. See also Sears 1993; cf. Page and Shapiro 1992.

25. Merelman 1995.

26. Cf. Dyson 1995, on rap music.

27. Kleiman and Riggs 1991.

28. Benton is more complicated than Dr. Cliff Huxtable on *Cosby* since, as noted in chapter 9, he does have some stereotypical "Black" traits, especially fathering a child out of wedlock, failing to be a stable presence in that child's life, and refusing to settle into marriage.

29. Bonner 1999.

30. Cf. Neuman 1991.

31. In this sense we are reversing the causal arrow in Putnam's (1993) argument that attention to television has undermined social capital; we are suggesting that lowered social capital may reduce attention to culturally integrative television news and other media productions.

32. Putnam 1993; Fukuyama 1995.

33. Bennett and Entman 2000.

References

Abernathy-Lear, Gloria. 1994. African Americans' Criticisms Concerning African Americans' Representations on Daytime Serials. *Journalism Quarterly* 71: 30–39.

Altheide, David L. 1991. The Impact of Television Formats on Social Policy. *Journal of Broadcasting and Electronic Media* 35 (1): 3–21.

Alvarez, R. Michael, and John Brehm. 1997. Are Americans Ambivalent Toward Racial Policies? *American Journal of Political Science* 41:45–74.

Anderson, Benedict R. O'G. 1991. *Imagined Communities: Reflections on the Origin and Spread of Nationalism*. London; New York: Verso.

Andersen, C. 1977. "Black Is Beautiful" and the Color Preferences of Afro-American youth. *Journal of Negro Education* 46 (winter): 76–88.

Andrews, David L. 1996. The Fact(s) of Michael Jordan's Blackness: Excavating a Floating Racial Signifier. *Sociology of Sport Journal* 13 (2): 125–58.

Andrews, Edmund L. 1993. Mild Slap at TV Violence. *New York Times*, 1 July, pp. 1, 7.

Appiah, K. Anthony, and Amy Gutmann. 1996. *Color Conscious: The Political Morality of Race*. Princeton: Princeton University Press.

Arlen, Michael J. 1980. *Thirty Seconds*. New York: Farrar, Straus, and Giroux.

Armstrong, Blake G., Kimberly A. Neuendorf, and James E. Brentar. 1992. TV Entertainment, News, and Racial Perceptions of College Students. *Journal of Communication* 42 (3): 53–76.

Atkin, David. 1992. An Analysis of Television Series with Minority-Lead Characters. *Critical Studies in Mass Communication* 9:37–49.

BBDO. 1998. BBDO's 13th Annual Report on Black Television Viewing. *PR Newswire*, 26 March.

Banaji, Mahzarin R., C. Hardin, and Alexander J. Rothman. 1993. Implicit Stereotyping In Person Judgment. *Journal of Personality and Social Psychology* 65 (2): 272–81.

Barber, Benjamin. 1984. *Strong Democracy: Participatory Politics for a New Age*. Berkeley: University of California Press.

Bartels, Larry. 1993. Messages Received—The Political Impact of Media Exposure. *American Political Science Review* 87 (2): 267–285.

Batson, Daniel C., Marina P. Polycarpou, Edie Harmon-Jones, Heidi J. Imhoff, Erin C. Mitchener, Lori L. Bednar, Tricia R. Klein, and Lori Highberger. 1997. Empathy and Attitudes: Can Feelings for a Member of a Stigmatized Group Improve Feelings Toward the Group? *Journal of Personality and Social Psychology* 72:105–18.

Bennett, W. Lance. 1996. *News: The Politics of Illusion*. 3rd ed. New York: Longman.

———. 1998. The Uncivic Culture: Communication, Identity, and the Rise of Lifestyle Politics. *P.S. Political Science and Politics* 31 (4): 741–61.

———. 1990. Toward a Theory of Press-State Relations. *Journal of Communication* 40:103–25.

Bennett, W. Lance, and Regina G. Lawrence. 1995. News Icons and the Mainstreaming of Social Change. *Journal of Communication* 45 (3): 20–39.

Bennett, W. Lance, and Robert M. Entman, eds. 2000. *Mediated Politics: Communication in the Future of Democracy*. New York: Cambridge University Press.

Bershtel, S., and A. Graubard. 1983. The Mystique of the Progressive Jew. *Working Papers*, 10:19–25.

Bierly, Margaret M. 1985. Prejudice Toward Contemporary Outgroups as a Generalized Attitude. *Journal of Applied Social Psychology* 15 (2): 89–99.

Binder, Amy. 1993. Constructing Racial Rhetoric: Media Depictions of Harm in Heavy Metal and Rap Music. *American Sociological Review* 58:53–68.

Blumrosen, Alfred W. 1995. Draft Report on Reverse Discrimination Commissioned by Labor Department: How the Courts Are Handling Reverse Discrimination Claims. *Daily Labor Report (BNA)*, 23 March.

Bobo, Lawrence. 1988. Group Conflict, Prejudice, and the Paradox of Contemporary Racial Attitudes. In *Eliminating Racism: Profiles in Controversy*, edited by Phyllis A. Katz and Dalmas A. Taylor. New York: Plenum.

Bobo, Lawrence, and James R. Kluegel. 1993. Opposition to Race-Targeting: Self-Interest, Stratification, Ideology, or Racial Attitudes? *American Sociological Review* 58:43–64.

Bogle, Donald. 1989. *Blacks in American Films and Television: An Encyclopedia*. New York: Simon & Schuster.

Bok, Sissela. 1994. TV Violence, Children, and the Press: Eight Rationales Inhibiting Public Policy Debates. Discussion Paper D-16, Joan Shorenstein Barone Center, Kennedy School of Government, Harvard University, April.

Bonney, Bill, and Helen Wilson. 1983. *Australia's Commercial Media*. Melbourne: Macmillan.

Bowen, William G., and Derek Bok. 1998. *The Shape of the River: Long-Term Consequences of Considering Race in College and University Admissions*. Princeton: Princeton University Press.

Boyd, Herb. 1996. African-American Images on Television and Film. *Crisis* 103 (2): 2–25.

Branigan, E. 1992. *Narrative Comprehension and Film*. New York: Routledge.

Branthwaite, Alan, and Lorraine Pierce. 1990. The Portrayal of Black People in British Television Advertisements. *Social Behavior* 5:327–34.

Braxton, Greg. 1997. Minority Leaders See Little to Celebrate in Oscar Nominations. *L.A. Times Entertainment*, 13 February.

References

Brennan, R. L., and W. Prediger. 1981. Coefficient Kappa: Some Uses, Misuses, and Alternatives. *Education and Psychological Measurement* 41 (3): 687–99.

Breslau, Daniel. 1990. Sources of Variation in Public Attitudes Toward Poverty and Public Assistance for the Poor: A Literature Review. Report to the Chicago Council on Urban Affairs.

Bristor, Julia M., Renee Gravois Lee, and Michelle R. Hunt. 1995. Race and Ideology: African-American Images in Television Advertising. *Journal of Public Policy and Marketing* 14 (1): 48–59.

Brodkin, Karen. 1999. *How the Jews Became White Folks*. New Brunswick, N.J.: Rutgers University Press.

Broh, C. Anthony. 1987. *A Horse of a Different Color: Television's Treatment of Jesse Jackson's 1984 Presidential Campaign*. Washington, D.C.: Joint Center for Political Studies.

Bronner, Ethan. 1999. Study Finds Resegregation in American Schools. *New York Times*, 13 April, p. A1.

Browning, Rufus P., Dale R. Marshall, and David H. Tabb. 1990. Can Blacks and Latinos Achieve Power in City Government? In *Racial Politics in American Cities*, edited by Rufus P. Browning, Dale R. Marshall, and David H. Tabb. New York: Longman.

Budd, Mike, and Clay Steinman. 1992. White Racism and the Cosby Show. *Jump Cut* 37:12–14.

Budd, Mike, Robert M. Entman, and Clay Steinman. 1990. The Affirmative Character of U.S. Cultural Studies. *Critical Studies in Mass Communication* 7 (2): 169–84.

Budd, Mike, Steve Craig, and Clay Steinman. 1999. *Consuming Environments*. New Brunswick, N.J.: Rutgers University Press.

Campbell, Christopher P. 1995. *Race, Myth and the News*. Thousand Oaks, Calif.: Sage.

Cappella, Joseph N., and Kathleen Hall Jamieson. 1994. Public Cynicism and News Coverage in Campaigns and Policy Debates: Three Field Experiments. Paper presented at the annual meeting of the American Political Science Association, Chicago.

Carmichael, Stokely, and Charles V. Hamilton. 1967. *Black Power: The Politics of Liberation in America*. New York: Random House.

Carmines, Edward G., and Geoffrey C. Layman. 1998. When Prejudice Matters: The Impact of Racial Stereotypes on the Racial Policy Preferences of Democrats and Republicans. In *Perception and Prejudice: Race and Politics in the United States*, edited by Jon Hurwitz and Mark Peffley. New Haven: Yale University Press.

Carmines, Edward G., and James A. Stimson. 1989. *Issue Evolution: Race and the Transformation of American Politics*. Princeton: Princeton University Press.

Carroll, Raymond L. 1989. Market Size and TV News Values. *Journalism Quarterly* 66:49–56.

References

Carson, C. 1994. The Politics of Relations Between African-Americans and Jews. In *Blacks and Jews: Alliances and Arguments*, edited by Paul Berman. New York: Delacorte.

Carter, Bill. 1996. Two Upstart Networks Courting Black Viewers. *New York Times*, 7 October, p. C11.

Centerwall, B. S. 1992. Television and Violence: The Scale of the Problem and Where to Go From Here. *Journal of the American Medical Association* 267 (22): 3059–63.

Charity, Arthur. 1996. *Doing Public Journalism*. New York: Guilford.

Chaudhary, Anju G. 1980. Press Portrayal of Black Officials. *Journalism Quarterly* 57:36–41.

Chicago Council on Urban Affairs. 1990. Report of Focus Group Results. Unpublished ms.

Chideya, Farai. 1995. *Don't Believe the Hype*. New York: Plume.

Cloud, D. L. 1992. The Limits of Interpretation: Ambivalence and the Stereotype in "Spenser for Hire." *Critical Studies in Mass Communication* 9 (4): 311–24.

Coltrane, S., and S. Adams. 1997. Work-Family Imagery and Gender Stereotypes: Television and the Reproduction of Difference. *Journal of Vocational Behavior* 50 (2): 323–47.

Commission on Freedom of the Press. 1947. *A Free and Responsible Press*. Chicago: University of Chicago Press.

Comstock, George, and Hae Jung Paik. 1991. *Television and the American Child*. San Diego: Academic.

Comstock, George, Steven Chaffee, Nathan Katzman, Maxwell McCombs, and Donald Roberts. 1978. *Television and Human Behavior*. New York: Columbia University Press.

Condit, Celeste Michelle, and J. Ann Selzer. 1985. The Rhetoric of Objectivity in the Newspaper Coverage of a Murder Trial. *Critical Studies in Mass Communication* 2:197–216.

Cook, Timothy. 1997. *Governing With the News*. Chicago: University of Chicago Press.

Corliss, Richard. 1996. The Invasion Has Begun! Independence Day Arrives to Lead the Assault of Science-Fiction Movies, TV Shows and Books On the Cultural Mainstream. *Time*, 8 July, p. 58.

Corner, John. 1995. *Television Form and Public Address*. London: Edward Arnold.

Cosby Jr., William H. 1995. 50 years of Blacks on TV. *Ebony* 51 (1): 215–17.

Cose, Ellis. 1993. *The Rage of a Privileged Class*. New York: HarperCollins.

Cruse, Harold. 1967. *The Crisis of the Negro Intellectual*. New York: Morrow.

Dahl, M. K., and W. Lance Bennett. 1995. Media Agency and the Use of Icons in the Agenda-Setting Process: News Representations of George Bush's Trade Mission to Japan. Paper presented at the annual meeting of the American Political Science Association, Chicago.

References

Danelian, L. 1992. Interest Groups in the News. In *Public Opinion, the Press, and Public Policy*, edited by J. David Kennamer. Westport, Conn.: Praeger.

Dates, Jannette L. 1993 [1990]. Advertising. In *Split Image: African Americans in the Mass Media*, edited by Jannette L. Dates and William Barlow. 2d ed. Washington, D.C.: Howard University Press.

Dawson, Michael C. 1994. *Behind the Mule: Race and Class in African-American Politics*. Princeton: Princeton University Press.

Delgado, Richard, and Jean Stepanic. 1997. *Critical White Studies: Looking Behind the Mirror*. Philadelphia: Temple University Press.

Delli Carpini, Michael X., and Bruce Williams. 2000. Let Us Infotain You: The Politics of the New Media Environment. In *Mediated Politics: Communication in the Future of Democracy*, edited by W. Lance Bennett and Robert M. Entman. New York: Cambridge University Press.

DeMott, Benjamin. 1995. *The Trouble With Friendship: Why Americans Can't Think Straight About Race*. New York: Atlantic Monthly.

Devine, Patricia G. 1989. Stereotypes and Prejudice: Their Automatic and Controlled Components. *Journal of Personality and Social Psychology* 56 (1): 5–18.

Dines, Gail, and Jean M. Humez, eds. 1995. *Gender, Race and Class in Media: A Text-Reader*. Thousand Oaks, Calif.: Sage.

Douglas, Mary. 1970 [1966]. *Purity and Danger: An Analysis of Concepts of Pollution and Taboo*. New York: Penguin.

———. 1992. *Risk and Blame: Essays in Cultural Theory*. London: Routledge.

Dovidio, John F., and Samuel L. Gaertner, eds. 1986. *Prejudice, Discrimination, and Racism: Theory and Research*. New York: Academic.

Dowden, Sue, and John P. Robinson. Age and Cohort Differences in American Racial Attitudes: The Generational Replacement Hypothesis Revisited. In *Prejudice, Politics, and the American Dilemma*, edited by Paul M. Sniderman, Philip E. Tetlock, and Edward G. Carmines. Stanford, Calif.: Stanford University Press.

Dyson, Michael Eric. 1996. *Between God and Gangsta Rap: Bearing Witness to Black Culture*. New York: Oxford University Press.

Edelman, Murray. 1988. *Constructing the Political Spectacle*. Chicago: University of Chicago Press.

Edley, Christopher. 1996. *Not All Black and White: Affirmative Action, Race, and American Values*. New York: Hill and Wang.

Edsall, Thomas Byrne, with Mary D. Edsall. 1992 [1991]. *Chain Reaction: The Impact of Race, Rights, and Taxes on American Politics*. 2d ed. New York: Norton.

EEOC. 1998. Race Based Charges, FY 1992–98. Washington, D.C.: U.S. Equal Employment Opportunity Commission. At <http://www.eeoc.gov/stats/race.html>.

Electronic Media. N.d. Network News Ratings. *Electronic Media*. Updates published regularly.

References

Elliot, Michael T. 1995. Differences in the Portrayal of Blacks: A Content Analysis of General Media Versus Culturally-Targeted Commercials. *Journal of Current Issues and Research in Advertising* 17 (1): 76–86.

Ellison, Christpher G., and Daniel A Powers. 1994. The Contact Hypothesis and Racial Attitudes Among Black Americans. *Social Science Quarterly* 75 (2): 385–400.

Entman, Robert M. 1989. *Democracy Without Citizens: Media and the Decay of American Politics*. New York: Oxford University Press.

———. 1990a. Depictions of Poverty in Local and National Television News. Report to the Chicago Council on Urban Affairs.

———. 1990b. Modern Racism and the Images of Blacks in Local Television News. *Critical Studies in Mass Communication* 7:32–45.

———. 1992a. Blacks in the News: Television, Modern Racism, and Cultural Change. *Journalism Quarterly* 69:41–61.

———. 1992b. Super Tuesday and the Future of Local Television News. In *The Future of News*, edited by Philip S. Cook, Douglas Gomery, and Lawrence W. Lichty. Baltimore, Md.: Johns Hopkins University Press.

———. 1993. Framing: Toward Clarification of a Fractured Paradigm. *Journal of Communication* 43 (4): 51–58.

———. 1994a. Representation and Reality in the Portrayal of Blacks on Network Television News. *Journalism Quarterly* 71:9–20.

———. 1994b. Violence in Local News and Reality Programming. Report to the Chicago Council on Urban Affairs.

———. 1994c. Whites' Attitudes Toward Blacks: Chicago and the Nation. Report to the Human Relations Foundation of Chicago.

———. 1995. Television, Democratic Theory and the Visual Construction of Poverty. *Research in Political Sociology* 7:39–59.

———. 1997. Manufacturing Discord: Media in the Affirmative Action Debate. *Harvard International Journal of Press / Politics* 2 (4): 32–51.

———. 1998. Affirming Discord: Media in the Affirmative Action Debate. In *A Communications Cornucopia*, edited by Monroe Price and Roger Noll. Washington, D.C.: Brookings Institution.

Entman, Robert M., and Benjamin I. Page. 1994. The News Before the Storm: The Iraq War Debate and the Limits to Media Independence. In *Taken by Storm: The Media, Public Opinion, and U.S. Foreign Policy in the Gulf War*, edited by W. Lance Bennett and David L. Paletz. Chicago: University of Chicago Press.

Entman, Robert M., and Constance L. Book. 2000. Light Makes Right: Skin Color and Racial Hierarchy in Television Advertising. In *Critical Studies in Media Commercialism*, edited by R. Andersen and L. Strate. New York: Oxford University Press.

Entman, Robert M., and Susan Herbst. 2000. Reframing Public Opinion as We Have Known It. In *Mediated Politics: Communication in the Future of Democracy*, edited by W. Lance Bennett and Robert M. Entman. New York: Cambridge University Press.

References

Entman, Robert M., Debra Burns Melican, Irma Munoz, Barbara Hanson Lang-
ford, Simone Boayue, Caryn Kennedy Groce, Anita Raman, Brian Kenner, and
Charles Merritt. 1998. *Media and Reconciliation.* Washington, D.C.: Report
submitted to the President's Advisory Commission on Race. Photocopy. Also
available at <http://www.raceandmedia.com.

Epstein, Edward J. 1973. *News from Nowhere: Television and the News.* New York:
Vintage.

Erikson, Kai T. 1966. *Wayward Puritans: A Study in the Sociology of Deviance.* New
York: Wiley.

Eron, Leonard D., and L. Rowell Huesmann. 1986. The Development of Aggres-
sion in American Children as a Consequence of Television Violence Viewing. In
Television and the Aggressive Child: A Cross-National Comparison, edited by
L. Rowell Huesmann and Leonard D. Eron. Hillsdale, N.J.: Erlbaum.

Ettema, James S. 1990. Press Rites and Race Relations: A Study of Mass-Mediated
Ritual. *Critical Studies in Mass Communication* 7:9–31.

Farley, Reynolds, Charlotte Steeh, Maria Krysan, Tara Jackson, and Keith Reeves.
1994. Stereotypes and Segregation: Neighborhoods in the Detroit Area. *American Journal of Sociology* 100 (3): 750–79.

Feagin, Joe R., and Hernan Vera. 1995. *White Racism: The Basics.* New York: Routledge.

Feagin, Joe R., and Melvin P. Sikes. 1994. *Living with Racism: The Black Middle-
Class Experience.* Boston: Beacon.

Federal Bureau of Investigation (FBI). 1998. *Uniform Crime Reports for the United
States 1997.* Washington, D.C.: U.S. Government Printing Office.

Ferguson, Thomas, and Joel Rogers. 1986. *Right Turn: The Decline of the Democrats
and the Future of American Politics.* New York: Hill and Wang.

Fiedler, Leslie. 1996. *Tyranny of the Normal: Essays on Bioethics, Theology, and
Myth.* Boston: Godine.

Fiske, John. 1994. *Media Matters: Everyday Culture and Political Change.* Minneapolis: University of Minnesota Press.

Fiske, Susan T., and Donald Kinder. 1981. Involvement, Expertise, and Schema
Use: Evidence from Political Cognition. In *Personality, Cognition, and Social
Interaction,* edited by Nancy Cantor and John F. Kihlstrom. Hillsdale, N.J.:
Erlbaum.

Fiske, Susan T., and Shelley E. Taylor. 1991 [1984]. *Social Cognition.* 2d ed. New
York: McGraw Hill.

Ford, Thomas E. 1997. Effects of Stereotypical Television Portrayals of African-
Americans on Person Perception. *Social Psychological Quarterly* 60 (3): 266–
75.

Frammolino, Ralph, Mark Gladstone, and Amy Wallace. 1996. Some Regents Seek
UCLA Admissions Priority for Friends. *Los Angeles Times,* 16 March, p. 1.

Franklin, Raymond. 1993. *Shadows of Race and Class.* Minneapolis: University of
Minnesota Press.

References

Friedman, Murray. 1995. *What Went Wrong? The Creation and Collapse of the Black-Jewish Alliance.* New York: Free Press.

Frymer, Paul. 1999. *Uneasy Alliances: Race and Party Competition in America.* Princeton: Princeton University Press.

Fukuyama, Francis. 1995. *Trust: The Social Virtues and the Creation of Prosperity.* New York: Free Press.

Gabriel, John. 1998. *Whitewash: Racialized Politics and the Media.* London and New York: Routledge.

Gaertner, Samuel L., and John F. Dovidio. 1986. The Aversive Form of Racism. In *Prejudice, Discrimination, and Racism,* edited by John F. Dovidio and Samuel L. Gaertner. Orlando, Fla: Academic.

Galbraith, James K. 1998. *Created Unequal: The Crisis in American Pay.* New York: Free Press.

Gamson, William A. 1992. *Talking Politics.* New York: Cambridge University Press.

Gamson, William, and Andre Modigliani. 1987. The Changing Culture of Affirmative Action. *Research in Political Sociology* 3:37–77.

Gandy Jr., Oscar. 1998. *Communication and Race.* London: Arnold.

Gans, Herbert J. 1979. *Deciding What's News.* New York: Pantheon.

———. 1995. *The War Against the Poor: The Underclass and Anti-poverty Policy.* New York: Basic Books.

Garfield, B. 1996a. Ikea Again Furnishes Ad Breakthrough. *Advertising Age* 67 (14): 61–65.

———. 1996b. Ad Review Staff Recalls its Kinder, Gentler 1996. *Advertising Age* 67 (52): 16–17.

———. 1997. Class Consciousness Hurts Denny's Ads. *Advertising Age* 68 (22): 49–53.

Garrow, David J. 1978. Protest at Selma: Martin Luther King, Jr., and the Voting Rights Act of 1965. New Haven: Yale University Press.

Gates Jr., Henry L. 1996. The Charmer. *New Yorker,* 29 April / 6 May, pp. 116–31.

Gerbner, George, and Larry Gross. 1976. Living with Television: The Violence Profile. *Journal of Communication* 26 (2): 73–99.

Gerbner, George, Hamid Mowlana, and Kaarle Nordenstreng, eds. 1993. *The Global Media Debate: Its Rise, Fall, and Renewal.* N.J.: Ablex.

Gerbner, George, M. Morgan, and N. Signorielli. 1994. Television Violence Profile No. 16: The Turning Point: From Research to Action. Unpublished ms., University of Pennsylvania.

Gilens, Martin. 1996. Race and Poverty in America. *Public Opinion Quarterly* 60:515–41.

———. 1998. Racial Attitudes and Race-Neutral Social Policies: White Opposition to Welfare and the Politics of Racial Inequality. In *Perception and Prejudice: Race and Politics in the United States,* edited by Jon Hurwitz and Mark Peffley. New Haven: Yale University Press.

References

————. 1999. *Why Americans Hate Welfare: Race, Media and the Politics of Anti-poverty Policy.* Chicago: University of Chicago Press.

Gilliam Jr., Frank D., Shanto Iyengar, Adam Simon, and Oliver Wright. 1996. Crime in Black and White: The Scary World of Local News. *Harvard International Journal of Press / Politics* 1 (3): 6–23.

Gitlin, Todd. 1980. *The Whole World Is Watching: Mass Media in the Making and Unmaking of the New Left.* Berkeley: University of California Press.

————. 1983. *Inside Prime Time.* New York: Pantheon Books.

Gleiberman L., E. Harburg, M. R. Frone, M. Russell, and M. L. Cooper. 1995. Skin Color, Measures of Socioeconomic-Status and Blood-Pressure among Blacks in Erie County, NY. *Annals of Human Biology* 22 (1): 69–73.

Goldberg, David T. 1993. *Racist Culture: Philosophy and the Politics of Meaning.* Cambridge, Mass.: Blackwell.

Goldman, Robert, and Stephen Papson. 1996. *Sign Wars: The Cluttered Landscape of Advertising.* New York: Guilford.

Goldstein, Patrick. 1996. Praying for Crossover Appeal; Movies: Disney's Holiday Wish Is for "The Preacher's Wife" to Attract Black and White Moviegoers. *Los Angeles Times,* 11 December, p. F1.

Goshorn, Kent, and Oscar H. Gandy Jr. 1995. Race, Risk and Responsibility: Editorial Constraint in the Framing of Inequality. *Journal of Communication* 45 (2): 33–51.

Grabe, Maria Elizabeth. 1999. Television News Magazine Crime Stories: A Functionalist Perspective. *Critical Studies in Mass Communication* 16 (2): 155–71.

Graber, Doris A. 1990. Seeing Is Remembering: How Visuals Contribute to Learning from Television News. *Journal of Communication* 40 (3): 34–56.

————. 1996a. Say It with Pictures. *Annals of the American Academy of Political and Social Science* 546:85–96.

————. 1996b. *Mass Media and American Politics.* 4th ed. Washington, D.C.: CQ Press.

Gray, Herman. 1989. Television, Black Americans, and the American Dream. *Critical Studies in Mass Communication* 6:76–86.

————. 1995. *Watching Race: Television and the Struggle for "Blackness."* Minneapolis: University of Minnesota Press.

Greenberg, Bradley S. 1988. Some Uncommon Television Images and the Drench Hypothesis. In *Television as a Social Issue: Applied Social Psychology Annual 8,* edited by Stuart Oskamp. Newbury Park, Calif.: Sage.

Greenberg, Bradley S., and J. E. Brand. 1992. U.S. Minorities and the News. Paper prepared for a Conference on Television News Coverage of Minorities, Aspen Institute, Wye, Md.

————. 1994. Minorities and the Mass Media: 1970s to 1990s. In *Media Effects: Advances in Theory and Research,* edited by Jennings Bryant and Dolf Zillman. Hillsdale, N.J.: Erlbaum.

Guerrero, Ed. 1993a. *Framing Blackness: The African American Image in Film.* Philadelphia: Temple University Press.

———. 1993b. The Black Image in Protective Custody: Hollywood's Biracial Buddy Films of the Eighties. In *Black American Cinema,* edited by M. Diawara. New York: Routledge.

Guinier, Lani. 1998. *Lift Every Voice: Turning a Civil Rights Setback into a New Vision of Social Justice.* New York: Simon & Schuster.

Haas, Nancy. 1998. A TV Generation Is Seeing Beyond Color. *New York Times,* 22 February, sec. 2, p. 1.

Hacker, Andrew. 1995 [1992]. *Two Nations: Black and White, Separate, Hostile, Unequal.* Expanded and updated ed. New York: Ballantine.

Hall, Patrick A. 1997. Not African-American, Just Americans. *Headway* 9 (11): 37–38.

Hall, Ronald. 1995. The Bleaching Syndrome. *Journal of Black Studies* 26 (2): 172–84.

Hall, Stuart. 1975. Introduction. In *Paper Voices: The Popular Press and Social Change, 1935–1965,* by A. C. H. Smith with Elizabeth Immirzi and Trevor Blackwell. London: Chatto & Windus.

———. 1990. The Whites of Their Eyes. In *The Media Reader,* edited by Manuel Alvarado and John O. Thompson. London: BFI.

———. 1997. *Representation.* London: Sage.

Hamamoto, Darrell Y. 1992. Kindred Spirits: The Contemporary Asian American Family on Television. *Amerasia Journal* 18 (2): 35–53.

Hamilton, James T. 1994. Violence and the Media: Research Perspectives and Policy Implications. Conference paper prepared for the Commission on Radio and Television Policy, Working Group on Autonomy and the State, Aspen Institute, Wye, Md., 4–7 May.

———. 1997. *Channeling Violence: The Economic Market for Violent Television Programming.* Princeton: Princeton University Press.

Hamm, N. H., D. O. Williams, and A. D. Dalhouse. 1973. Preference for Black Skin among Negro Adults. *Psychological Reports* 32 (3, part 2): 1171–75.

Hammonds, Keith. 1998. Invisible in the Executive Suite. *Business Week,* 21 December, p. 68.

Hartmann, Paul G., and Charles Husband. 1974. *Racism and the Mass Media.* London: Davis-Poynter.

Herbst, Susan. 1993. *Numbered Voices: How Opinion Polling Has Shaped American Politics.* Chicago: University of Chicago Press.

Herman, Edward S., and Noam Chomsky. 1988. *Manufacturing Consent: The Political Economy of the Mass Media.* New York: Pantheon.

Hickey, Neil. 1998. Money Lust: How Pressure for Profit Is Perverting Journalism. *Columbia Journalism Review* 37 (July / August): 28–36.

Hilton, James L., and William von Hippel. 1996. Stereotypes. *Annual Review of Psychology* 47:237–72.

References

Hinckley, Barbara. 1981. *Coalitions and Politics*. New York: Harcourt Brace Jovanovich.

Hoberman, John M. 1997. *Darwin's Athletes: How Sport Has Damaged Black America and Preserved the Myth of Race*. Boston: Houghton Mifflin.

Hochschild, Jennifer L. 1995. *Facing Up to the American Dream*. Princeton: Princeton University Press.

Hooks, Bell. 1991. Micheaux: Celebrating Blackness. *Black American Literature Forum* 25 (2): 351–60.

————. 1992. *Black Looks: Race and Representation*. Boston: South End Press.

Hughes, Michael, and Bradley R. Hertel. 1990. The Significance of Color Remains: A Study of Life Chances, Mate Selection and Ethnic Consciousness Among Black Americans. *Social Forces* 68 (4): 1105–20.

Hunt, Darnell. 1997. *Screening the Los Angeles "Riots": Race, Seeing and Resistance*. New York: Cambridge University Press.

————. 1999. *O.J. Simpson Facts and Fictions: News Rituals in the Construction of Reality*. New York : Cambridge University Press.

Hurwitz, Jon, and Mark Peffley. 1997. Public Perceptions of Race and Crime: The Role of Racial Stereotypes. *American Journal of Political Science* 41: 375–401.

————, eds. 1998. *Perception and Prejudice: Race and Politics in the United States*. New Haven: Yale University Press.

Huston, Aletha, Edward Donnerstein, Halford Fairchild, Norma D. Feshbach, Phyllis A. Katz, John P. Murray, Eli A. Rubinstein, Brian L. Wilcox, and Diana Zuckerman. *Big World, Small Screen: The Role of Television in American Society*. Lincoln: University of Nebraska.

Innis, Leslie B., and Joe R. Feagin. 1995. The Cosby Show: The View from the Black Middle Class. *Journal of Black Studies* 25:692–711.

Internet Movie Database. 1999. The Top-Grossing Movies of All Time at the U.S.A. Box Office. At <http://us.imdb.com / Charts / usatopmovies>.

Iyengar, Shanto. 1990. Framing Responsibility for Political Issues: The Case of Poverty. *Political Behavior* 12 (1): 1–22.

————. 1991. *Is Anyone Responsible? How Television Frames Political Issues*. Chicago: University of Chicago Press.

Iyengar, Shanto, and Donald R. Kinder. 1987. *News That Matters: Television and American Opinion*. Chicago: University of Chicago Press.

Iyengar, Shanto, and William J. McGuire, eds. 1993. *Explorations in Political Psychology*. Durham, N.C.: Duke University Press.

Jamieson, Kathleen H. 1992. *Dirty Politics: Deception, Distraction, and Democracy*. New York: Oxford University Press.

Jencks, Christopher. 1991. Is the American Underclass Growing? In *The Urban Underclass*, edited by Christopher Jencks and Paul Peterson. Washington, D.C.: Brookings Institution.

————. 1992. *Rethinking Social Policy*. Cambridge, Mass.: Harvard University Press.

References

Jet. 1997. More than Half of Teens Who Date Have Dated Interracially: Study. *Jet* 93 (1): 32.

Jhally, Sut, and Justin Lewis. 1992. *Enlightened Racism*. Boulder, Colo.: Westview.

Jones, Jacquie. 1993. The Construction of Black Sexuality. In *Black American Cinema*, edited by M. Diawara. New York: Routledge.

Kahneman, Daniel, Paul Slovic, and Amos Tversky, eds. 1982. *Judgment under Uncertainty: Heuristics and Biases*. New York: Cambridge University Press.

Kaniss, Phyllis. 1991. *Making Local News*. Chicago: University of Chicago Press.

Katz, Phyllis A., and Dalmas A. Taylor, eds. 1988a. *Eliminating Racism*. New York: Plenum.

———. 1988b. Introduction. In *Eliminating Racism*, edited by Phyllis A. Katz and Dalmas A. Taylor. New York: Plenum.

Kawachi, Ichiro, Bruce P. Kennedy, K. Lochner, and D. Prothrow-Stith. 1997. Social Capital, Income Inequality, and Mortality. *American Journal of Public Health* 87:1491–99.

Kawakami, Kerry, Kenneth L. Dion, and John F. Dovidio. 1998. Racial Prejudice and Stereotype Activation. *Personality and Social Psychology Bulletin* 24 (4): 407–16.

Keith, V. M., and C. Herring. 1991. Skin Tone and Stratification in the Black Community. *American Journal of Sociology* 97 (3): 760–78.

Kern-Foxworth, Marilyn. 1994. *Aunt Jemima, Uncle Ben, and Rastus*. Westport, Conn.: Praeger.

Kern-Foxworth, Marilyn, and Oscar Gandy. 1994. Assessing the Managerial Roles of Black Female Public Relations Practitioners. *Journal of Black Studies* 24 (4): 416–34.

Kerner Commission. 1968. Report of the U.S. National Advisory Commission on Civil Disorders. Washington, D.C.: U.S. Government Printing Office.

Kinder, Donald R., and Lynn M. Sanders. 1990. Mimicking Political Debate with Survey Questions: The Case of White Opinion on Affirmative Action for Blacks. *Social Cognition* 8 (1): 73–103.

———. 1996. *Divided by Color: Racial Politics and Democratic Ideals*. Chicago: University of Chicago Press.

Klag, M. J., and P. K. Whelton. 1991. The Association of Skin Color with Blood Pressure in U.S. Blacks with Low Socioeconomic Status. *Journal of the American Medical Association* 265 (5): 599–602.

Kleiman, Vivian, and Marlon Riggs. 1991. *Color Adjustment*. San Francisco: California Newsreel.

Klite, Paul, Robert A. Bardwell, and Jason Salzman. 1997. Local TV News: Getting Away With Murder. *Harvard International Journal of Press / Politics* 2 (2): 102–12.

Kluegel, James E., and Lawrence Bobo. 1993. Dimensions of Whites' Beliefs about the Black-White Socioeconomic Gap. In *Prejudice, Politics, and the American Dilemma*, edited by Paul M. Sniderman, Philip E. Tetlock, and Edward G. Carmines. Stanford, Calif.: Stanford University Press.

Knight-Ridder Newspapers. 1991. Study Dispels Stereotypes of Child Poverty. *Chicago Tribune,* 3 June, pp. 1, 13.

Kochman, Thomas. 1981. *Black and White Styles in Conflict.* Chicago: University of Chicago Press.

Kubey, Robert, and Milan Csikszentmihalyi. 1990. *Television and the Quality of Life: How Viewing Shapes Everyday Experience.* Hillsdale, N.J.: Erlbaum.

Kuklinski, James H., Paul M. Sniderman, Kathleen Knight, Thomas Piazza, Philip E. Tetlock, G. R. Lawrence, and B. Mellers. 1997. Racial Prejudice and Attitudes toward Affirmative Action. *American Journal of Political Science* 41:2–19.

Lafayette, J. 1994. Stations Clean Up Newscasts. *Electronic Media,* 21 February, pp. 1, 2.

Lakoff, George. 1996. *Moral Politics.* Chicago: University of Chicago Press.

———. 1987. *Women, Fire, and Dangerous Things: What Categories Reveal about the Mind.* Chicago: University of Chicago Press.

Lambert, Pam. 1996. What's Wrong with This Picture? Exclusion of Minorities Has Become a Way of Life in Hollywood. *People,* 18 March, pp. 41–52.

Larson, Stephanie G. 1994. Black Women on *All My Children. Journal of Popular Film and Television* 22 (1): 44–48.

Lee, Taeku. 1998. The Backdoor and the Backlash: Campaign Finance and the Politicization of Chinese-Americans. Unpublished paper presented at Kennedy School, Harvard University, 2 November 1998.

Lewis, Dan A., and Greta Salem. 1986. *Fear of Crime: Incivility and the Production of a Social Problem.* New Brunswick, N.J.: Transaction Books.

Littleton, Cynthia. 1999. NAACP: Webs' Fall Skeds a Whitewash. *Daily Variety,* 13 July, p. 1.

Longino, Bill. 1997. Big Four Beef Up Minority Roles, Changing the Face of Network TV. *Charlotte Observer,* 30 July, p. E6.

Los Angeles Times. 1995. Poll described in *CQ Researcher* 5 (16): 69–92, 28 April 1995.

Lyman, S. L. 1990. Race, Sex and Servitude: Images of Blacks in American Cinema. *International Journal of Politics, Culture, and Society* 4 (1): 49–77.

MacDonald, J. Fred. 1992 [1983]. *Blacks and White TV: African Americans in Television Since 1948.* 2d ed. Chicago: Nelson-Hall.

Malkki, Lisa H. 1995. *Purity and Exile: Violence, Memory and National Cosmology Among Hutu Refugees in Tanzania.* Chicago: University of Chicago Press.

Manheim, Jarol. 1976. Can Democracy Survive Television? *Journal of Communication* 26 (2): 84–90.

———. 1991. *All of the People, All the Time: Strategic Communication and American Politics.* Armonk, N.Y.: M.E. Sharpe.

Marin, Rick, and Allison Samuels. 1996. White Nights. *Newsweek,* 29 January, p. 60.

Martilla and Kiley, Inc. 1992. Survey on Anti-Semitism and Prejudice in America. Under sponsorship of the Anti-Defamation League of B'nai B'rith.

References

Marx, Anthony W. 1998. *Making Race and Nation: A Comparison of the United States, South Africa, and Brazil.* New York: Cambridge University Press.

Massey, Douglas S., and Nancy A. Denton. 1993. *American Apartheid: Segregation and the Making of the Underclass.* Cambridge, Mass.: Harvard University Press.

Masters, Kim. 1996. Testing the Faith: Can "The Preachers Wife" Shake up Hollywood's Firm Belief That Whites Won't Go to Black Movies? *Time,* 16 December, p. 73.

McCarthy, Cameron R., A. P. Rodriguez, Edward Buendia, S. Meacham, H. Godina, K. E. Supriya, and Carrie Ann Wilson-Brown. 1997. Danger in the Safety Zone: Notes on Race, Resentment, and the Discourse of Crime, Violence and Suburban Security. *Cultural Studies* 11 (2): 274–95.

McConahay, John B. 1986. Modern Racism, Ambivalence, and the Modern Racism Scale. In *Prejudice, Discrimination, and Racism: Theory and Research,* edited by John F. Dovidio and Samuel L. Gaertner. New York: Academic.

Mediaweek. 1996. What They Watch. *Mediaweek,* 22 April, p. 30.

Mendelberg, Tali. 1997. Executing Hortons: Racial Crime in the 1988 Presidential Campaign. *Public Opinion Quarterly* 61:134–57.

Merelman, Richard M. 1995. *Representing Black Culture: Racial Conflict and Cultural Politics in the US.* New York: Routledge.

Messaris, Paul. 1997. *Visual Persuasion: The Role of Images in Advertising.* Newbury Park, Calif.: Sage.

Miller, Cyndee. 1992. Special K Loves Kristi, but Will Asian Heritage Hinder Other Endorsements? *Marketing News,* 30 March, p. 1.

Mollenkopf, John. 1995. New York: The Great Anomaly. Paper presented to the annual meeting of the American Political Science Association, Chicago.

Morley, David. 1986. *Family Television: Cultural Power and Domestic Leisure.* London: Comedia.

Morris, Norval. 1993. Race, Drugs, and Imprisonment. *Chicago Tribune,* 30 March, p. 13.

Morrison, Toni, and Claudia Brodsky Lacour, eds. 1997. *Birth of a Nation'hood : Gaze, Script, and Spectacle in the O.J. Simpson Case.* New York: Pantheon Books.

Myers Garth, Thomas Klak, and Timothy Koehl. 1996. The Inscription of Difference: News Coverage of the Conflicts in Rwanda and Bosnia. *Political Geography* 15 (1): 21–46.

Nacos, Brigitte, and Natasha Hritzuk. 1998. The Portrayal of Black America in the Mass Media: Perception and Reality. Paper presented to the annual meeting of the American Political Science Association, Boston.

Nadeau, Richard, and Richard G. Niemi. 1993. Innumeracy about Minority Populations. *Public Opinion Quarterly* 57:332–49.

Nation of Islam. 1991. *The Secret Relationship between Blacks and Jews.* Vol. I. Chicago: Nation of Islam.

Neal, A. M., and M. L. Wilson. (1989). The Role of Skin Color and Features in the Black Community: Implications for Black Women and Therapy. *Clinical Psychology Review* 9:323–33.

Neuman, W. Russell. 1991. *The Future of the Mass Audience.* New York: Cambridge University Press.

Neuman, W. Russell, Marion R. Just, and Ann N. Crigler. 1992. *Common Knowledge: News and the Construction of Reality.* Chicago: University of Chicago Press.

News and Observer. 1998. Diversity Trouble. *Raleigh News and Observer,* 5 January, p. 2A.

Nielsen, A. C. Co. 1989. *Nielsen Station Index (Chicago Metered Market Service for February 1989).* New York: Nielsen Media Research.

Noelle-Neumann, Elisabeth. 1993. *The Spiral Of Silence: Public Opinion, Our Social Skin.* Chicago: University of Chicago Press.

NORC. 1964. Anti-Semitism in the United States. Survey Research Center, University of California, Berkeley. Under sponsorship of the Anti-Defamation League of B'nai B'rith.

Norris, Pippa. 1996. Does Television Erode Social Capital? A Reply to Putnam. *P.S., Political Science and Politics* 29:74–80.

O'Barr, William M. 1994. *Culture and the Ad: Exploring Otherness in the World of Advertising.* Boulder, Colo.: Westview.

Ofori, Kofi A. 1999. When Being Number 1 is Not Enough: The Impact of Advertising Practices on Minority-Owned and Minority-Formatted Broadcast Stations. Submitted to the Office of Communications Business Opportunities, Federal Communications Commission (2 March). At <http://www.civilrightsforum.org/fccadvertising.htm>.

Ogbu, John U. 1978. *Minority Education and Caste: The American System in Cross-Cultural Perspective.* New York: Academic.

Oliver, Mary Beth. 1994. Portrayals Of Crime, Race, and Aggression in "Reality-Based" Police Shows: A Content Analysis. *Journal of Broadcasting & Electronic Media* 38 (2): 179–93.

———. 1999. Caucasian Viewers' Memory of Black and White Criminal Suspects in the News. *Journal of Communication* 49 (3): 46–60.

Omi, Michael, and Howard Winant. 1994. *Racial Formation in the United States: From the 1960s to the 1990s.* 2d ed. New York: Routledge.

Orfield, Gary, Susan Eaton, and the Harvard Project on Desegregation. 1996. *Dismantling Desegregation: The Quiet Reversal of Brown v. Board of Ed.* New York: New Press.

Page, Benjamin I. 1996. *Who Deliberates? Mass Media in a Modern Democracy.* Chicago: University of Chicago Press.

Page, Benjamin I., and Robert Y. Shapiro. 1992. *The Rational Public.* Chicago: University of Chicago Press.

Page, Benjamin I., Robert Y. Shapiro, and Glenn R. Dempsey. 1987. What Moves Public Opinion? *American Political Science Review* 81 (1): 23–43.

Paletz, David L., and Robert M. Entman. 1981. *Media Power Politics.* New York: Free Press.

Pan, Zhongdang, and Gerald M. Kosicki. 1996. Assessing News Media Influences on the Formation of Whites' Racial Policy Preferences. *Communication Research* 23 (2): 47–78.

Parks, M. R. 1982. Ideology in Interpersonal Communication: Off the Couch and into the World. In *Communication Yearbook,* edited by Michael Burgoon. New Brunswick, N.J.: Transaction Books.

Patterson, Orlando. 1997. *The Ordeal of Integration: Progress and Resentment in America's "Racial" Crisis.* Washington, D.C.: Civitas.

Patterson, Thomas E. 1993. *Out of Order.* New York: Knopf.

Peffley, Mark, and Jon Hurwitz. 1998. Whites' Stereotypes of Blacks: Sources and Political Consequences. In *Perception and Prejudice: Race and Politics in the United States,* edited by Jon Hurwitz and Mark Peffley. New Haven: Yale University Press.

Peffley, Mark, and Jon Hurwitz. 1997. Racial Stereotypes and Whites' Political Views of Blacks in the Context of Welfare and Crime. *American Journal of Political Science* 41 (1): 30–60.

Peffley, Mark, Todd Shields, and Bruce Williams. 1996. The Intersection of Race and Crime in Television News Stories: An Experimental Study. *Political Communication* 13:9–27.

Pettigrew, Thomas F. 1998. Intergroup Contact Theory. *Annual Review of Psychology* 9:65–85.

Pew Research Center for the People and the Press. 1997. *Press "Unfair, Inaccurate and Pushy."* Washington, D.C.: Pew Research Center (21 March).

———. 1998. *Turned Off Public Tuned Out Impeachment.* Washington, D.C.: Pew Research Center (22 December).

Philips, Chuck. 1992. The Uncivil War: The Battle between the Establishment and Supporters of Rap Music Reopens Old Wounds of Race and Class. *Los Angeles Times,* 19 July, p. 6.

Philo, Greg. 1990. *Seeing and Believing: The Influence of Television.* New York: Routledge.

Pieterse, Jan Nederveen. 1992. *White on Black: Images of Africa and Blacks in Western Popular Culture.* New Haven: Yale University Press.

Pines, Jim. 1995. Black Cops and Black Villains in Film and TV Crime Fiction. In *Crime and the Media: The Post-Modern Spectacle,* edited by David Kidd-Hewitt and Richard Osborne. London: Pluto.

Pinkney, Alphonso. 1984. *The Myth of Black Progress.* New York: Cambridge University Press.

Plous, Scott, and Tyrone Williams. 1995. Racial Stereotypes from the Days of American Slavery: A Continuing Legacy. *Journal of Applied Social Psychology* 25:795–817.

Power, J. Gerard, Sheila T. Murphy, and Gail Coover. 1996. Priming Prejudice: How Stereotypes and Counter-Stereotypes Influence Attribution of Responsibility and Credibility among Ingroups and Outgroups. *Human Communication Research* 23 (1): 6–58.

Price, Vincent. 1989. Social Identification and Public Opinion: Effects of Communicating Group Conflict. *Public Opinion Quarterly* 53 (2): 197–224.

Pride, Richard A. 1999. Redefining the Problem of Racial Inequality. *Political Communication* 16 (2): 147–67.

Protess, David L. et al. 1991. *The Journalism of Outrage: Investigative Reporting and Agenda Building in America.* New York: Guilford.

Putnam, Robert D. 1993. *Making Democracy Work.* Princeton: Princeton University Press.

———. 1995. Bowling Alone, Revisited. *Responsive Community* 5 (2): 18–33.

Rainville, Raymond E., and Edward McCormick. 1977. Extent of Covert Racial Prejudice in Pro Football Announcers' Speech. *Journalism Quarterly* 54:10–26.

Reed Jr., Adolph L. 1986. *The Jesse Jackson Phenomenon: The Crisis of Purpose in Afro-American Politics.* New Haven: Yale University Press.

Reed, Ishmael. 1993. *Airing Dirty Laundry.* Reading, Mass.: Addison-Wesley.

Reeves, Jimmie L., and Richard Campbell. 1994. Cracked Coverage. Durham, N.C.: Duke University Press.

Reeves, Keith. 1997. *Voting Hopes or Fears?: White Voters, Black Candidates and Racial Politics in America.* New York: Oxford University Press.

Reibstein, Larry. 1994. The Battle of the TV News Magazine Shows. *Newsweek,* 1 April, pp. 60–65.

Reinarman, Craig, and Harry Levine. 1995. The Crack Attack: Politics and Media in America's Latest Drug Scare, 1986–1992. In *Images of Issues: Typifying Contemporary Social Problems,* edited by Joel Best. New York: Aldine De Gruyter.

Rhines, Jesse Algernon. 1995. The Political Economy of Black Film. *Cineaste* 21 (3): 38–40.

Ricks, Delthia. 1998. The Health Divide / Medical Myths / Black Patients Fight against Harmful "Silent Curriculum." *Newsday,* 6 December, p. A4.

Robinson, John, and Mark Levy. 1986. *The Main Source: Learning from Television News.* Beverly Hills, Calif.: Sage.

Rojecki, Andrew. 1996. Deadly Embrace. Paper presented at the annual conference of the International Communication Association, Chicago.

———. 1999. *Silencing the Opposition: Anti-Nuclear Movements and the Media in the Cold War.* Urbana, Ill.: University of Illinois Press.

Romer, Daniel, Kathleen H. Jamieson, and N. J. de Coteau. 1998. The Treatment of Persons of Color in Local Television News—Ethnic Blame Discourse or Realistic Group Conflict? *Communication Research* 25 (3): 286–305.

Romer, Daniel, Kathleen H. Jamieson, Catharine Riegner, Mika Emori, and Brigette Rouson. 1997. Blame Discourse versus Realistic Conflict as Explana-

References

tions of Ethnic Tension in Urban Neighborhoods. *Political Communication* 14 (3): 273–92.

Rosch, Eleanor. 1981. Prototype Classification and Logical Classification: The Two Systems. In *New Trends in Cognitive Representation: Challenges to Piaget's Theory,* edited by E. Scholnick. Hillsdale, N.J.: Erlbaum.

Rosensteil, Tom, Carl Gottlieb, and Lee Ann Brady. 1998. Local TV News: What Works, What Flops, and Why. *Columbia Journalism Review* 37 (January / February): 65–70.

Roth, Byron M. 1990. Social Psychology's "Racism." *Public Interest* 98 (winter): 6–36.

Rothbart, Myron, and Oliver P. John. 1993. Intergroup Relations and Stereotype Change. In *Prejudice, Politics, and the American Dilemma,* edited by Paul M. Sniderman, Philip E. Tetlock, and Edward G. Carmines. Stanford, Calif.: Stanford University Press.

Russell, Katheryn K. 1998. *The Color of Crime: Racial Hoaxes, White Fear, Black Protectionism, Police Harassment, and Other Macroaggressions.* New York: New York University Press.

Russell, Kathy, Midge Wilson, and Ronald Hall. 1992. *The Color Complex: The Politics of Skin Color among African Americans.* New York: Harcourt Brace Jovanovich.

Sabato, Larry. 1991. *Feeding Frenzy: How Attack Journalism Has Transformed American Politics.* New York: Free Press.

Samuels, Allison, and John Leland. 1999. They've Got Next. *Newsweek,* 5 April, p. 66.

Schattschneider, Elmer E. 1975 [1960]. *The Semi-Sovereign People: A Realist's View of Democracy in America.* Hinsdale, Ill.: Dryden.

Schlossberg, Howard. 1993. Many Marketers Still Consider Blacks "Dark-Skinned Whites." *Marketing News,* 18 January, p. 1.

Schlozman, Kay Lehman, and John T. Tierney. 1986. *Organized Interests and American Democracy.* New York: Harper & Row.

Schram, Martin. 1987. *The Great American Video Game: Presidential Politics in the Television Age.* New York: William Morrow.

Schuman, Howard, Charlotte Steeh, Lawrence Bobo, and Maria Krysan. 1998. *Racial Attitudes in America: Trends and Interpretations.* Cambridge, Mass.: Harvard University Press.

Sciara, F. J. 1983. Skin Color and College Student Prejudice. *College Student Journal* 17 (4): 390–94.

Scott, Sandra Davidson. 1994. Beavis and Butthead: We Didn't Start the Fire. *Media Law Notes* 21 (spring): 8.

Sears, David O. 1988. Symbolic Racism. In *Eliminating Racism,* edited by Phyllis A. Katz and Dalmas A. Taylor. New York: Plenum.

Sears, David O., and Tom Jessor. 1996. Whites' Racial Policy Attitudes: The Role of White Racism. *Social Science Quarterly* 77 (4): 751–59.

References

Sears, David O., Collette Van-Laar, Mary Carrillo, and Rick Kosterman. 1997. Is It Really Racism? The Origins of White Americans' Opposition to Race-Targeted Policies. *Public Opinion Quarterly* 61 (1): 16–53.

Seib, Gerald F., and Joe Davidson. 1994. Whites, Blacks Agree on Problems; the Issue is How to Resolve Them. *Wall Street Journal,* 29 September, pp. A1, A6.

Seiter, Ellen. 1995. Different Children, Different Dreams: Racial Representation in Advertising. In *Gender, Race and Class in Media: A Text—Reader,* edited by Gail Dines and Jean M. Humez. Thousand Oaks, Calif.: Sage.

Seltzer, Richard, and Robert C. Smith. 1992. Color Differences in the Afro-American Community and the Differences They Make. *Journal of Black Studies* 21 (3): 279–86.

Shedler, Jonathon, and Melvin Manis. 1986. Can the Availability Heuristic Explain Vividness Effects? *Journal of Personality and Social Psychology* 51 (1): 6–36.

Shohat, Ella, and Robert Stam. 1994. *Unthinking Eurocentrism: Multiculturalism and the Media.* London: Routledge.

Shrum, L. J. 1996. Psychological Processes Underlying Cultivation Effects: Further Tests of Construct Accessibility. *Human Communication Research* 22: 482–509.

Sidanius, Jim, and Felicia Pratto. 1993. The Inevitability of Oppression and the Dynamics of Social Dominance. In *Prejudice, Politics, and the American Dilemma,* edited by Paul M. Sniderman, Philip E. Tetlock, and Edward G. Carmines. Stanford, Cal: Stanford University Press.

Sigelman, Lee, and Susan Welch. 1993. The Contact Hypothesis Revisited: Black–White Interaction and Positive Racial Attitudes. *Social Forces* 71 (3): 81–795.

Slaby, R. 1993. Violence and Youth: Psychology's Response. Report of the American Psychological Association Commission on Violence and Youth. Washington, D.C.: American Psychological Association.

Smith, A. C. H., with Elizabeth Immirzi and Trevor Blackwell. 1975. *Paper Voices: The Popular Press and Social Change, 1935–1965.* London: Chatto and Windus.

Smith, Erna. 1994. Transmitting Race in the Los Angeles Riots. Harvard University, Kennedy School of Government, Shorenstein Center, Paper R-11.

Sniderman, Paul M. 1991. *National Race and Politics Survey.* <http://socrates. berkeley.edu:7502/cgi-bin12/hsda?harcsrc+natlrace>.

Sniderman, Paul M., and Thomas Piazza. 1993. *The Scar of Race.* Cambridge, Mass.: Harvard University Press.

Sniderman, Paul M., Philip E. Tetlock, Edward G. Carmines, and Randall S. Peterson. 1993. The Politics of the American Dilemma: Issue Pluralism. In *Prejudice, Politics, and the American Dilemma,* edited by Paul M. Sniderman, Philip E. Tetlock, and Edward G. Carmines. Stanford, Calif.: Stanford University Press.

Sniderman, Paul M., Richard Brody, and Philip Tetlock. 1991. *Reasoning and Choice: Explorations in Political Psychology.* New York: Cambridge University Press.

Sniderman, Paul M., with Michael Gray Hagen. 1985. *Race and Inequality: A Study in American Values.* Chatham, N.J.: Chatham House.

References

Sonenshein, Raphael J. 1993. *Politics in Black and White: Race and Power in Los Angeles.* Princeton: Princeton University Press.

Spigner, Clarence. 1994. Black Impressions: Television and Film Imagery. *Crisis* 101 (1): 8–16.

Spindler, Amy. 1997. Models of Color Still Stuck in the "Exotic" Pigeonhole. *Raleigh News and Observer,* 19 June, p. 5E.

Stallybrass, Peter, and Allon White. 1986. *The Politics and Poetics of Transgression.* London: Methuen.

Steeh, Charlotte, and Maria Krysan. 1996. The Polls: Trends: Affirmative Action and the Public, 1970–1995. *Public Opinion Quarterly* 60 (1): 128–58.

Steele, S. 1990. A Negative Vote on Affirmative Action. *New York Times Magazine* 139 (4823): 46–51.

Sterngold, James. 1998. A Racial Divide Widens on Network TV. *New York Times,* 29 December, sec. A, p. 1.

Stone, Vernon. 1997. Women Gain, Minorities Lose in TV News. In *Facing Difference: Race, Gender and Mass Media,* edited by Shirley Biagi and Marilyn Kern-Foxworth. Thousand Oaks, Calif.: Pine Forge.

Streisand, Betsy. 1997. True Story, Big Studio, Black Film. *U.S. News and World Report,* 10 March, p. 66.

Sturm, Susan, and Lani Guinier. 1996. The Future of Affirmative Action: Reclaiming the Innovative Ideal. *California Law Review* 84 (4): 953–1036.

Subervi-Velez, Federico A. 1994. Mass Communication and Hispanics. In *Handbook of Hispanic Cultures in the United States: Sociology,* edited by Nicholas Kanellos and Claudio Esteva-Fabregat. Houston, Tex.: Arte Publico.

Tajfel, Henri, ed. 1982. *Social Identity and Intergroup Relations.* Cambridge and New York: Cambridge University Press.

Tan, Alexis, Yuki Fujioka, and Nancy Lucht. 1997. Native American Stereotypes, TV Portrayals, and Personal Contact. *Journalism and Mass Communication Quarterly* 74:265–84.

Tarrow, Sidney. 1996. Making Social Science Work across Space and Time: A Critical Reflection on Robert Putnam's *Making Democracy Work. American Political Science Review* 90: 389–97.

Thernsrom, Stephan, and Abigail Thernstrom. 1997. We Have Overcome. *New Republic* 217 (15): 23–27.

Tiemens, Robert K. 1991. Examining Visual Content: Theoretical and Technical Considerations. Paper presented at the annual conference of the International Communication Association, Chicago.

Tobenkin, David. 1996. Latinos Unhappy with TV Portrayal, Representation. *Broadcasting & Cable,* 9 January, pp. 81–82.

Todorov, Tzvetan, and Catherine Porter. 1993. *On Human Diversity.* Cambridge, Mass.: Harvard University Press.

Trigoboff, Dan. 1998. Survey: Viewers Applaud Their Local News. *Broadcasting & Cable,* 21 December, p. 60.

References

Trotter Society. 1990. The Role of the Media in Racial Stereotyping. *Trotter Review* 4, special issue (spring).

Tuchman, Gaye. 1977. Objectivity as Strategic Ritual: An Examination of Newsmen's Notions of Objectivity. *American Journal of Sociology* 7:60–79.

———. 1978. *Making News: A Study in the Construction of Reality.* New York: Free Press.

Turner, Patricia A. 1993. *I Heard It through the Grapevine: Rumor in African-American Culture.* Berkeley: University of California Press.

Turner, Victor W. 1967. *The Forest of Symbols.* Ithaca, N.Y.: Cornell University Press.

Turow, Joseph. 1997. *Breaking Up America: Advertisers and the New Media World.* Chicago: University of Chicago Press.

Tversky, Amos, and Daniel Kahneman. 1973. Availability: A Heuristic for Judging Frequency and Probability. *Cognitive Psychology* 5 (2): 207–32.

U.S. Bureau of the Census. 1997. *Statistical Abstract of the United States* (October).

U.S. Department of Justice. 1998. *Sourcebook of Criminal Justice Statistics.* Washington, D.C.: Bureau of Justice Statistics.

U.S. Federal Glass Ceiling Commission. 1995. *Good for Business: Making Full Use of the Nation's Human Capital.* Washington, D.C.: Federal Glass Ceiling Commission.

U.S. House. Subcommittee on Telecommunications and Finance. 1994. Survey Finds Parents Not Routinely Receiving "Violence Advisories" in Advance of Programs. News release. 14 January.

USA Today. 1997. Poll Underscores a Change in Attitude. *USA Today,* 3 November, p. 10A.

Valentino, Nicholas A. 1999. Crime News and the Priming of Racial Attitudes During Evaluations of the President. *Public Opinion Quarterly* 63:293–320.

Verhovek, Sam Howe. 1997. In Poll, Americans Reject Means But Not Ends of Racial Diversity. *New York Times,* 14 December, sec. 1, p. 1.

Virtanen, S. V., and L. Huddy. 1998. Old Fashioned Racism and New Forms of Racial Prejudice. *Journal of Politics* 60 (2): 311–32.

Voakes, Paul S. 1997. *The Newspaper Journalists of the 90s.* American Society of Newspaper Editors. Available at <http://www.asne.org/kiosk/reports/97reports/journalists90s/coverpage.html>.

Wachtel, Paul L. 1999. *Race in the Mind of America.* New York: Routledge.

Weigel, Russell H., Eleanor L. Kim, and Jill L. Frost. 1995. Race Relations on Prime Time Reconsidered: Patterns of Continuity and Change. *Journal of Applied Social Psychology* 25 (3): 223–36.

Weston, Mary Ann. 1996. Native Americans in the News: Images of Indians in the Twentieth Century Press. Westport, Conn.: Greenwood Press.

Wetherell, Margaret, and Jonathan Potter. 1992. *Mapping the Language of Racism: Discourse and the Legitimation of Exploitation.* New York and London: Harvester Wheatsheaf.

References

Wilkes, Robert E., and Humberto Valencia. 1989. Hispanics and Blacks in Television Commercials. *Journal of Advertising* 18 (1): 9–25.

Wilson, William J. 1996. *When Work Disappears: The World of the New Urban Poor.* New York: Knopf.

Winant, Howard. 1994. *Racial Conditions: Politics, Theory, Comparisons.* Minneapolis: University of Minnesota Press.

Witkin, Gordon. 1998. The Crime Bust. *US News and World Report* 124 (20): 28–35.

Wolverton, Brad. 1997. So Far, She's Not the Venus de Moola. *Business Week,* 19 September, p. 189.

Wonsek, Pamela L. 1992. College Basketball on Television: A Study of Racism in the Media. *Media, Culture, and Society* 14:49–61.

Wynter, Leon E. 1998. Business and Race: Ads Tend to Ignore Trend Toward Interracial Dating. *Wall Street Journal,* 7 January, p. B1.

Yankelovich, Skelley, and White. 1981. Anti-Semitism in the United States. Poll under sponsorship of the American Jewish Committee.

Zaller, John. 1992. *The Nature and Origins of Mass Opinion.* New York: Cambridge University Press.

Zinkhan, George M., William J. Qualls, and Abhijit Biswas. 1990. The Use of Blacks in Magazine and Television Advertising: 1946 to 1986. *Journalism Quarterly* 67:47–53.

Index

Page numbers in italics refer to tables.

Asians
in advertising, 165, 260n. 8, 263n. 25
in movies, 192–93, 193
in news reports, 63, 86, 117, 248n. 13
population percentage of, 265n. 17
Aspen Institute's Communications and
Society Program, xvii
assumptions of study, 13–15
attitudes, continuum of, 16–22. *See also
specific attitudes*
audience, need for critical awareness in,
217, 222
aversive racism theory, 5, 17

Babatunde, Obba, 203
Baer, Neil, 158–59
Barry, Marion, 138, 139, 141, 209, 217
benign neglect, 33
Bennett, W. Lance, 126
Best Man, The (movie), 203
BET. *See* Black Entertainment Television
(BET)
Beulah (TV show), 160
biological racism, 29–30
black, uses of word, 65–68
Black Entertainment Television (BET),
164–65, 167, 171–72, 174–75
Black politics
local level, 135–38
national level, 125–35, 138–41, 142–
43, 209
power and, 9–10, 141–42
Black racism, xii–xiii
Blacks
as experts in news reports, 13, 68–69, 73
focus on, xi–xii
as media personnel, 57, 69, 86–88, 106
as movie-going audience, 202
percentage in U.S. population, 25, 29
qualities needed for success, 206–8
social conditions and, 56
as synonymous with poverty, 9, 102–3,
105

See also liminality of Blacks
Black women in movies, 184, 191, 198, 199
Blue Streak (movie), 203
Bobo, Lawrence, 6, 22, 46–47, 113
Bochco, Steven, 148
Booty Call (movie), 202
Boston Common (TV show), 148
box office returns, 193–94
Brody, Richard, 79
Brokaw, Tom, 108
brotherhood, 11
buddy films, 183
Bullock, Sandra, 185
Bureau of Media Research (Indiana Uni-
versity), xviii
Bush, George, 53, 92, 126

cable television, 45, 210
Castro, Fidel, 132
categorical thinking, 163
CBS Evening News (TV news), 115, 117–
18
Chicago
Cabrini Green, 35
Michael Reese Hospital, 101
politics in, 130
poverty and racial attitudes in, 102–3
South Side, 96
See also local television news
Chicago Community Trust's Human Rela-
tions Foundation, xvii, xviii
Chicago Sun-Times (newspaper), 88–89, 99
Chicago Tribune (newspaper), 88–90, 99,
129–30
children in ads, 173
City of Angels (TV show), 148
class bias in local television news, 84–85
Clinton, Bill, 1–2, 76–77, 109, 113, 115,
127, 135, 221
clothing of defendants, 83
Cochran, Johnnie, 148
cognitive miser view, 57–58
Coleman, Milton, 127, 129

Index

  Blacks equated with poverty in, 102
  conflict frame for affirmative action
    and, 117
  of criminals, 74, 82, 85
  image clusters, 96–99
  newspapers and, 99–100
  of poverty, 95
  transfer of information and, 101
Vogue (magazine), 179

Waiting to Exhale (movie), 193, 195,
    267n. 31
Washington, Denzel, 193, 194–95, 200,
    203
Washington Post (newspaper), 127, 190
Wattenberg, Ben, 132
Wayans Brothers, The (TV show), 148
WB (Warner Brothers Television Net-
    work), 33, 45
web sites
  authors', xiv
  movie databases, 265n. 14
welfare
  percentage of U.S. budget going to, 25,
    27
  television news and, 8–9, 34–35,
    73

"Whiteness," 241–42n. 5
Whites
  anxiety in due to economy, 76–77
  collective guilt of, 12
  fear of being controlled in, 125
  priority of studying racial animosity in,
    xiii, 4
  racial privilege of, 38, 42–43, 118–19,
    123–24, 137–38
Wild Wild West (movie), 203
Wilson, William Julius, 116
Wilson (Woodrow) International Center
    for Scholars, xvii
Winant, Howard, 71, 75
Winfrey, Oprah, 29, 30, 54, 158
Wintour, Anna, 179
women and affirmative action, 117, 119
Woods, Tiger, 29
Wright, Oliver, 215

Yamaguchi, Kristi, 263n. 25
Young, Andrew, 131
youth culture of 1990s, 220

zero-sum conflict of interest
  affirmative action and, 115, 118–20
  Black compared to White politicians
    and, 137